nakaba
suzuki
presents

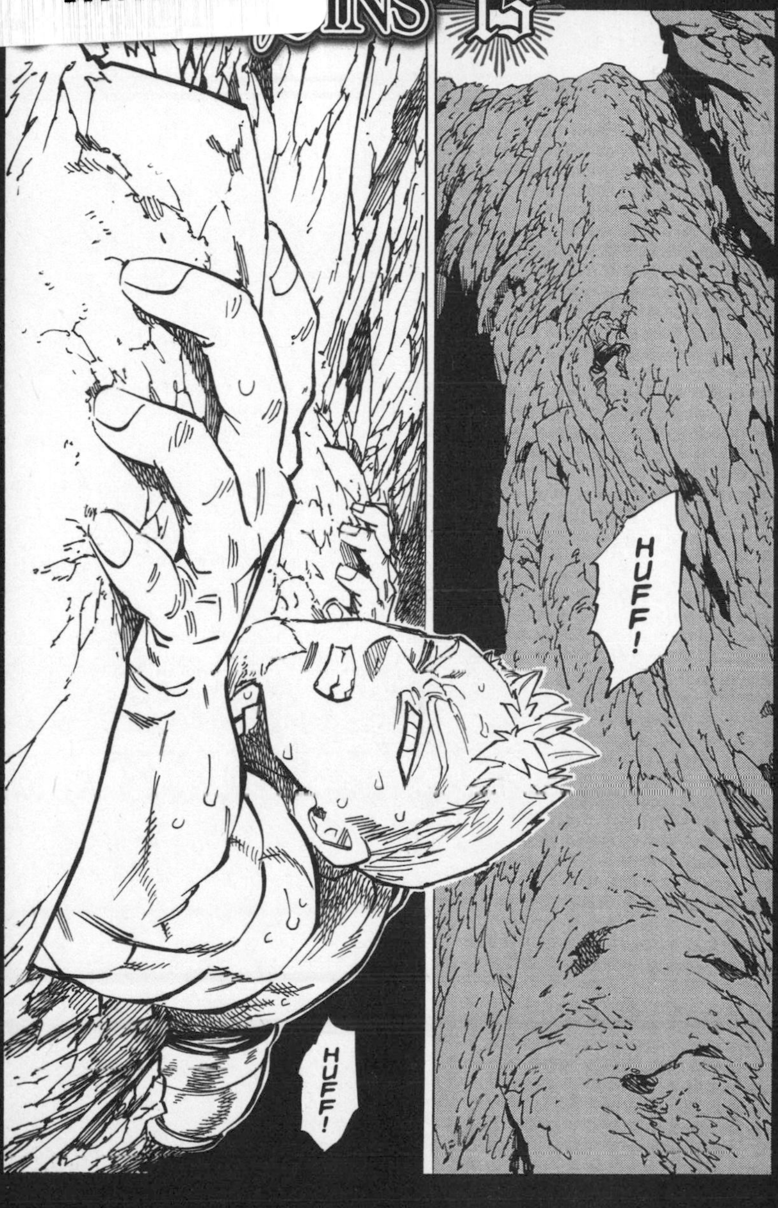
HUFF!
HUFF!

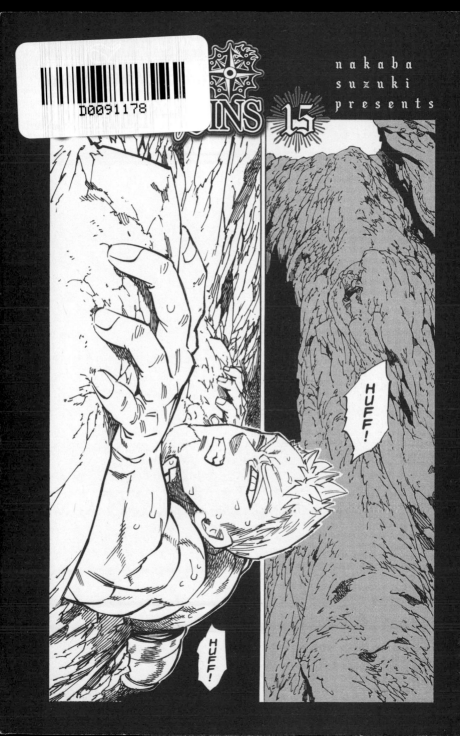

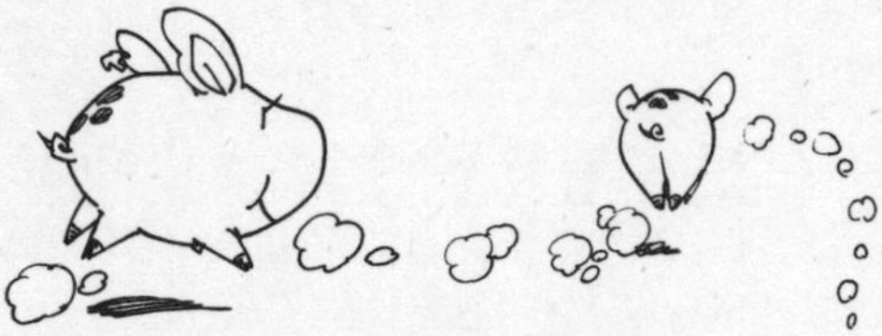

THE SEVEN DEADLY SINS

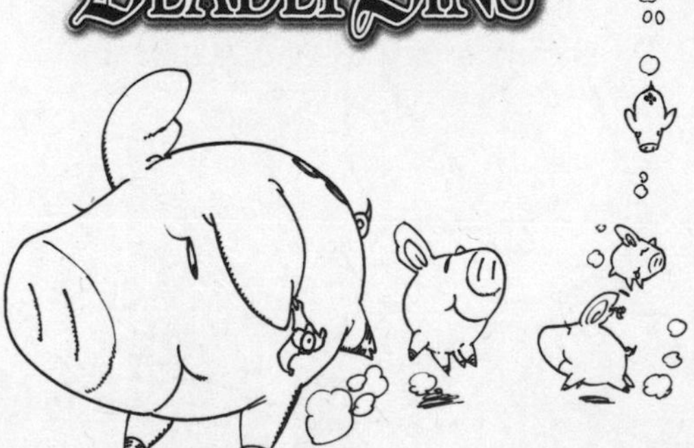

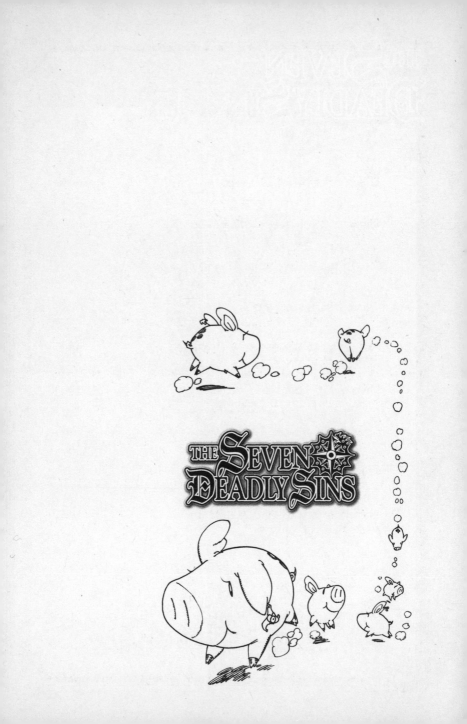

CONTENTS

BOAR HAT

The Seven Deadly Sins

RED DEMONS

Among the ranks of Demons, these are the most inferior. However, their powers exceed those of Holy Knights.

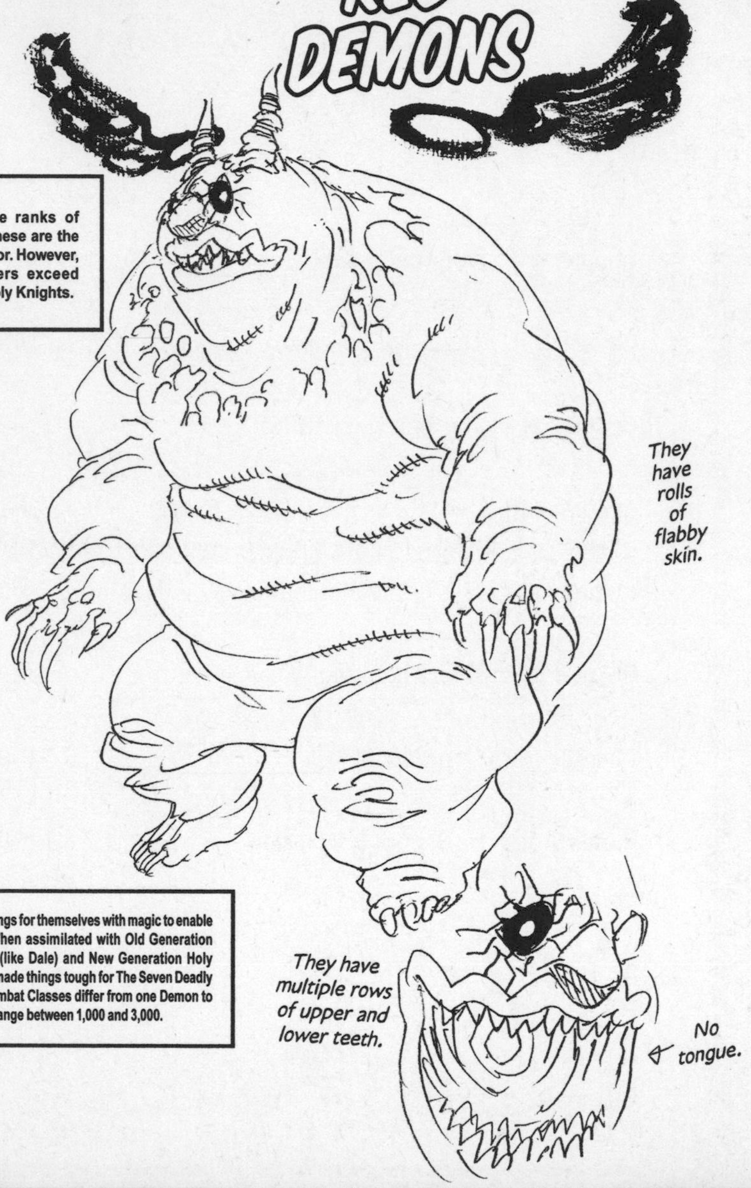
They have rolls of flabby skin.
They have multiple rows of upper and lower teeth.
No tongue.

They create wings for themselves with magic to enable them to fly. When assimilated with Old Generation Holy Knights (like Dale) and New Generation Holy Knights, they made things tough for The Seven Deadly Sins. Their Combat Classes differ from one Demon to the next, and range between 1,000 and 3,000.

Chapter 114 - The Lost Heroes

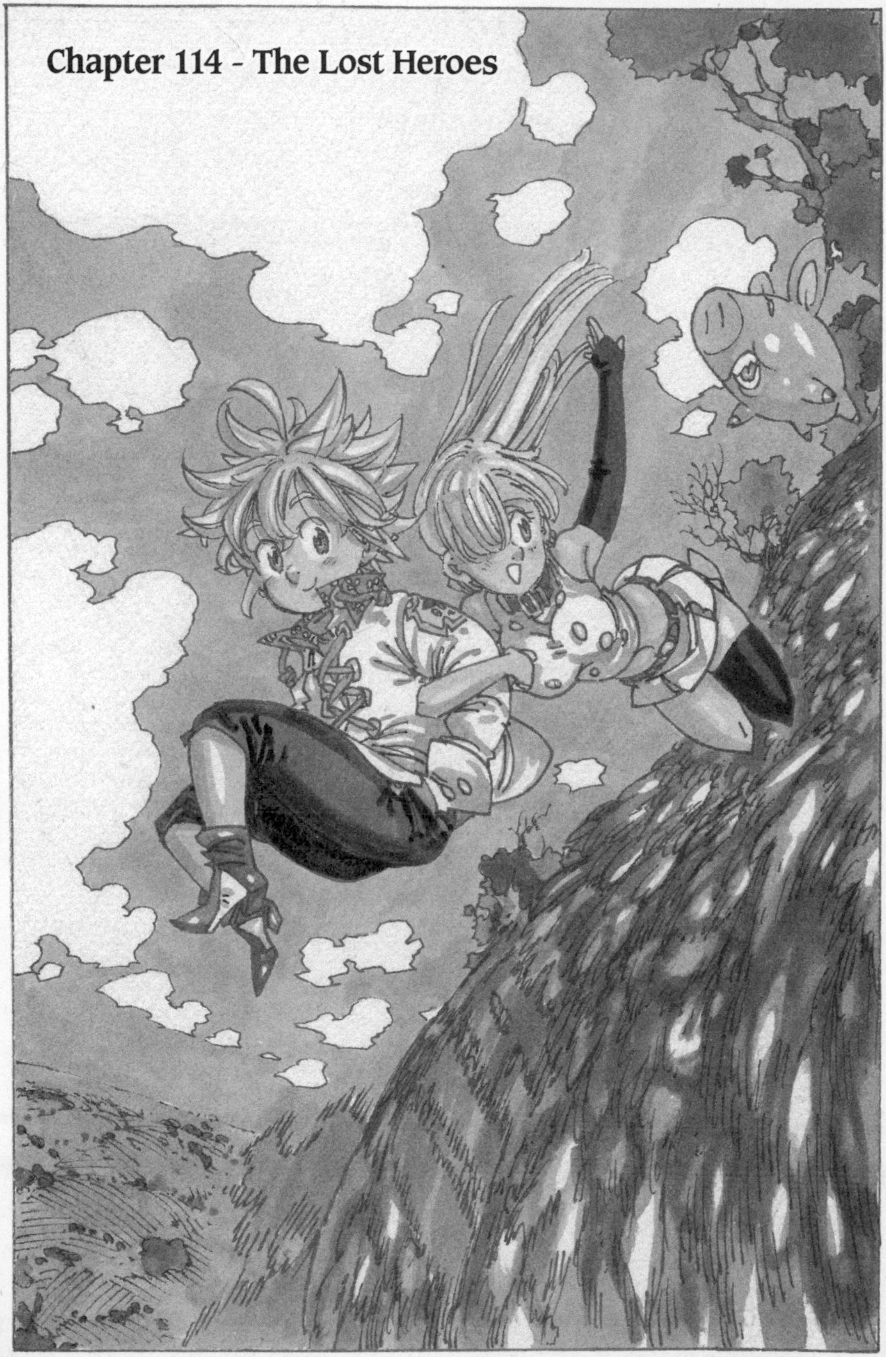

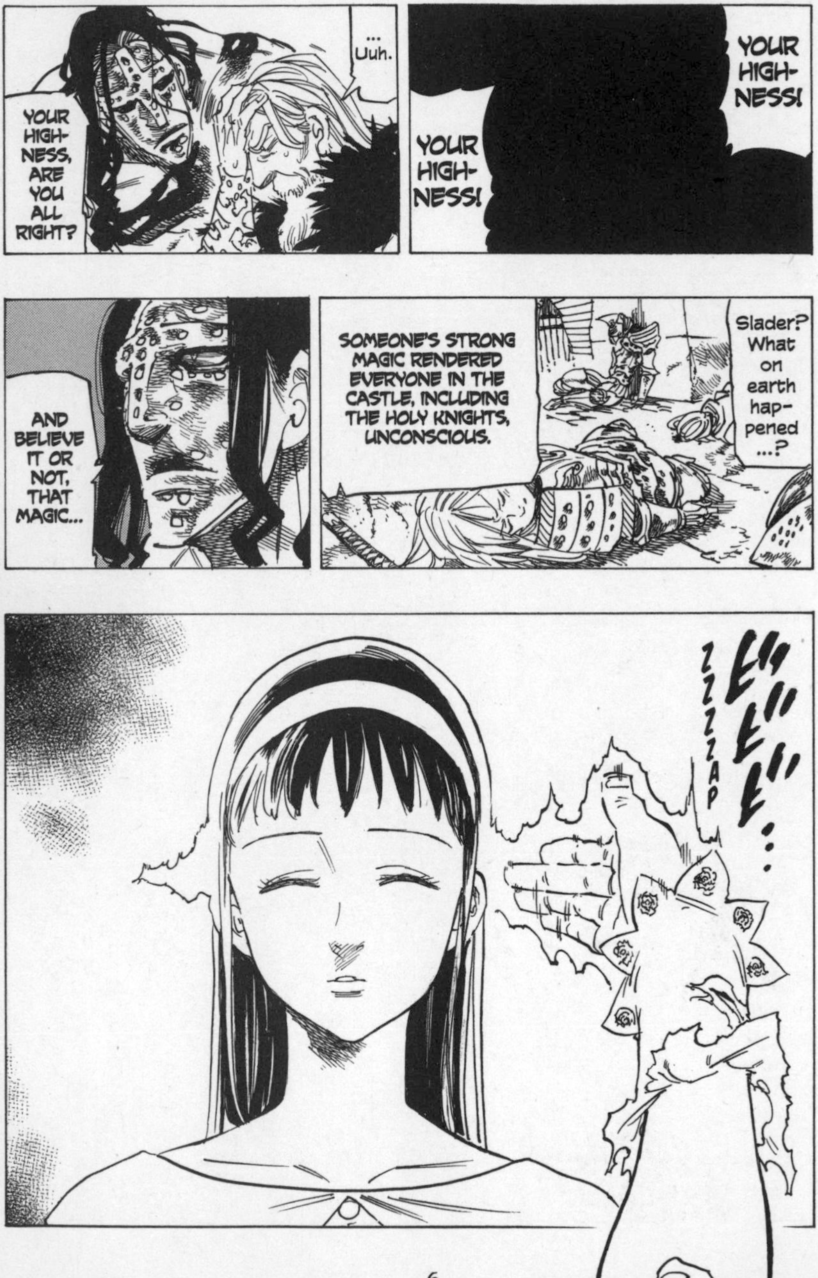
YOUR HIGH-NESS!
YOUR HIGH-NESS!
... Uuh.
YOUR HIGH-NESS, ARE YOU ALL RIGHT?
Slader? What on earth hap-pened ...?
SOMEONE'S STRONG MAGIC RENDERED EVERYONE IN THE CASTLE, INCLUDING THE HOLY KNIGHTS, UNCONSCIOUS.
AND BELIEVE IT OR NOT, THAT MAGIC...
ZZZZZAP

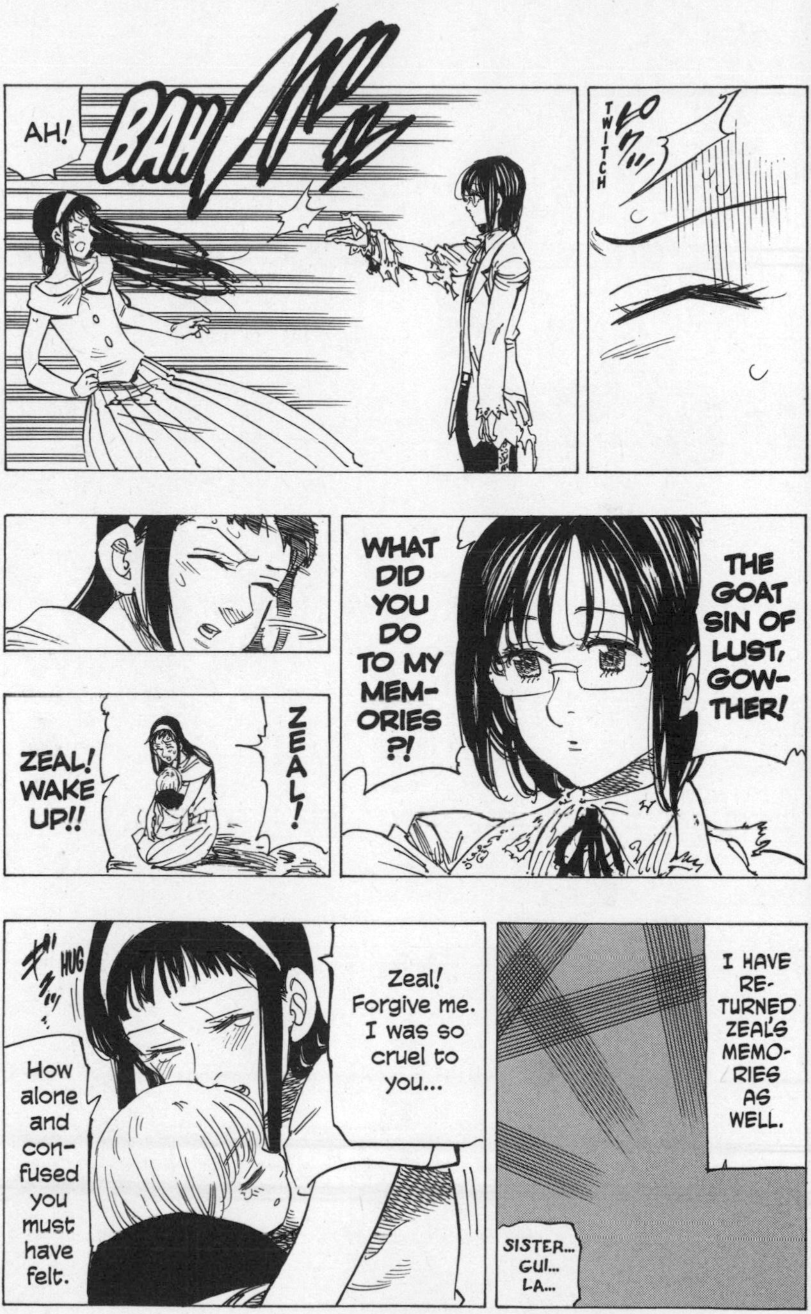
TWITCH
BAH
AH!
THE GOAT SIN OF LUST, GOWTHER!
WHAT DID YOU DO TO MY MEMORIES?!
ZEAL!
ZEAL! WAKE UP!!
I HAVE RETURNED ZEAL'S MEMORIES AS WELL.
SISTER... GUI... LA...
HUG
Zeal! Forgive me. I was so cruel to you...
How alone and confused you must have felt.

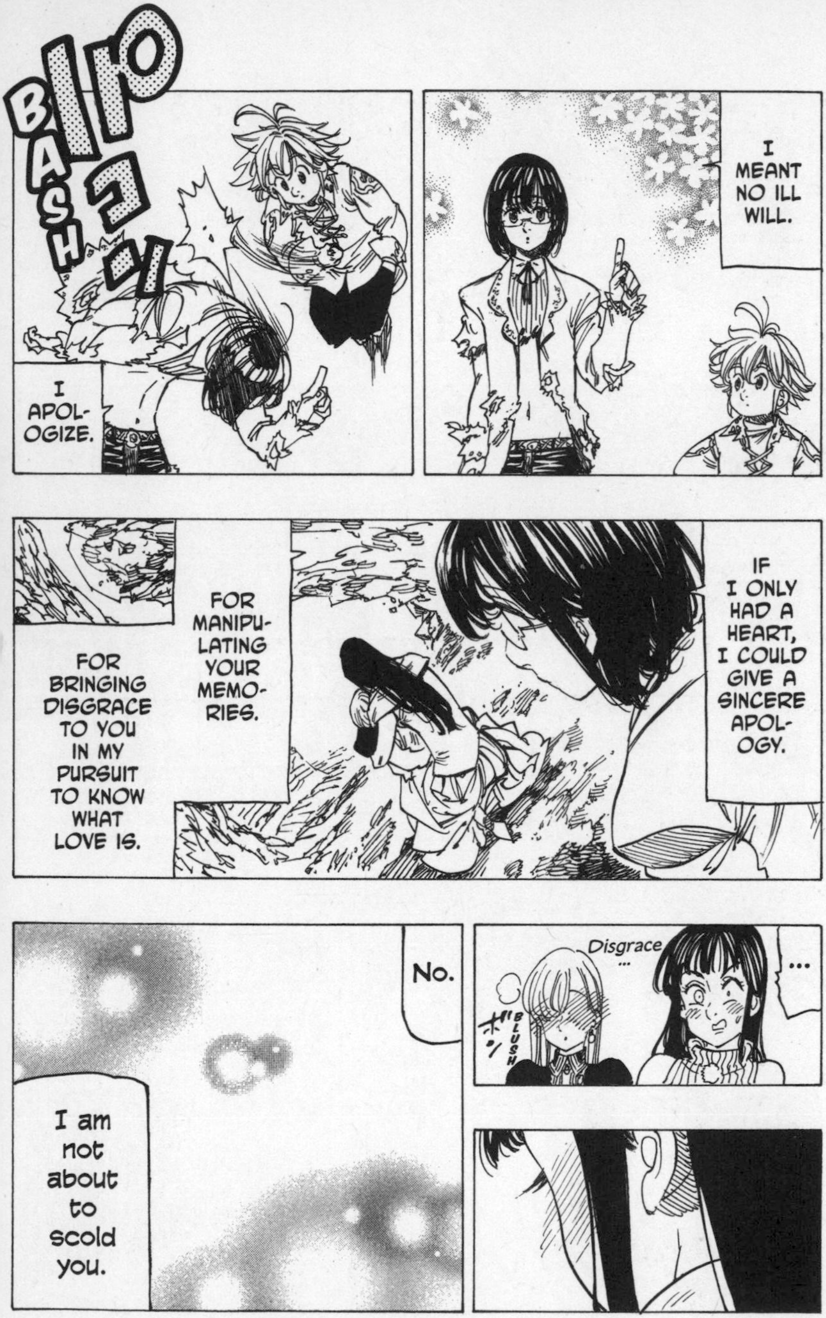
I MEANT NO ILL WILL.
BASH
I APOLOGIZE.
IF I ONLY HAD A HEART, I COULD GIVE A SINCERE APOLOGY.
FOR MANIPULATING YOUR MEMORIES.
FOR BRINGING DISGRACE TO YOU IN MY PURSUIT TO KNOW WHAT LOVE IS.
...
Disgrace...
BLUSH
No.
I am not about to scold you.

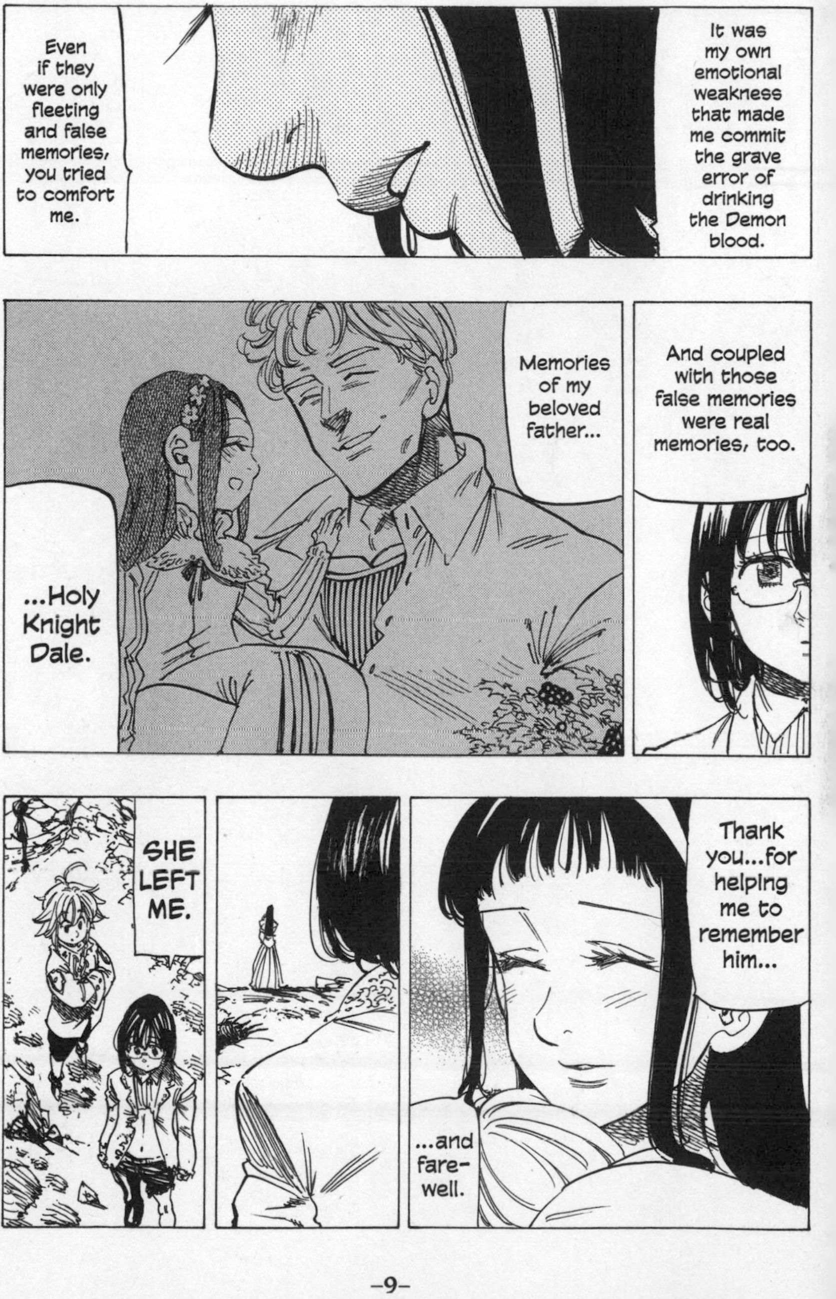
It was my own emotional weakness that made me commit the grave error of drinking the Demon blood.
Even if they were only fleeting and false memories, you tried to comfort me.
And coupled with those false memories were real memories, too.
Memories of my beloved father...
...Holy Knight Dale.
Thank you...for helping me to remember him...
...and fare-well.
SHE LEFT ME.

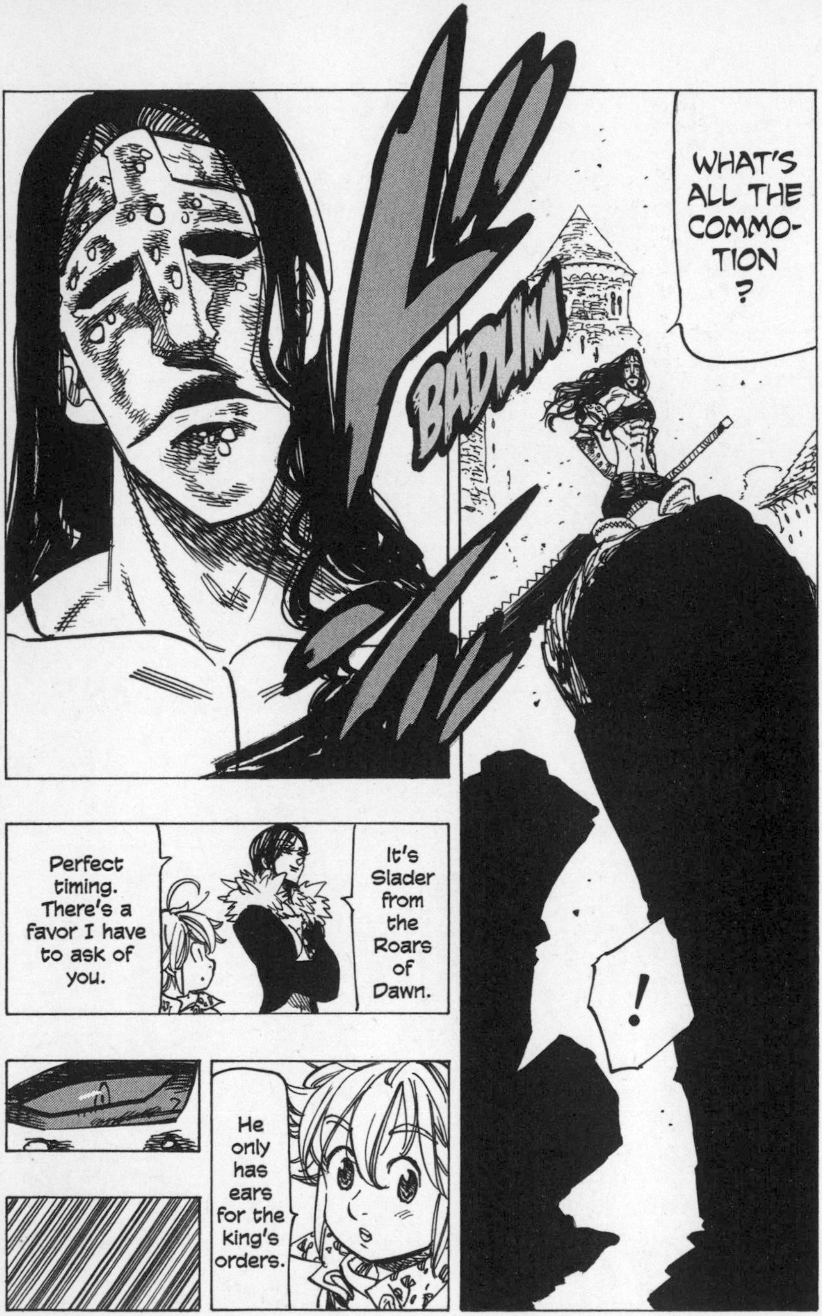
WHAT'S ALL THE COMMOTION?
BADUM
!
It's Slader from the Roars of Dawn.
Perfect timing. There's a favor I have to ask of you.
He only has ears for the king's orders.

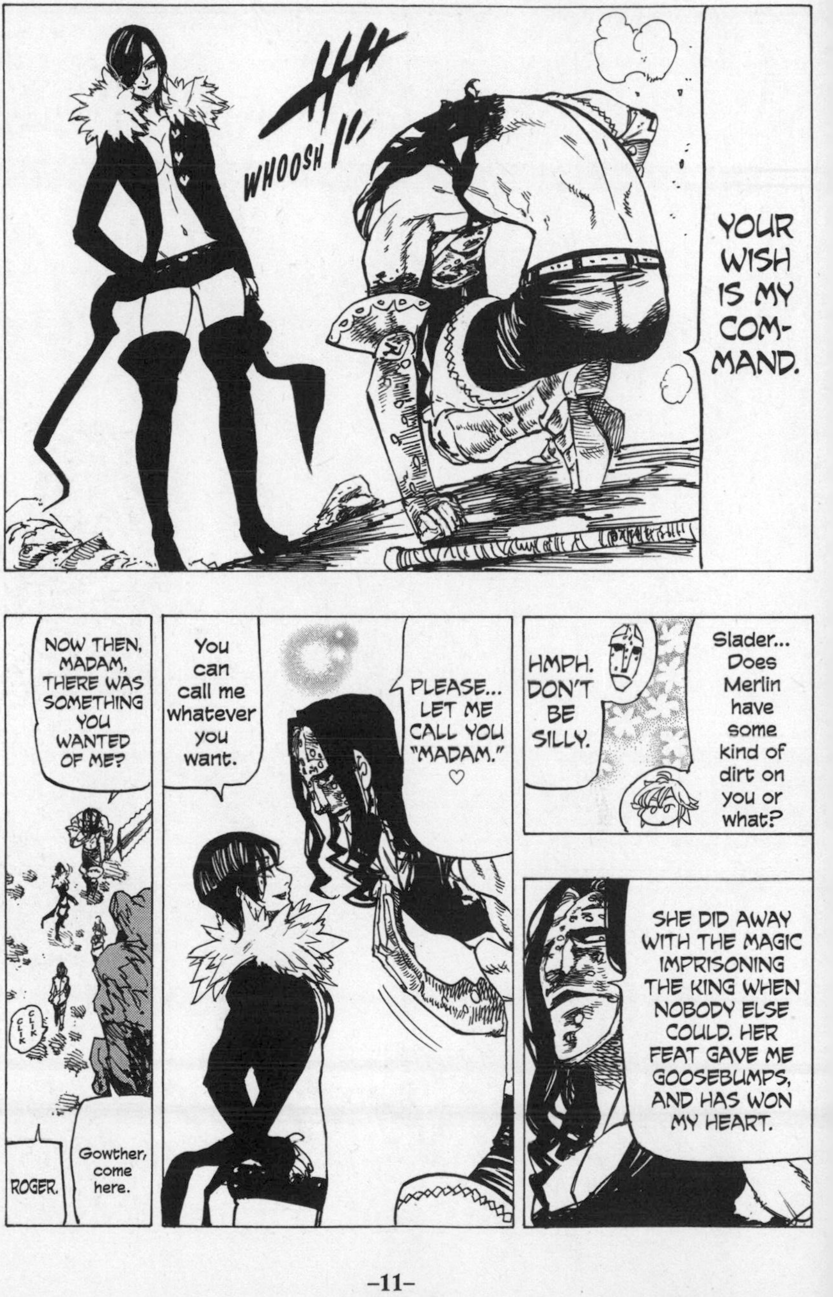
YOUR WISH IS MY COM-MAND.
WHOOSH
Slader... Does Merlin have some kind of dirt on you or what?
HMPH. DON'T BE SILLY.
SHE DID AWAY WITH THE MAGIC IMPRISONING THE KING WHEN NOBODY ELSE COULD. HER FEAT GAVE ME GOOSEBUMPS, AND HAS WON MY HEART.
PLEASE... LET ME CALL YOU "MADAM." ♡
You can call me whatever you want.
NOW THEN, MADAM, THERE WAS SOMETHING YOU WANTED OF ME?
CLIK CLIK
Gowther, come here.
ROGER.

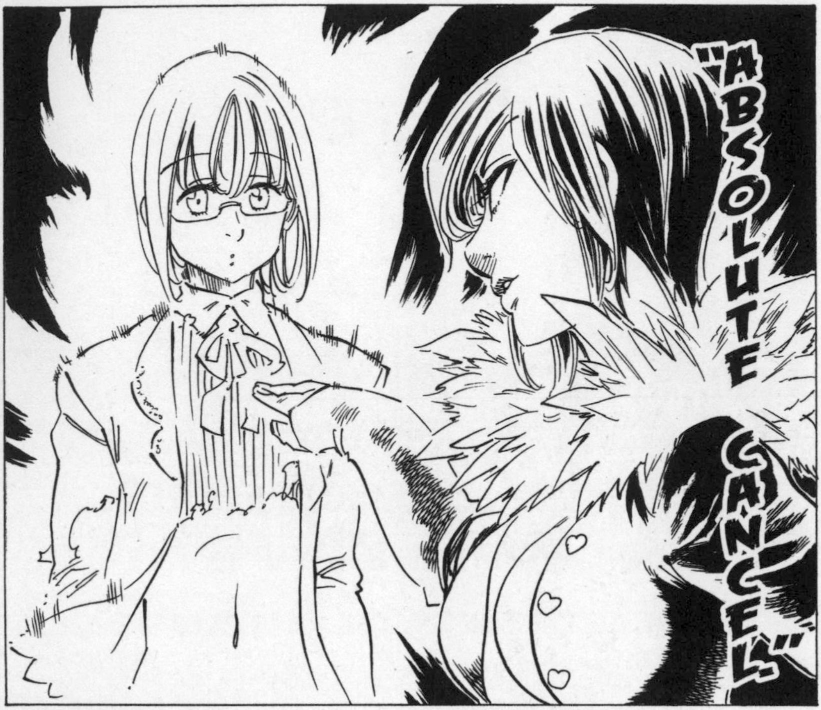
"ABSOLUTE CANCEL."
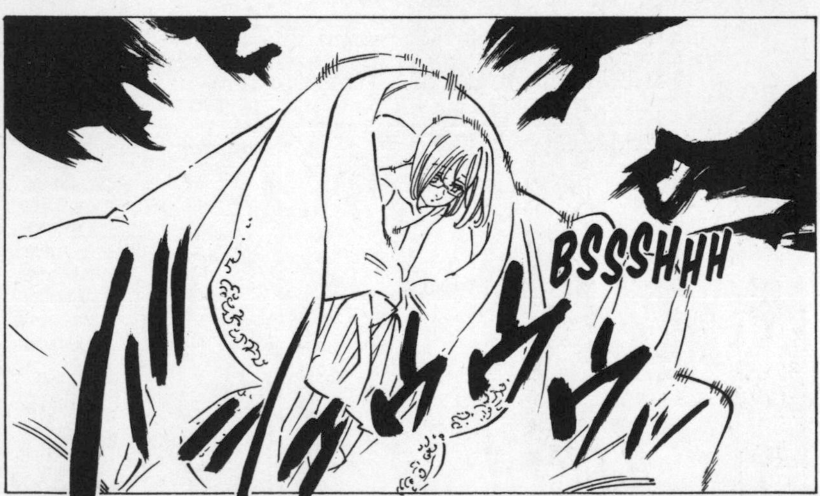
BSSSHHH

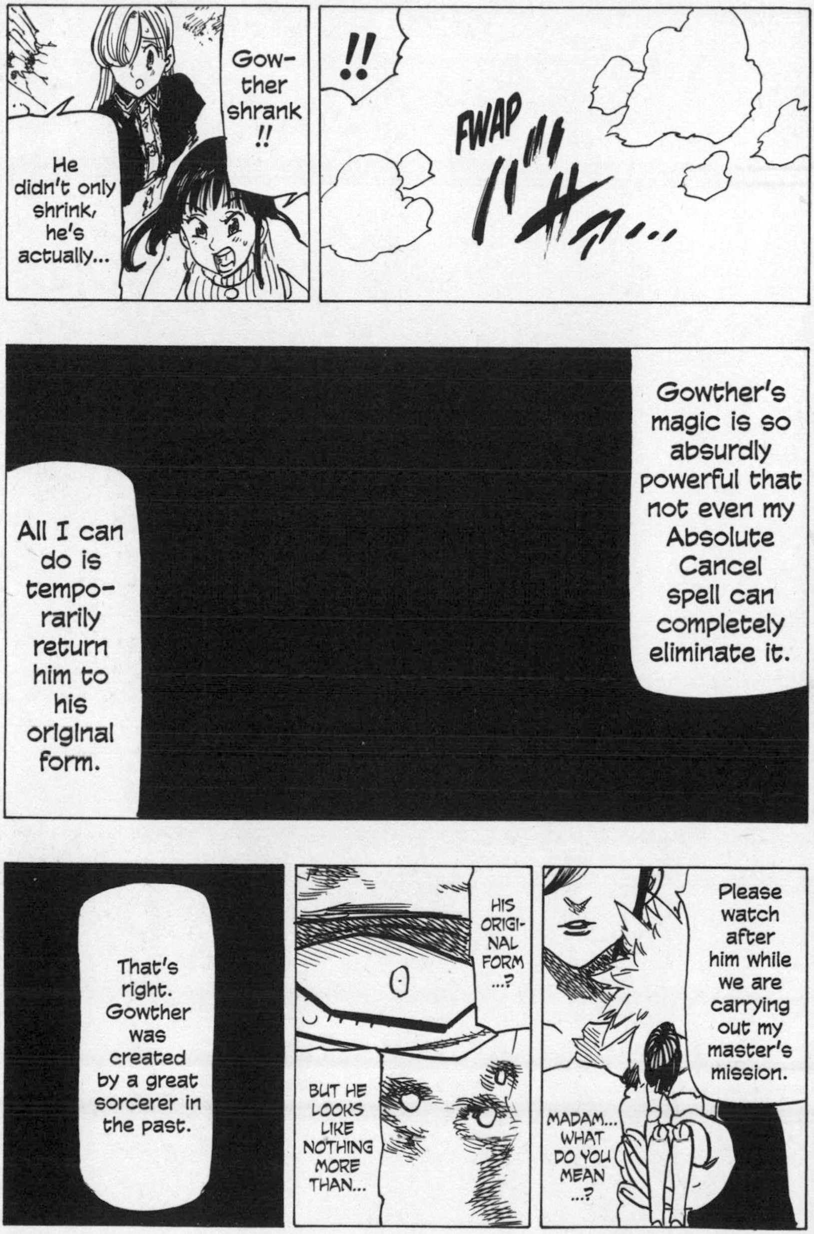
!!
FWAP
Gow-ther shrank!!
He didn't only shrink, he's actually...
Gowther's magic is so absurdly powerful that not even my Absolute Cancel spell can completely eliminate it.
All I can do is tempo-rarily return him to his original form.
Please watch after him while we are carrying out my master's mission.
MADAM... WHAT DO YOU MEAN ...?
HIS ORIGI-NAL FORM ...?
BUT HE LOOKS LIKE NOTHING MORE THAN...
That's right. Gowther was created by a great sorcerer in the past.

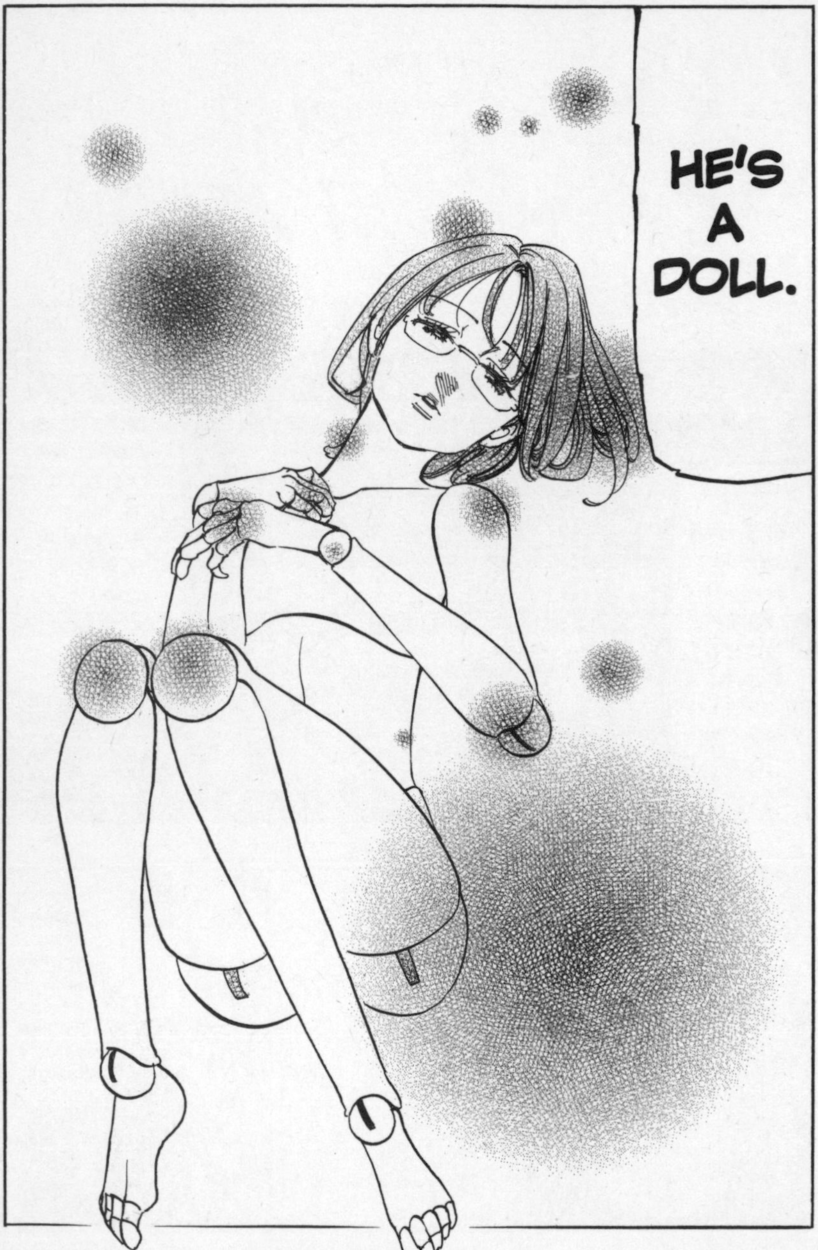
HE'S A DOLL.

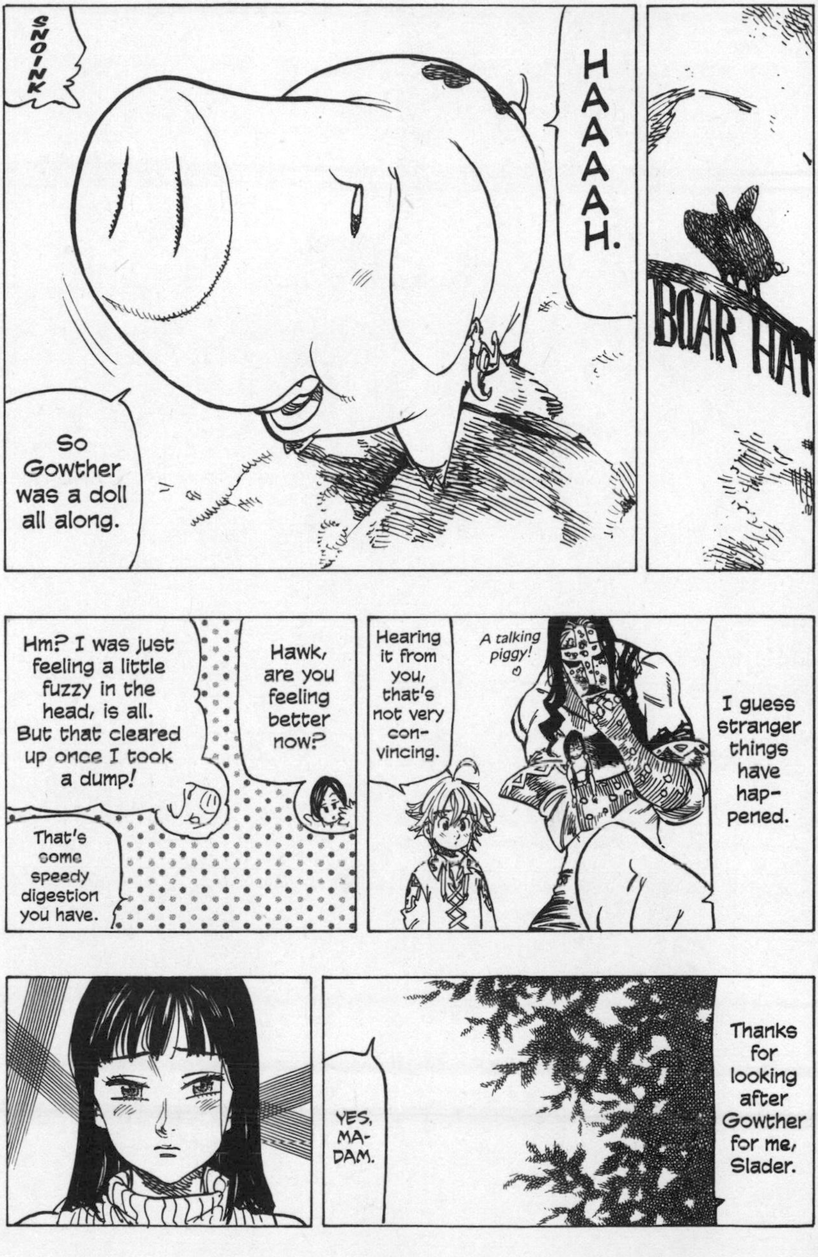
BOAR HAT
HAAAAH.
SNOINK
So Gowther was a doll all along.
I guess stranger things have hap-pened.
A talking piggy! ♡
Hearing it from you, that's not very con-vincing.
Hawk, are you feeling better now?
Hm? I was just feeling a little fuzzy in the head, is all. But that cleared up once I took a dump!
That's some speedy digestion you have.
Thanks for looking after Gowther for me, Slader.
YES, MA-DAM.

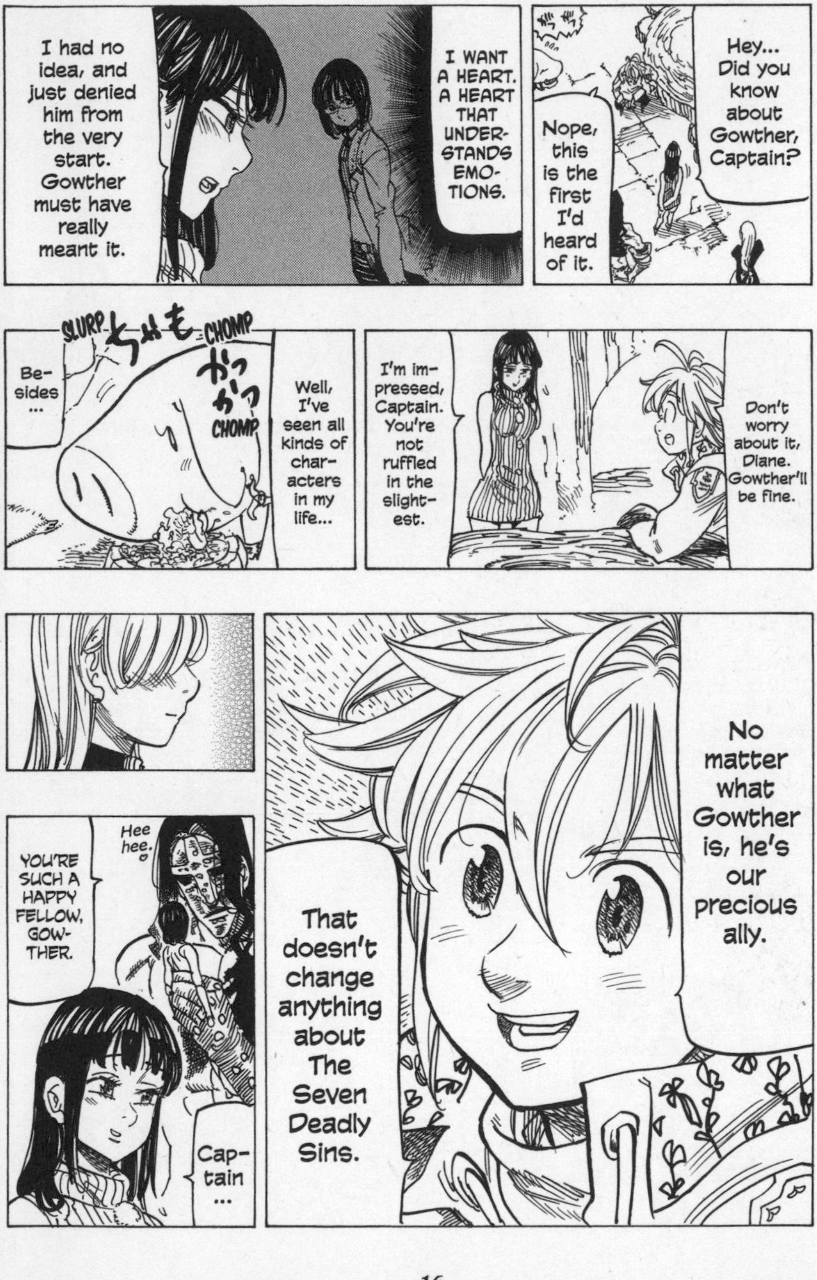
Hey... Did you know about Gowther, Captain?
Nope, this is the first I'd heard of it.
I WANT A HEART. A HEART THAT UNDERSTANDS EMOTIONS.
I had no idea, and just denied him from the very start. Gowther must have really meant it.
Don't worry about it, Diane. Gowther'll be fine.
I'm impressed, Captain. You're not ruffled in the slightest.
Well, I've seen all kinds of characters in my life...
SLURP
CHOMP
CHOMP
Besides...
No matter what Gowther is, he's our precious ally.
That doesn't change anything about The Seven Deadly Sins.
Captain...
Hee hee.
YOU'RE SUCH A HAPPY FELLOW, GOWTHER.

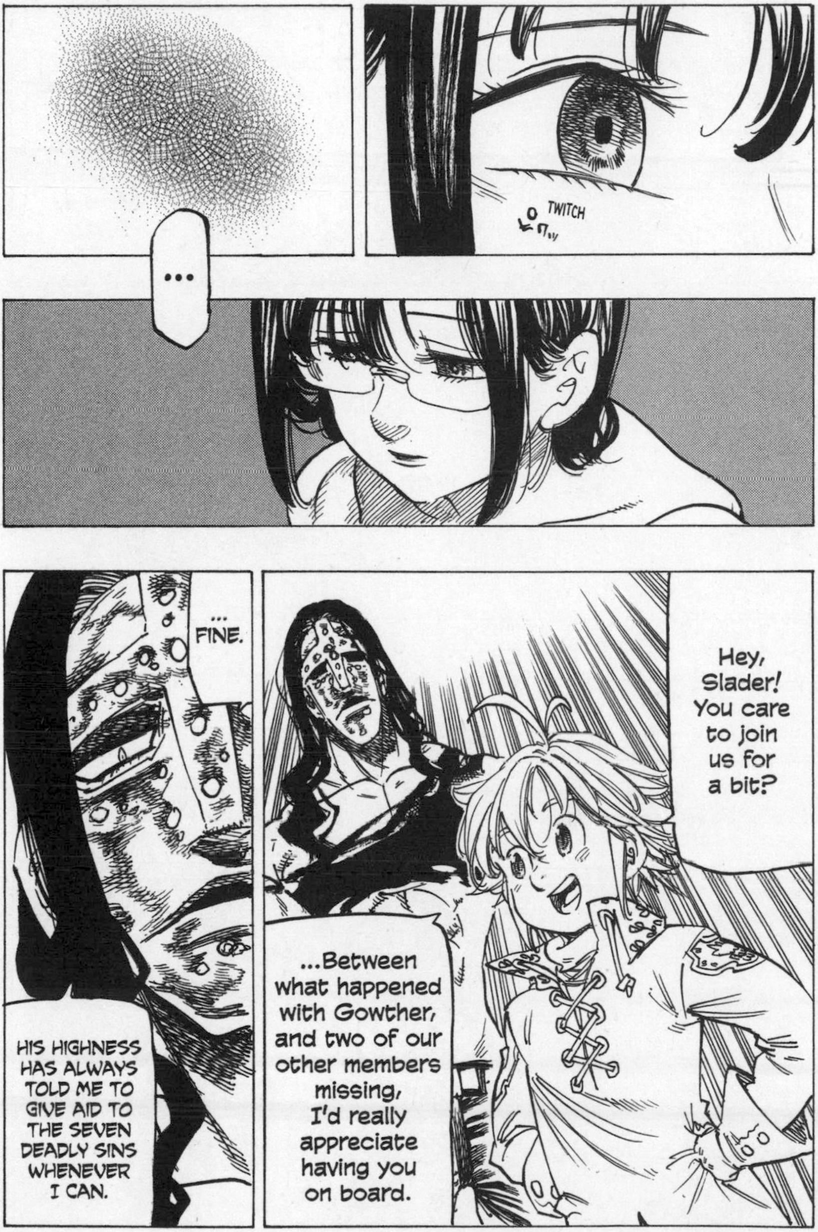
TWITCH
...
Hey, Slader! You care to join us for a bit?
...Between what happened with Gowther, and two of our other members missing, I'd really appreciate having you on board.
... FINE.
HIS HIGHNESS HAS ALWAYS TOLD ME TO GIVE AID TO THE SEVEN DEADLY SINS WHENEVER I CAN.

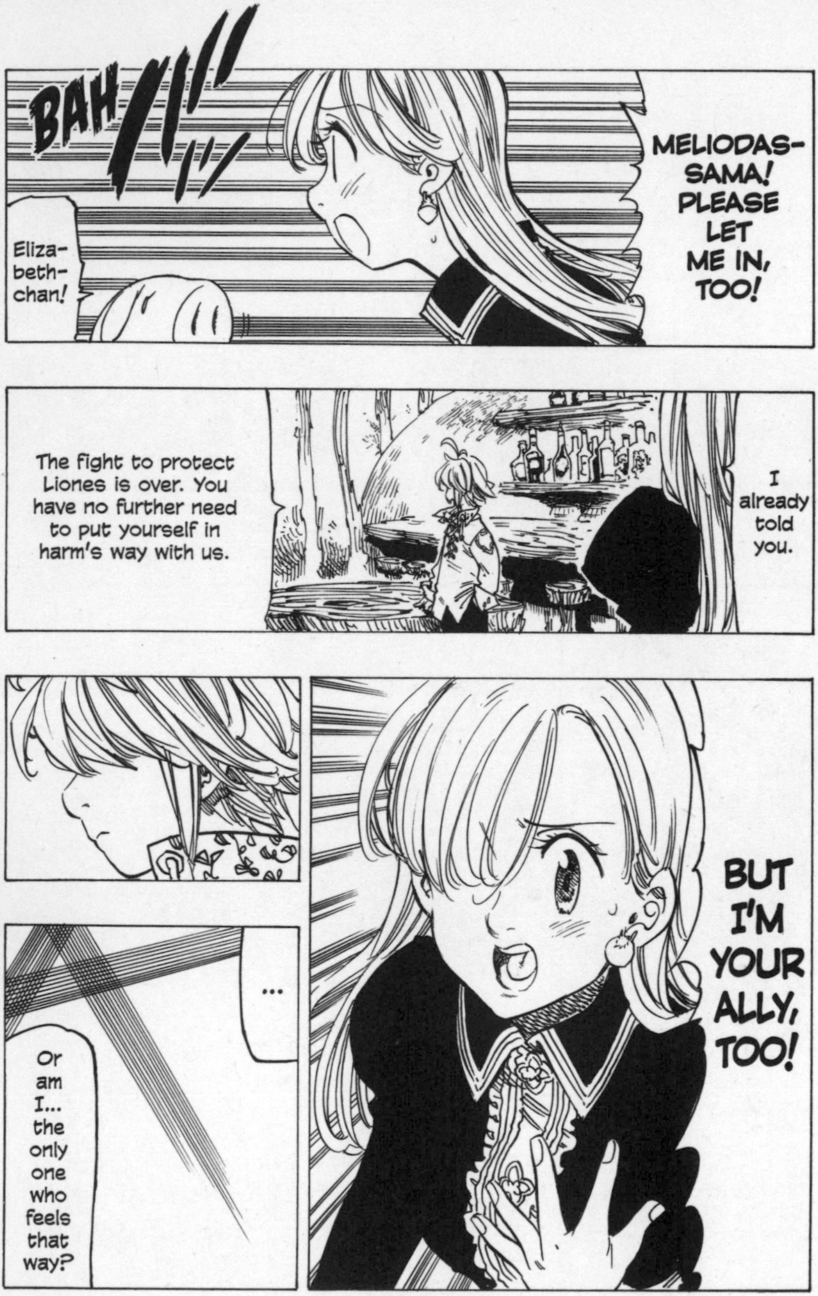
MELIODAS-SAMA! PLEASE LET ME IN, TOO!
BAH
Eliza-beth-chan!
I already told you.
The fight to protect Liones is over. You have no further need to put yourself in harm's way with us.
BUT I'M YOUR ALLY, TOO!
...
Or am I... the only one who feels that way?

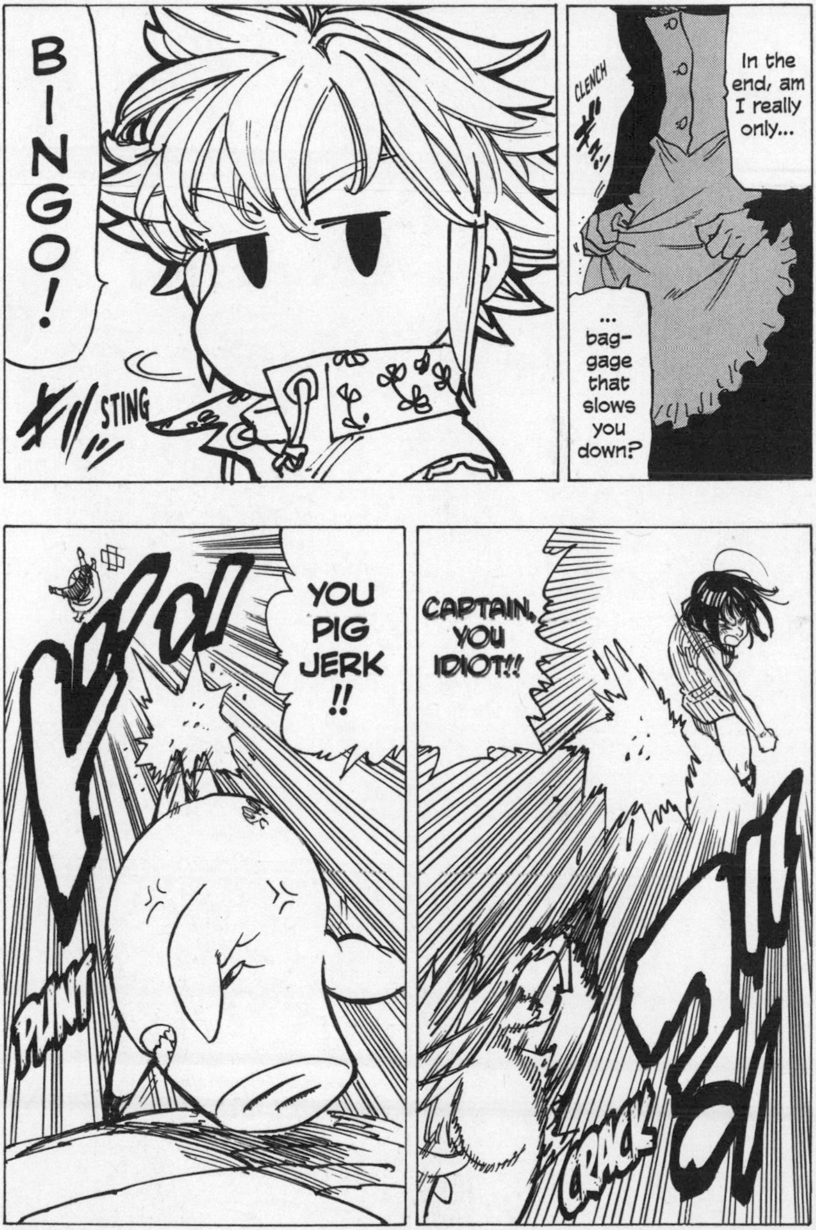
In the end, am I really only...
CLENCH
... bag-gage that slows you down?
BINGO!
STING
CAPTAIN, YOU IDIOT!!
CRACK
YOU PIG JERK!!
PUNT

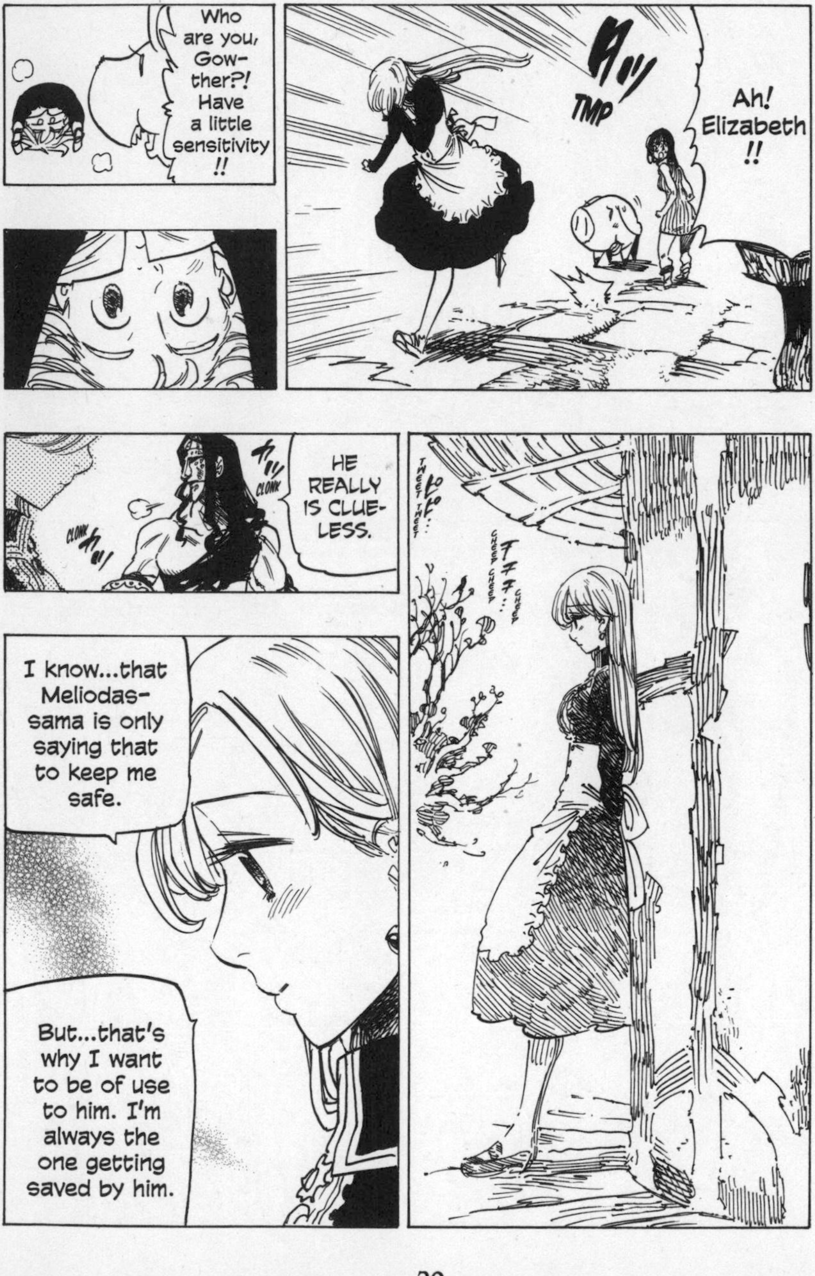
TMP
Ah! Elizabeth!!
Who are you, Gowther?! Have a little sensitivity!!
TWEET TWEET
CHEEP CHEEP CHEEP
CLONK
HE REALLY IS CLUELESS.
CLONK
I know...that Meliodas-sama is only saying that to keep me safe.
But...that's why I want to be of use to him. I'm always the one getting saved by him.

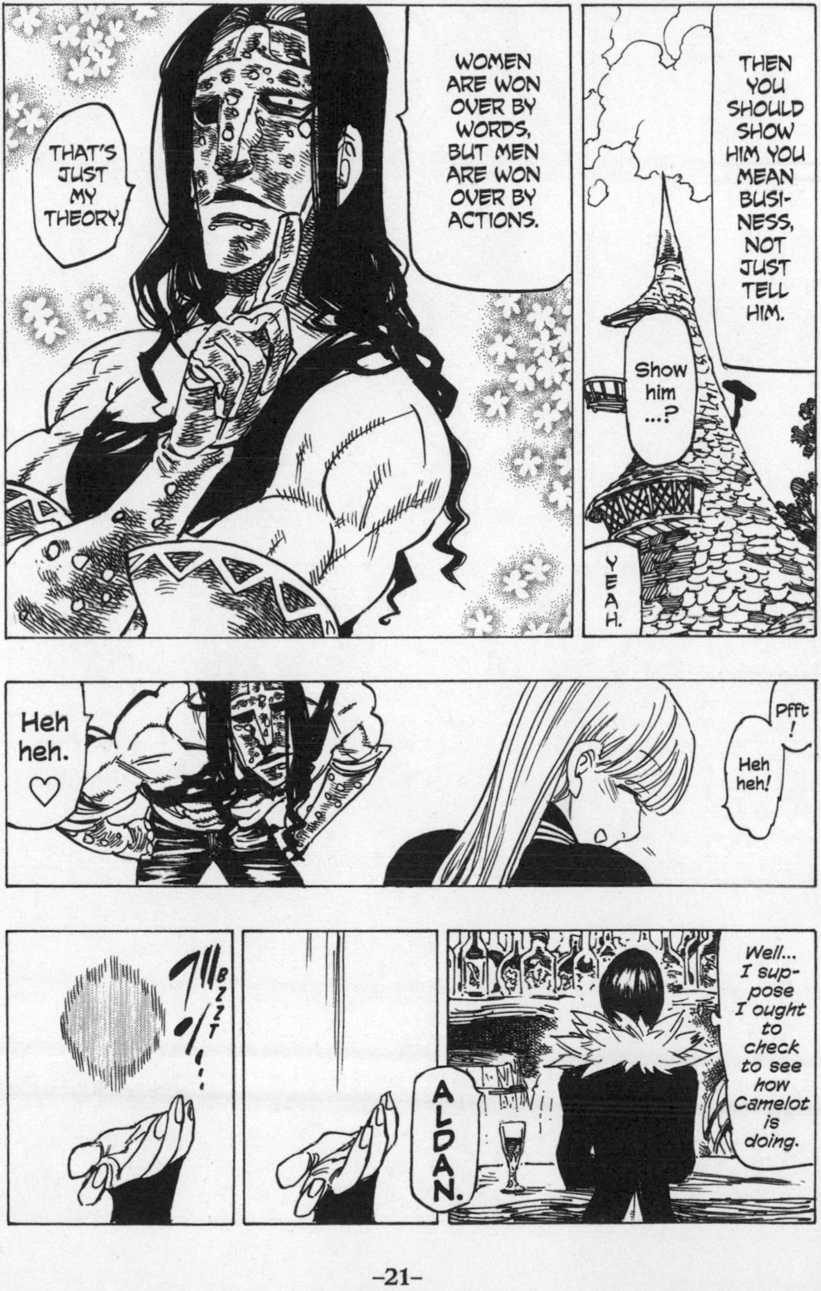
THEN YOU SHOULD SHOW HIM YOU MEAN BUSINESS, NOT JUST TELL HIM.
Show him ...?
YEAH.
WOMEN ARE WON OVER BY WORDS, BUT MEN ARE WON OVER BY ACTIONS.
THAT'S JUST MY THEORY.
Pfft!
Heh heh!
Heh heh. ♡
Well... I suppose I ought to check to see how Camelot is doing.
ALDAN.
BZZT

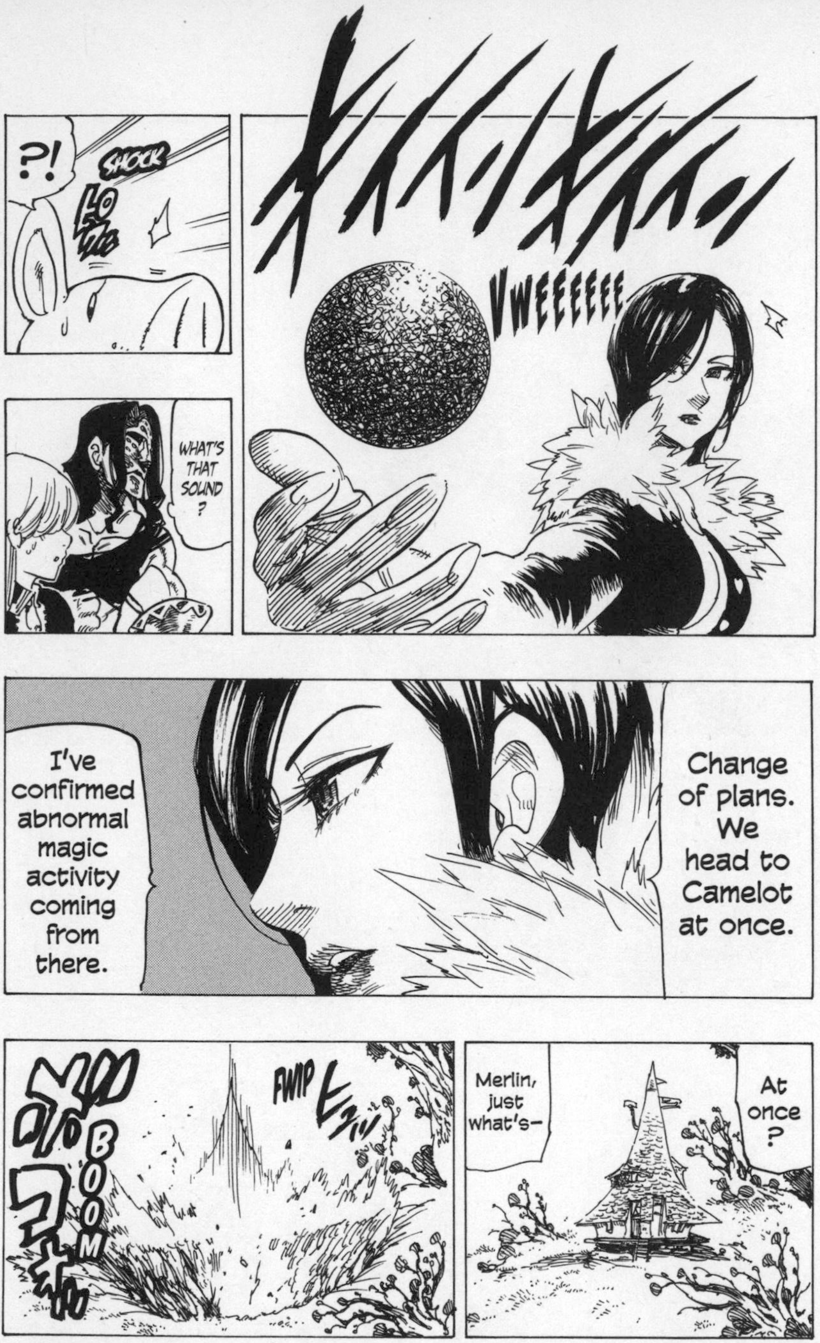
VWEEEEE
?!
SHOCK
WHAT'S THAT SOUND?
Change of plans. We head to Camelot at once.
I've confirmed abnormal magic activity coming from there.
At once?
Merlin, just what's—
FWIP
BOOM

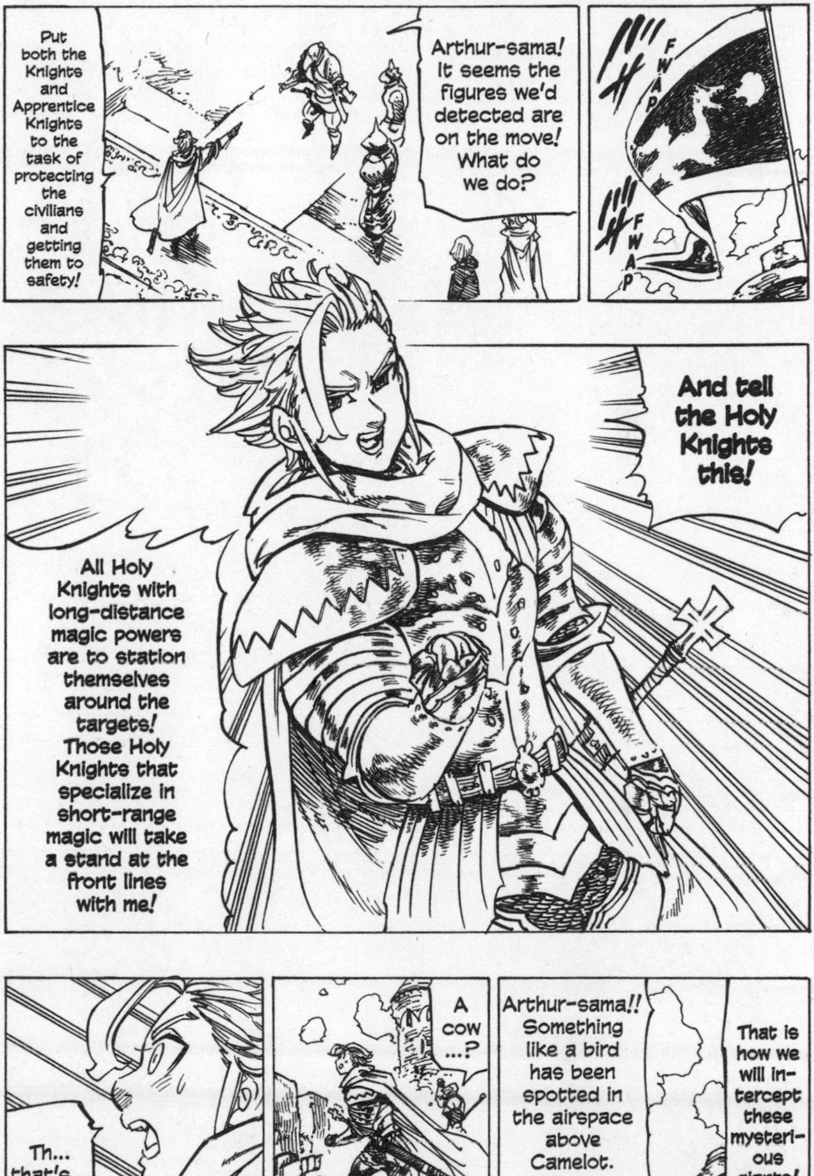
FWAP
FWAP
Arthur-sama! It seems the figures we'd detected are on the move! What do we do?
Put both the Knights and Apprentice Knights to the task of protecting the civilians and getting them to safety!
And tell the Holy Knights this!
All Holy Knights with long-distance magic powers are to station themselves around the targets! Those Holy Knights that specialize in short-range magic will take a stand at the front lines with me!
That is how we will intercept these mysterious giants!
Arthur-sama!! Something like a bird has been spotted in the airspace above Camelot. Wait...no, it's...
A cow...?
Th... that's...

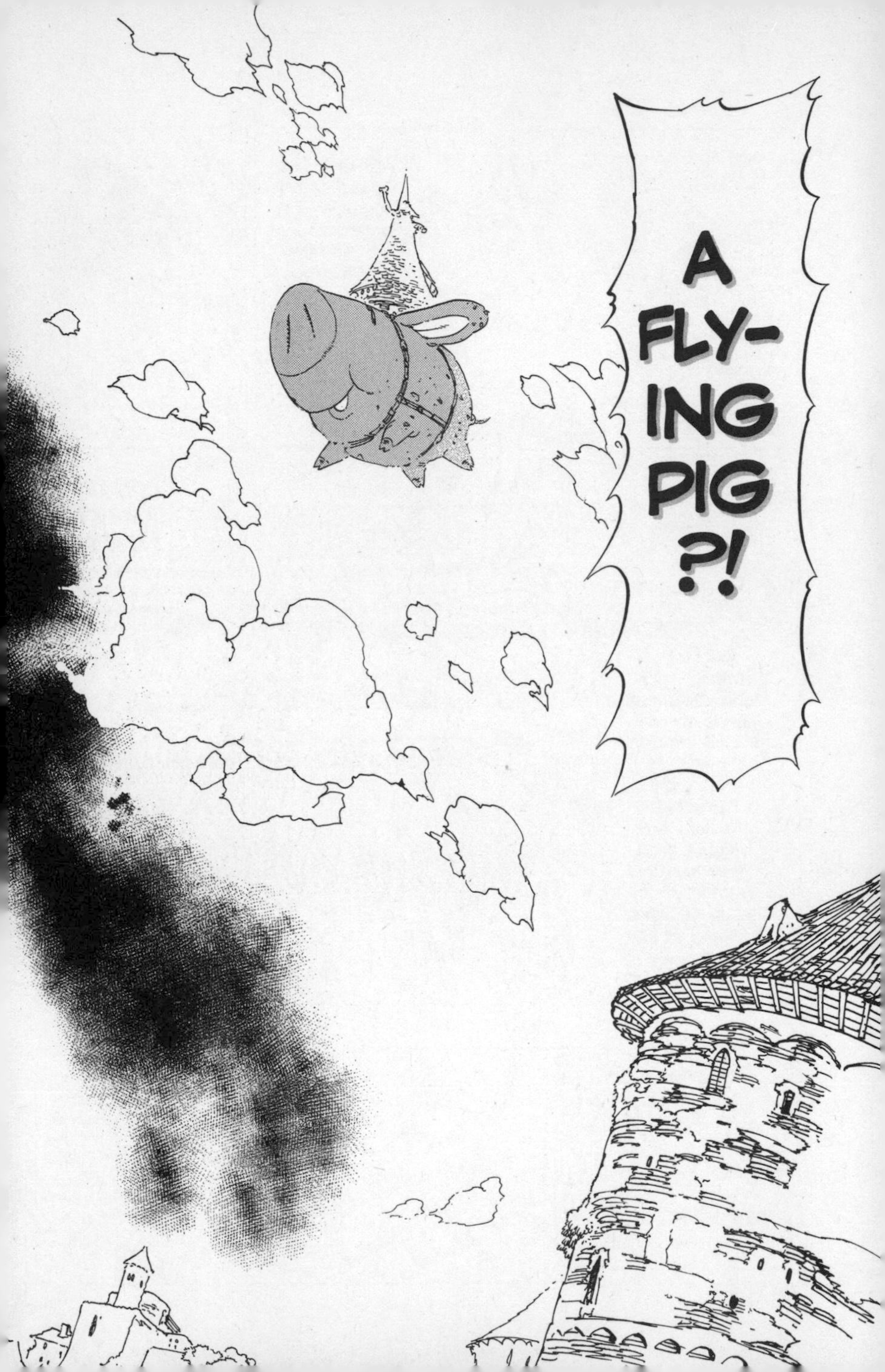
A FLY-ING PIG?!

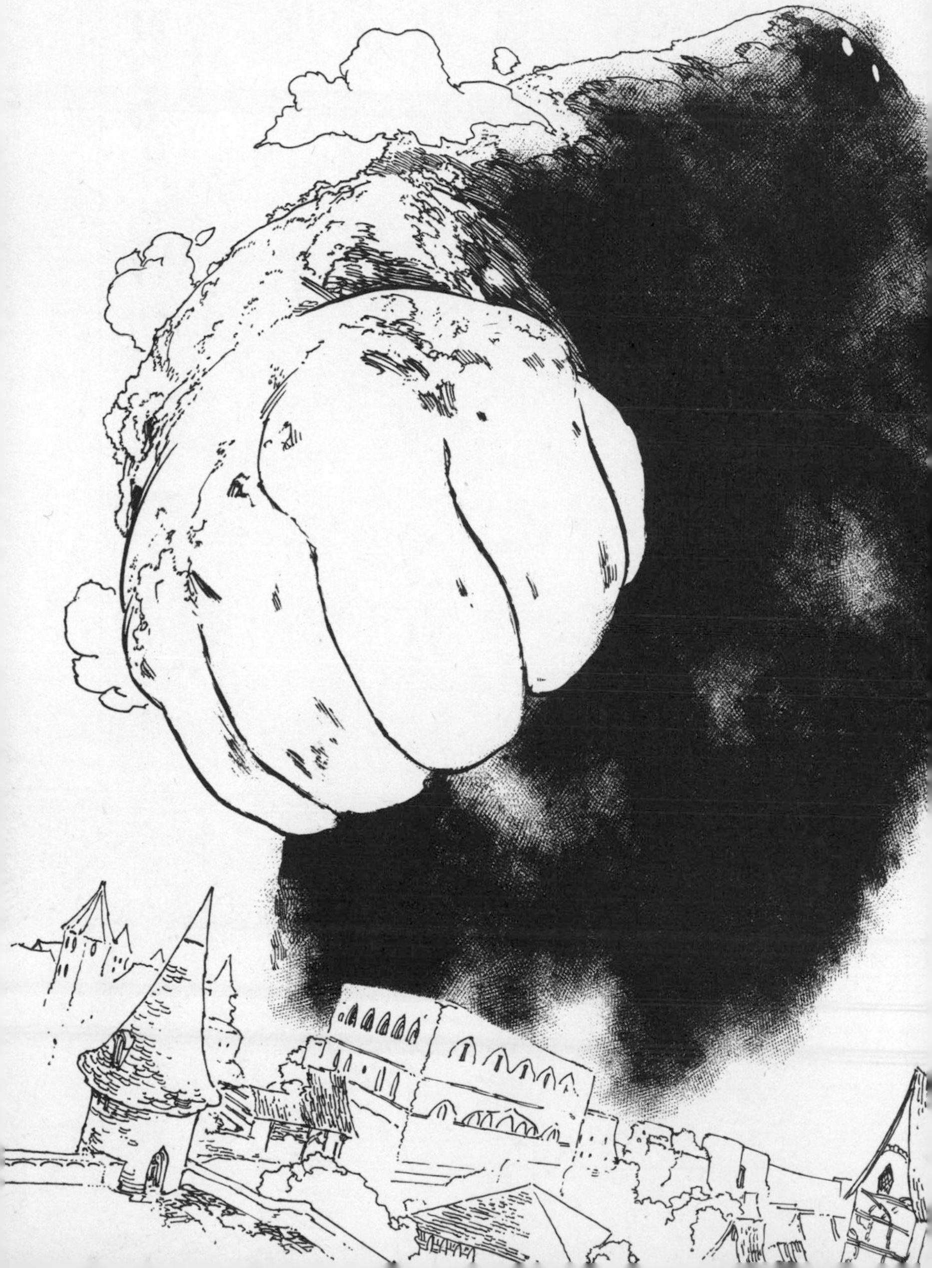

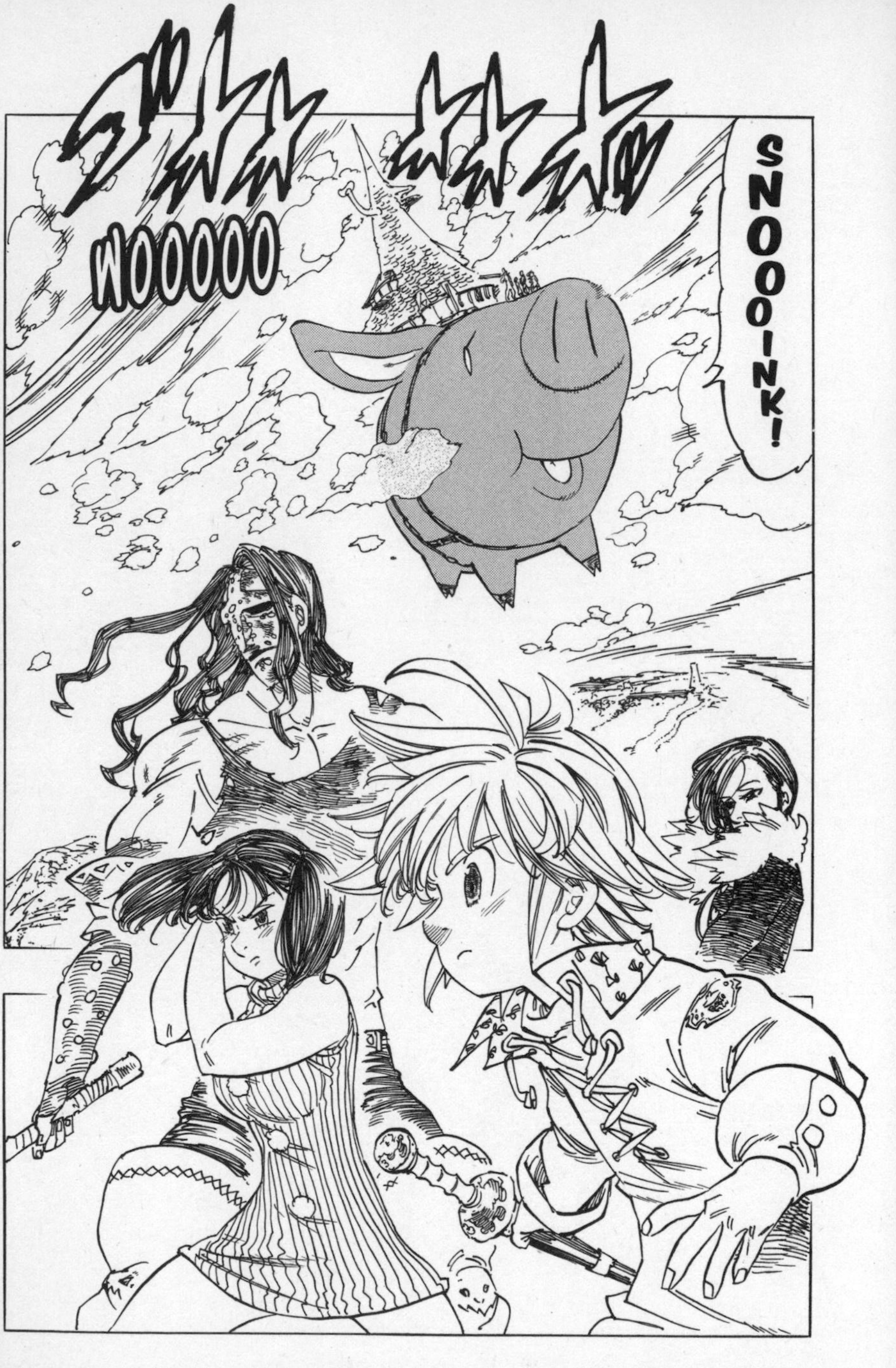
WOOOOO
SNOOOOINK!

Chapter 115 - Nightmare Take Two

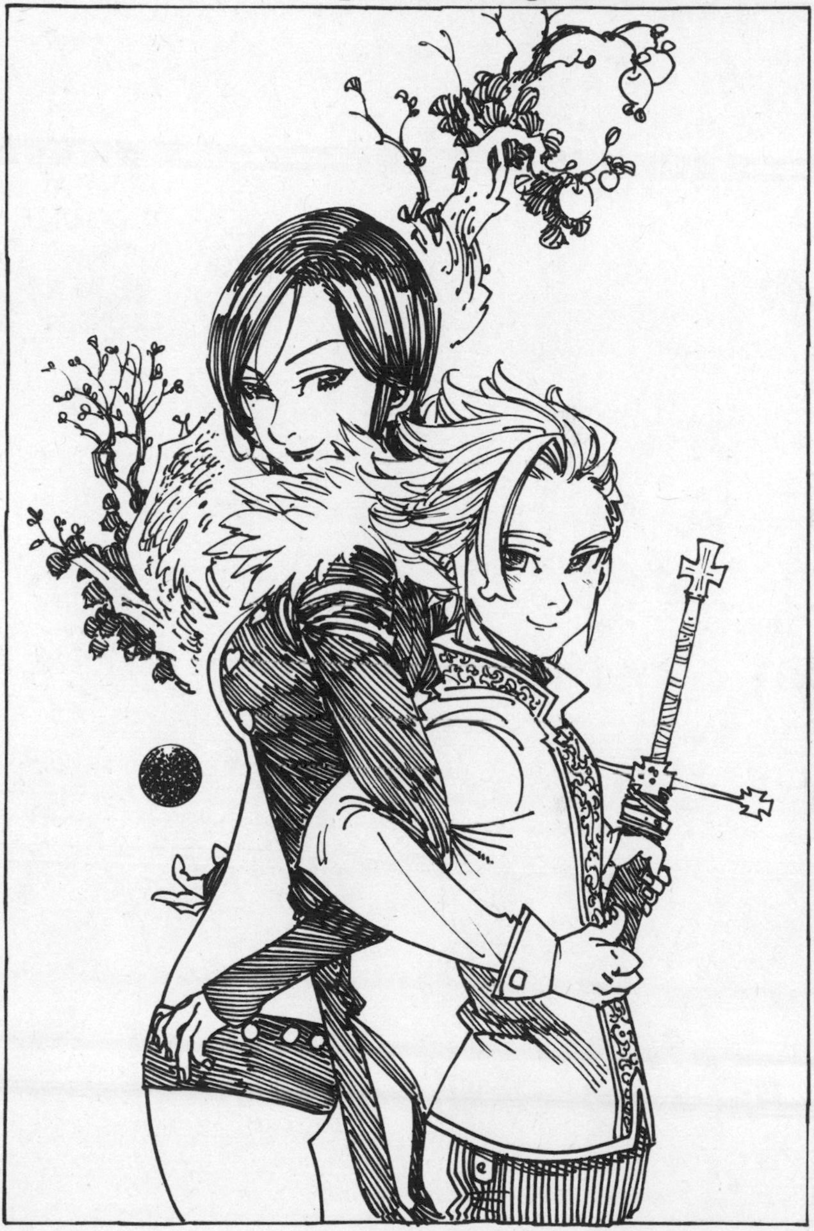

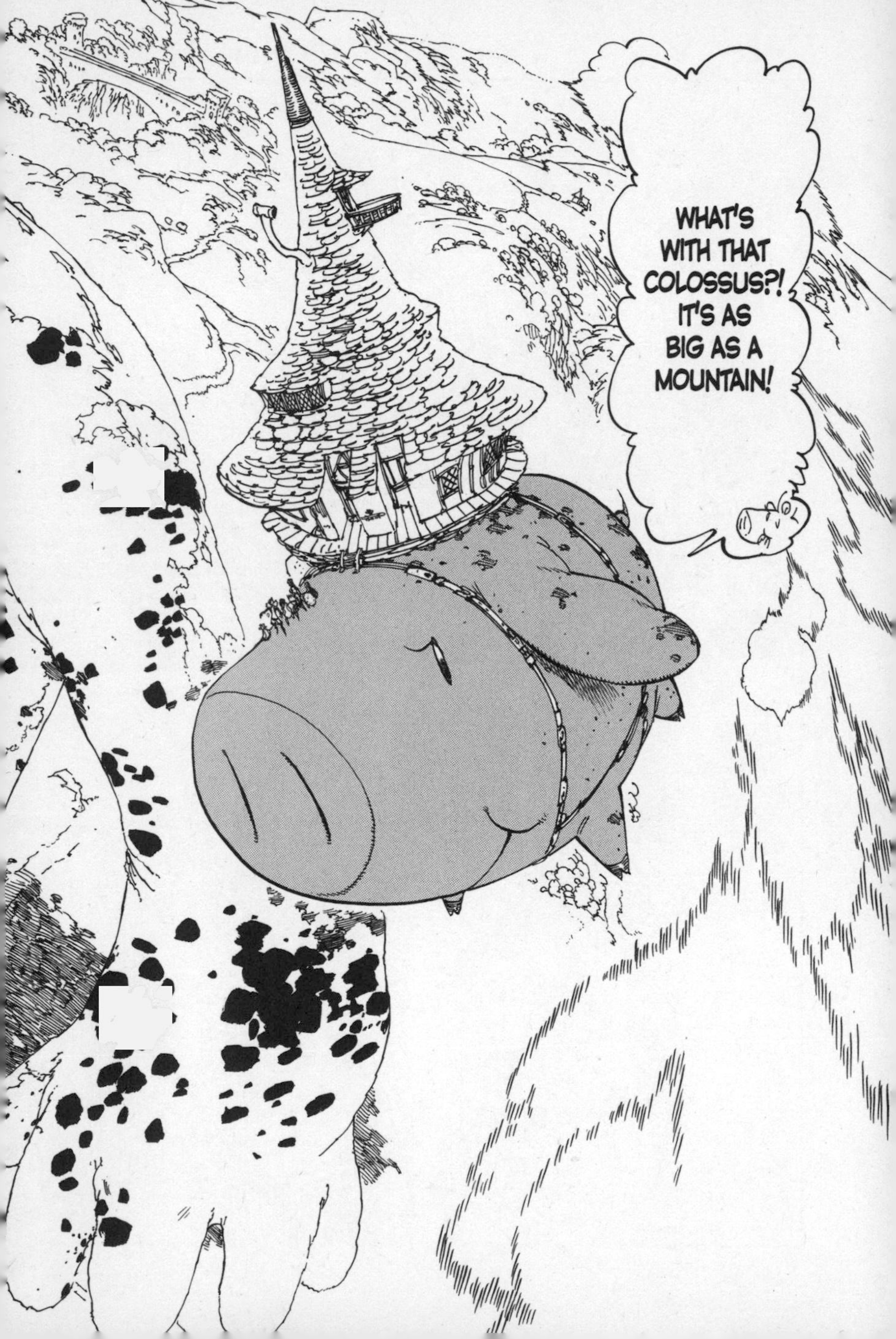
WHAT'S WITH THAT COLOSSUS?! IT'S AS BIG AS A MOUNTAIN!

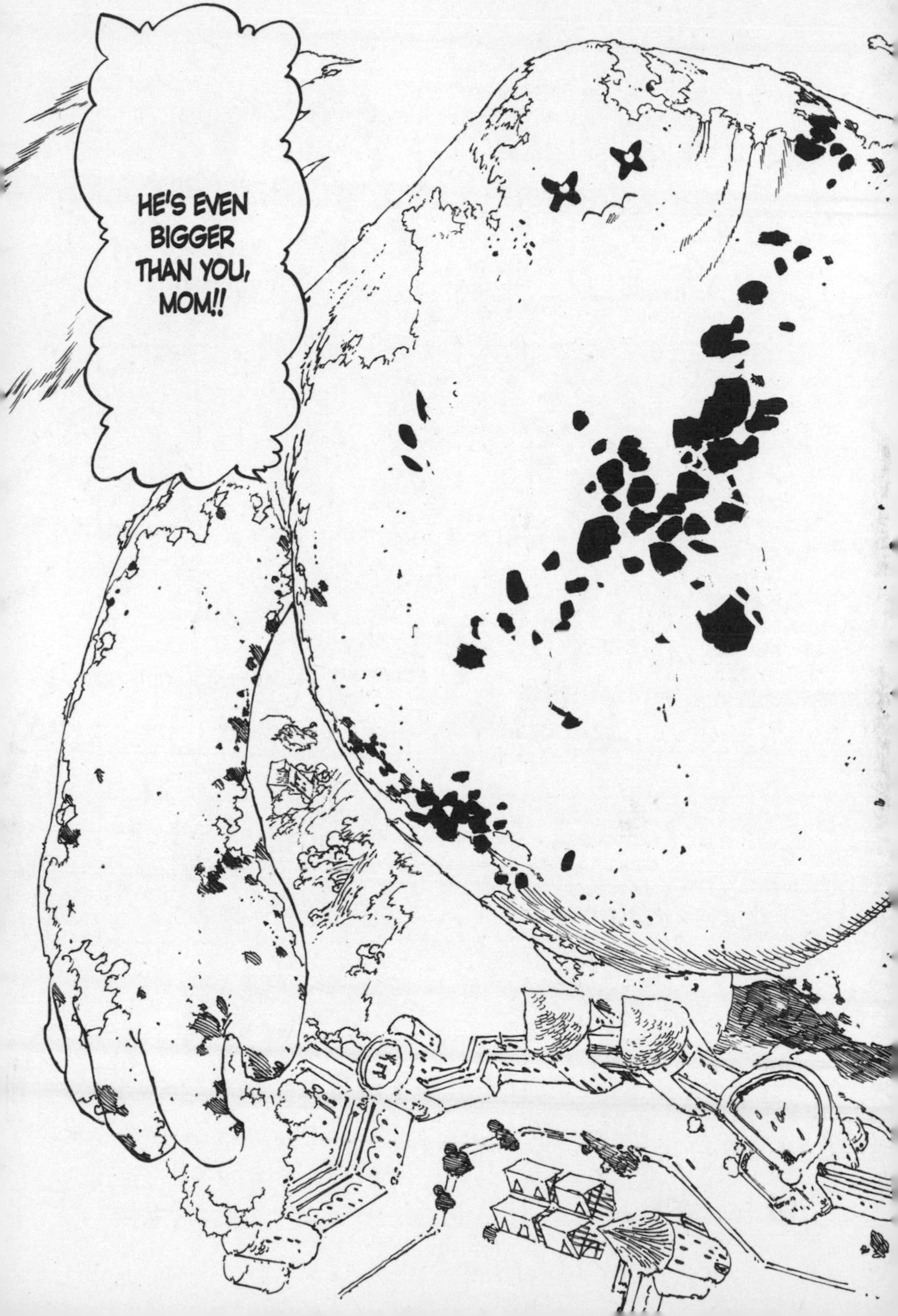
HE'S EVEN BIGGER THAN YOU, MOM!!

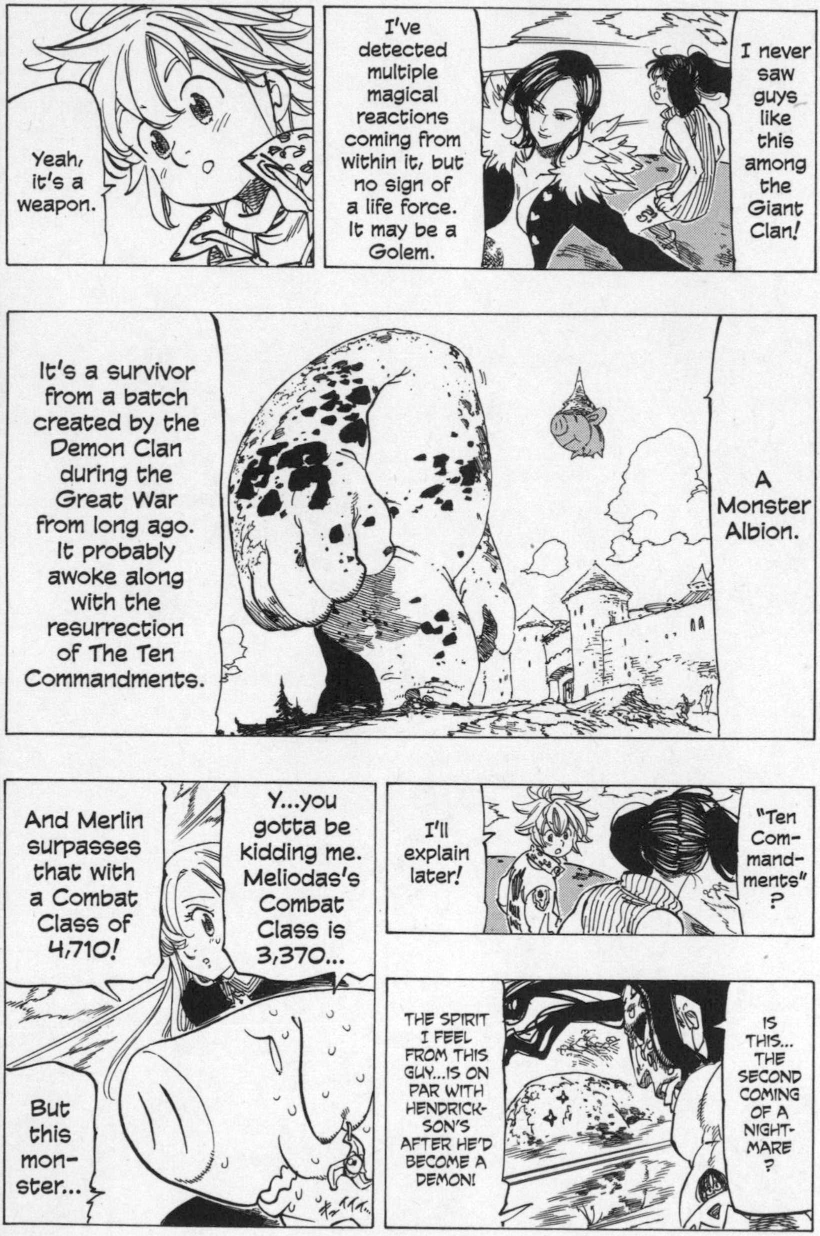
I never saw guys like this among the Giant Clan!
I've detected multiple magical reactions coming from within it, but no sign of a life force. It may be a Golem.
Yeah, it's a weapon.
A Monster Albion.
It's a survivor from a batch created by the Demon Clan during the Great War from long ago. It probably awoke along with the resurrection of The Ten Commandments.
"Ten Commandments"?
I'll explain later!
IS THIS... THE SECOND COMING OF A NIGHTMARE?
THE SPIRIT I FEEL FROM THIS GUY...IS ON PAR WITH HENDRICKSON'S AFTER HE'D BECOME A DEMON!
Y...you gotta be kidding me. Meliodas's Combat Class is 3,370...
And Merlin surpasses that with a Combat Class of 4,710!
But this monster...

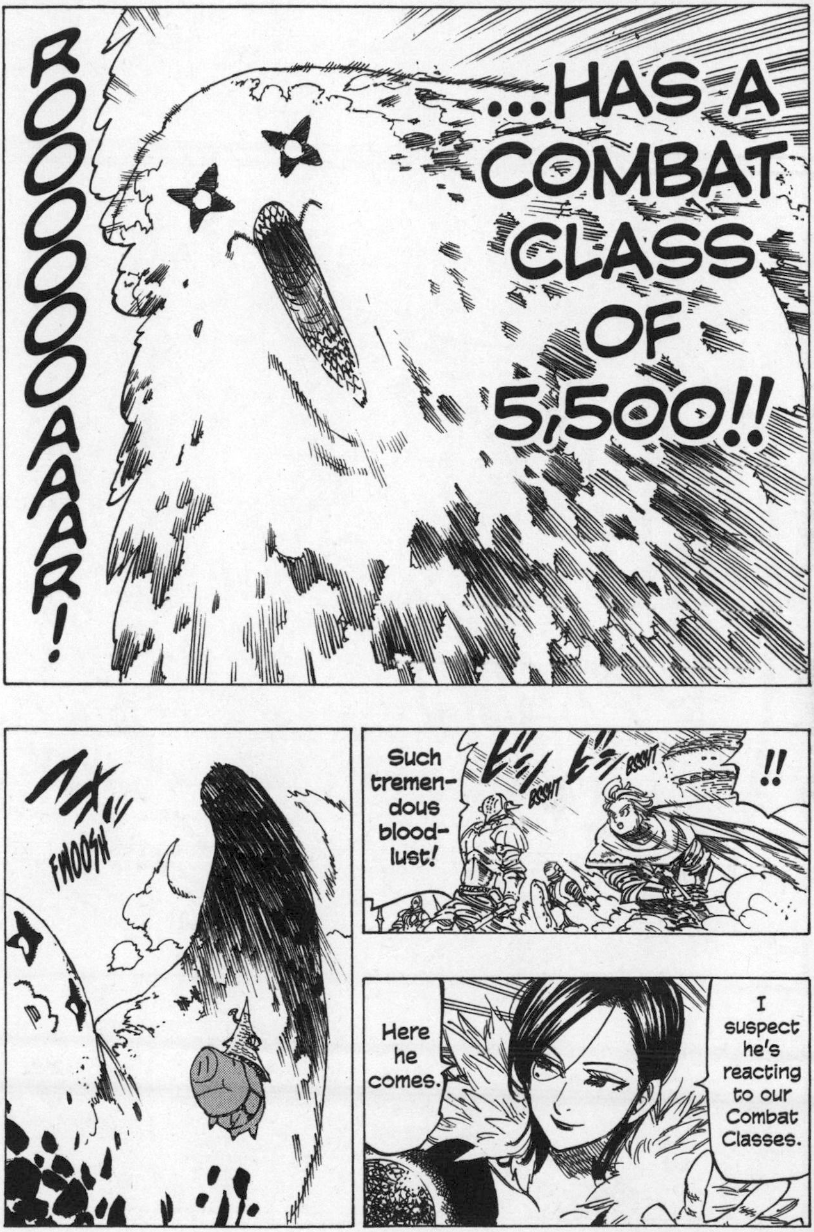
...HAS A COMBAT CLASS OF 5,500!!
ROOOOOOOAAAR!
BSSHT
BSSHT
!!
Such tremendous bloodlust!
I suspect he's reacting to our Combat Classes.
Here he comes.
FWOOSH

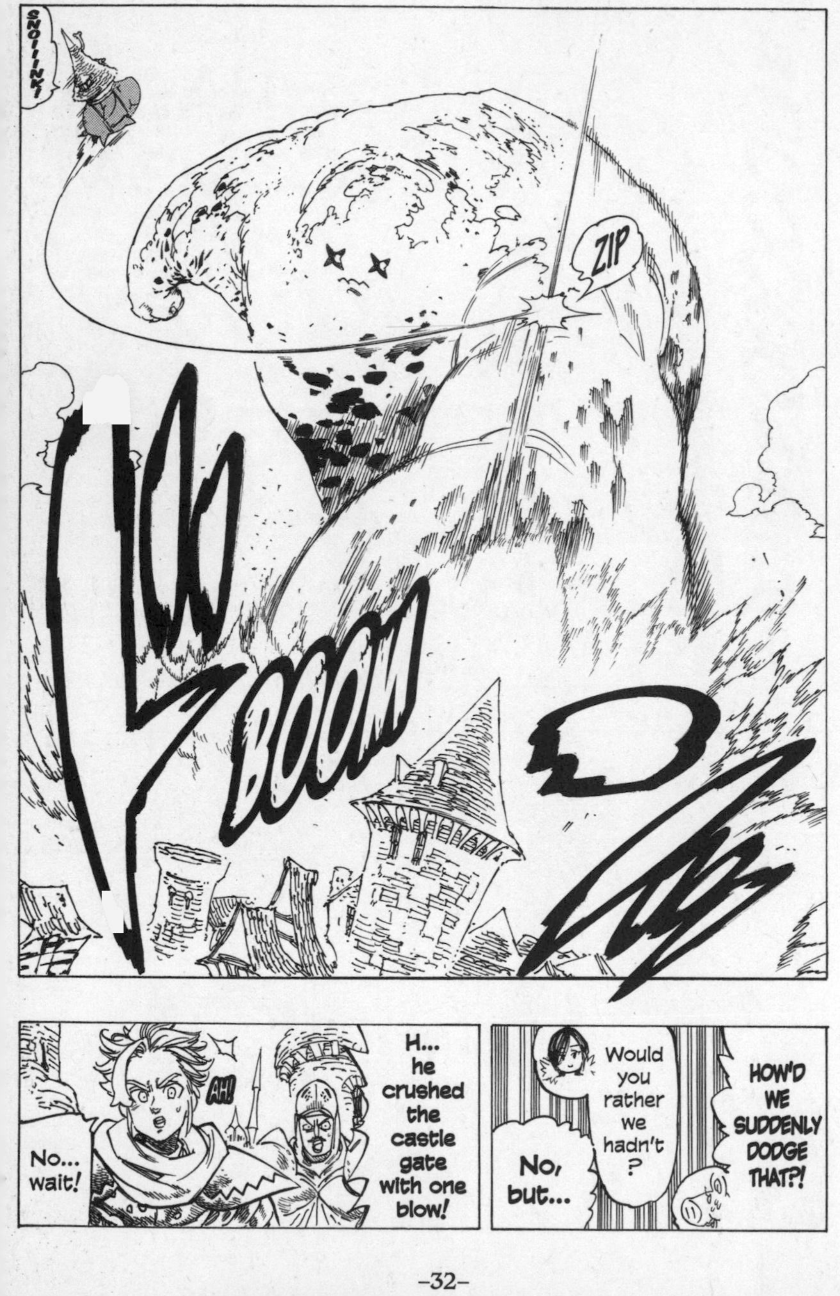
SNOIIINK!
ZIP
BOOM
HOW'D WE SUDDENLY DODGE THAT?!
Would you rather we hadn't?
No, but...
H... he crushed the castle gate with one blow!
AH!
No... wait!

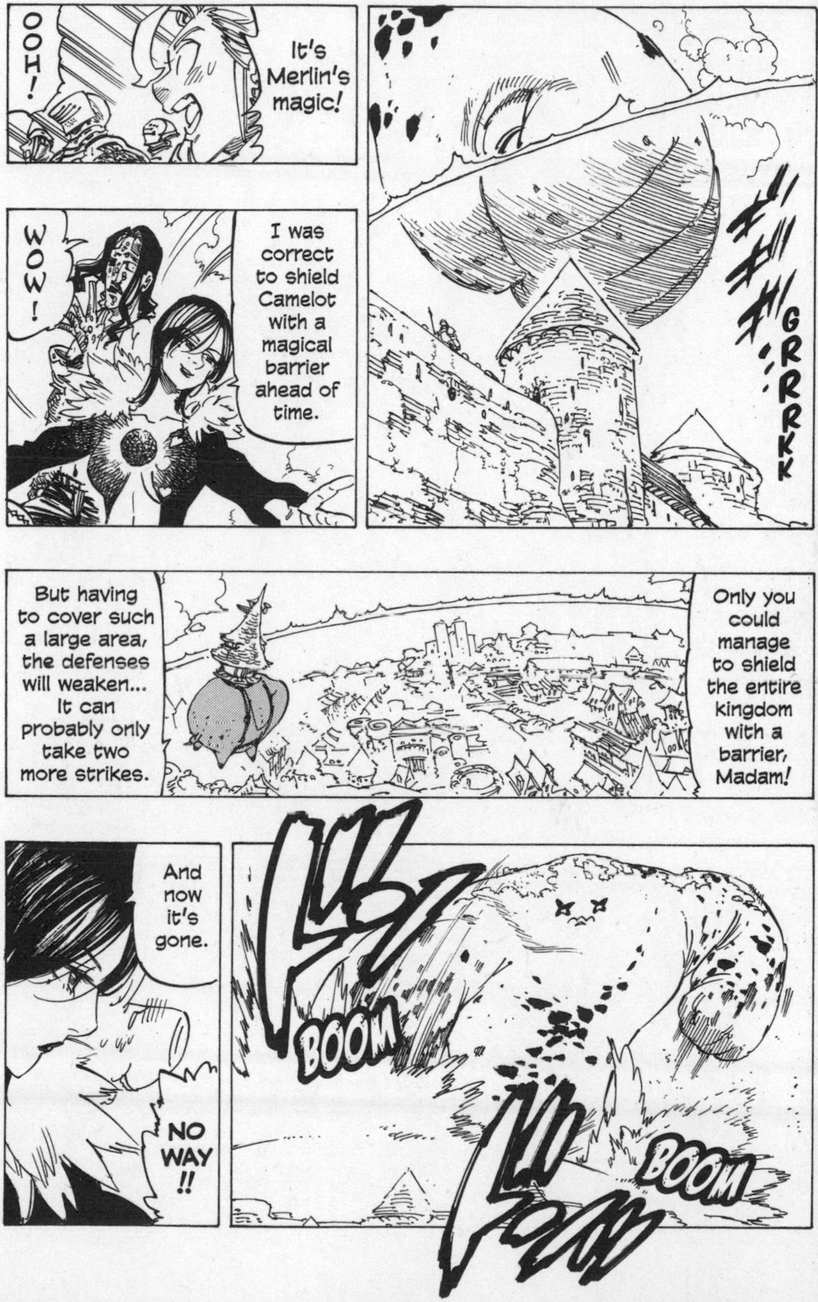
GRRRKK
OOH!
It's Merlin's magic!
WOW!
I was correct to shield Camelot with a magical barrier ahead of time.
Only you could manage to shield the entire kingdom with a barrier, Madam!
But having to cover such a large area, the defenses will weaken... It can probably only take two more strikes.
BOOM
BOOM
And now it's gone.
NO WAY!!

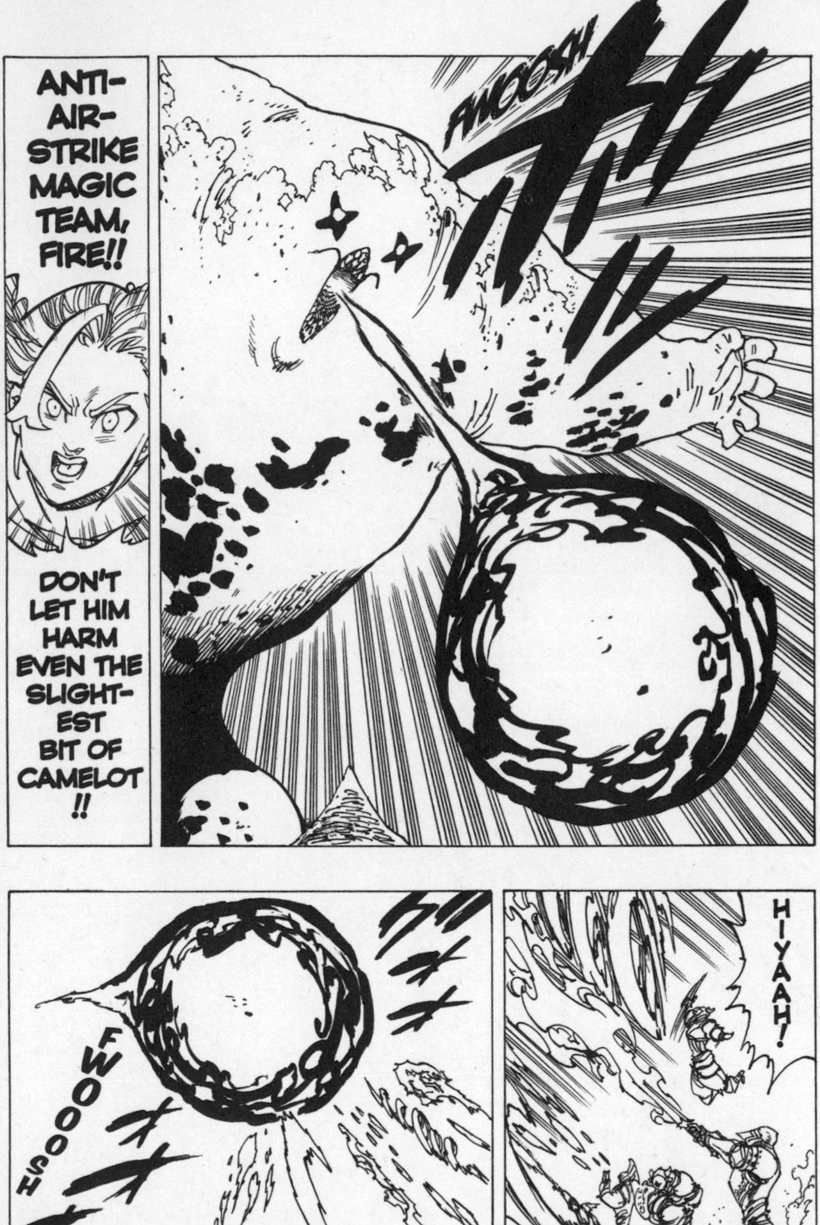
FWOOOSH
ANTI-AIR-STRIKE MAGIC TEAM, FIRE!!
DON'T LET HIM HARM EVEN THE SLIGHTEST BIT OF CAMELOT!!
HIYAAH!
FWOOOSH

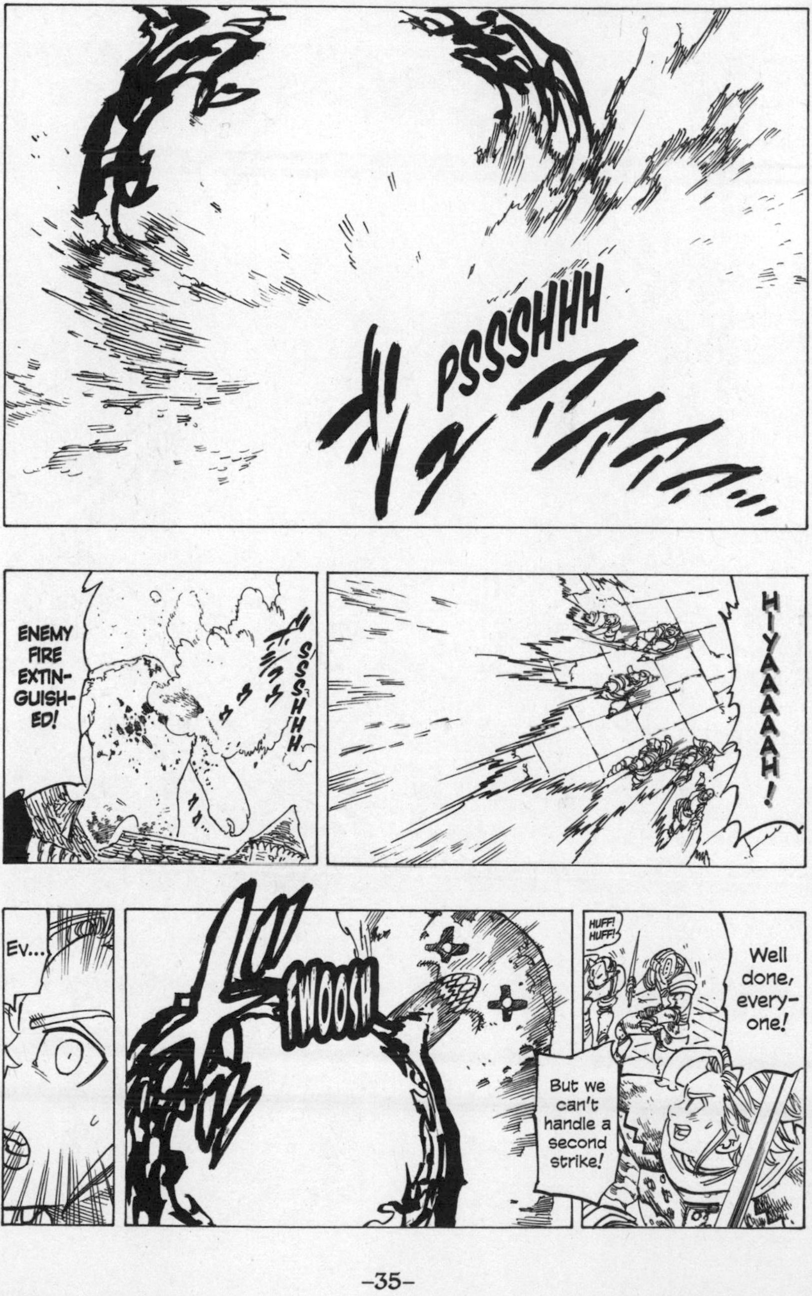
PSSSHHH
HIYAAAAAH!
SSSHHH
ENEMY FIRE EXTIN-GUISH-ED!
HUFF! HUFF!
Well done, every-one!
But we can't handle a second strike!
FWOOSH
Ev...

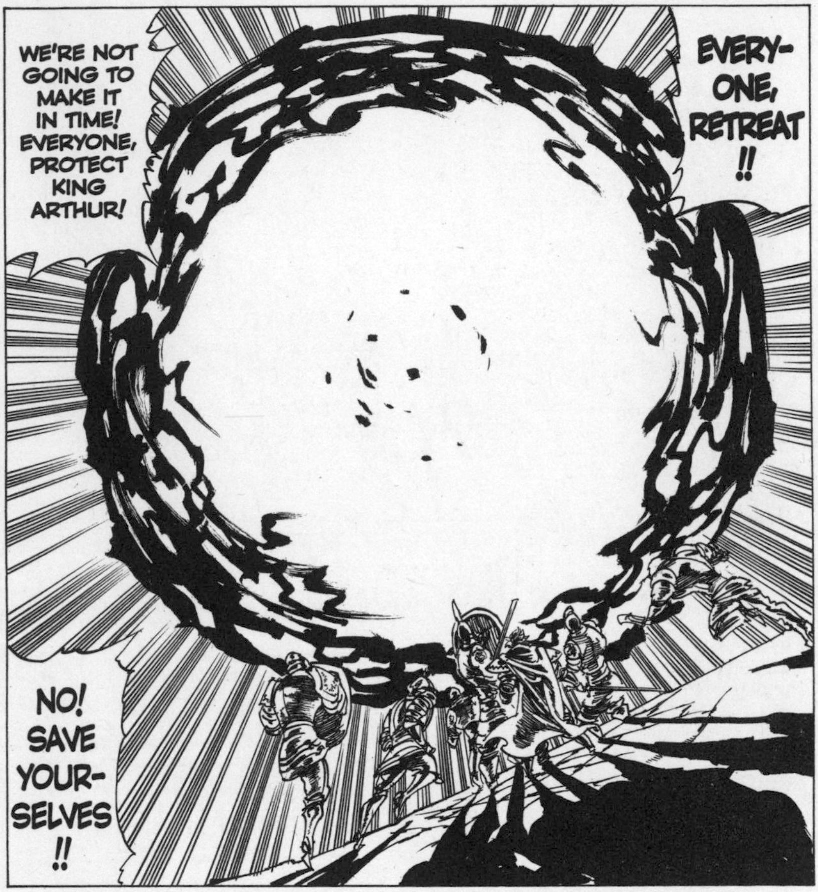
EVERY-
ONE,
RETREAT
!!
WE'RE NOT
GOING TO
MAKE IT
IN TIME!
EVERYONE,
PROTECT
KING
ARTHUR!
NO!
SAVE
YOUR-
SELVES
!!

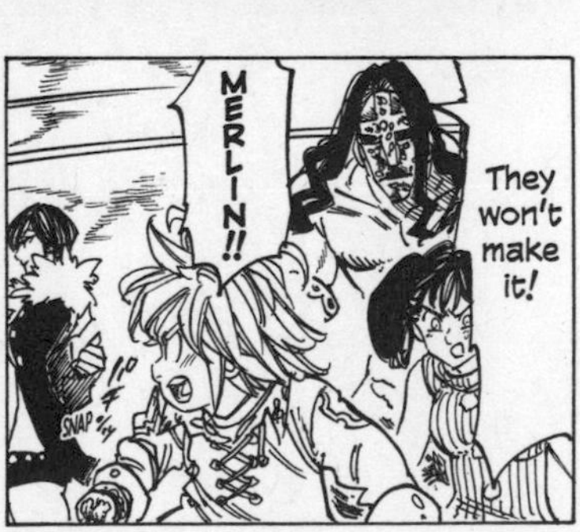
MERLIN!!
They won't make it!
SNAP

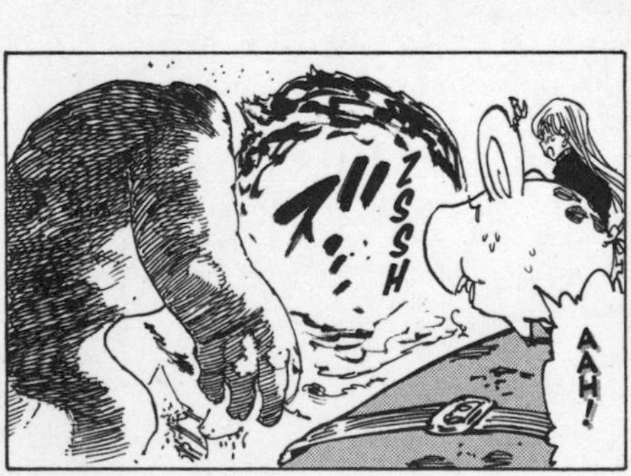
ZSSH
AAH!

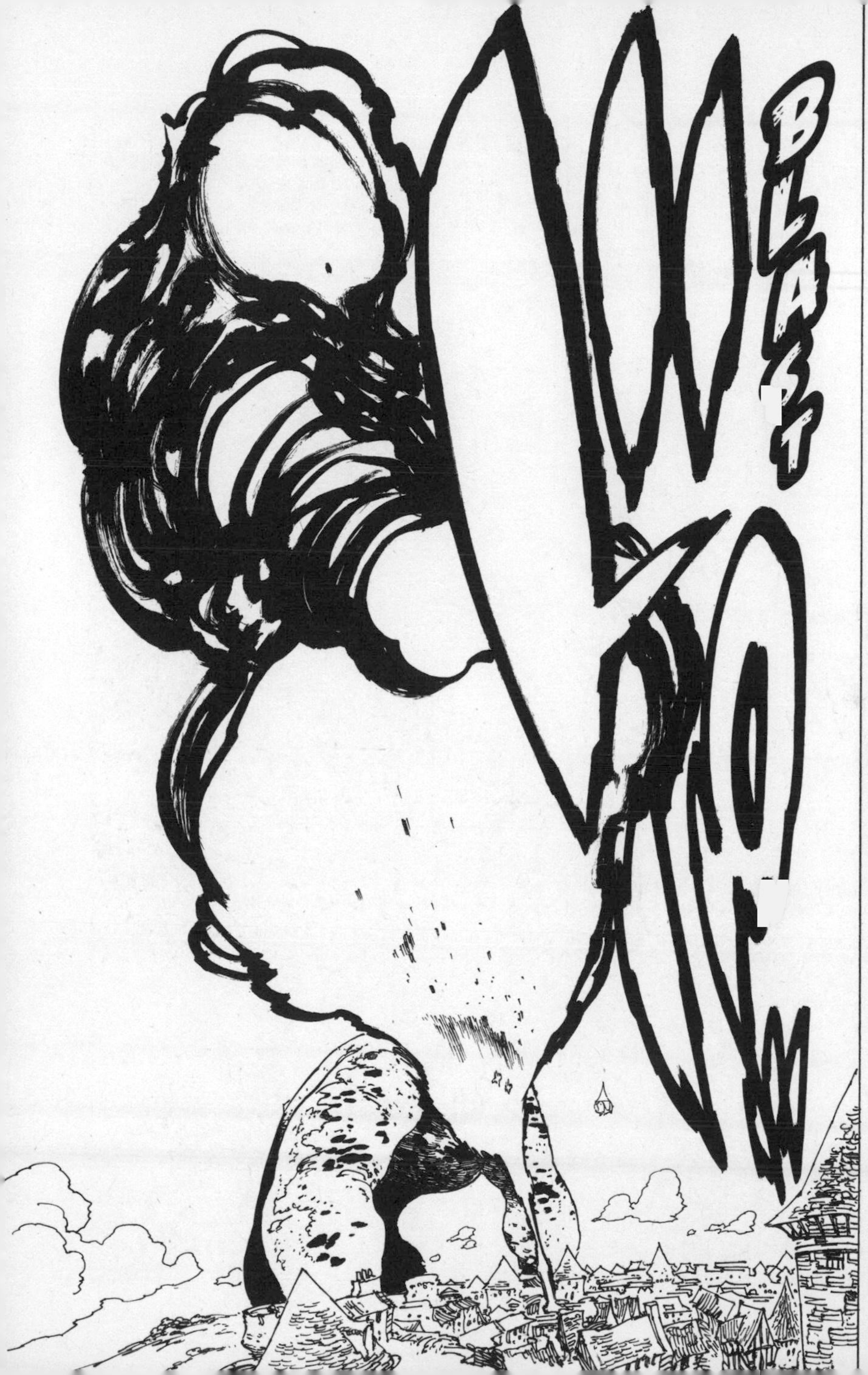
BLAST

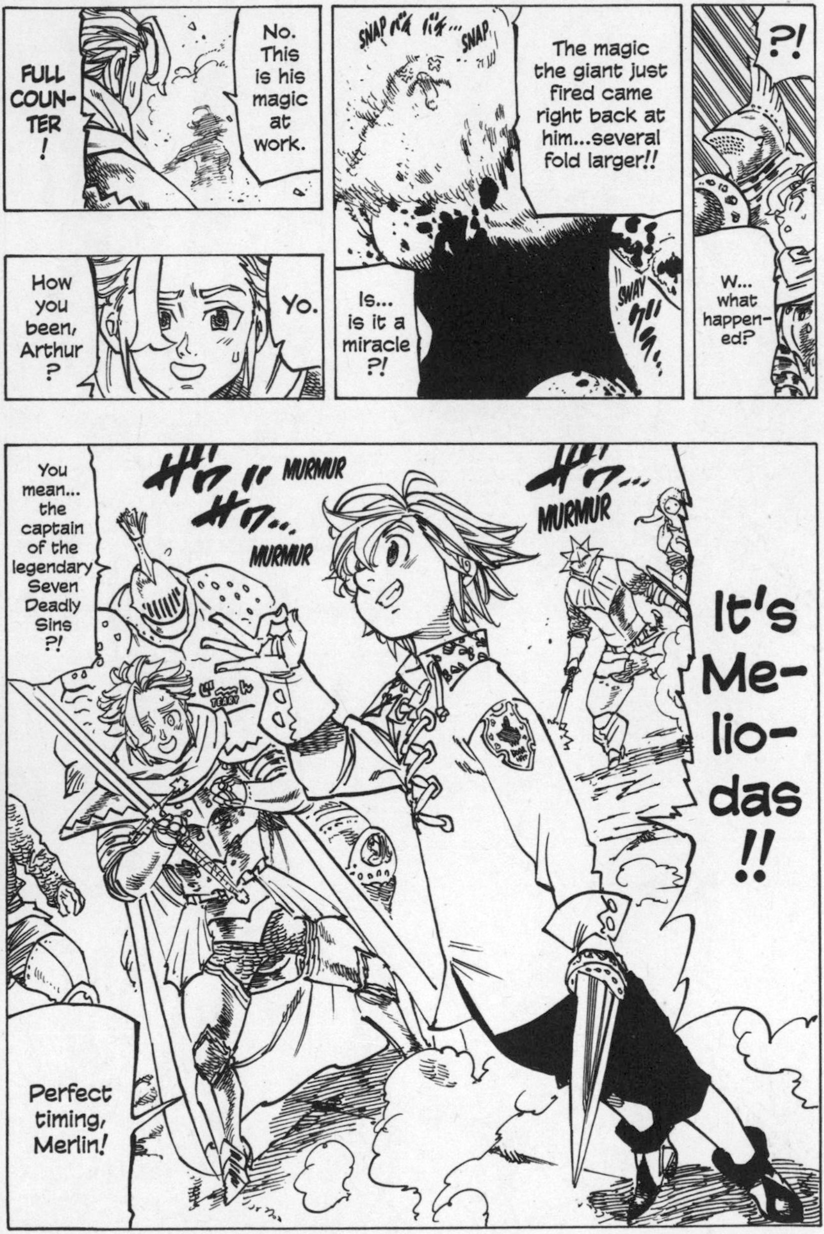
?!
W... what happened?
SNAP
SNAP
The magic the giant just fired came right back at him...several fold larger!!
SWAY
Is... is it a miracle?!
No. This is his magic at work.
FULL COUNTER!
Yo.
How you been, Arthur?
MURMUR
It's Me-lio-das!!
MURMUR
MURMUR
You mean... the captain of the legendary Seven Deadly Sins?!
TEARY
Perfect timing, Merlin!

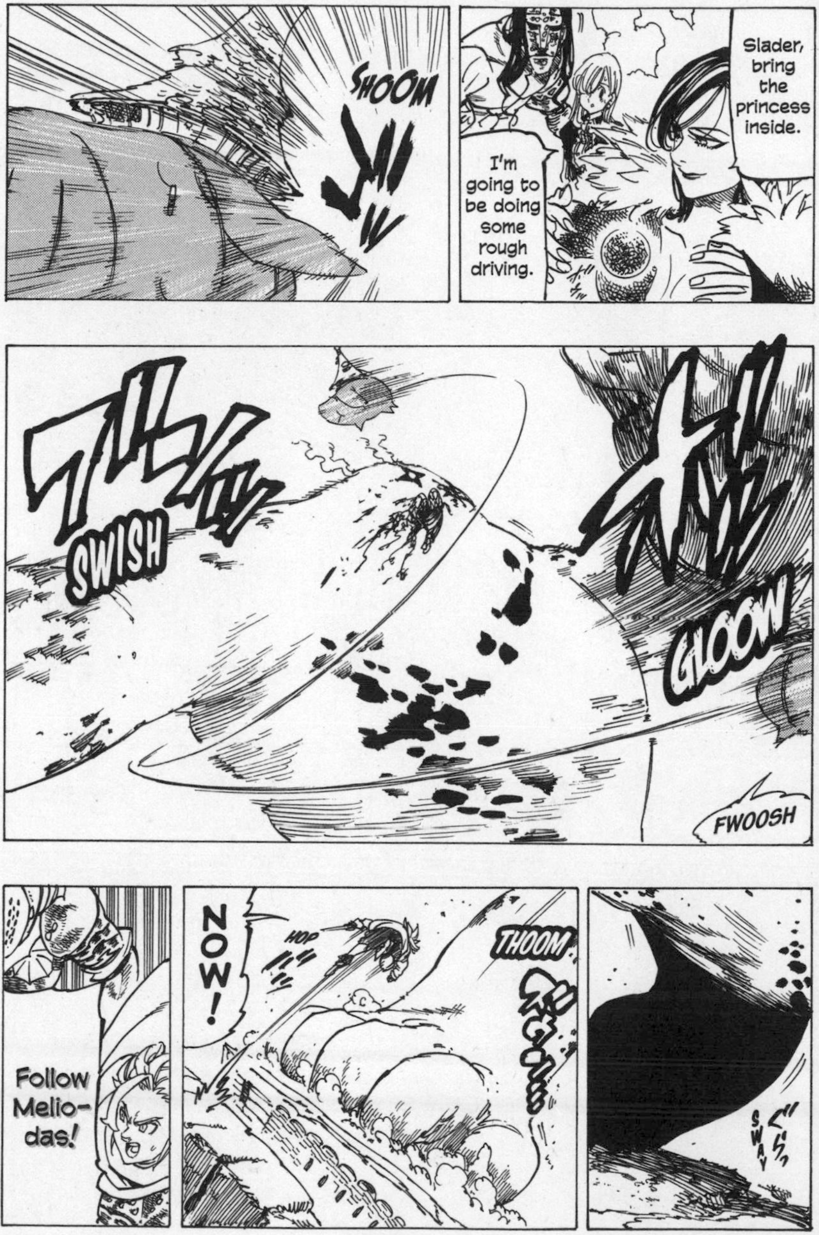
Slader, bring the princess inside.
I'm going to be doing some rough driving.
SHOOM
GLOOW
FWOOSH
SWISH
SWAY
THOOM
NOW!
HOP
Follow Melio-das!

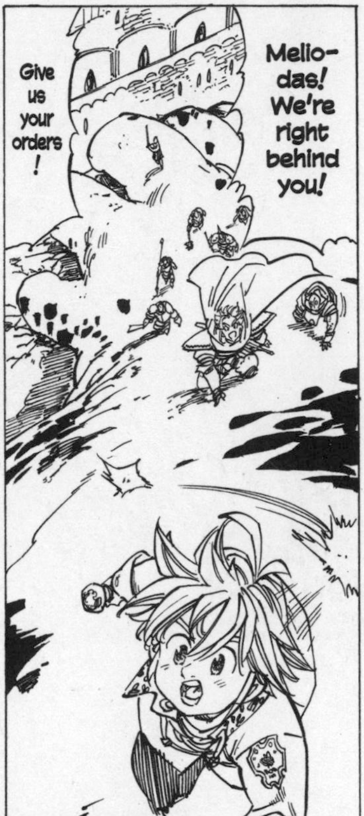
Melio-das! We're right behind you!
Give us your orders!
This giant's an Albion. That means his weak spot is the core hidden in his chest! We've got to scale him and crush it in one blow!
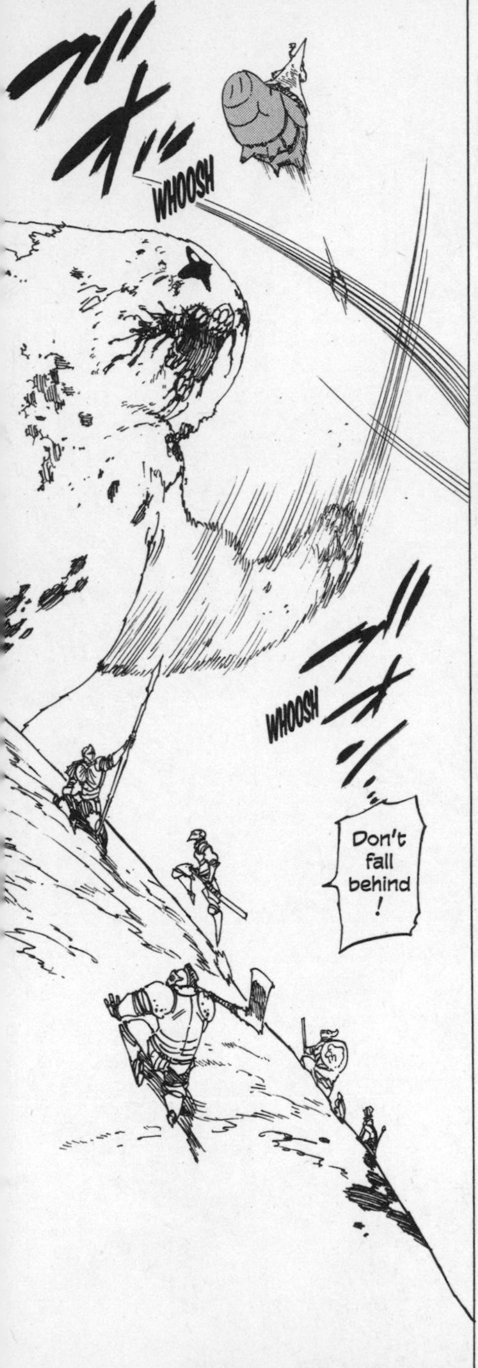
WHOOSH
WHOOSH
Don't fall behind!

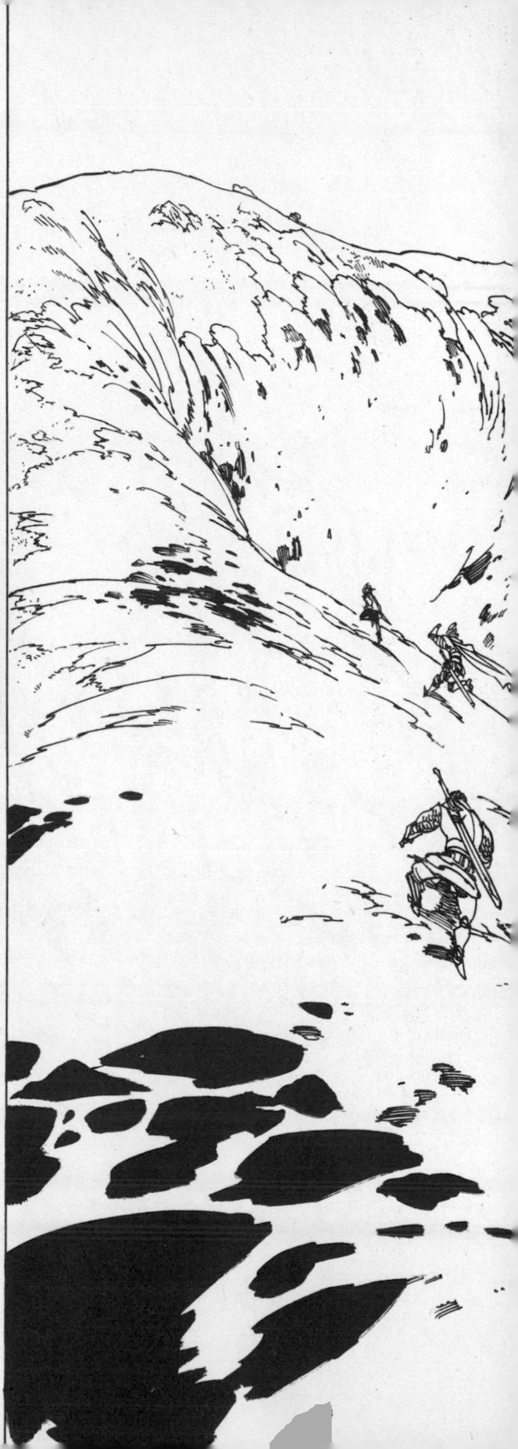
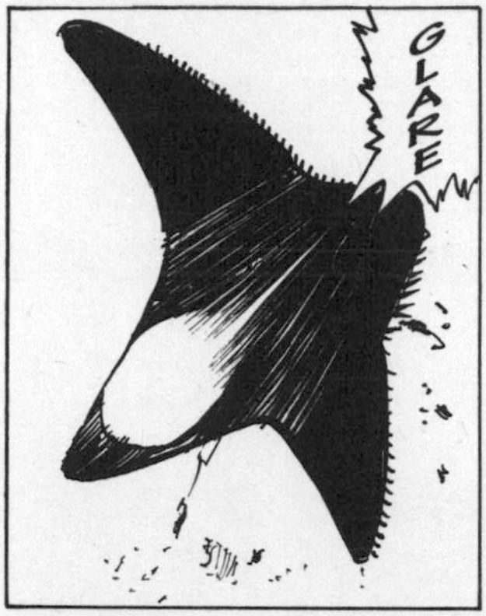
GLARE
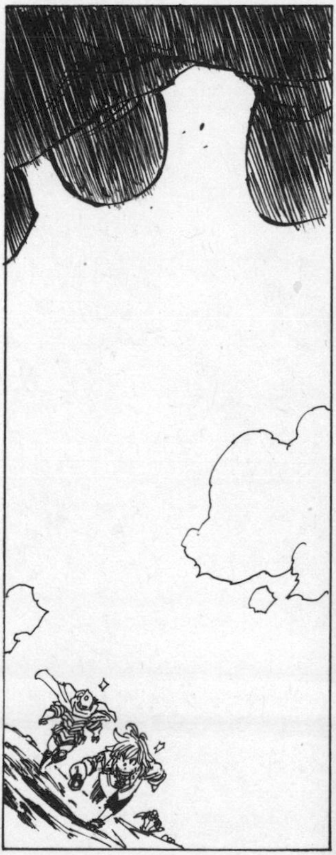

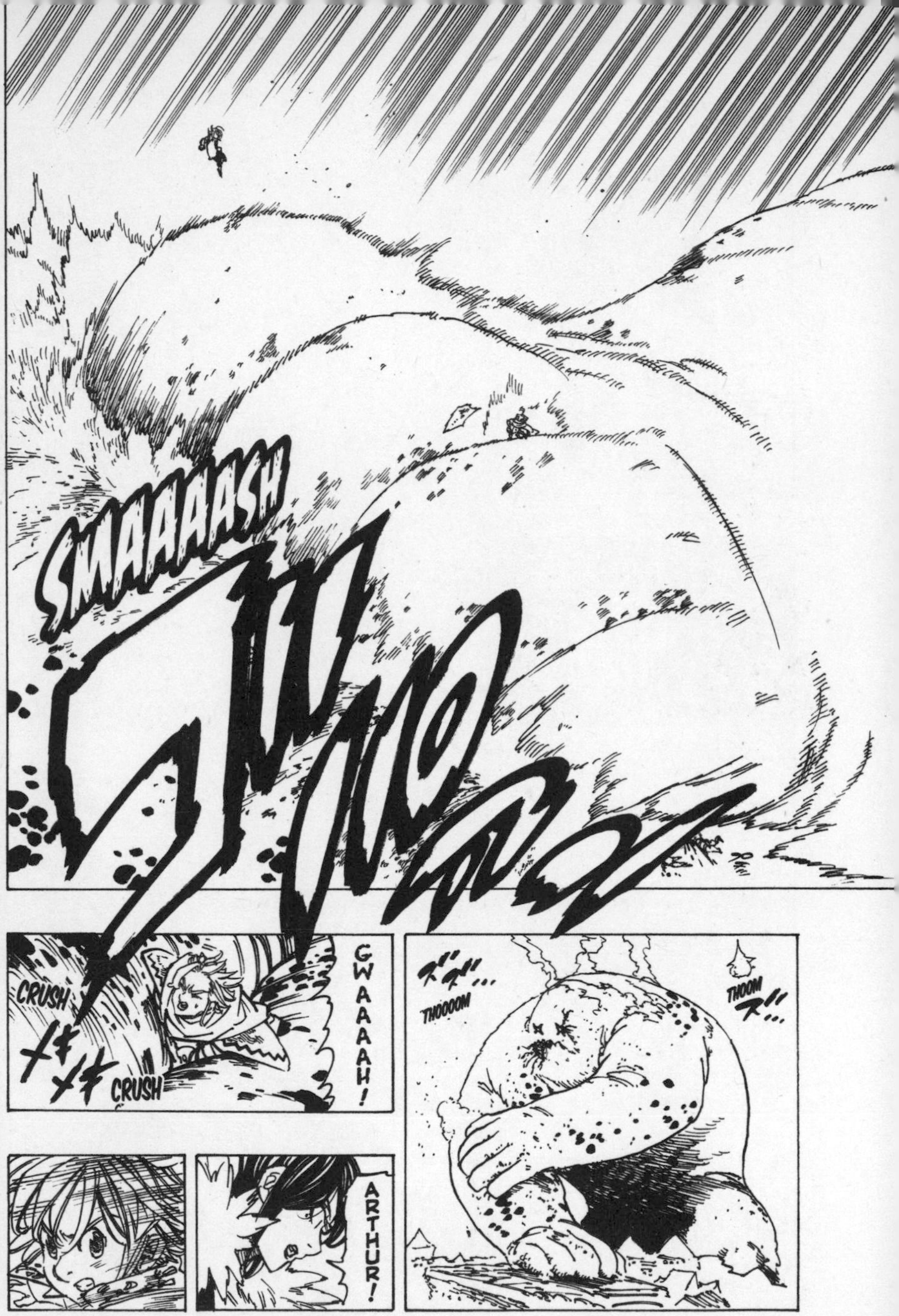
SMAAAASH
ズズ...
THOOOOM
THOOM
ズ!!...
GWAAAAAH!
CRUSH
メキ
メキ
CRUSH
ARTHUR!

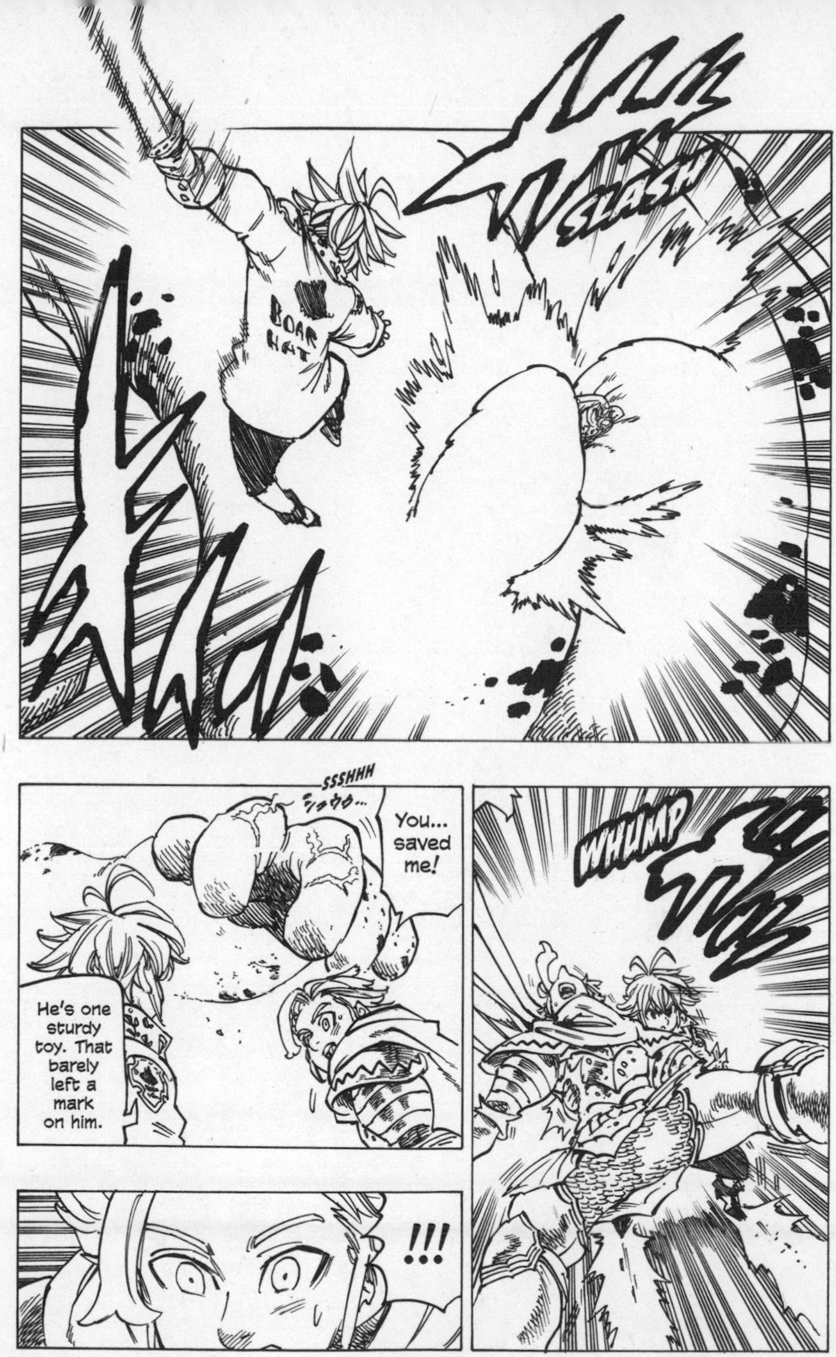
SLASH
WHUMP
SSSHHH
You... saved me!
He's one sturdy toy. That barely left a mark on him.
!!!

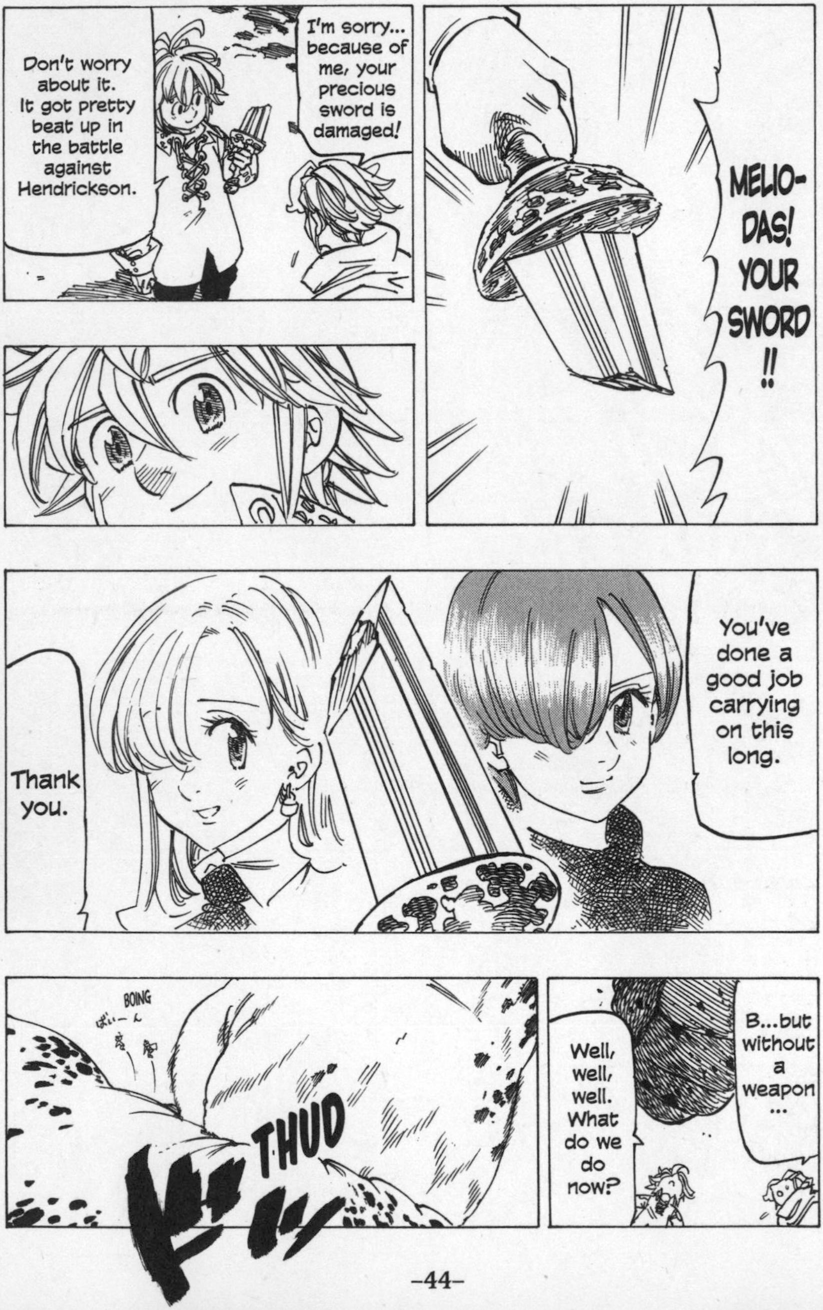
MELIO-DAS! YOUR SWORD!!
I'm sorry... because of me, your precious sword is damaged!
Don't worry about it. It got pretty beat up in the battle against Hendrickson.
You've done a good job carrying on this long.
Thank you.
B...but without a weapon...
Well, well, well. What do we do now?
BOING
THUD

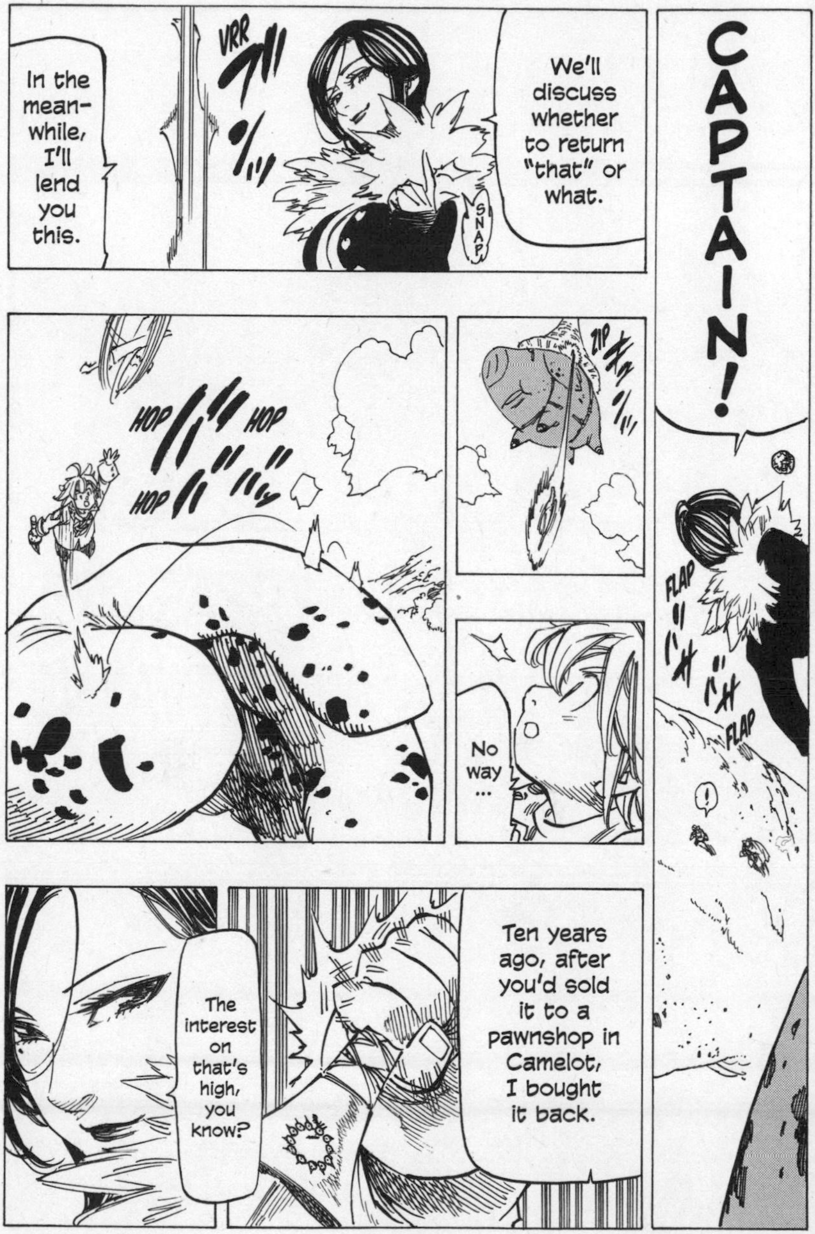
CAPTAIN!
FLAP
FLAP
We'll discuss whether to return "that" or what.
SNAP
VRR
In the mean-while, I'll lend you this.
ZIP
No way ...
HOP
HOP
HOP
Ten years ago, after you'd sold it to a pawnshop in Camelot, I bought it back.
The interest on that's high, you know?

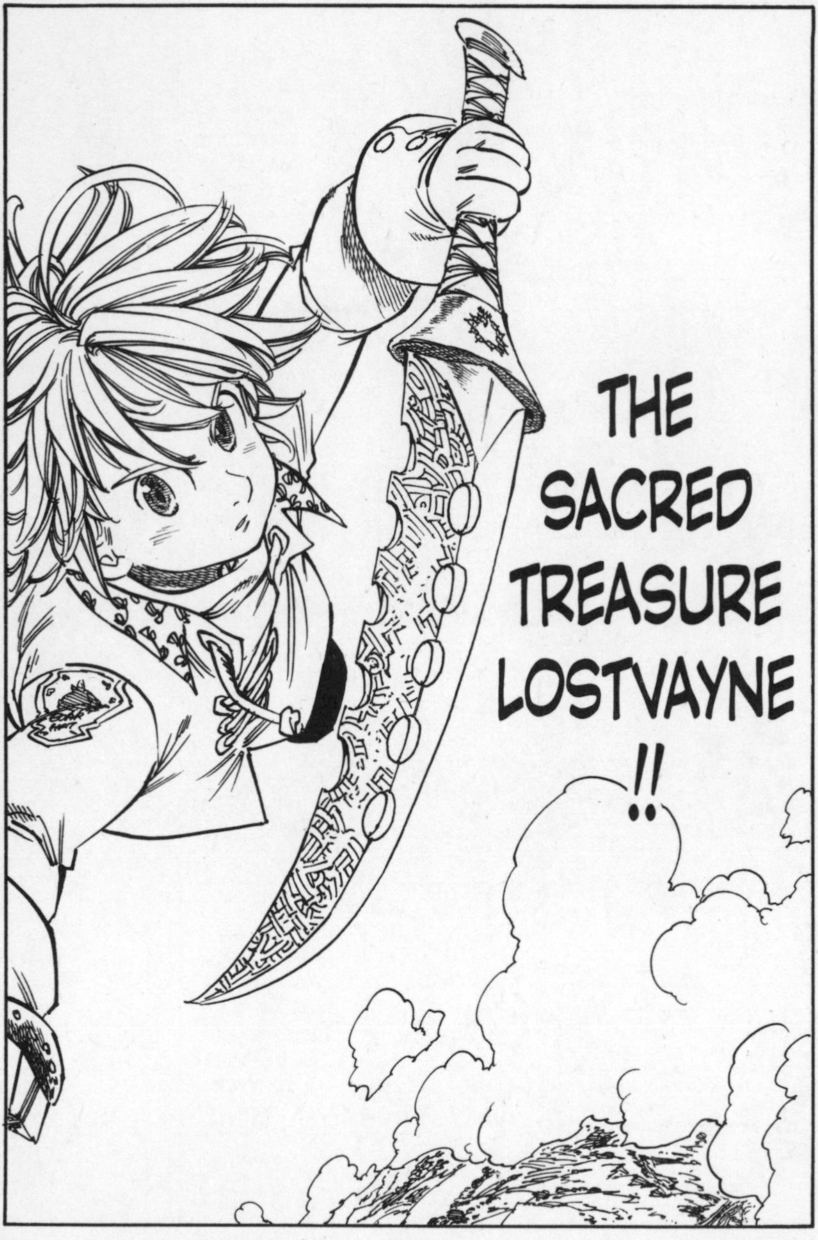
THE SACRED TREASURE LOSTVAYNE !!

OLD GENERATION
DALE

The Holy Knight Dale volunteered himself for Hendrickson's experiments, which transformed him into a Demon.

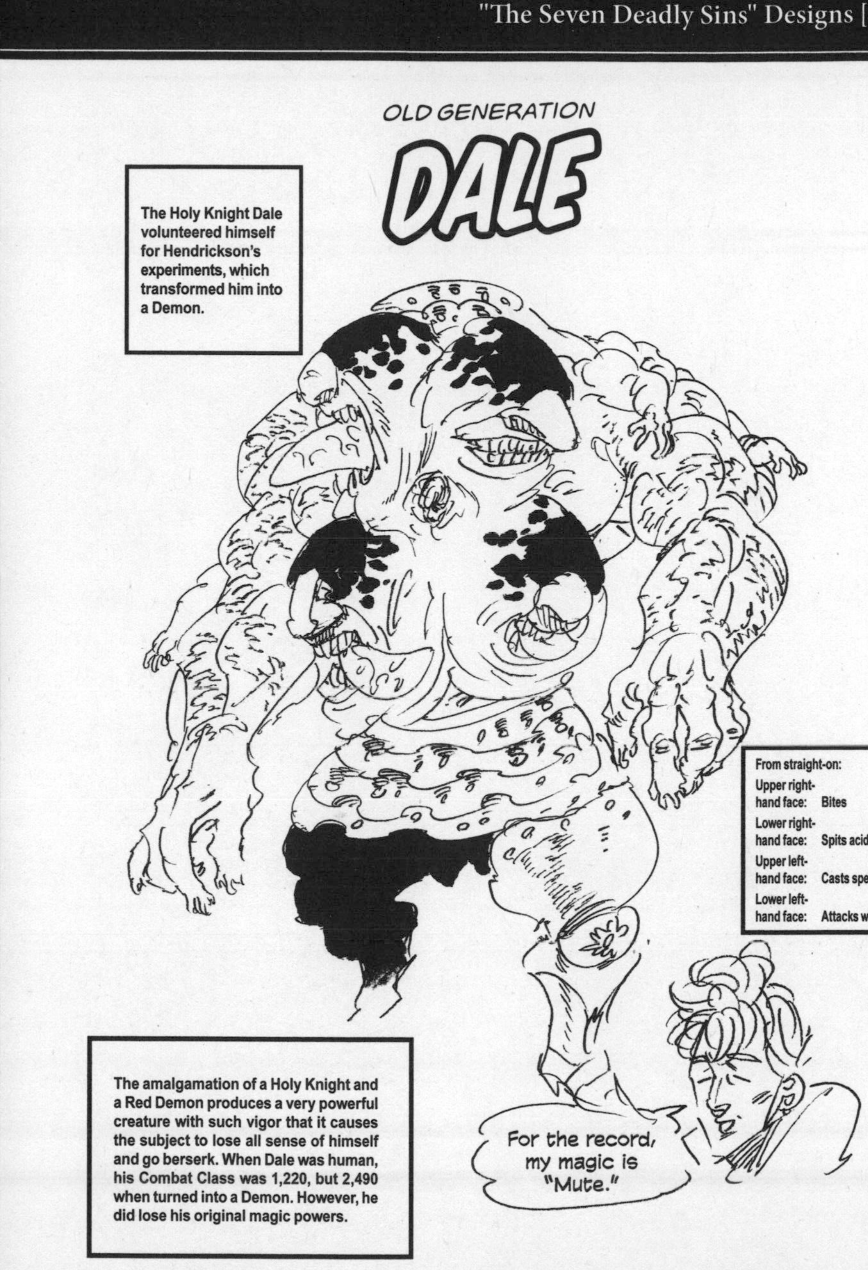
For the record, my magic is "Mute."

From straight-on:

Upper right-hand face:	Bites
Lower right-hand face:	Spits acid
Upper left-hand face:	Casts spells
Lower left-hand face:	Attacks with ice

The amalgamation of a Holy Knight and a Red Demon produces a very powerful creature with such vigor that it causes the subject to lose all sense of himself and go berserk. When Dale was human, his Combat Class was 1,220, but 2,490 when turned into a Demon. However, he did lose his original magic powers.

Chapter 116 - The Sacred Treasure Lostvayne

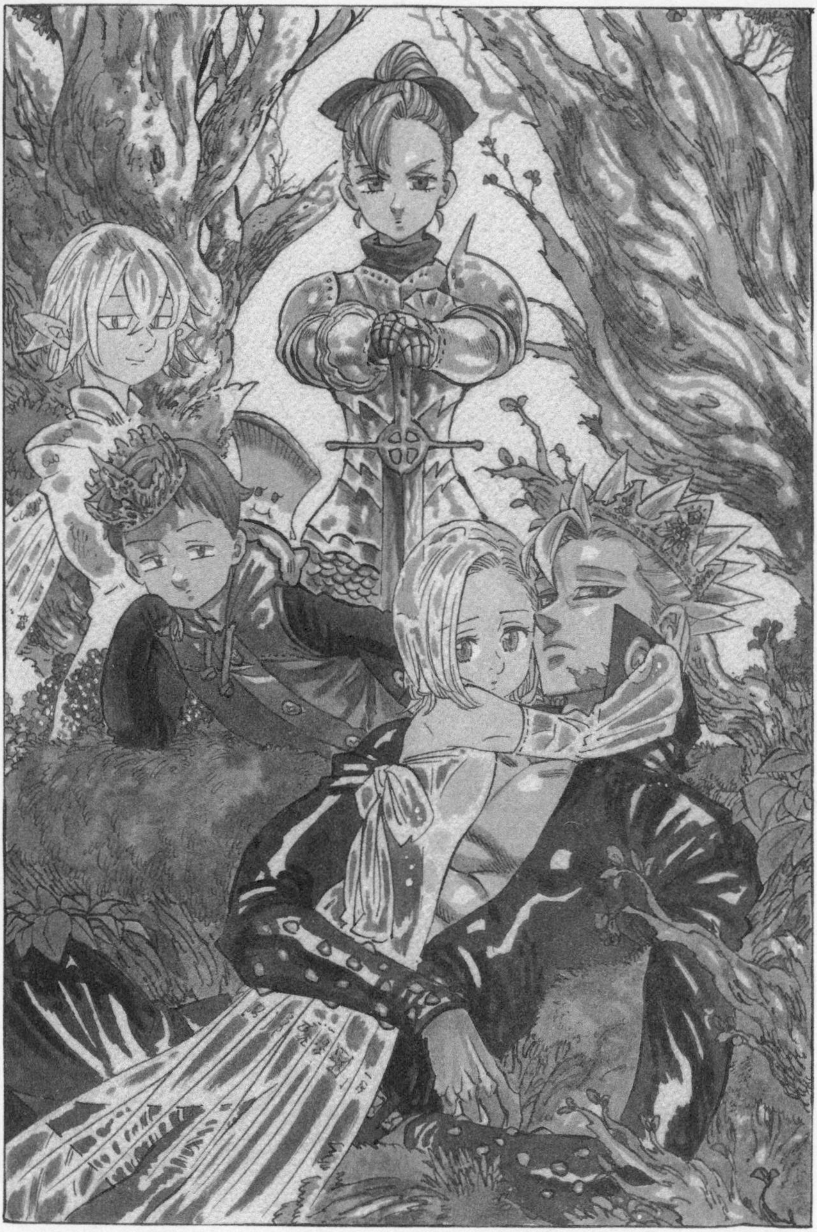

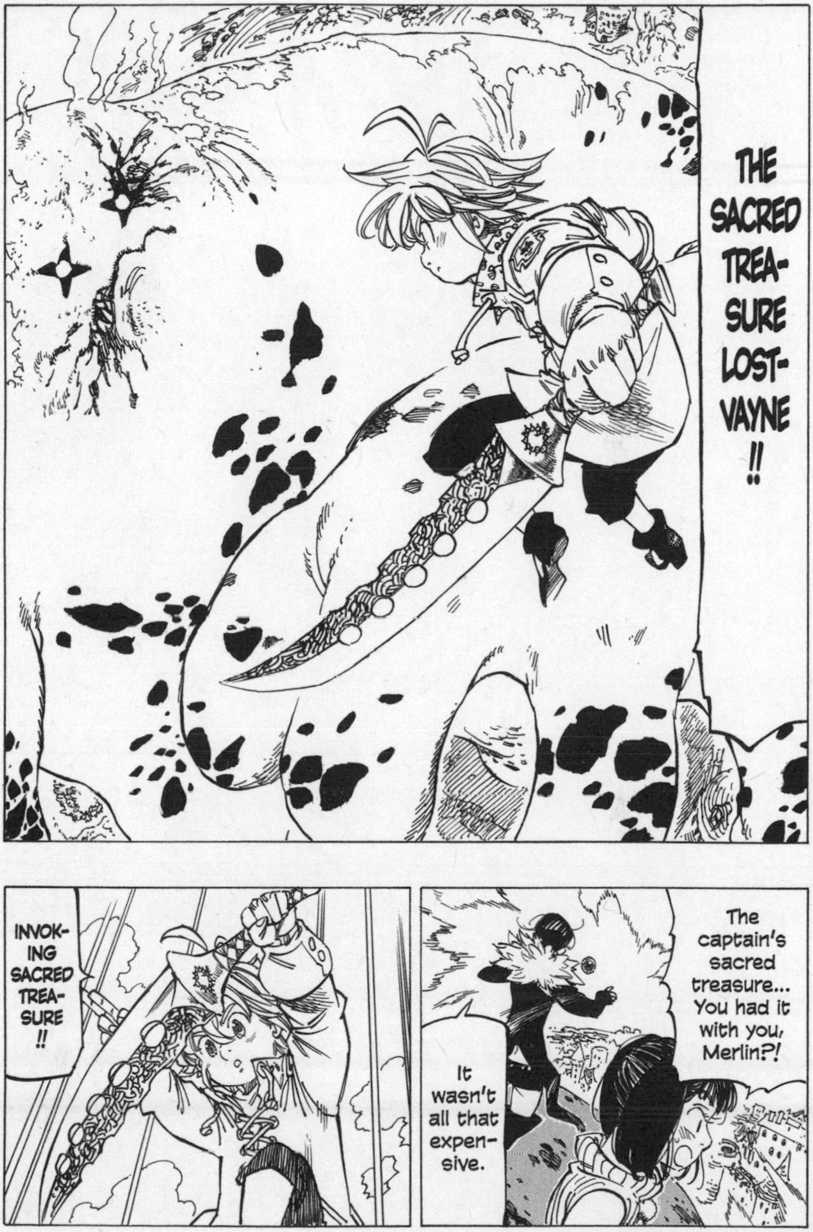
THE SACRED TREA-SURE LOST-VAYNE!!
The captain's sacred treasure... You had it with you, Merlin?!
It wasn't all that expen-sive.
INVOK-ING SACRED TREA-SURE!!

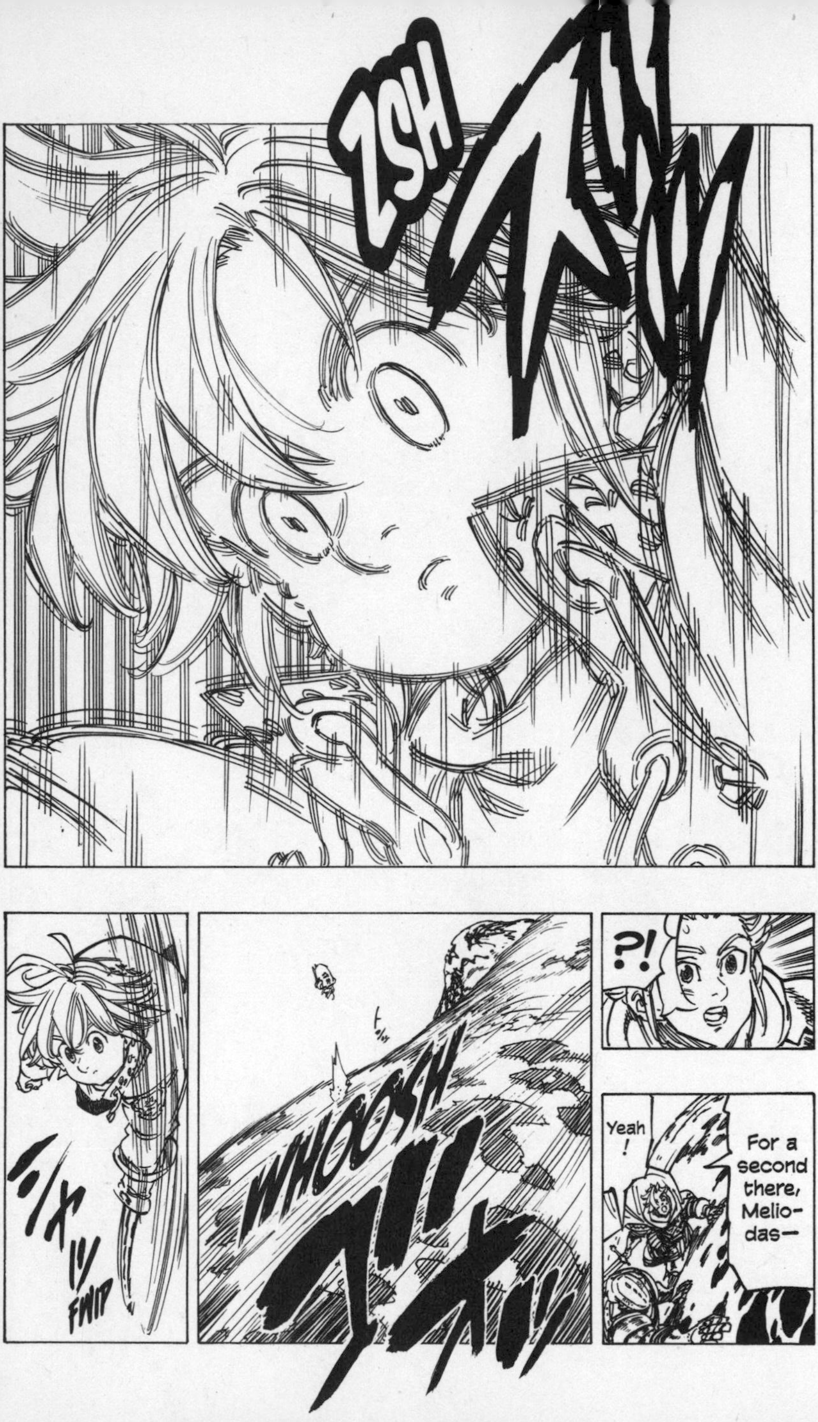
ZSH
?!
For a second there, Melio-das—
Yeah!
WHOOSH
FWIP

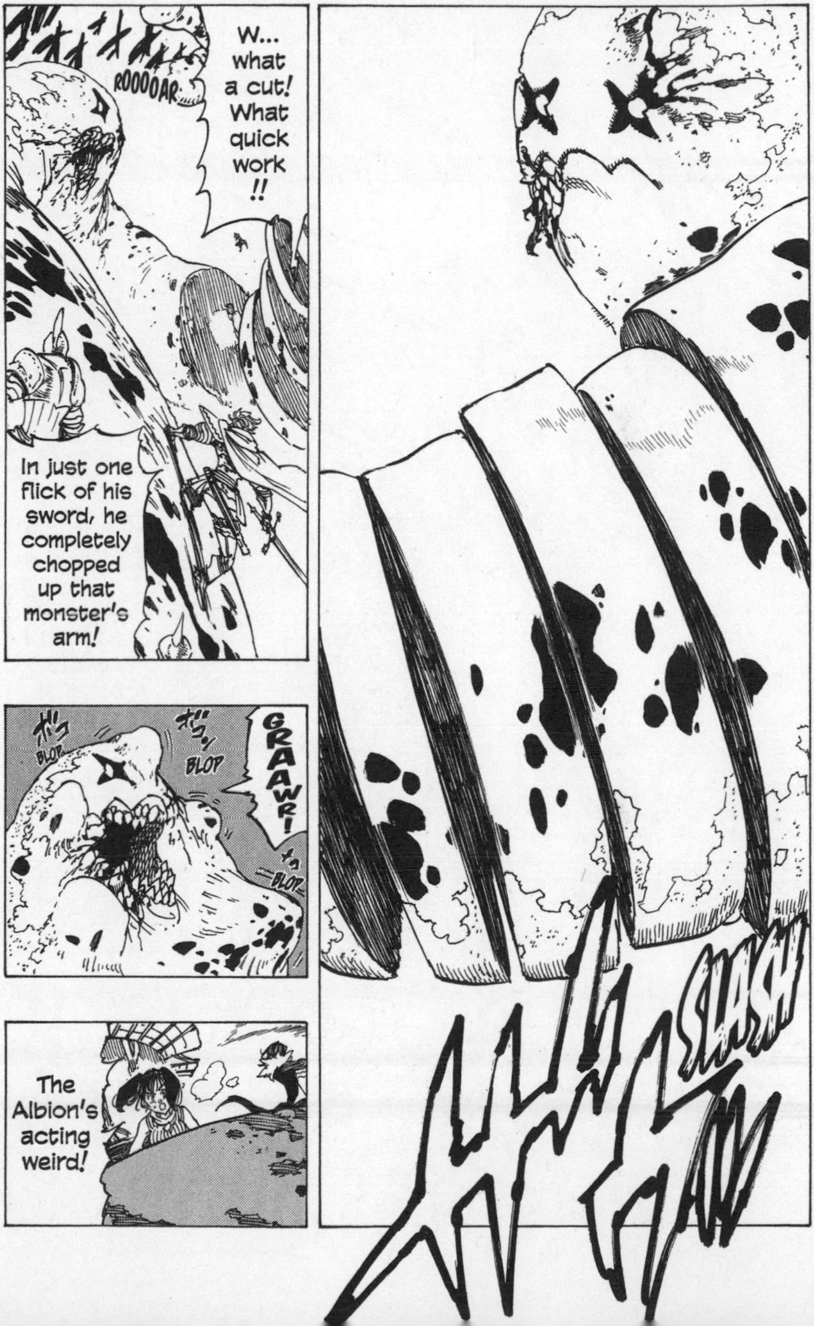
SLASH
ROOOOAR
W... what a cut! What quick work!!
In just one flick of his sword, he completely chopped up that monster's arm!
BLOP
BLOP
GRAAAWR!
BLOP
The Albion's acting weird!

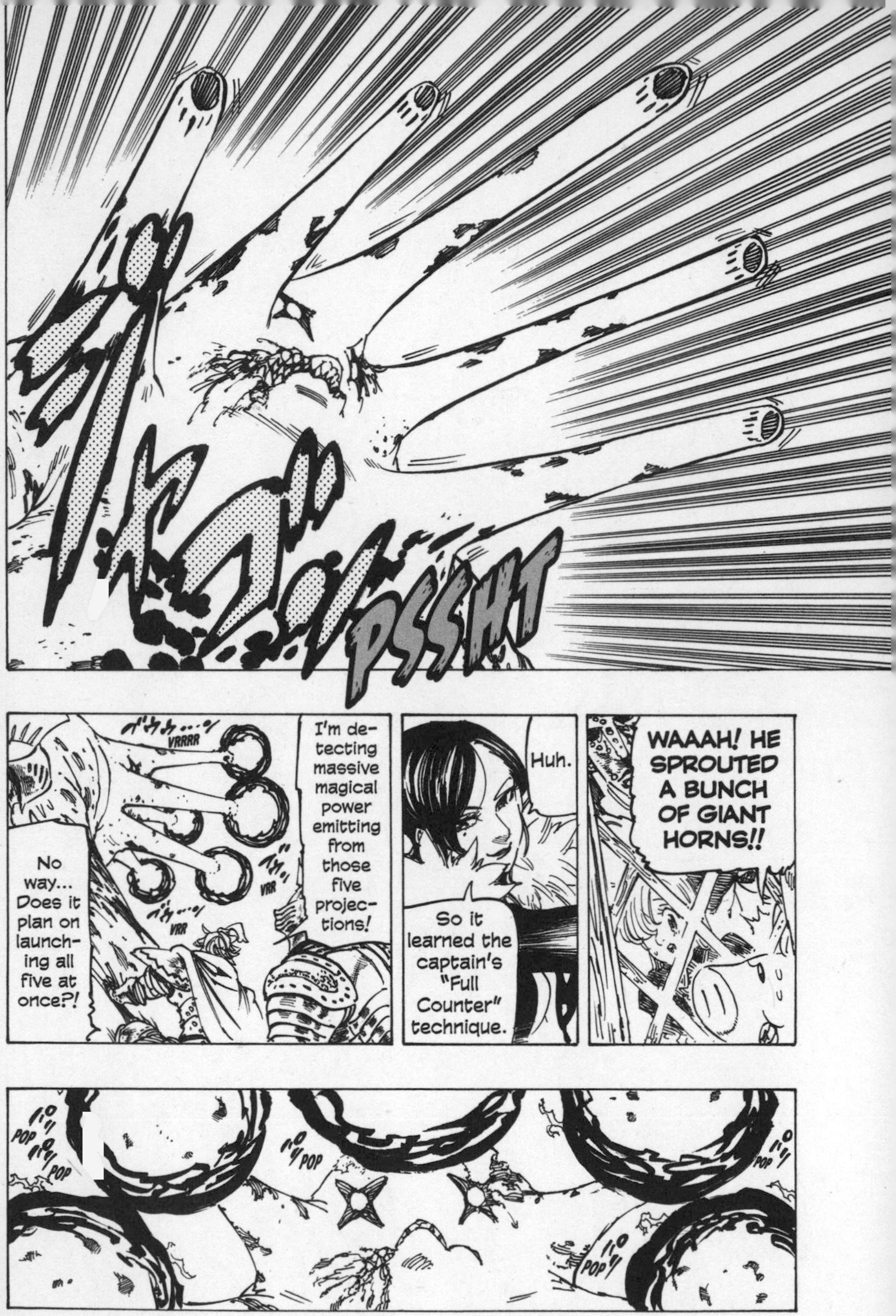
PSSHT
WAAAH! HE SPROUTED A BUNCH OF GIANT HORNS!!
Huh.
So it learned the captain's "Full Counter" technique.
I'm detecting massive magical power emitting from those five projections!
VRRRR
VRR
VRR
No way... Does it plan on launching all five at once?!
POP
POP
POP
POP
POP
POP

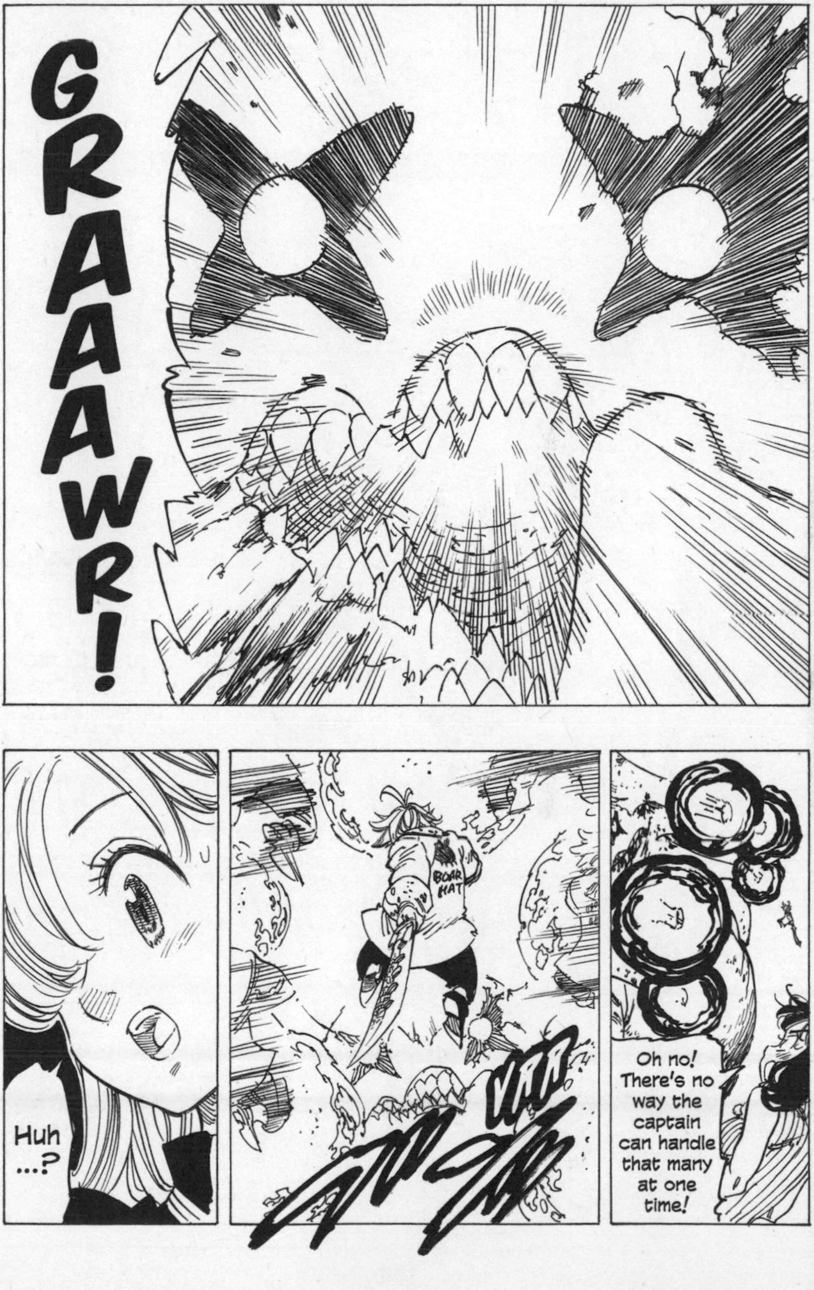
GRAAAWR!
Oh no! There's no way the captain can handle that many at one time!
VRR
Huh ...?

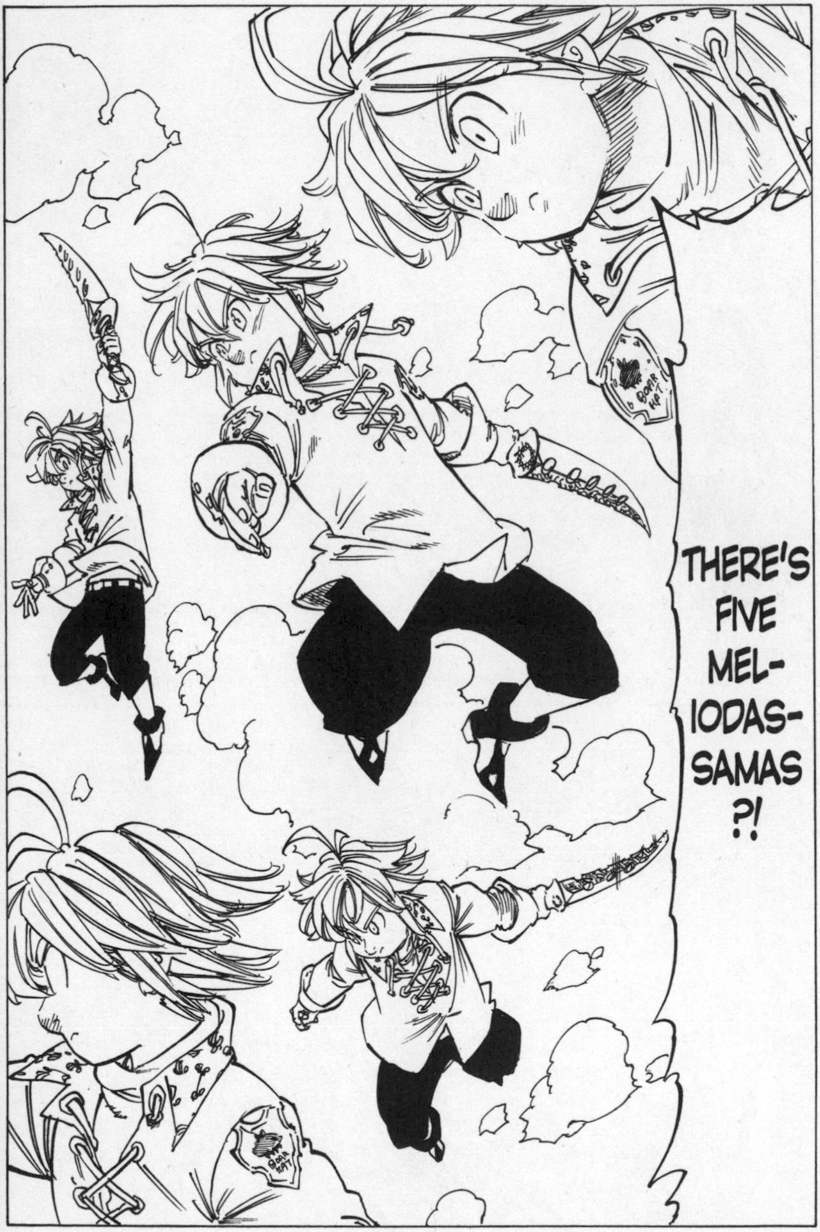
THERE'S FIVE MEL-IODAS-SAMAS ?!

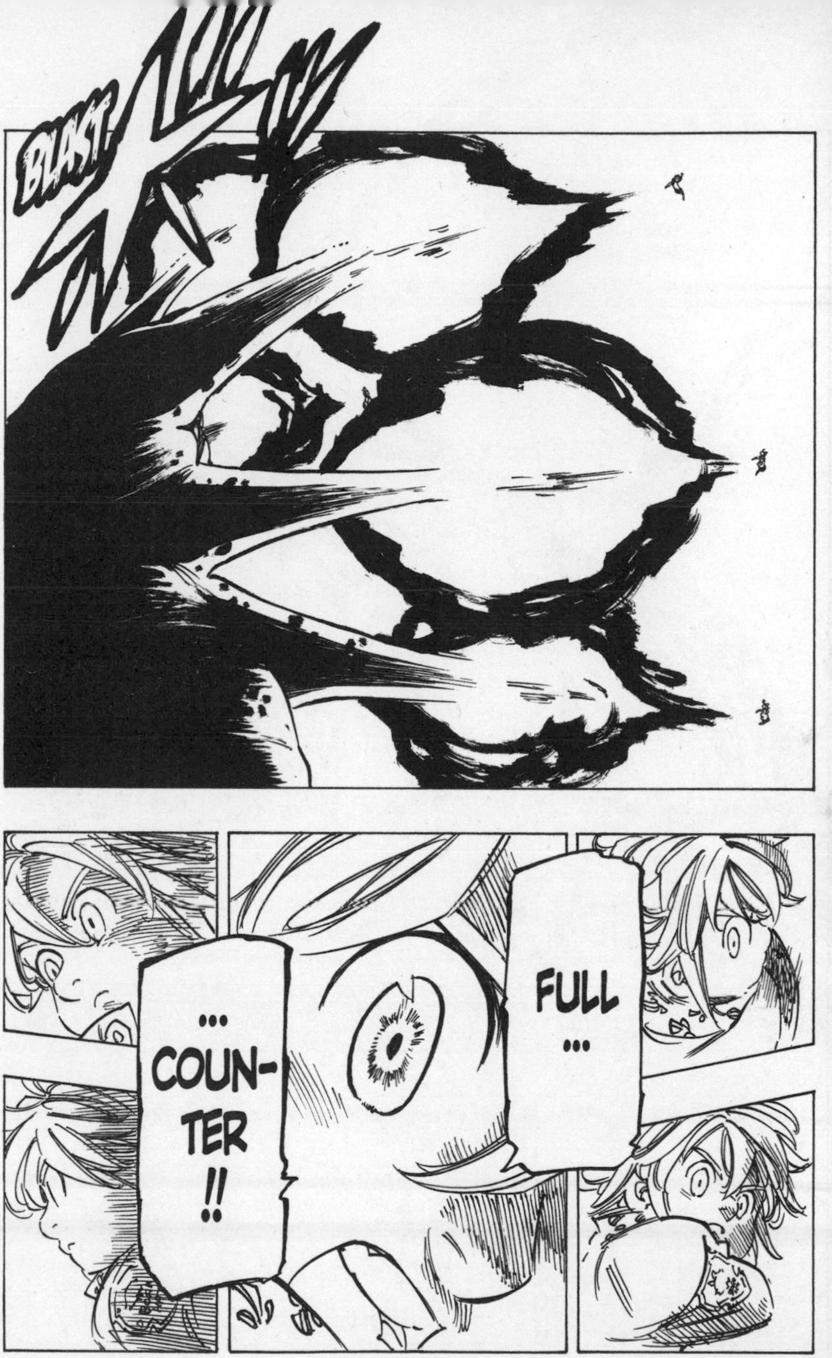
BLAST
FULL ...
... COUN-TER !!

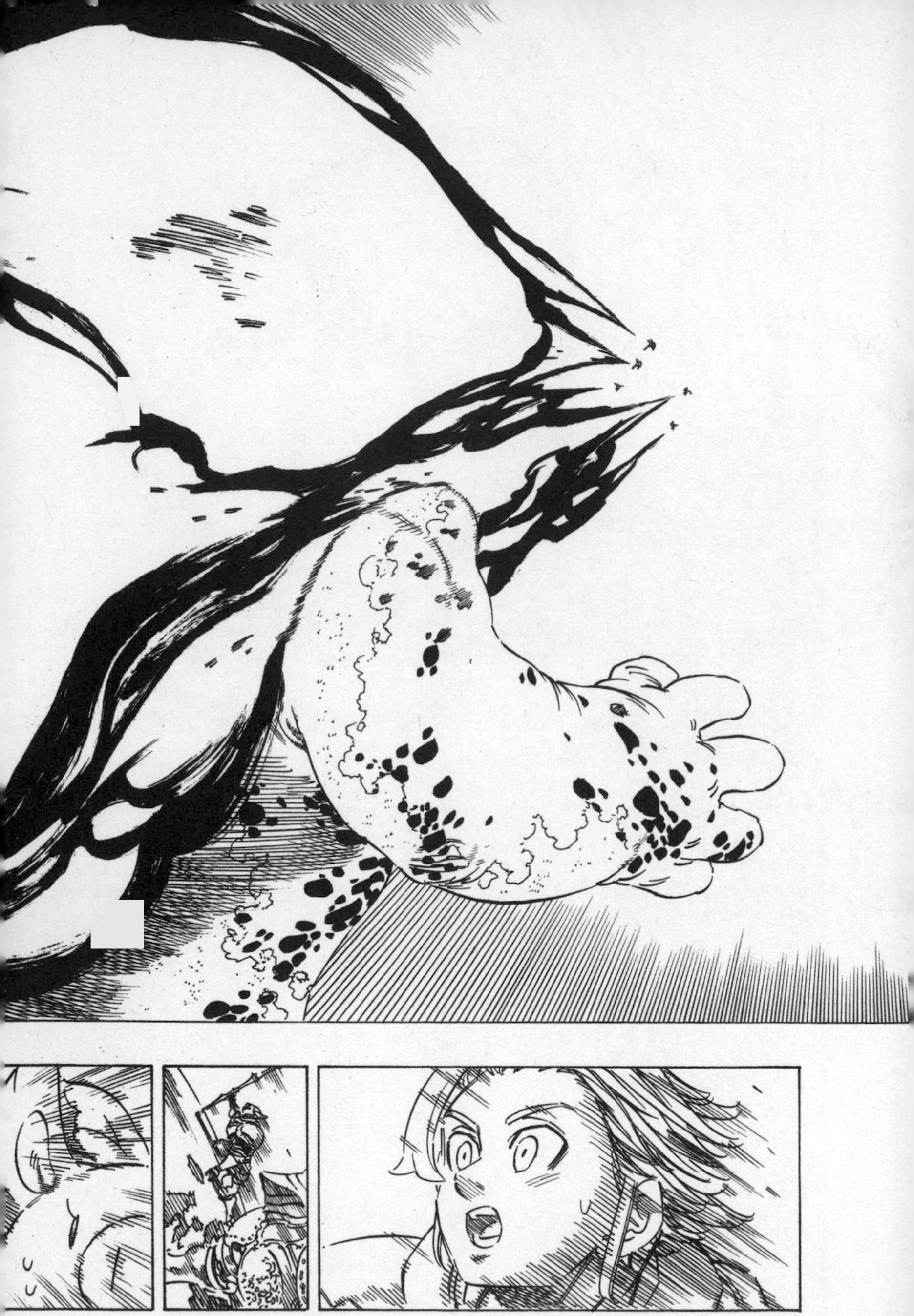

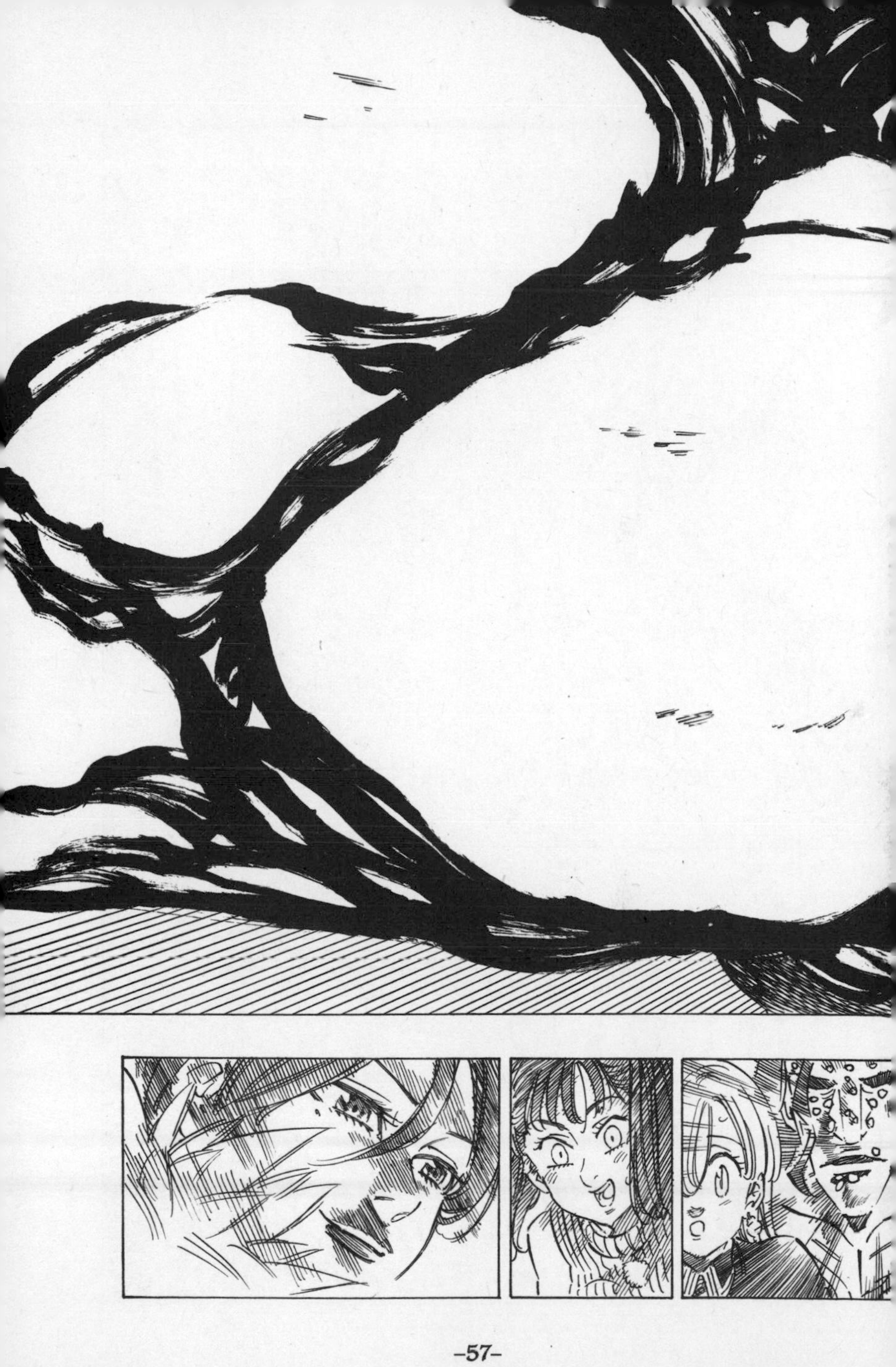

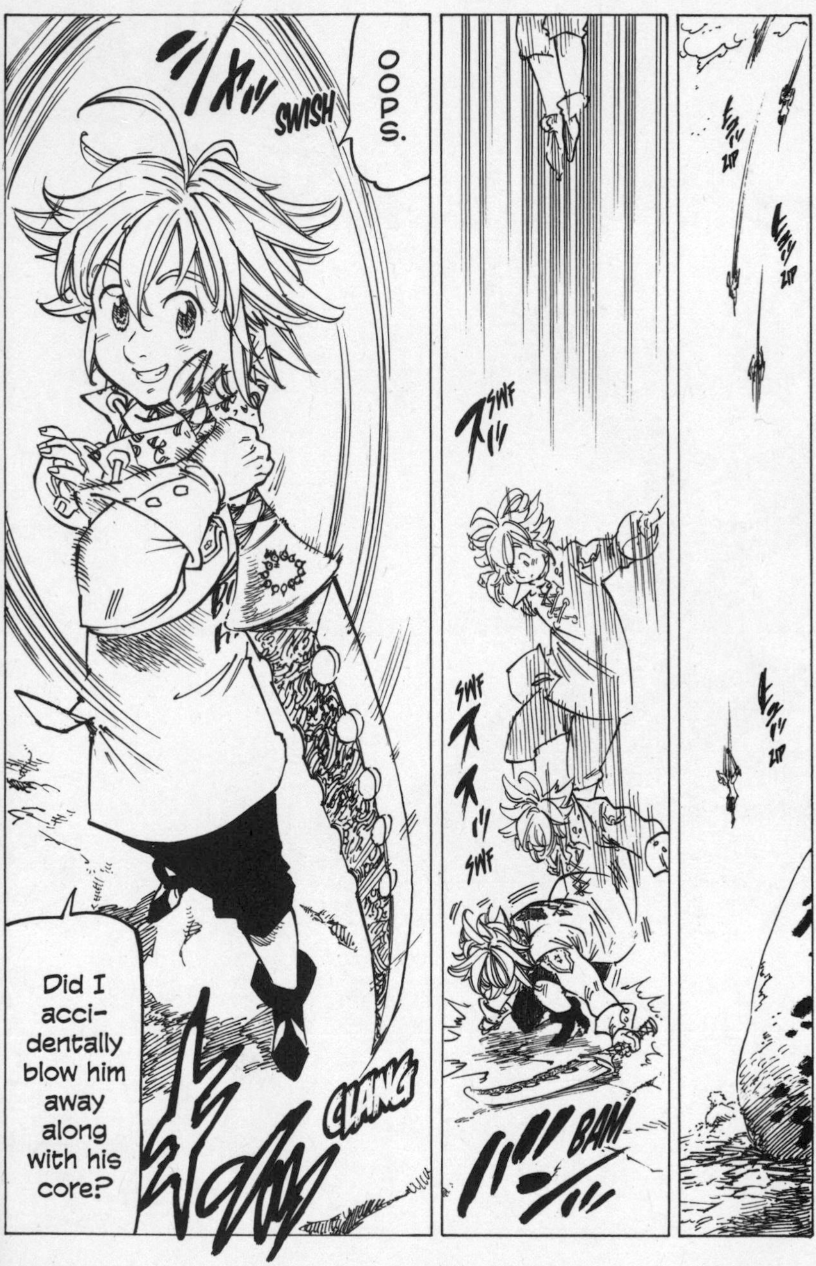
ZIP
ZIP
ZIP
SWF
SWF
SWF
BAM
OOPS.
SWISH
Did I accidentally blow him away along with his core?
CLANG

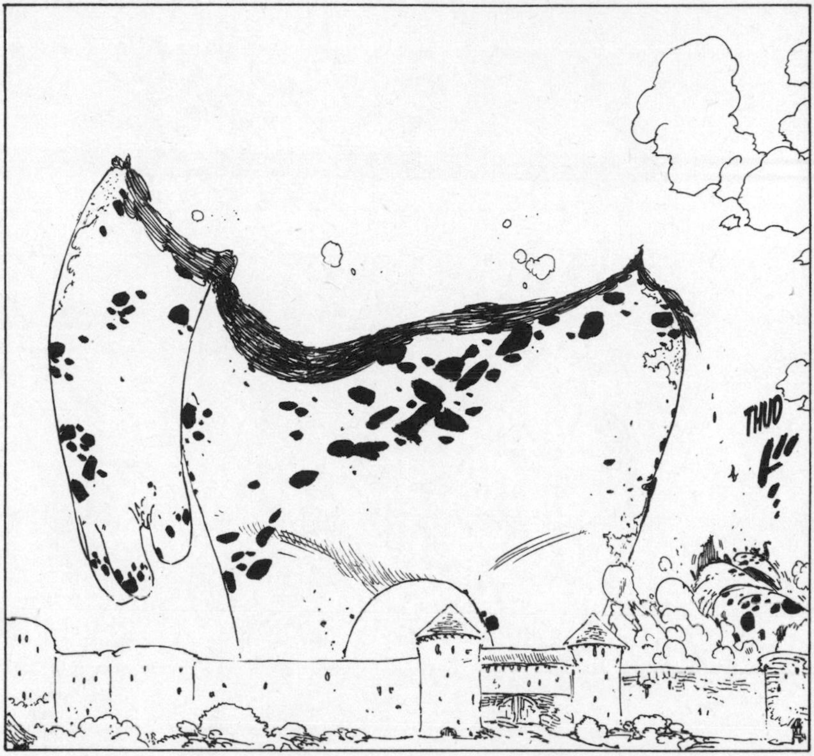
THUD

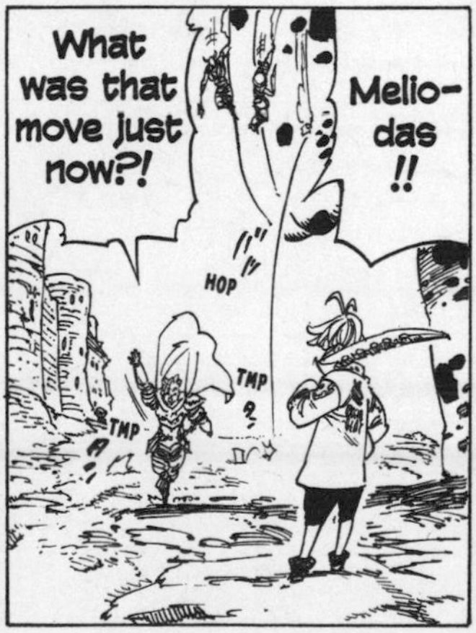
Melio-das!!
What was that move just now?!
HOP
TMP
TMP

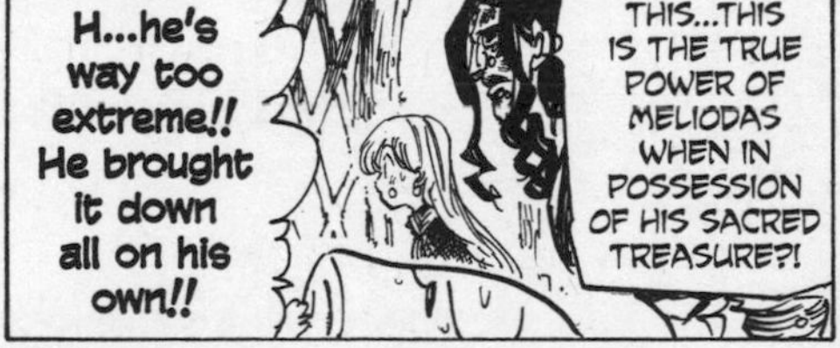
THIS...THIS IS THE TRUE POWER OF MELIODAS WHEN IN POSSESSION OF HIS SACRED TREASURE?!
H...he's way too extreme!! He brought it down all on his own!!

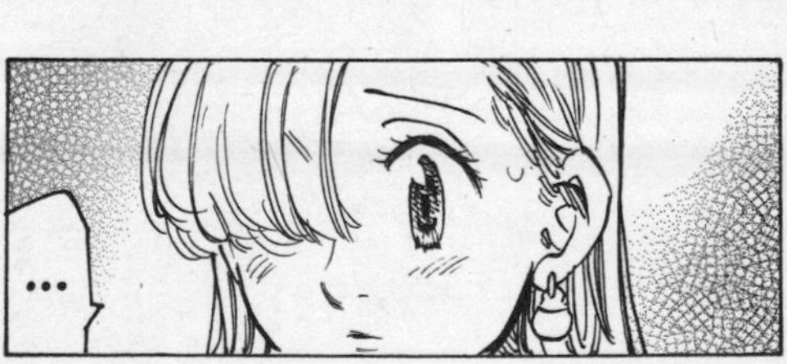
...

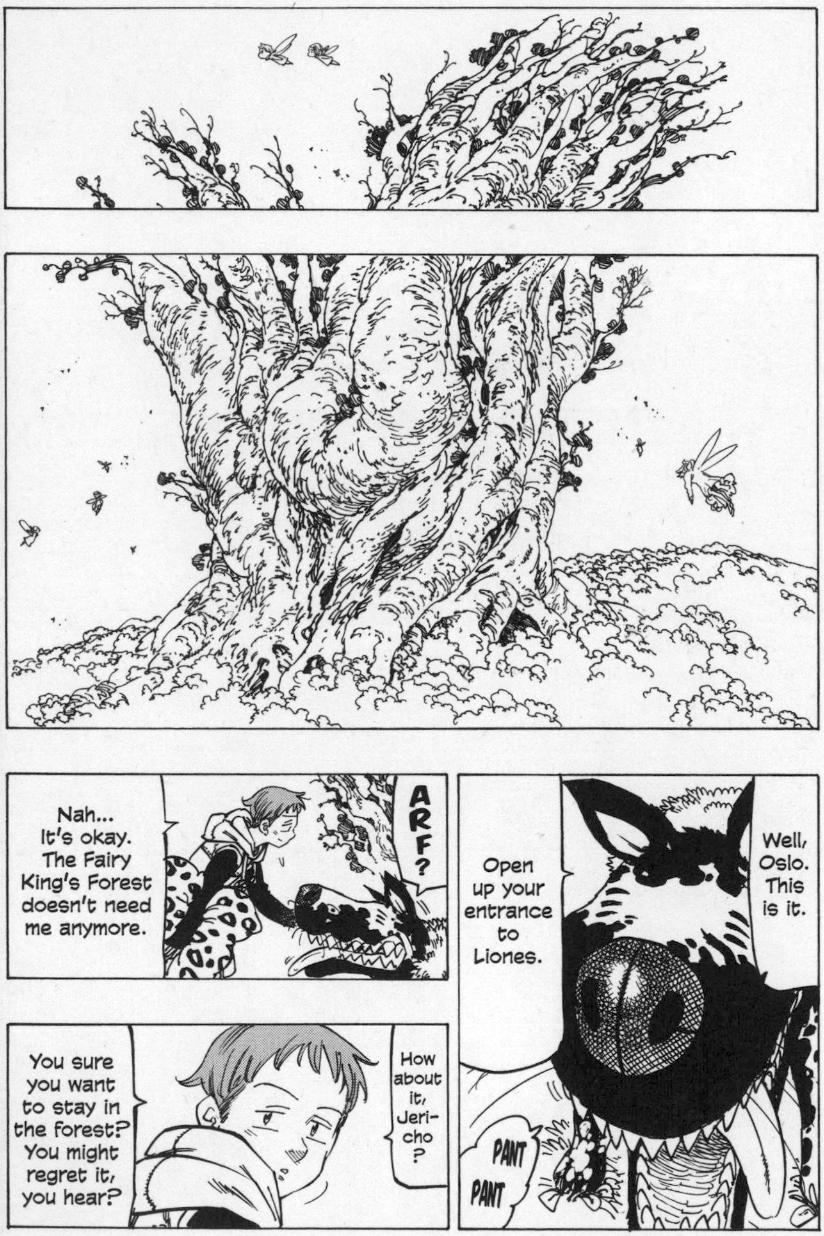
Well, Oslo. This is it.
Open up your entrance to Liones.
PANT
PANT
ARF?
Nah... It's okay. The Fairy King's Forest doesn't need me anymore.
How about it, Jeri-cho?
You sure you want to stay in the forest? You might regret it, you hear?

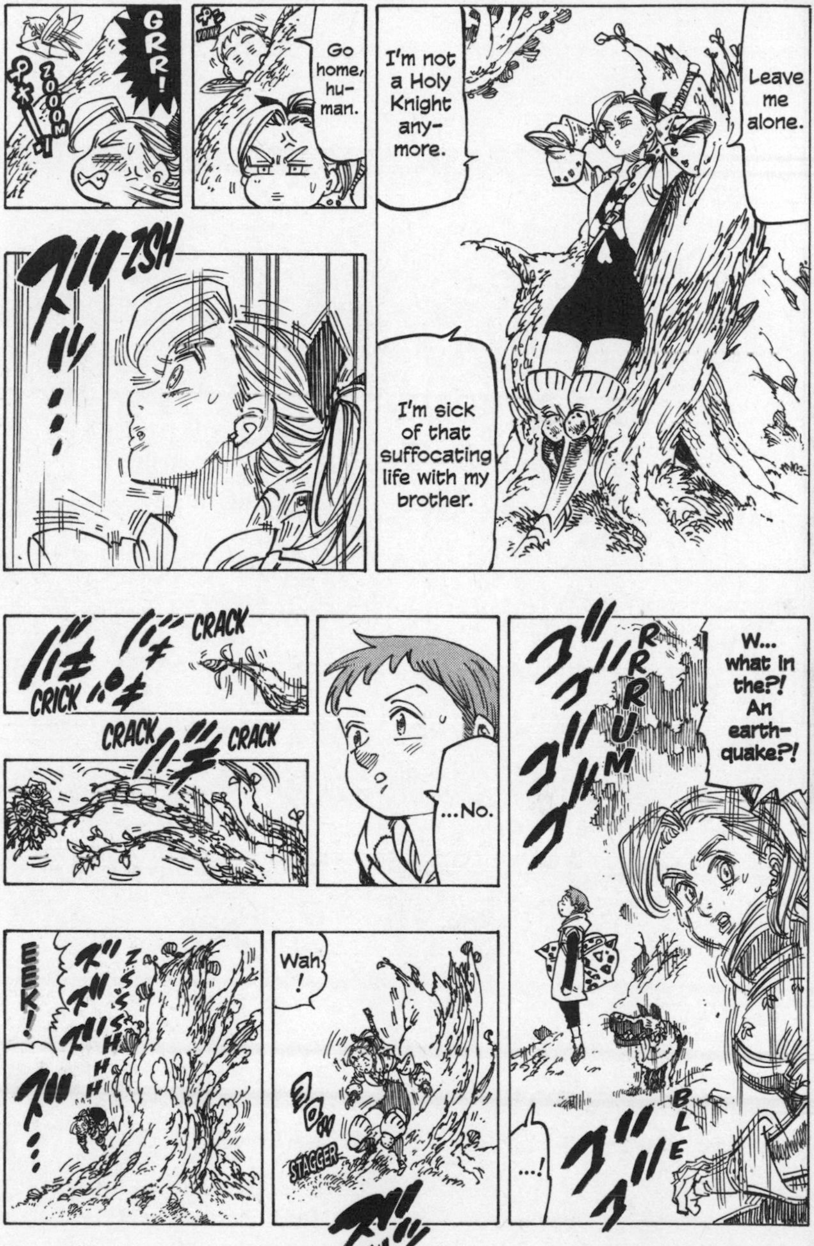
Leave me alone.
I'm not a Holy Knight anymore.
I'm sick of that suffocating life with my brother.
YOINK
Go home, human.
GRR!
ZOOOM
ZSH
RRRUMBLE
W... what in the?! An earthquake?!
...!
...No.
CRACK
CRICK
CRACK
CRACK
Wah!
STAGGER
ZSH
EEK!
ZSSSHHHH

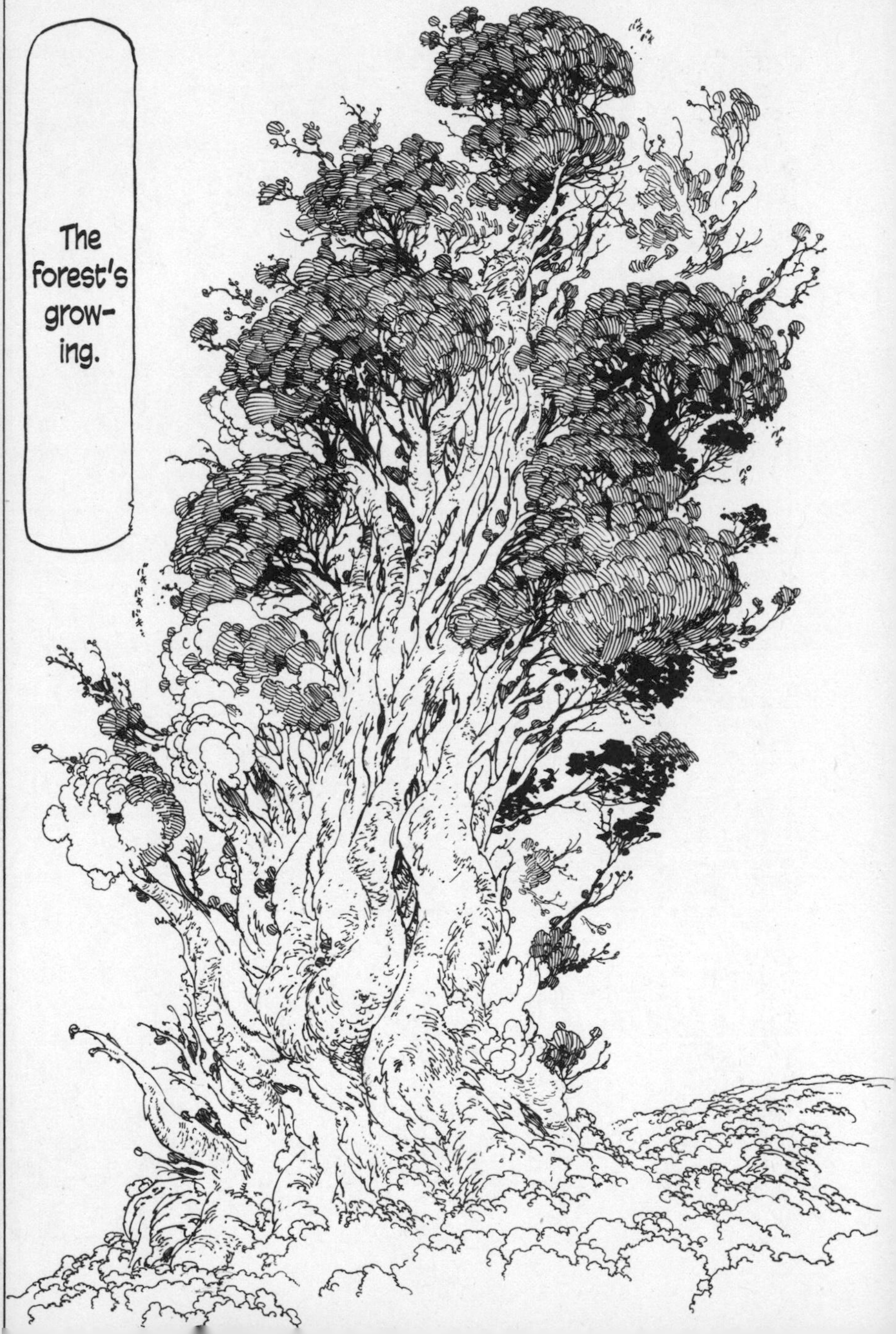
The forest's growing.

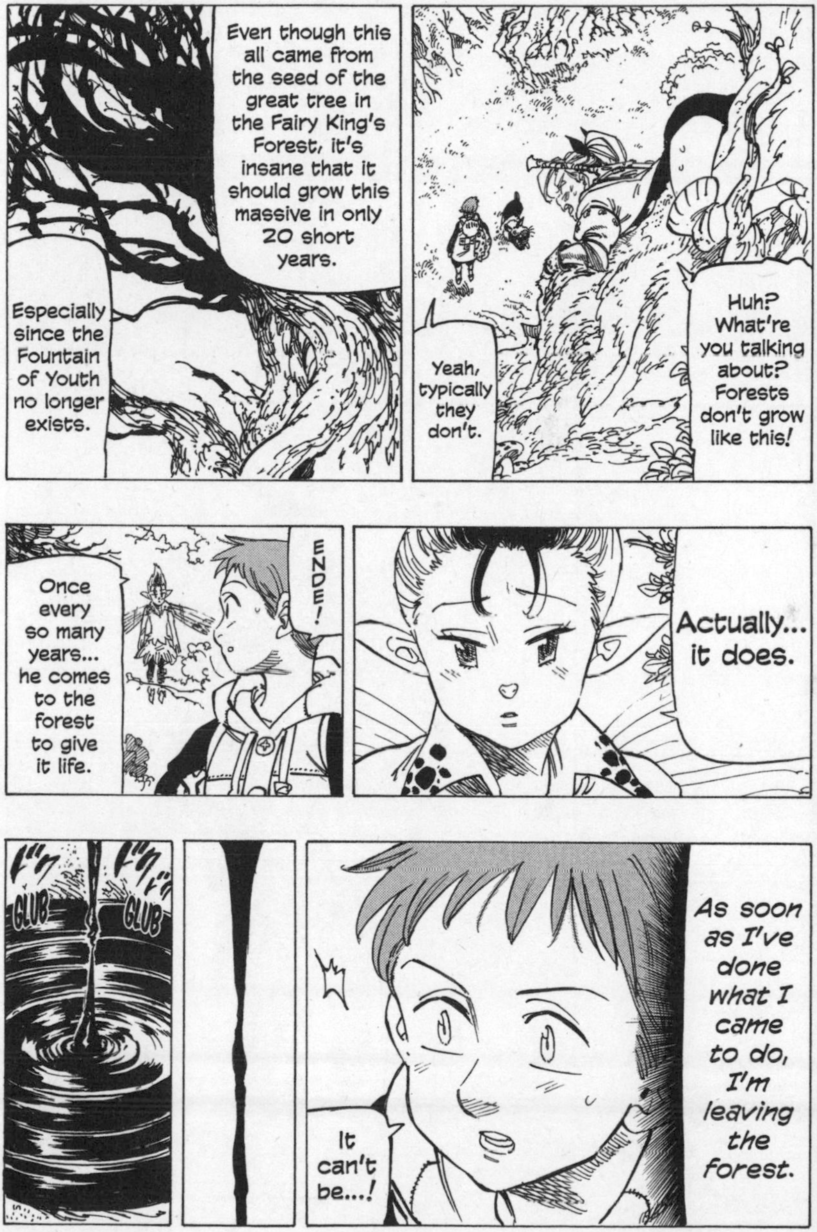
Huh? What're you talking about? Forests don't grow like this!
Yeah, typically they don't.
Even though this all came from the seed of the great tree in the Fairy King's Forest, it's insane that it should grow this massive in only 20 short years.
Especially since the Fountain of Youth no longer exists.
Actually... it does.
ENDE!
Once every so many years... he comes to the forest to give it life.
As soon as I've done what I came to do, I'm leaving the forest.
It can't be...!
GLUB
GLUB

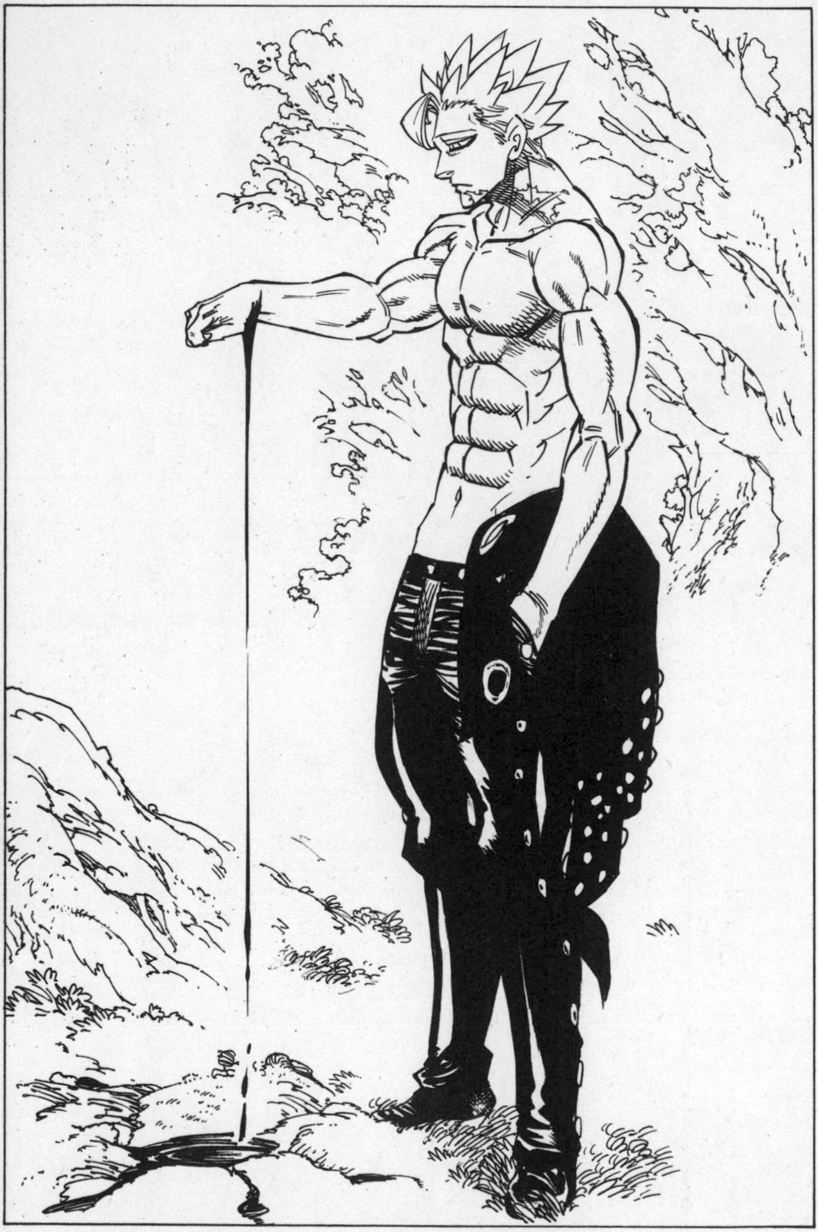

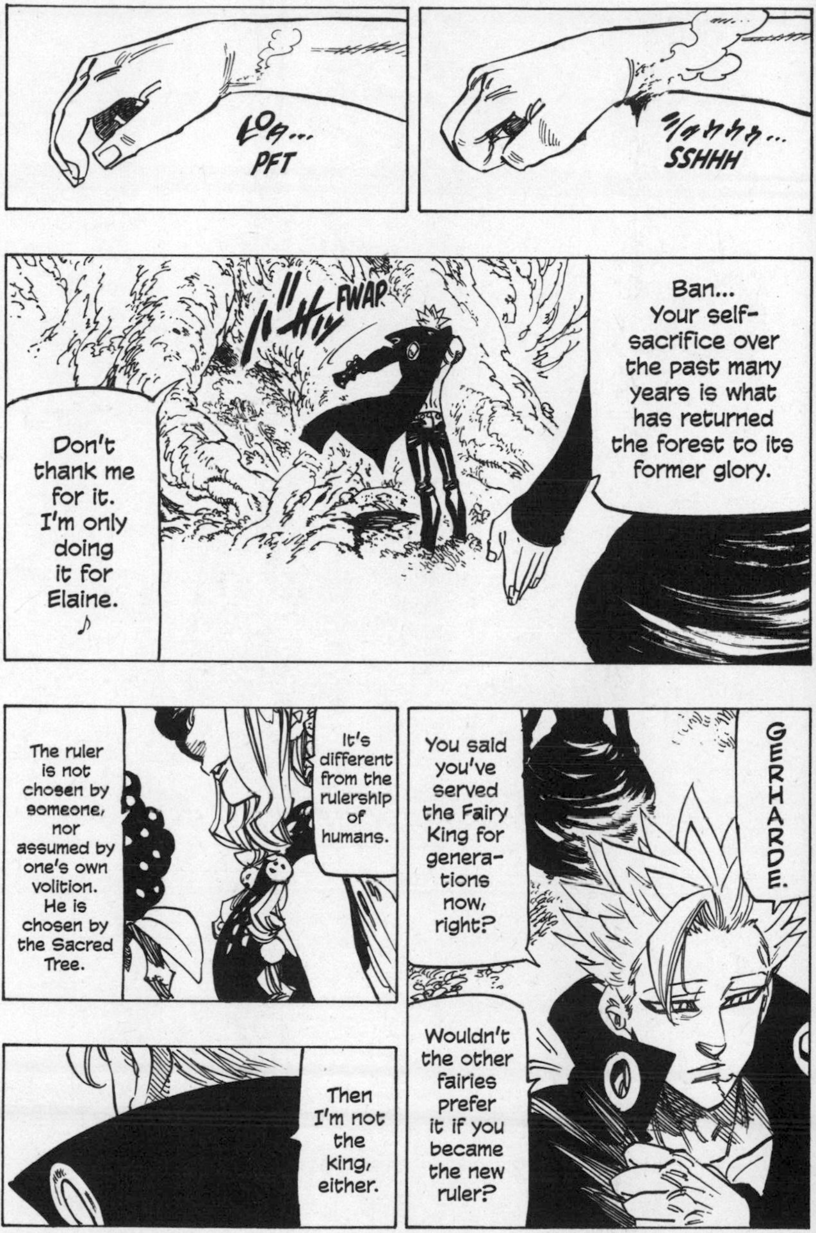
SSHHH
PFT
Ban... Your self-sacrifice over the past many years is what has returned the forest to its former glory.
FWAP
Don't thank me for it. I'm only doing it for Elaine. ♪
GERHARDE.
You said you've served the Fairy King for generations now, right?
Wouldn't the other fairies prefer it if you became the new ruler?
It's different from the rulership of humans.
The ruler is not chosen by someone, nor assumed by one's own volition. He is chosen by the Sacred Tree.
Then I'm not the king, either.

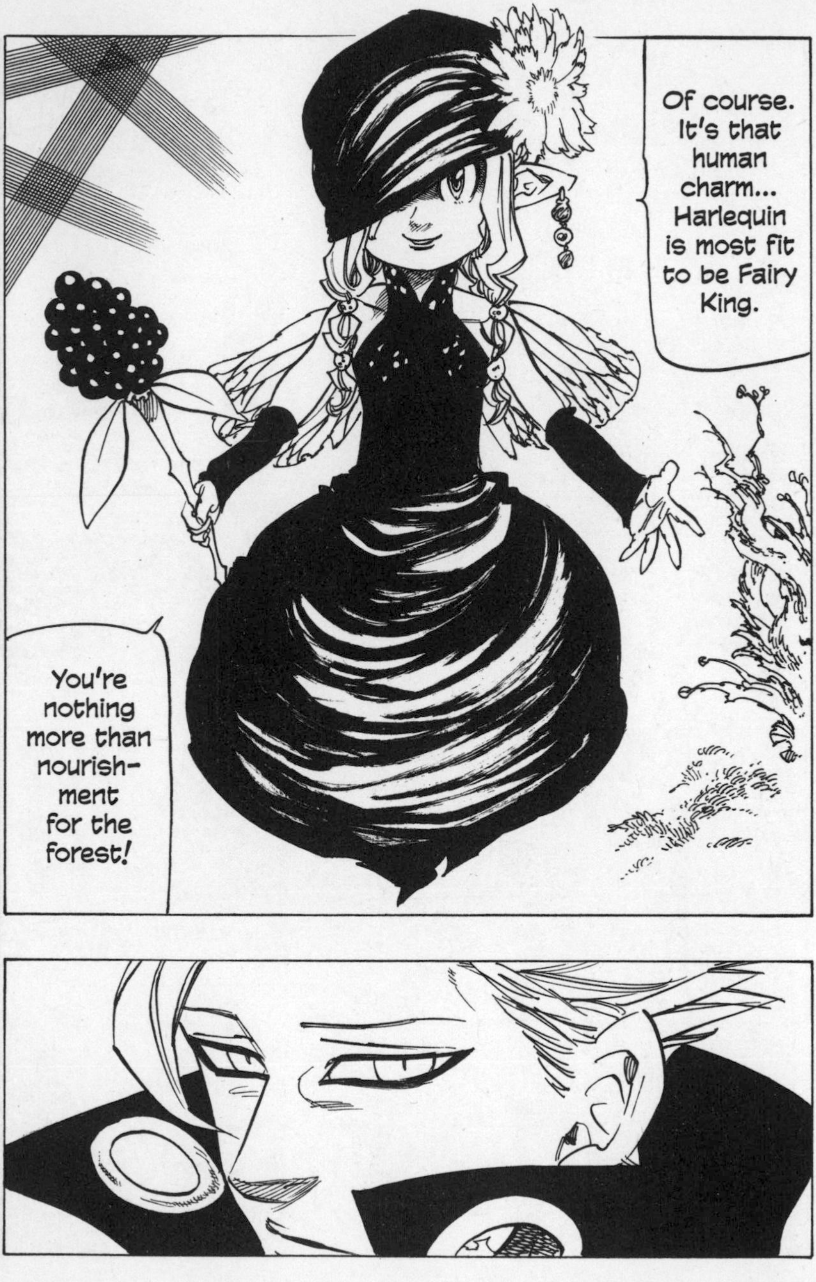
Of course. It's that human charm... Harlequin is most fit to be Fairy King.
You're nothing more than nourish-ment for the forest!

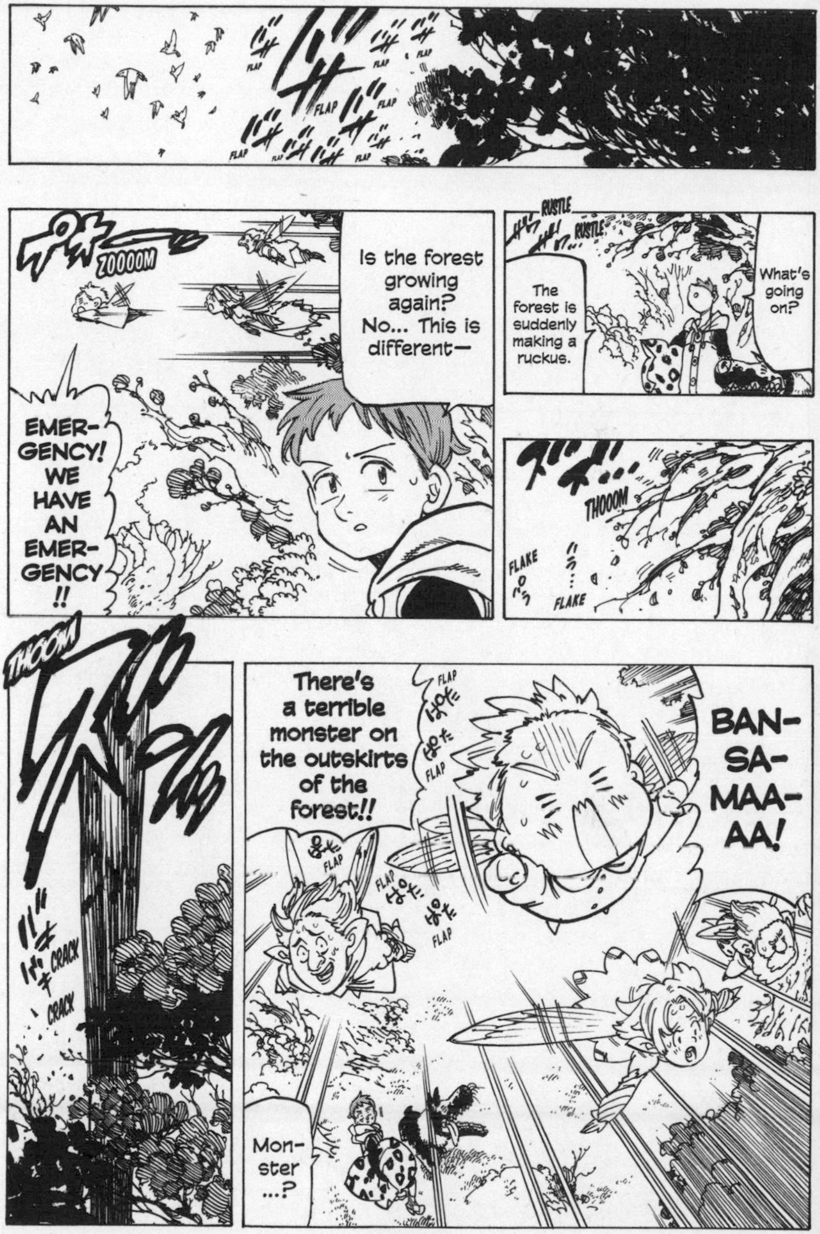
FLAP
FLAP
FLAP
FLAP
FLAP
FLAP
RUSTLE
RUSTLE
What's going on?
The forest is suddenly making a ruckus.
THOOOM
FLAKE
FLAKE
ZOOOOM
Is the forest growing again? No... This is different—
EMERGENCY! WE HAVE AN EMERGENCY!!
BAN-SA-MAAA-AA!
FLAP
FLAP
There's a terrible monster on the outskirts of the forest!!
FLAP
FLAP
FLAP
Mon-ster ...?
THOOM
CRACK
CRACK

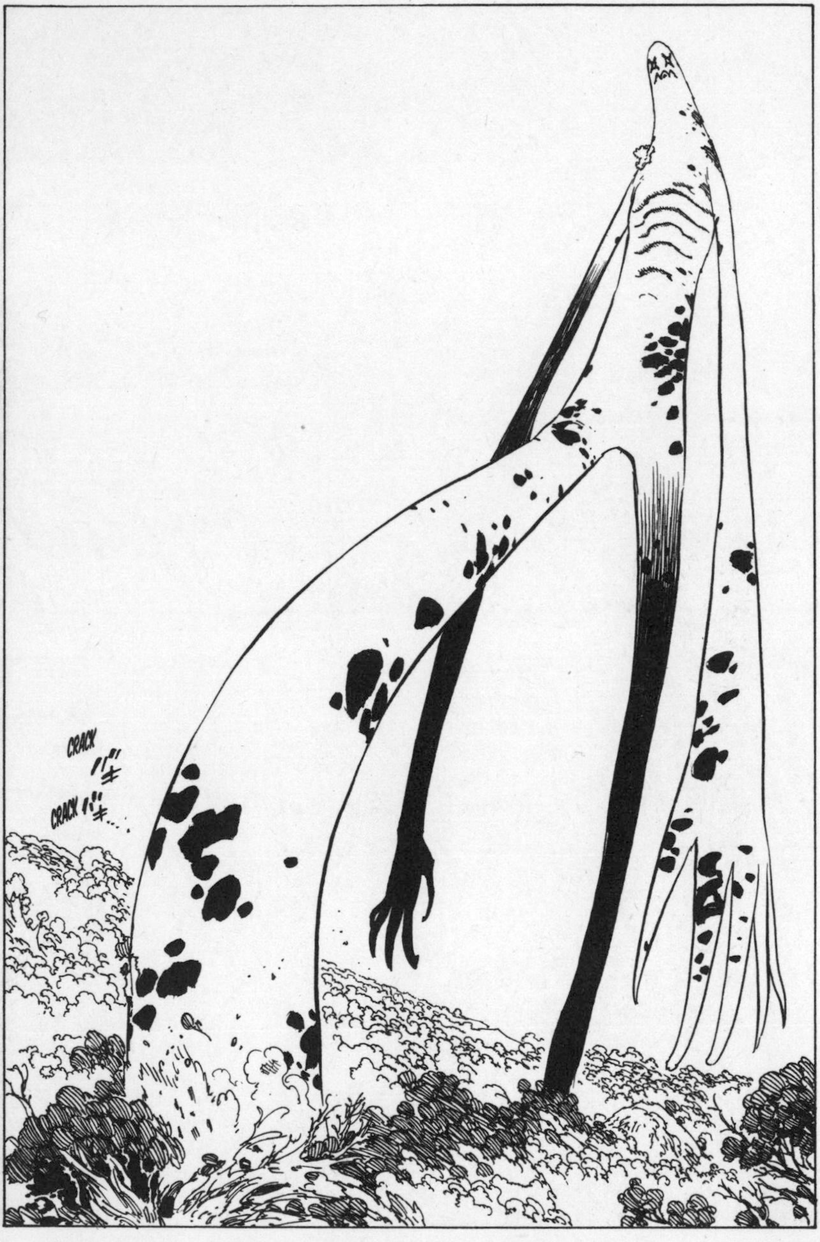
CRACK
バキ
CRACK
バキ...

Chapter 117 - The Two Fairy Kings

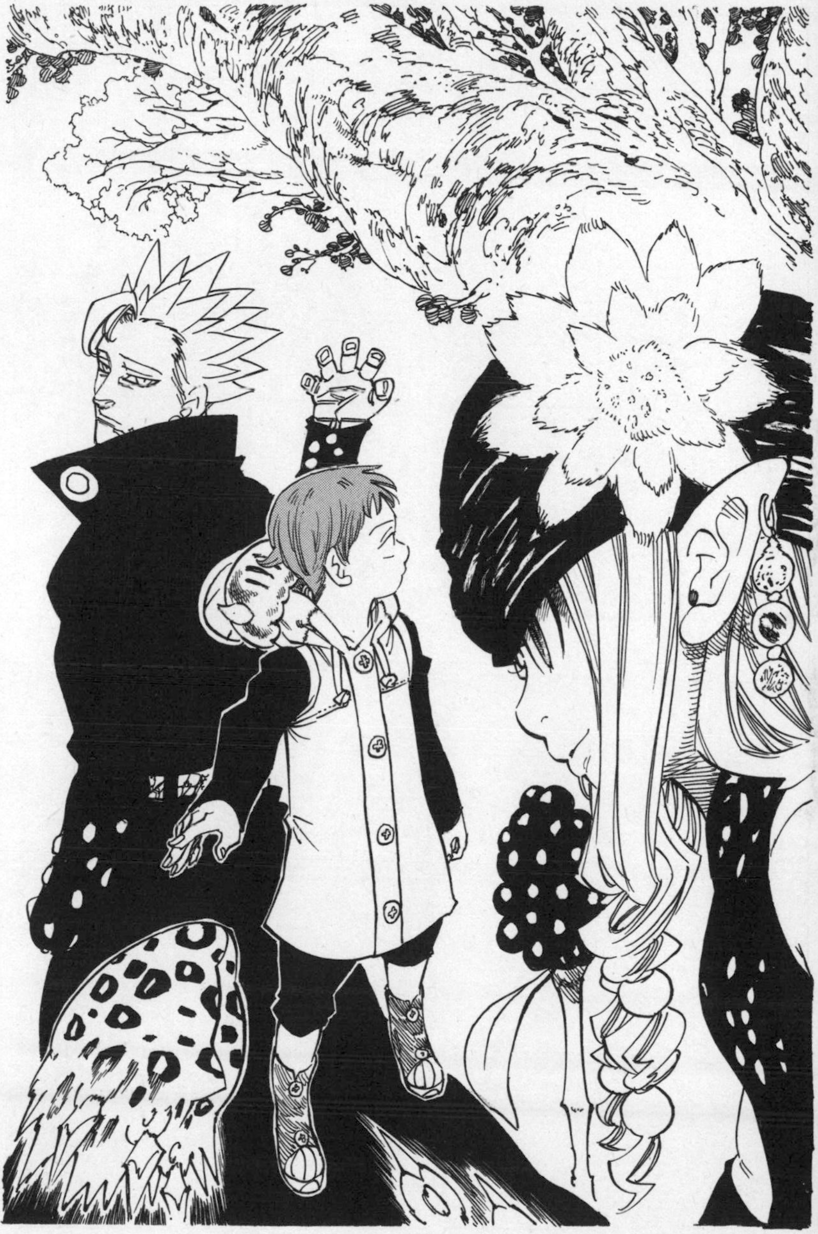

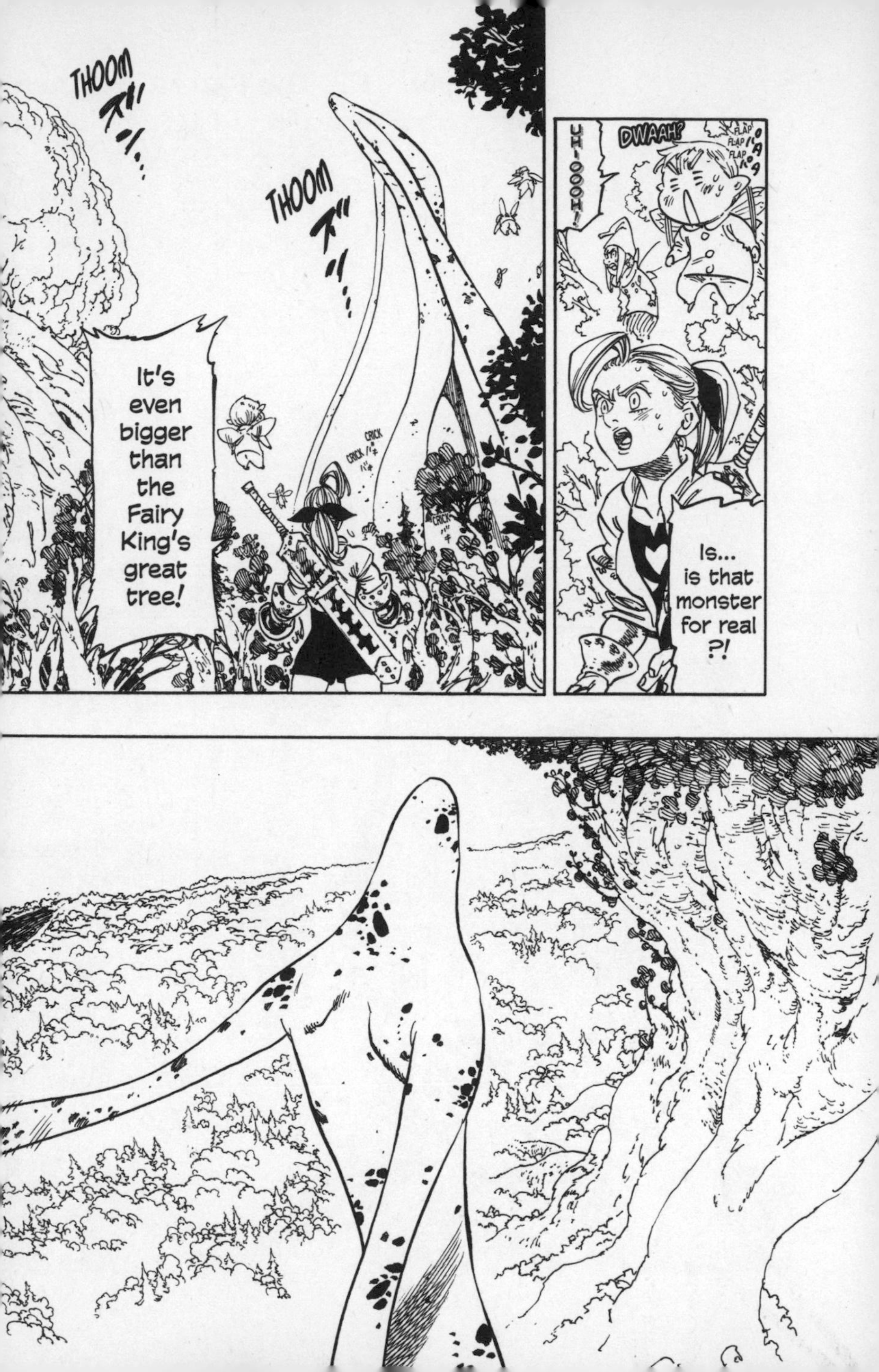
DWAAH?
FLAP FLAP FLAP
UHI-OOOOH!
Is... is that monster for real?!
THOOM
THOOM
CRICK CRICK
CRICK
It's even bigger than the Fairy King's great tree!

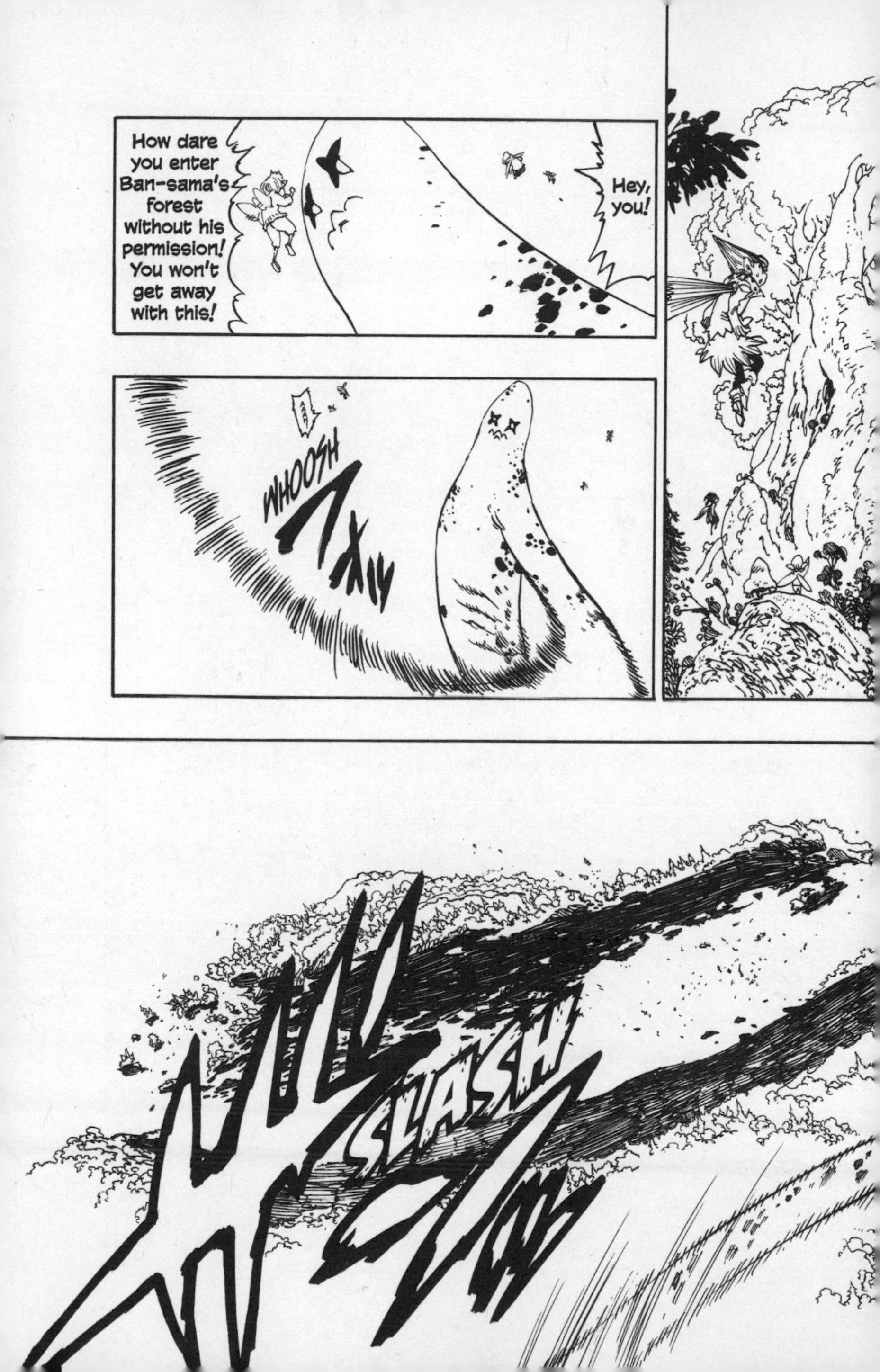
Hey, you!
How dare you enter Ban-sama's forest without his permission! You won't get away with this!
WHOOSH
SLASH

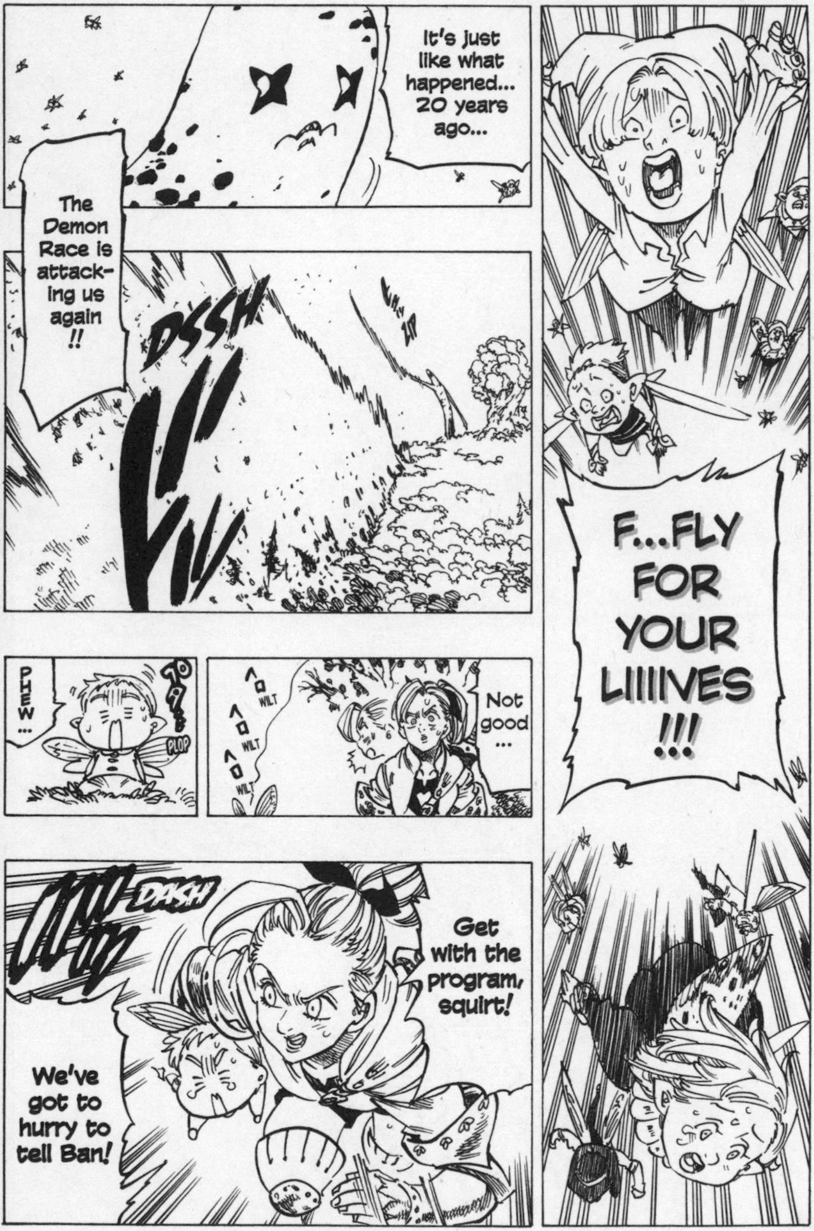

F...FLY FOR YOUR LIIIVES !!!
It's just like what happened... 20 years ago...
The Demon Race is attacking us again !!
DSSH
WILT
WILT
WILT
Not good ...
PLOP
PHEW...
DASH
Get with the program, squirt!
We've got to hurry to tell Ban!

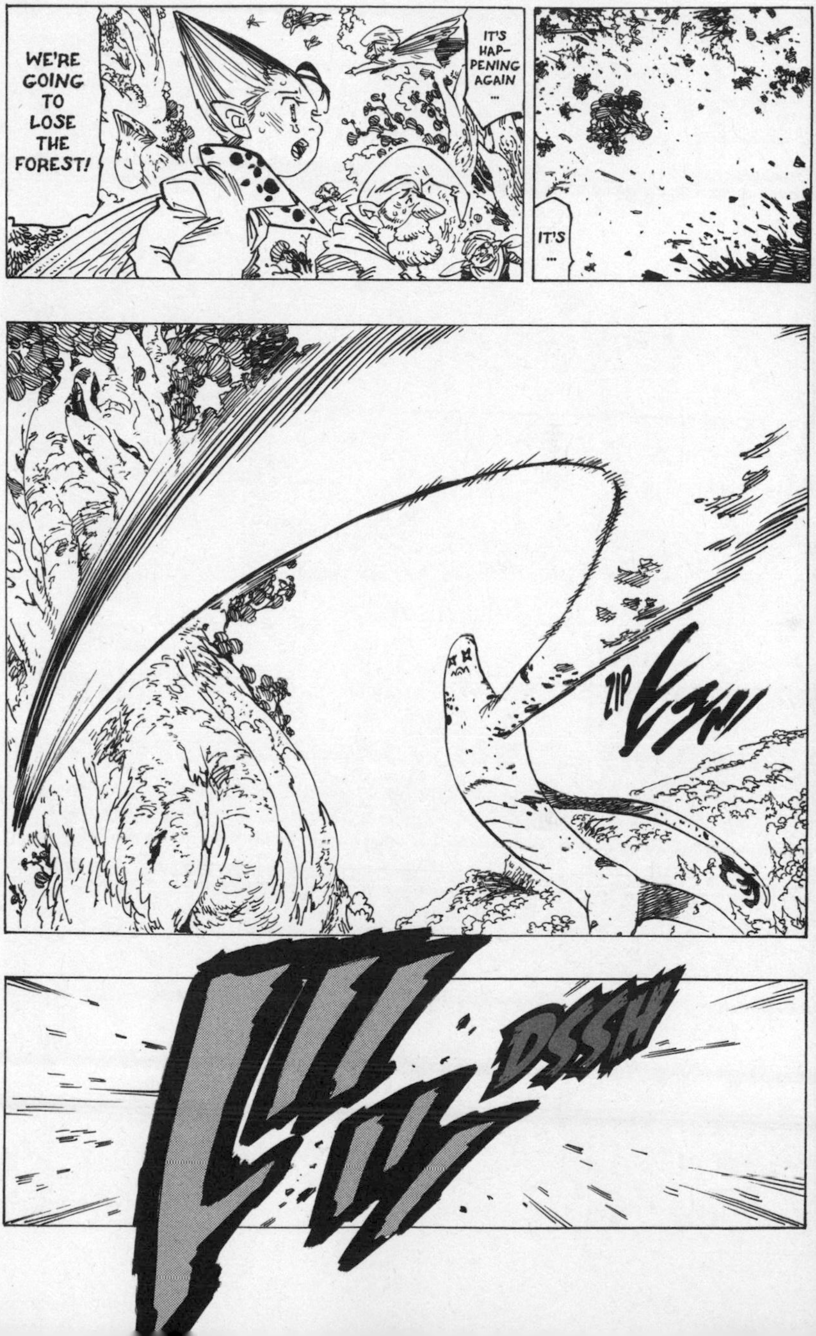
IT'S ...
IT'S HAPPENING AGAIN ...
WE'RE GOING TO LOSE THE FOREST!
ZIP
DSSH

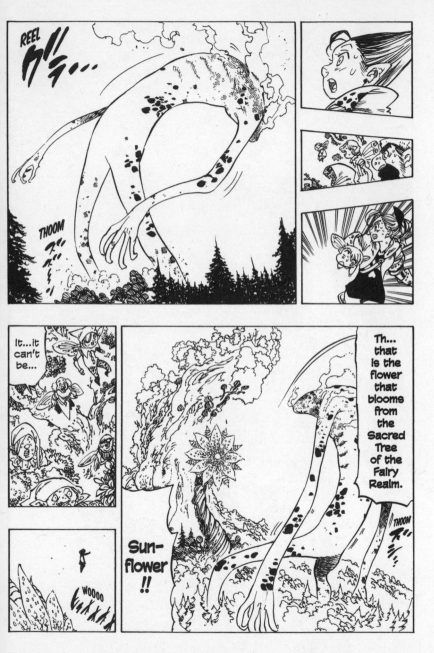

REEL

THOOM

It...it can't be...

Sun-flower !!

WOOOO

Th... that is the flower that blooms from the Sacred Tree of the Fairy Realm.

THOOM

-74-

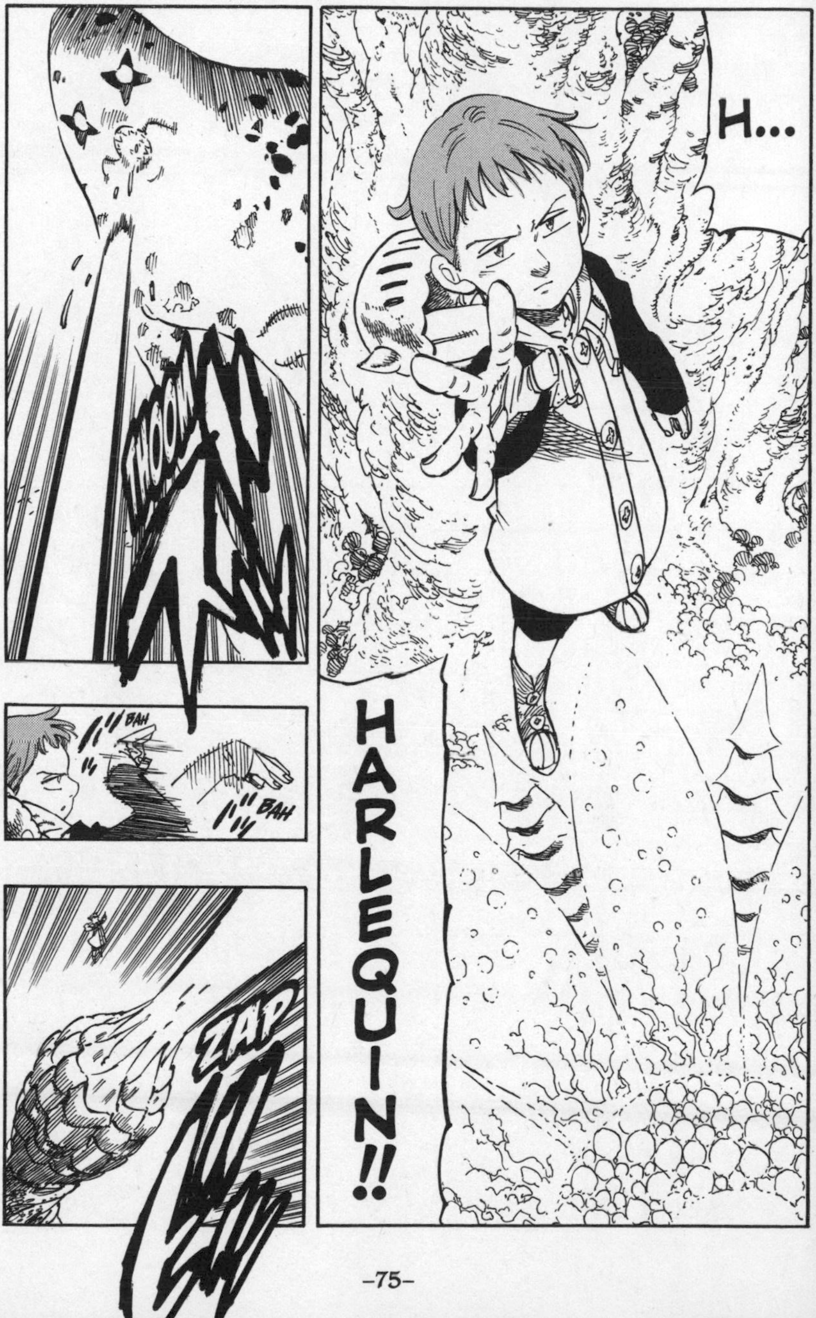
H...
HARLEQUIN!!
THOOM
BAH
BAH
ZAP

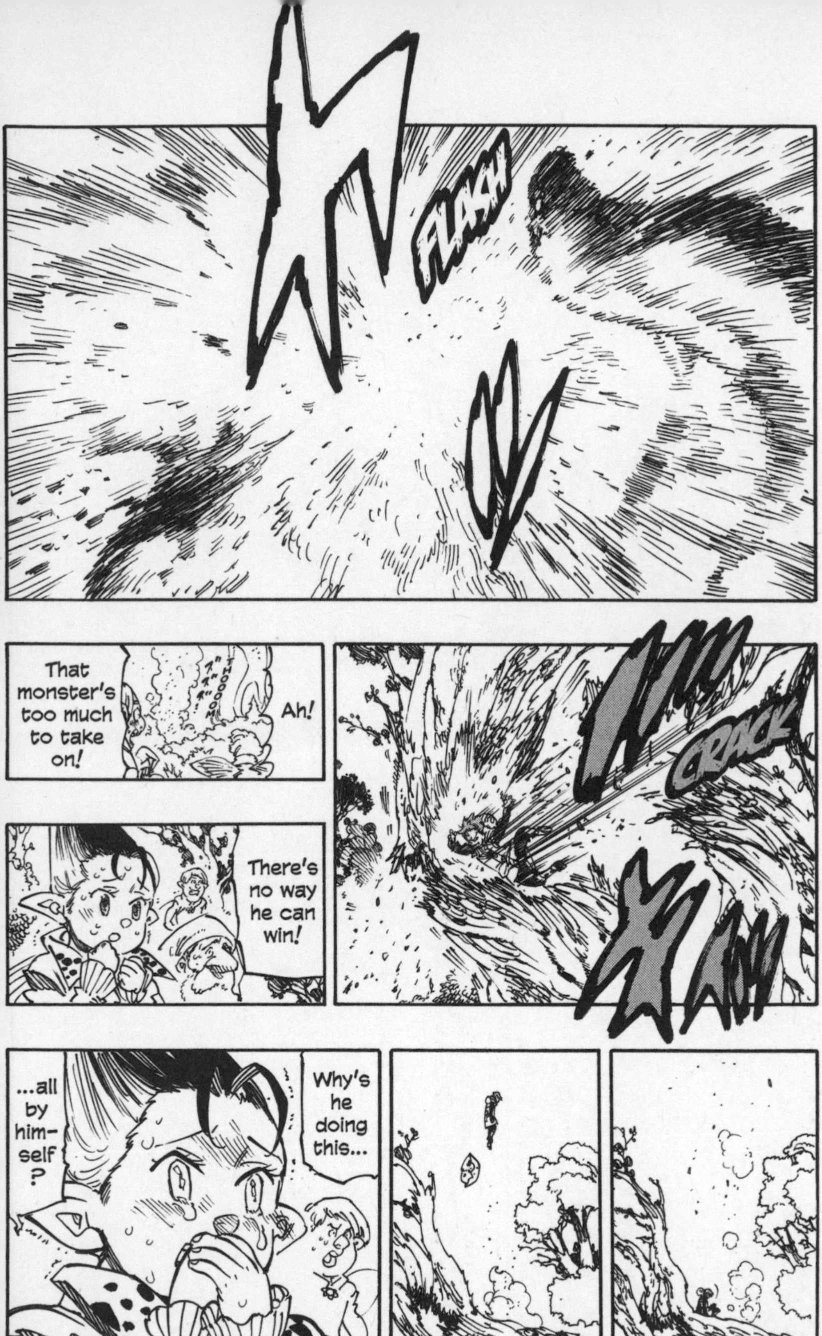
FLASH
CRACK
Ah!
That monster's too much to take on!
There's no way he can win!
Why's he doing this...
...all by him-self?

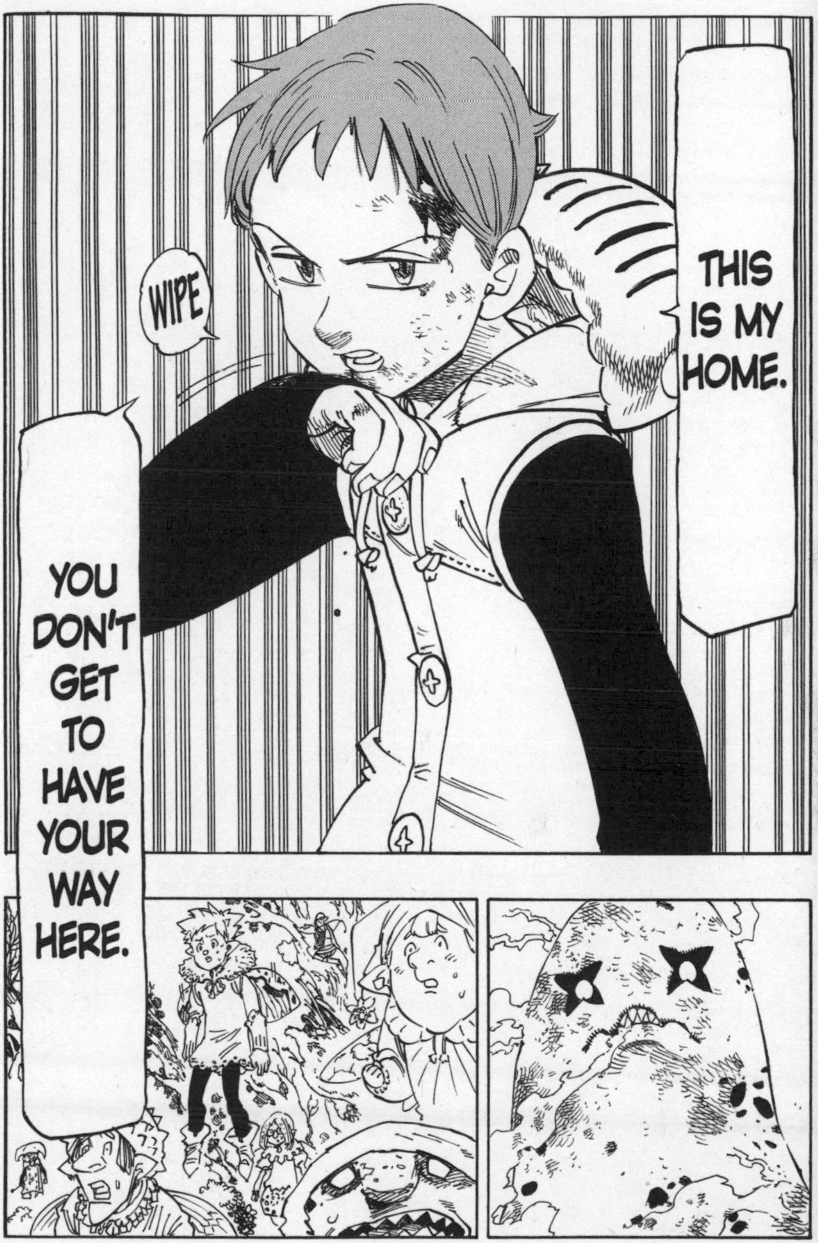
THIS IS MY HOME.
WIPE
YOU DON'T GET TO HAVE YOUR WAY HERE.

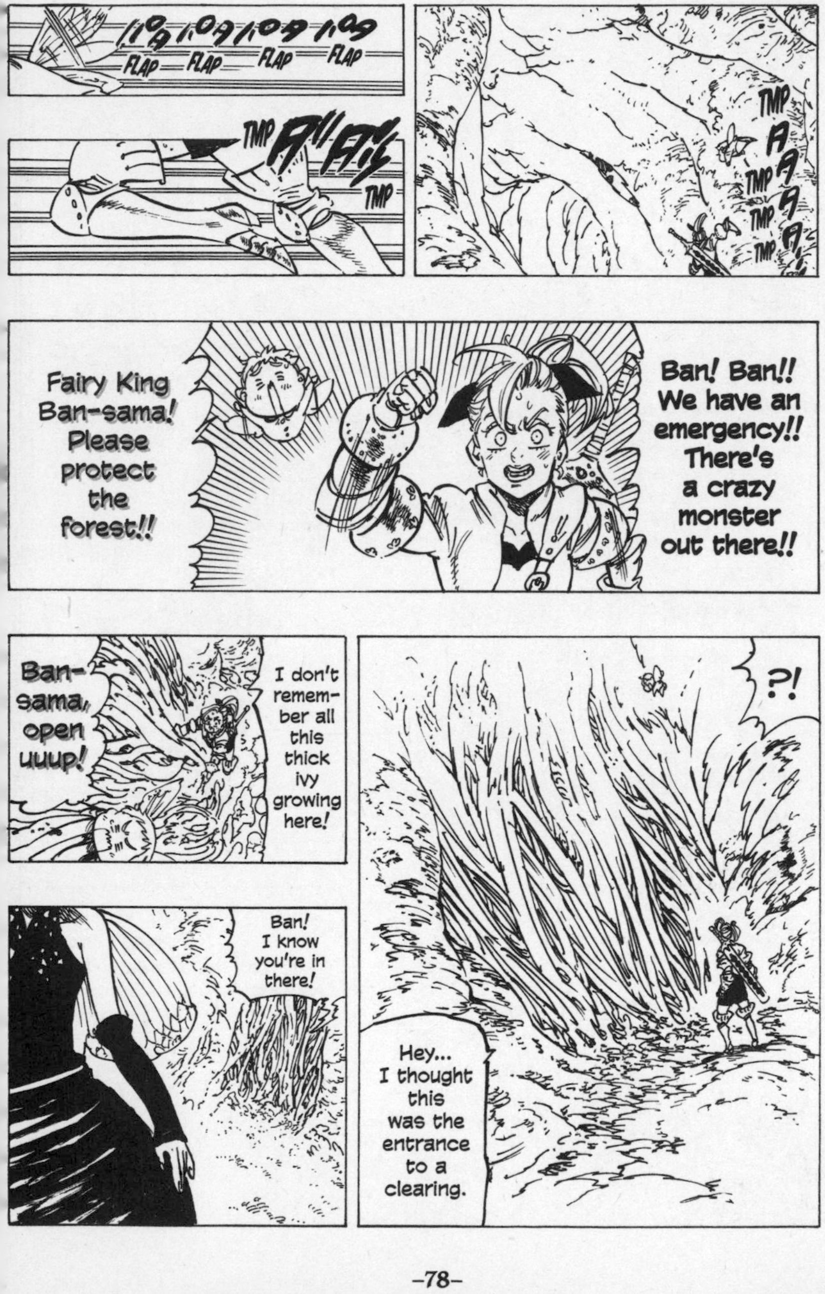
TMP
TMP
TMP
TMP
FLAP FLAP FLAP FLAP
TMP
TMP
Ban! Ban!! We have an emergency!! There's a crazy monster out there!!
Fairy King Ban-sama! Please protect the forest!!
?!
Hey... I thought this was the entrance to a clearing.
I don't remember all this thick ivy growing here!
Ban-sama, open uuup!
Ban! I know you're in there!

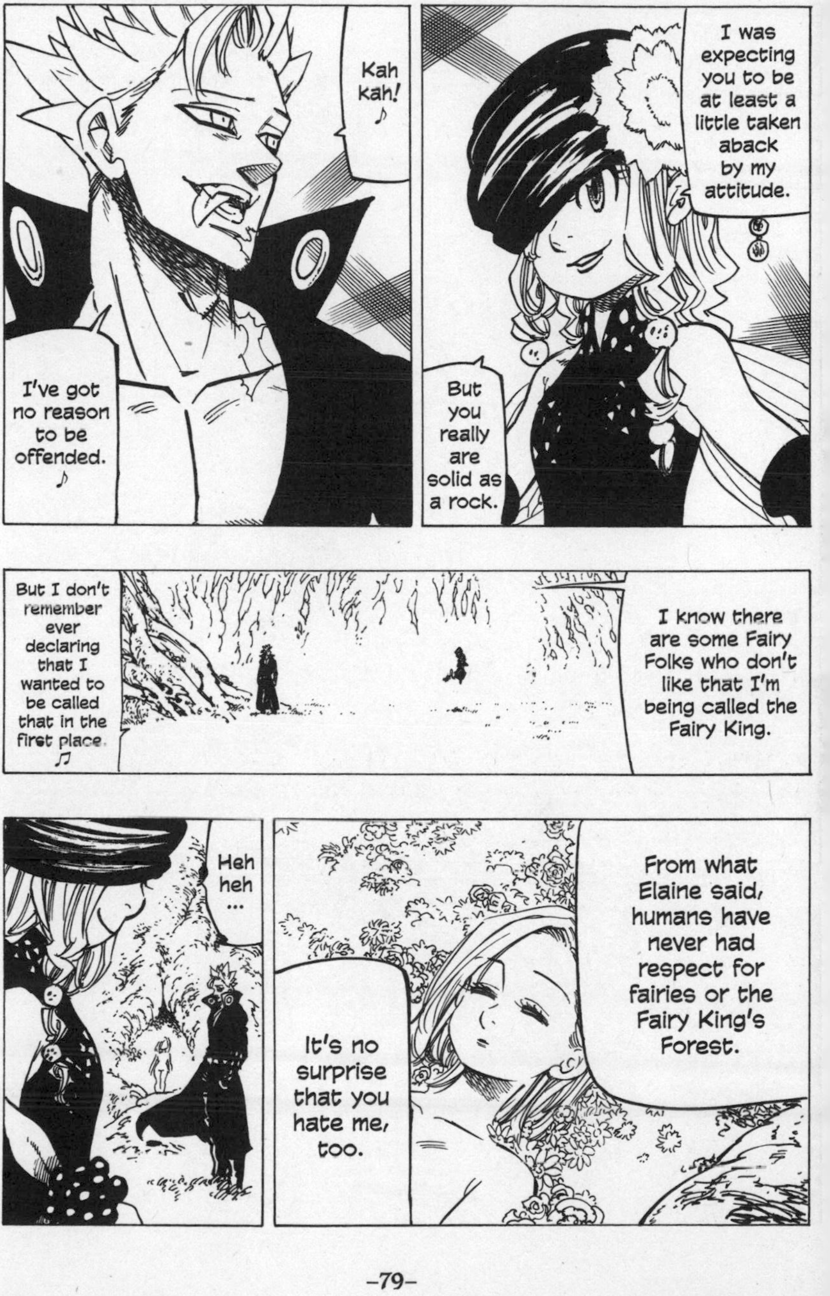
I was expecting you to be at least a little taken aback by my attitude.
But you really are solid as a rock.
Kah kah! ♪
I've got no reason to be offended. ♪
I know there are some Fairy Folks who don't like that I'm being called the Fairy King.
But I don't remember ever declaring that I wanted to be called that in the first place. ♫
From what Elaine said, humans have never had respect for fairies or the Fairy King's Forest.
It's no surprise that you hate me, too.
Heh heh ...

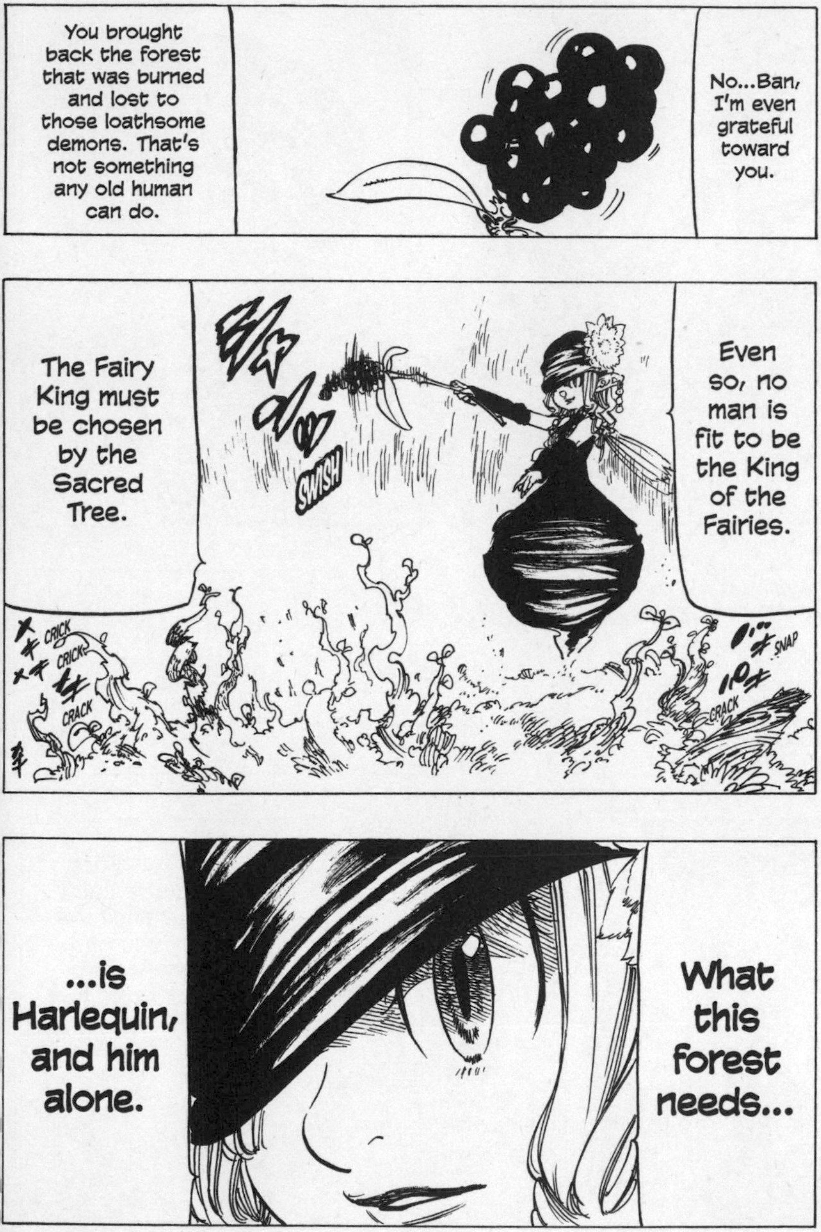
No...Ban, I'm even grateful toward you.
You brought back the forest that was burned and lost to those loathsome demons. That's not something any old human can do.
Even so, no man is fit to be the King of the Fairies.
SWISH
The Fairy King must be chosen by the Sacred Tree.
SNAP
CRACK
CRICK
CRICK
CRACK
What this forest needs...
...is Harlequin, and him alone.

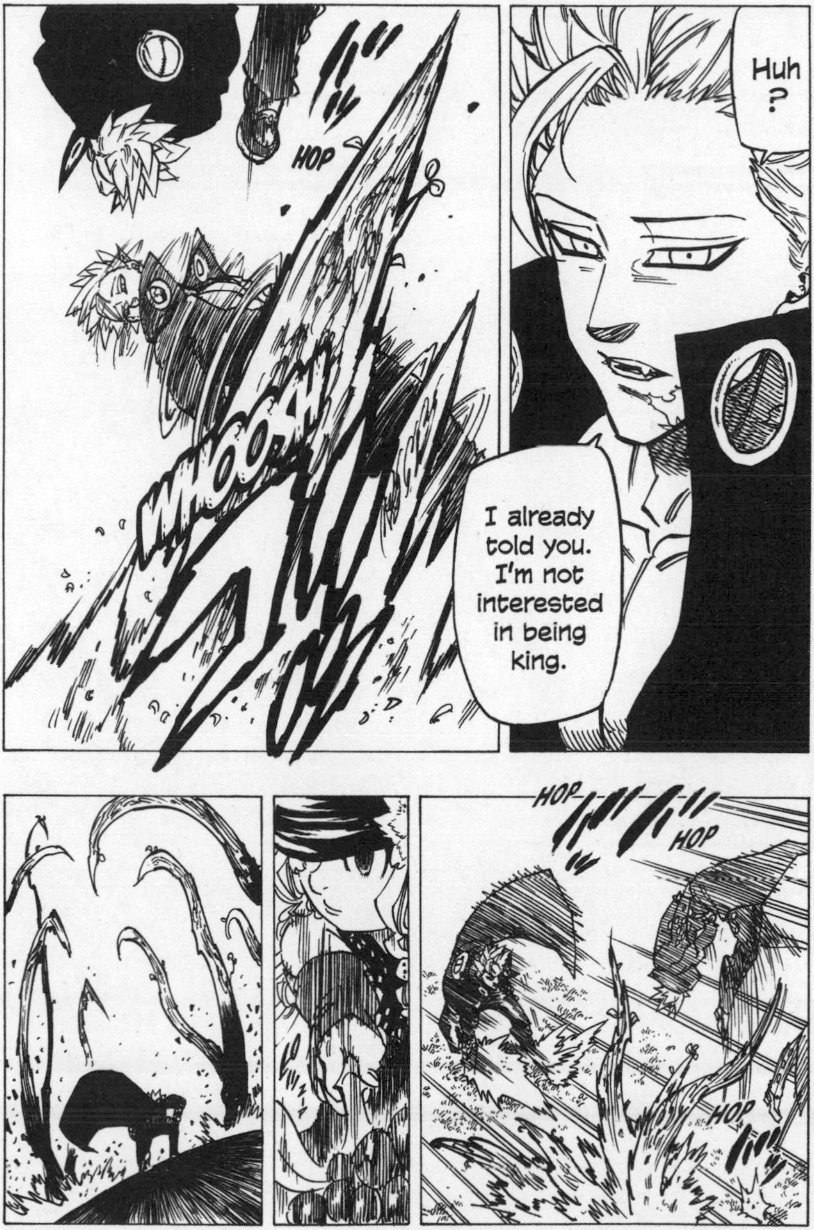
Huh?
I already told you. I'm not interested in being king.
HOP
HOP
HOP
HOP

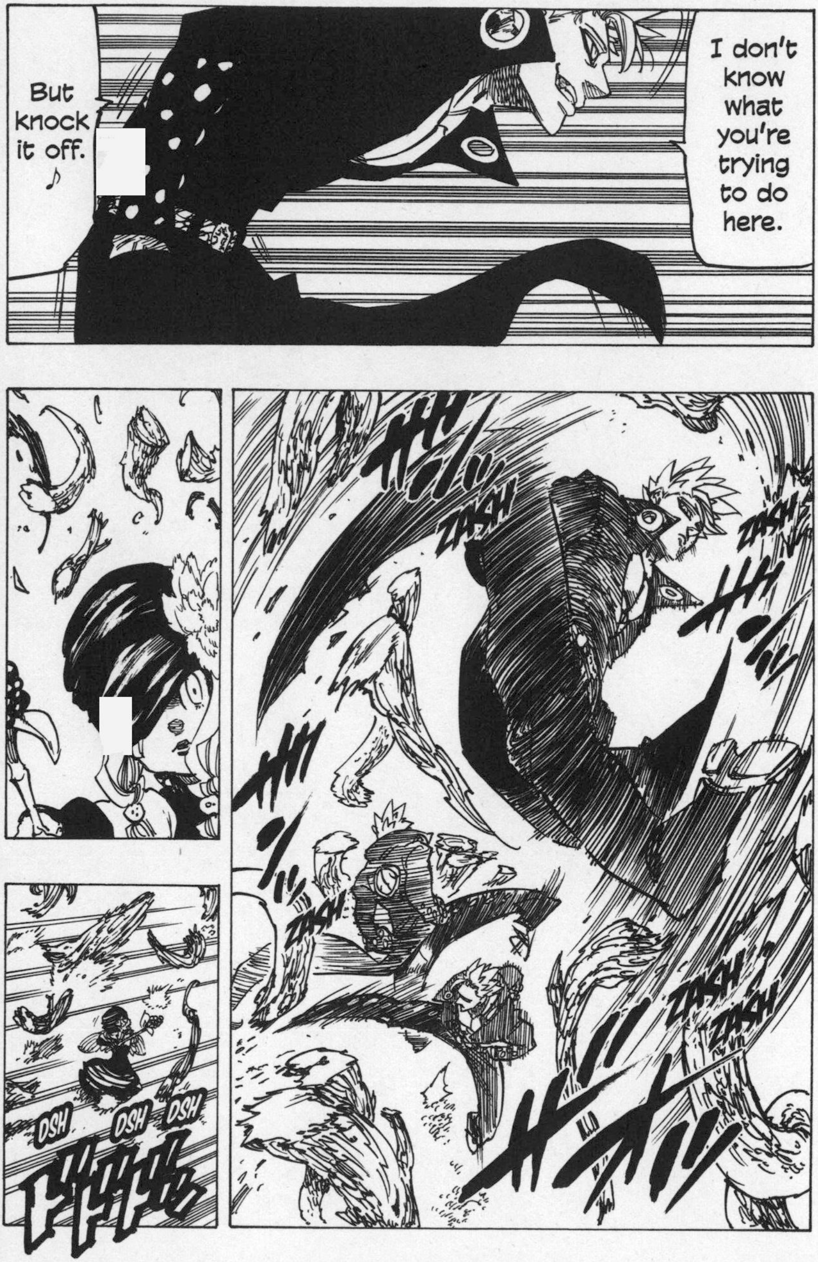
I don't know what you're trying to do here.
But knock it off. ♪
ZASH
ZASH
ZASH
ZASH
ZASH
DSH
DSH
DSH

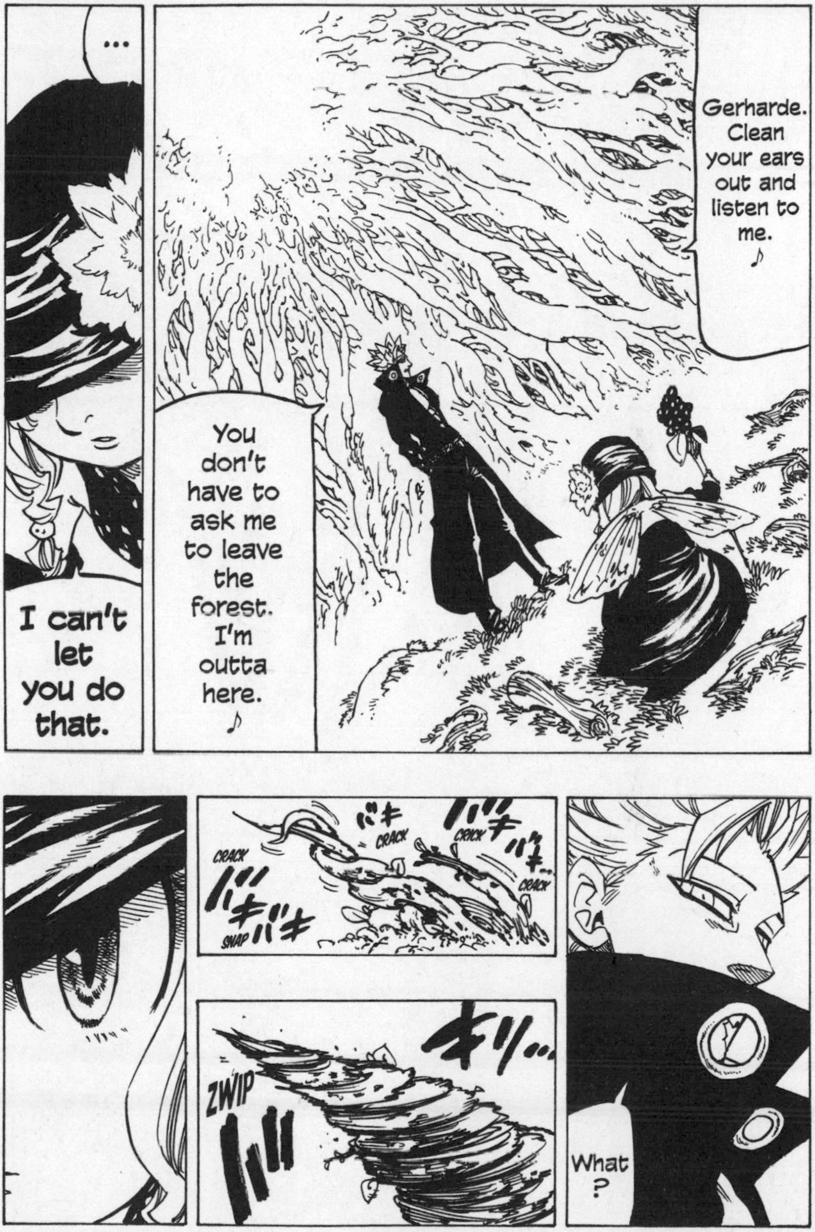
Gerharde. Clean your ears out and listen to me. ♪
You don't have to ask me to leave the forest. I'm outta here. ♪
...
I can't let you do that.
What?
CRACK
CRICK
CRACK
CRACK
SNAP
ZWIP

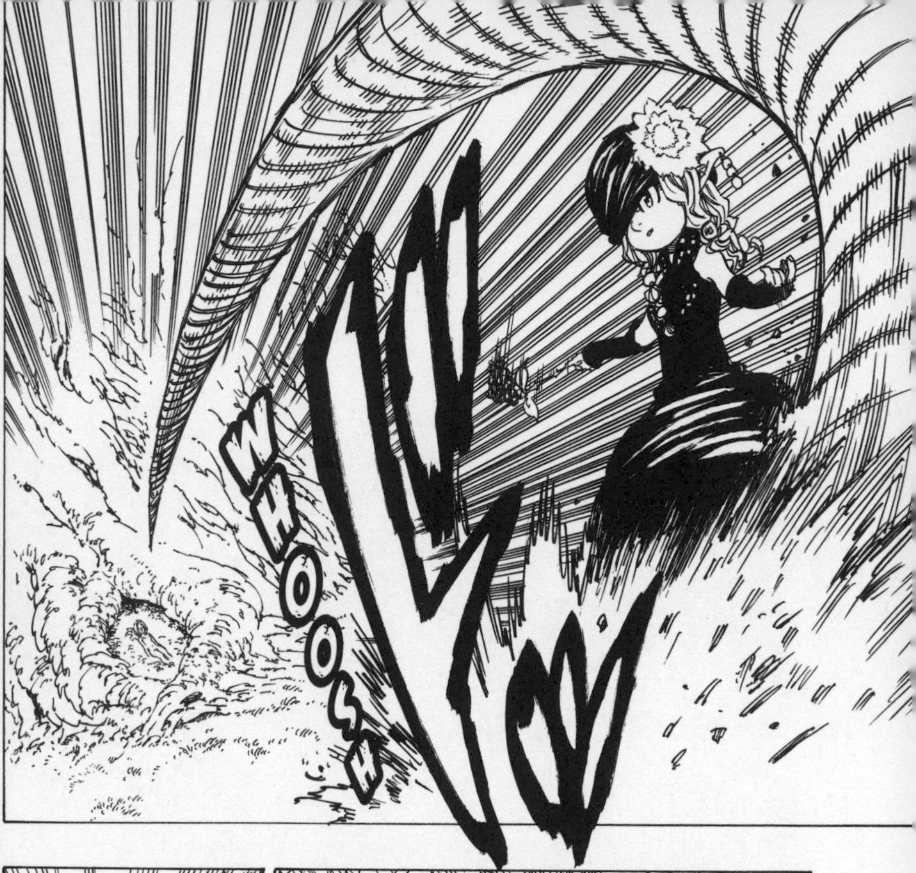
WHOOSH

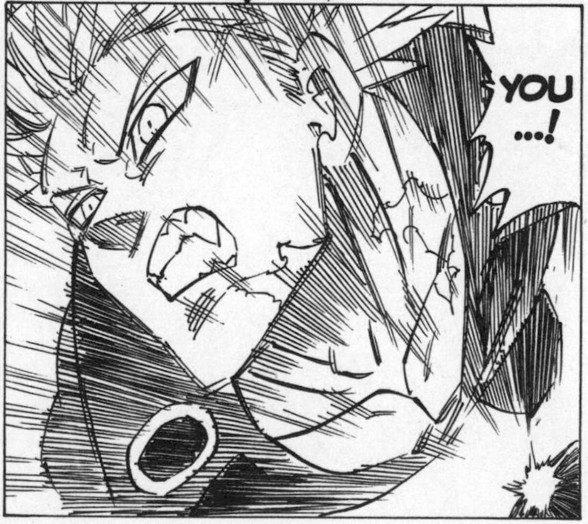
YOU ...!

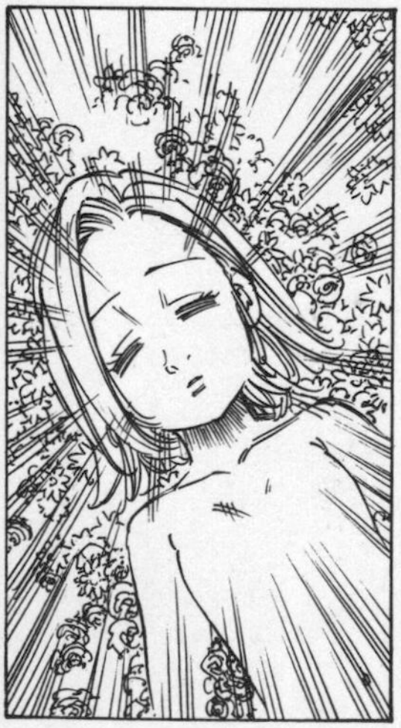

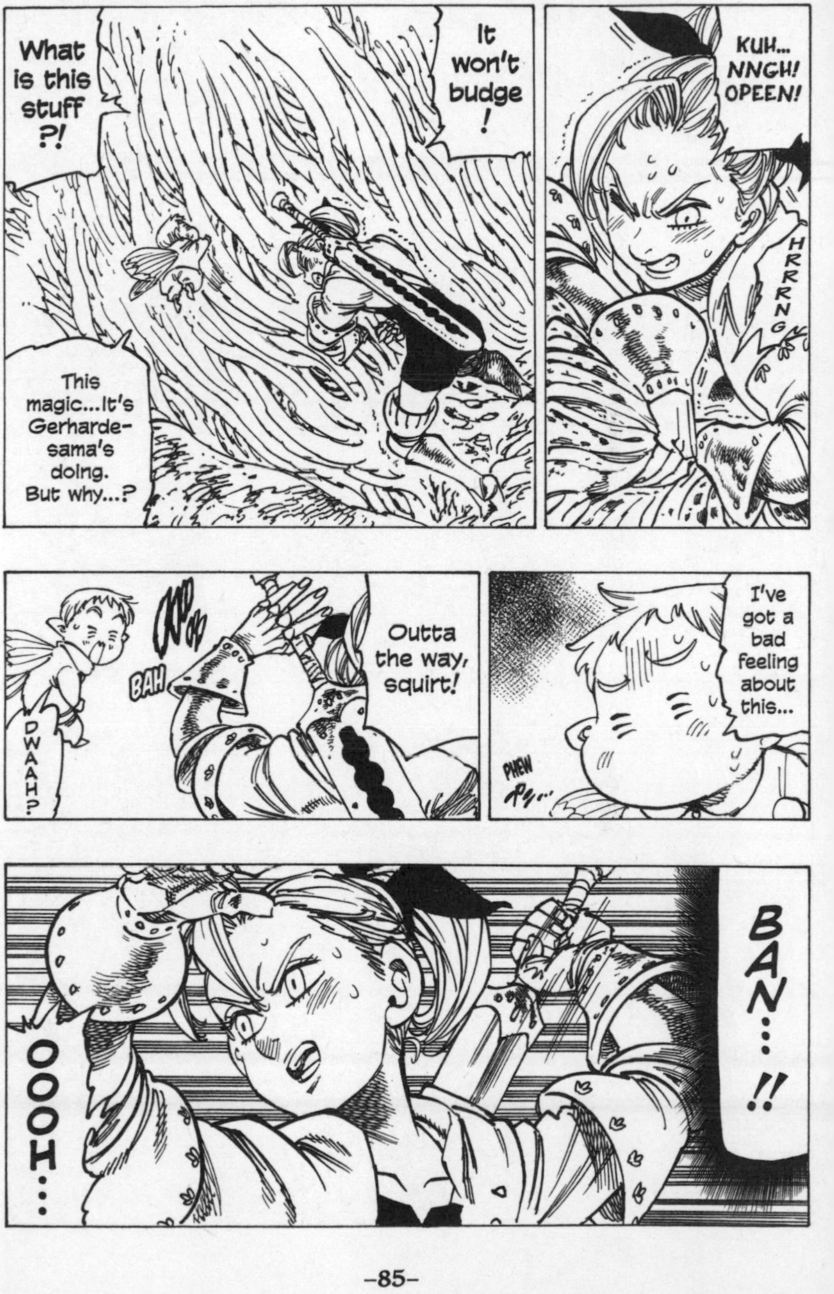
KUH... NNGH! OPEEN!
HRRRNG
It won't budge!
What is this stuff?!
This magic...It's Gerharde-sama's doing. But why...?
I've got a bad feeling about this...
PHEW
Outta the way, squirt!
BAH
DWAAH?
BAN...!!
OOOOH...

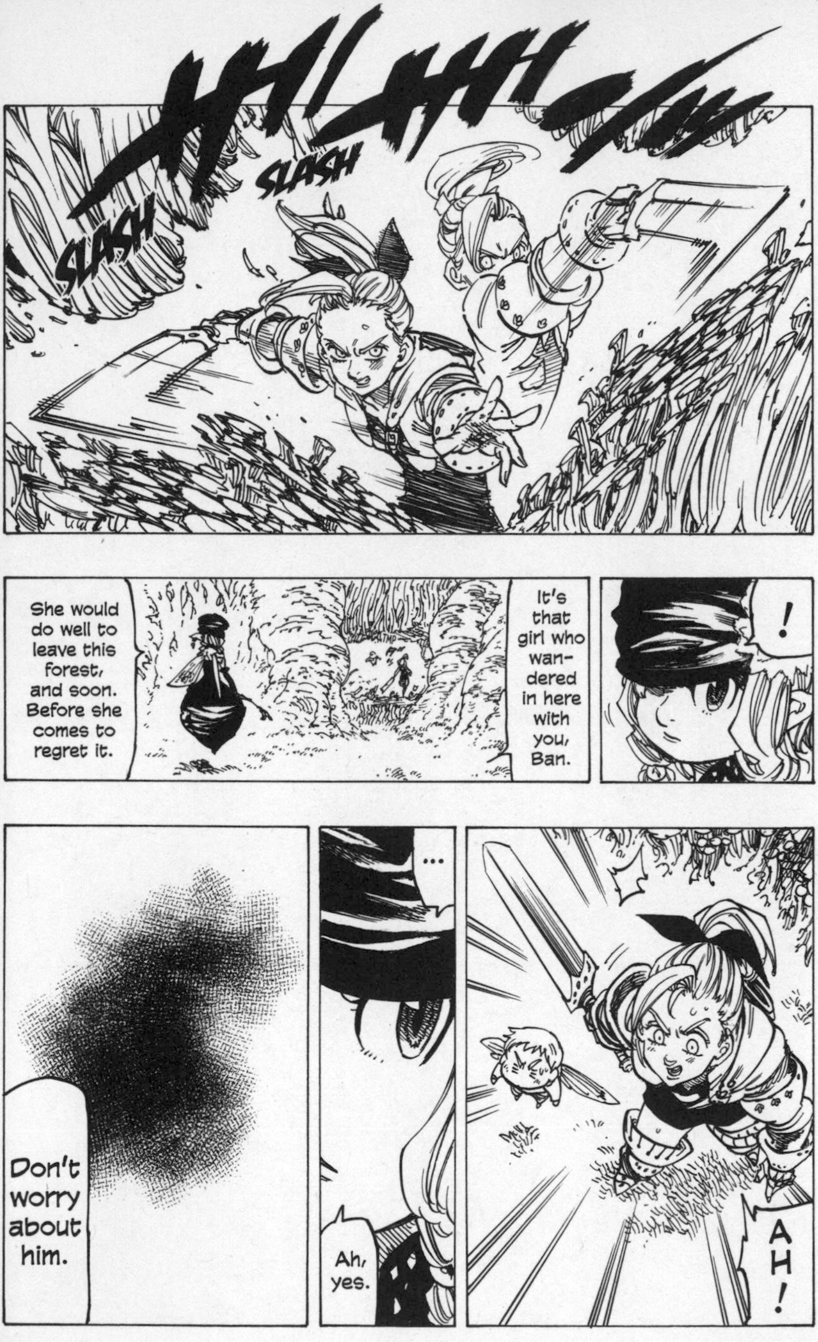
SLASH
SLASH
!
It's that girl who wandered in here with you, Ban.
She would do well to leave this forest, and soon. Before she comes to regret it.
AH!
...
Ah, yes.
Don't worry about him.

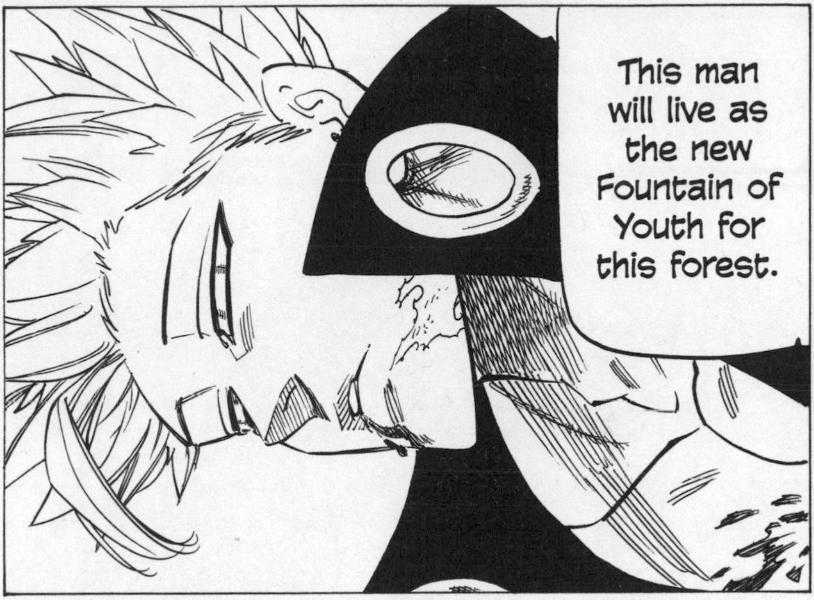
This man will live as the new Fountain of Youth for this forest.
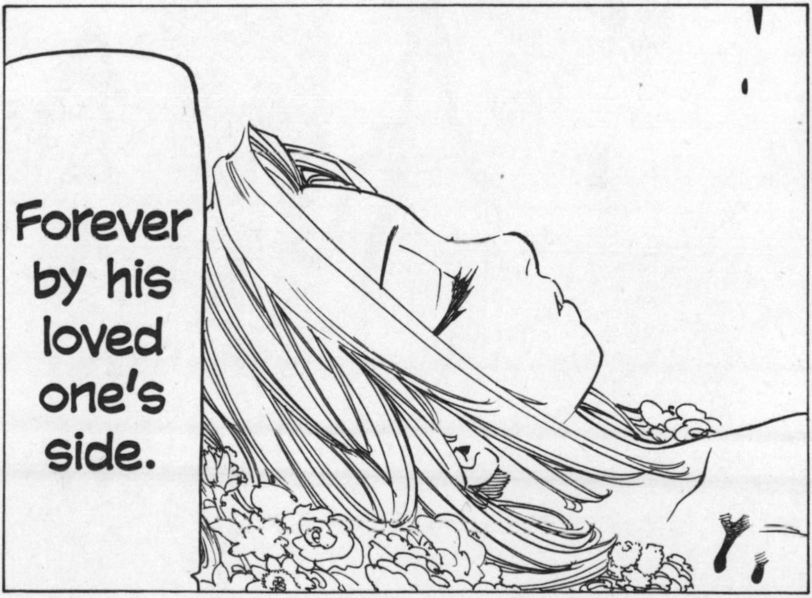
Forever by his loved one's side.

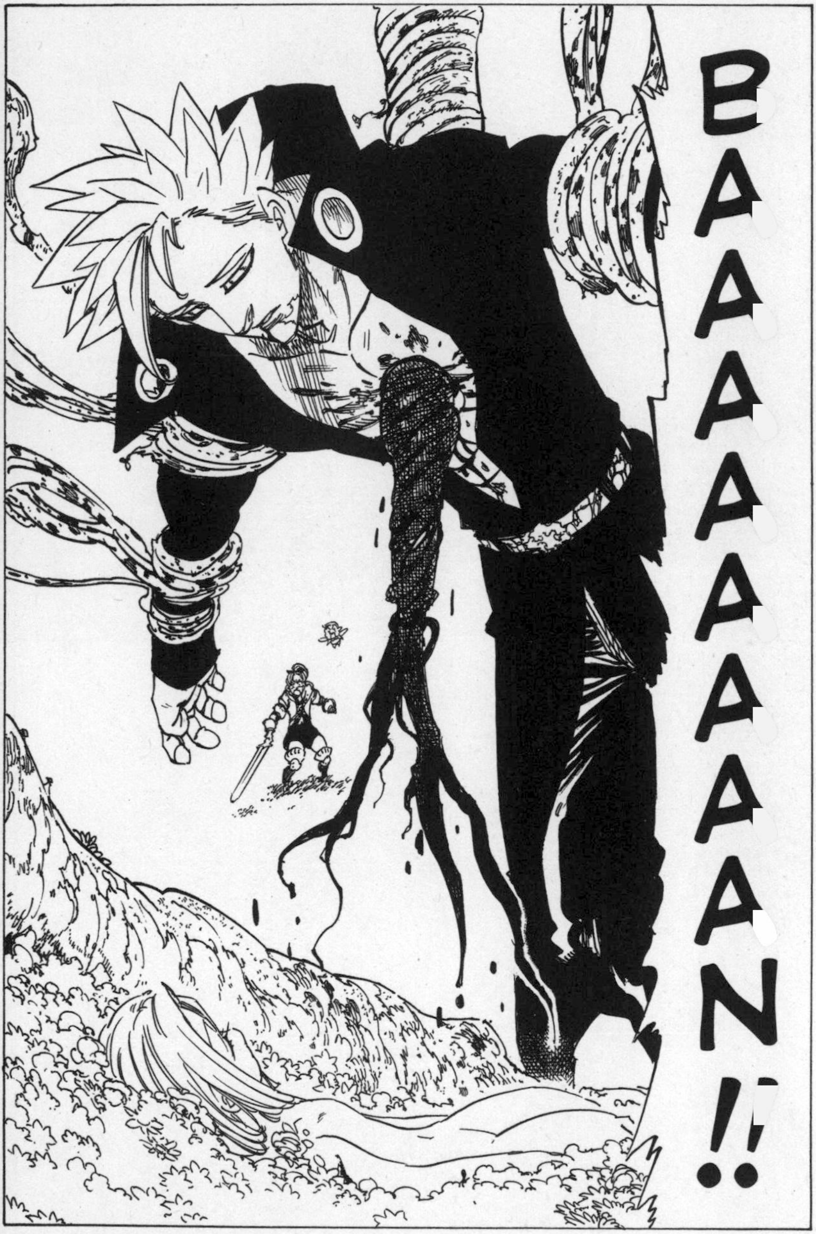
BAAAAAAAN!!

Chapter 118 - Clash!! The Fairy King's Forest

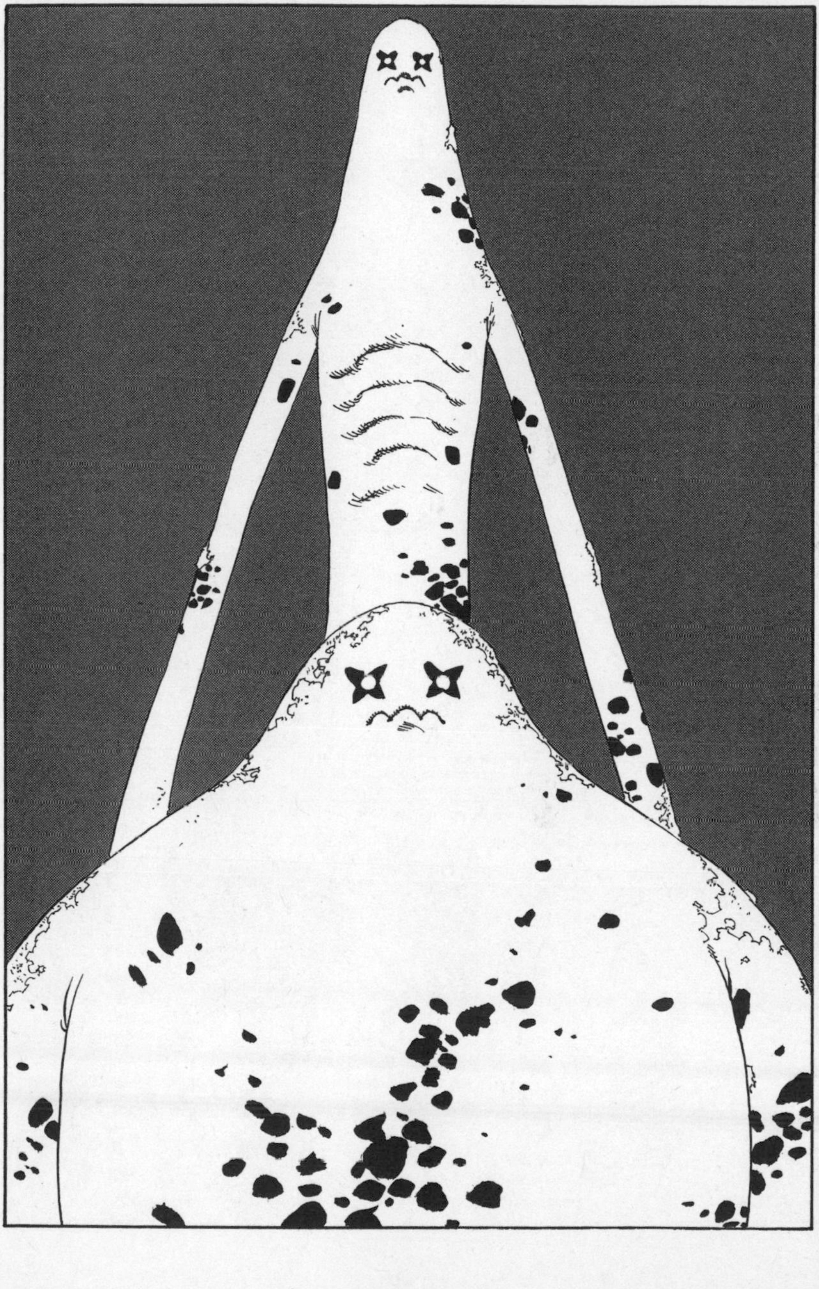

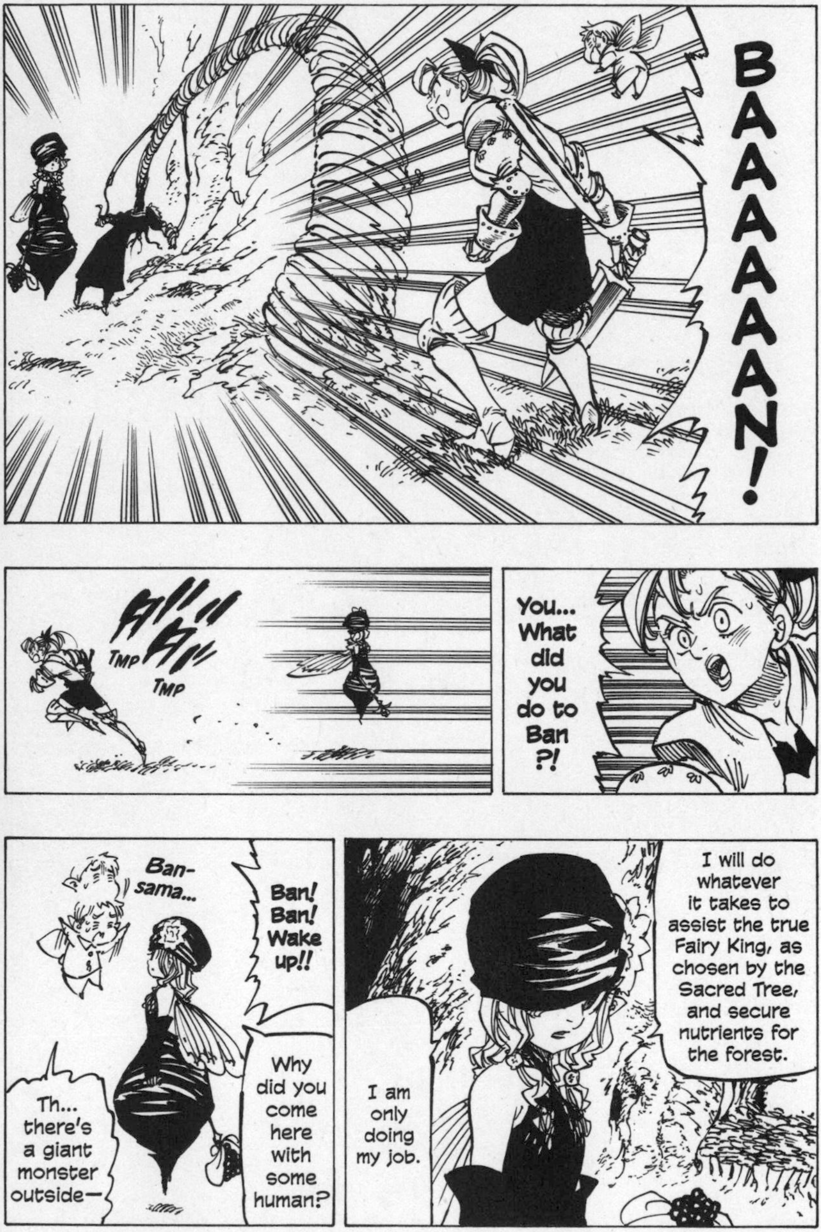
BAAAAAAN!
You... What did you do to Ban ?!
TMP
TMP
I will do whatever it takes to assist the true Fairy King, as chosen by the Sacred Tree, and secure nutrients for the forest.
I am only doing my job.
Ban! Ban! Wake up!!
Ban-sama...
Why did you come here with some human?
Th... there's a giant monster outside—

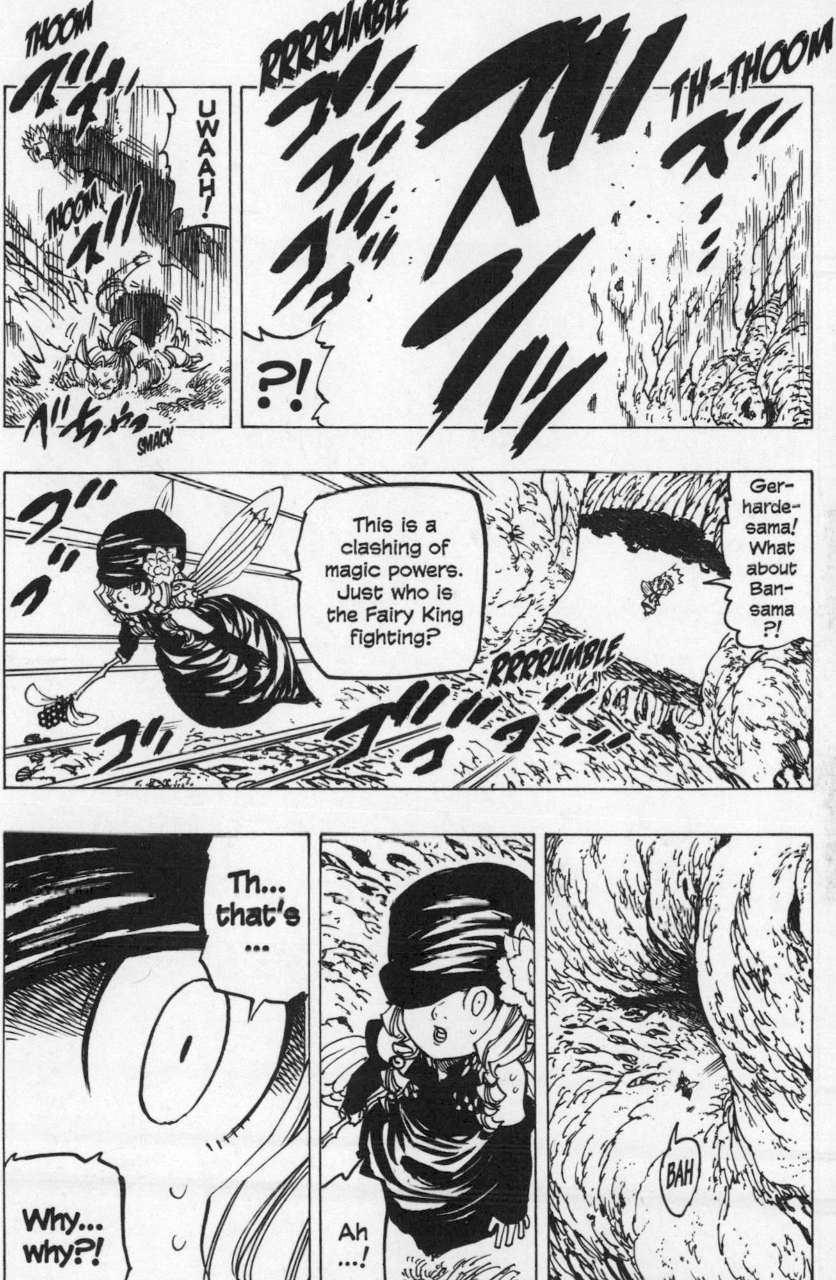
RRRRUMBLE
TH-THOOM
?!
THOOM
UWAAH!
THOOM
SMACK
Ger-harde-sama! What about Ban-sama?!
RRRRUMBLE
This is a clashing of magic powers. Just who is the Fairy King fighting?
BAH
Ah...!
Th... that's...
Why... why?!

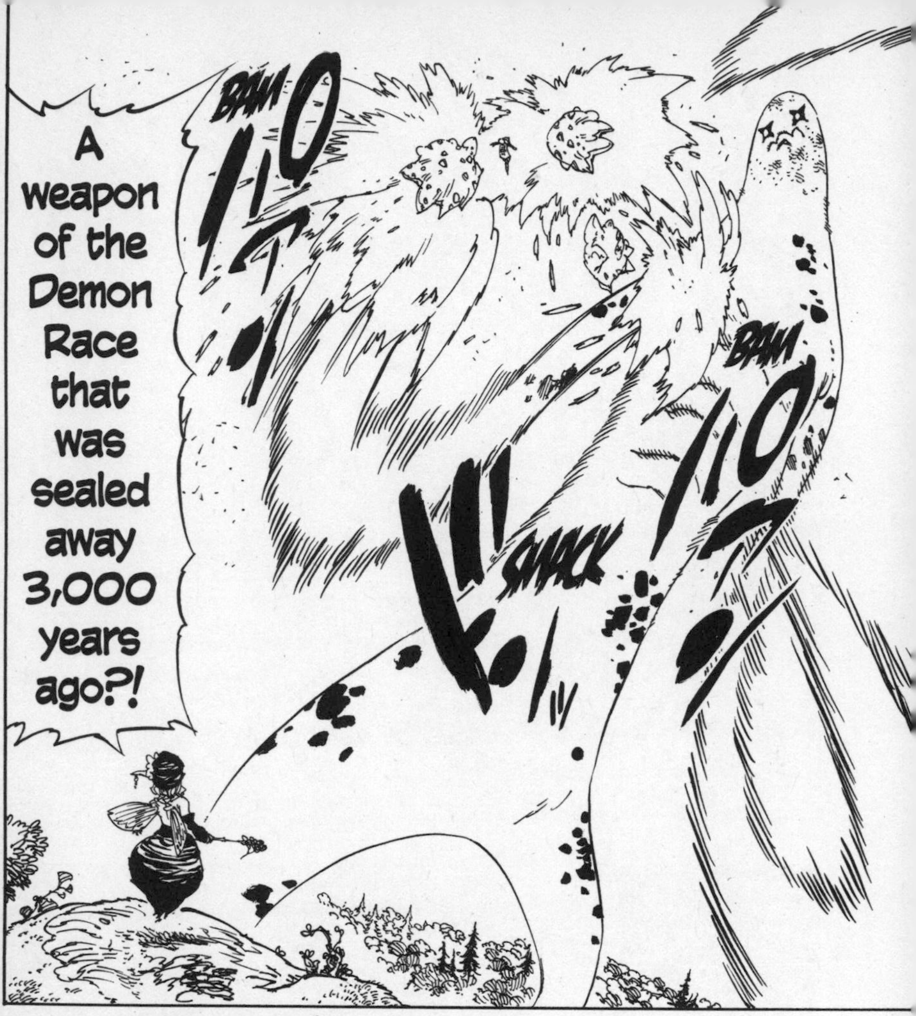
BAM
A weapon of the Demon Race that was sealed away 3,000 years ago?!
BAM
SMACK

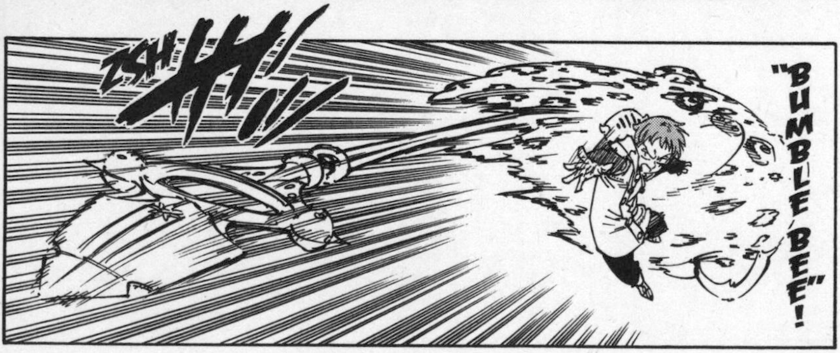
"BUMBLE BEE"!
ZSH

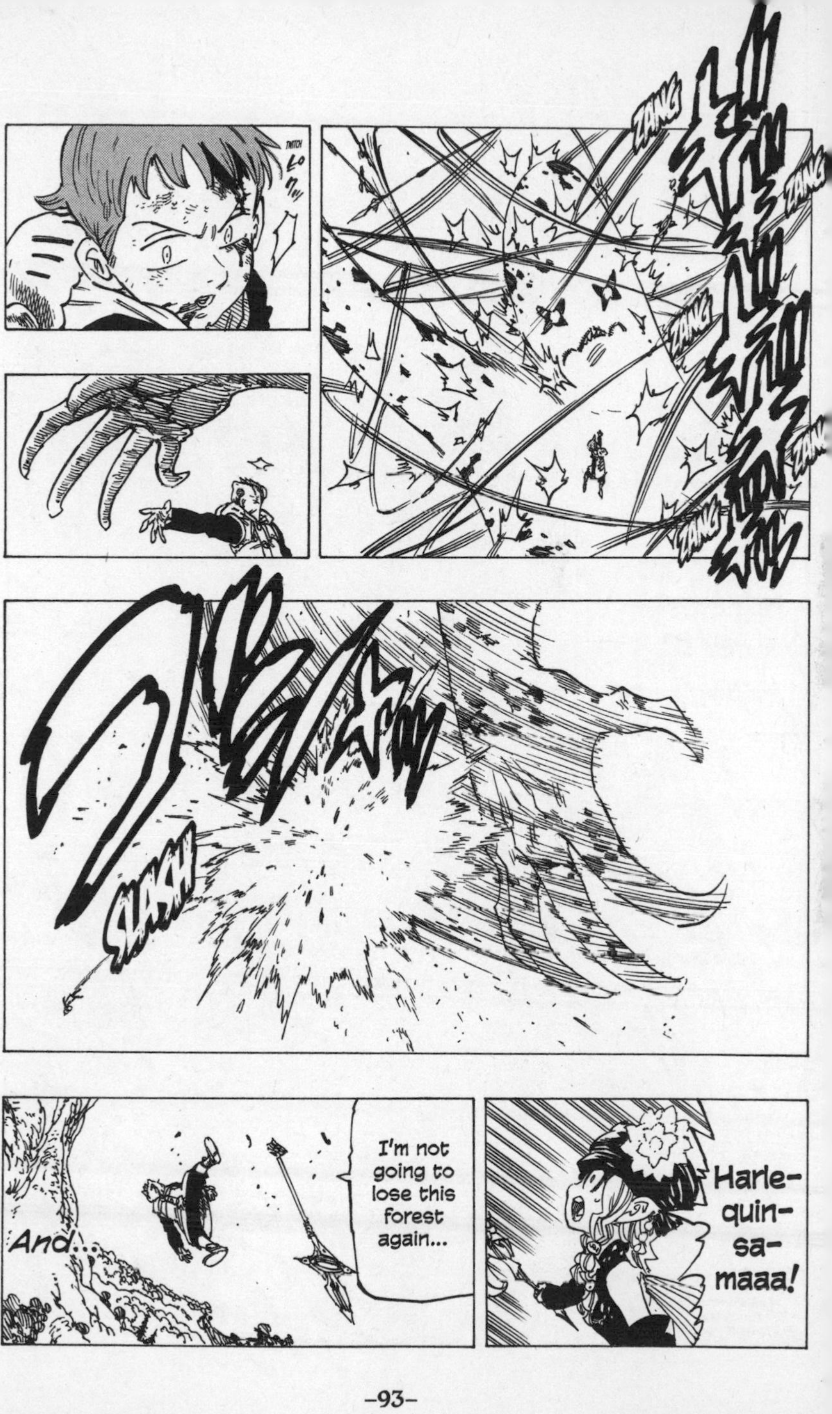
ZANG
ZANG
ZANG
ZANG
ZANG
TWITCH
SLASH
Harle-
quin-
sa-
maaa!
I'm not
going to
lose this
forest
again...
And...

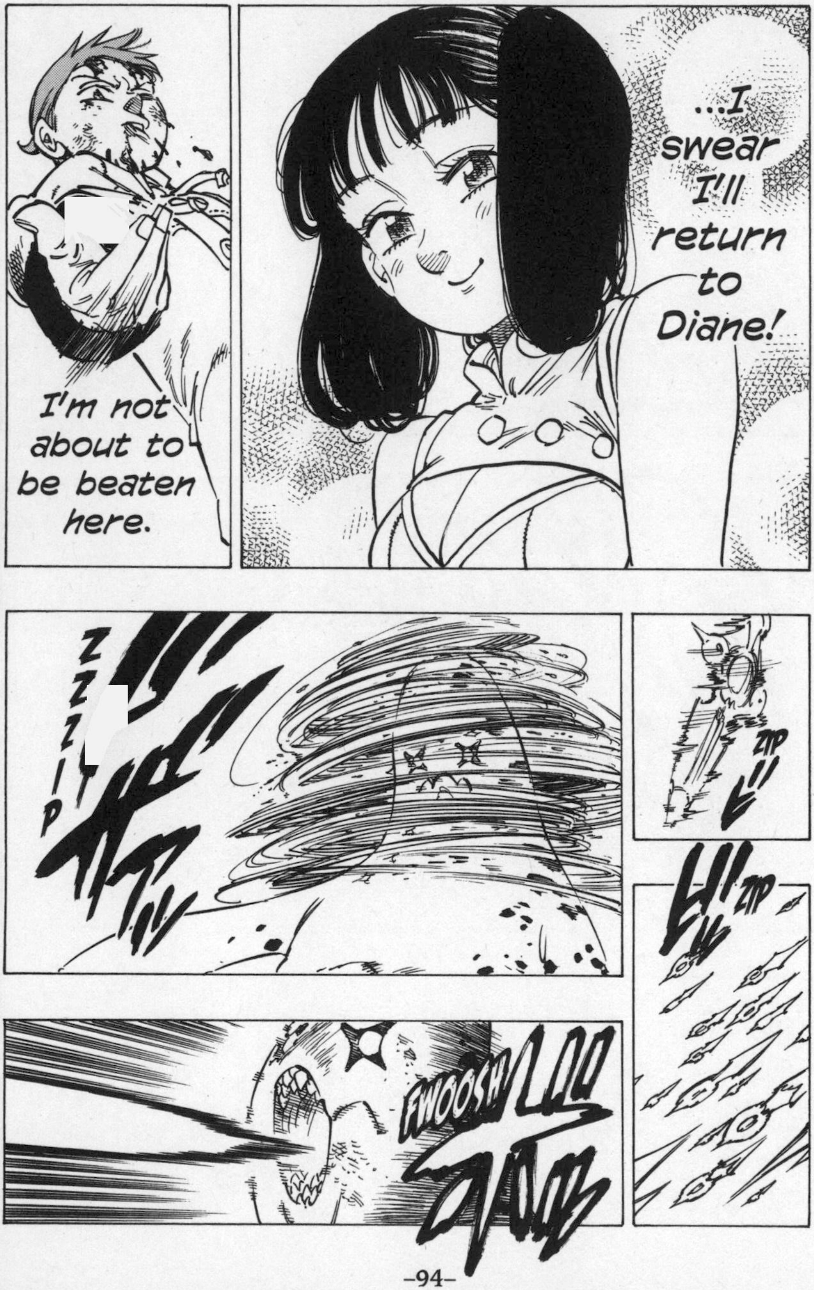
...I swear I'll return to Diane!
I'm not about to be beaten here.
ZIP
ZZZIP
ZIP
FWOOSH

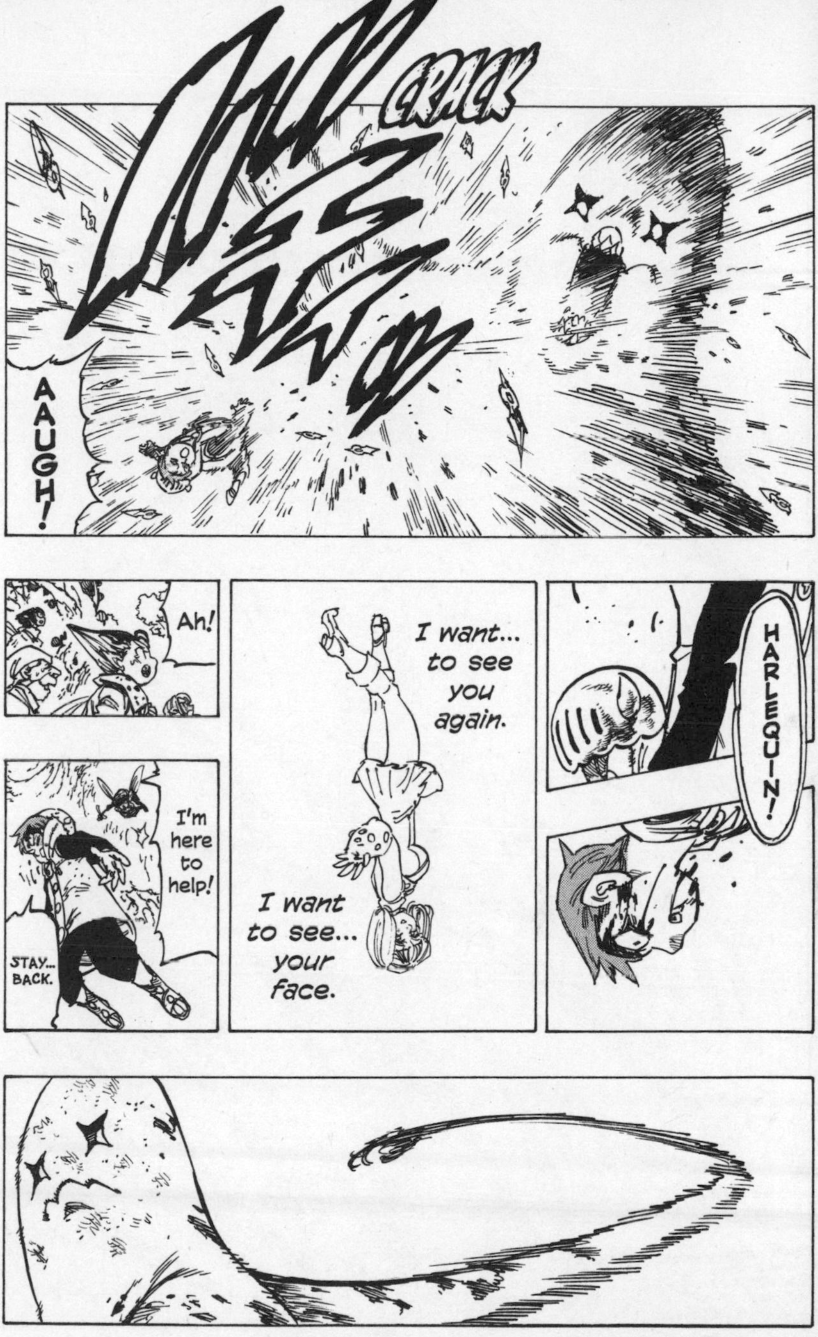
CRACK
AAUGH!
HARLEQUIN!
I want... to see you again.
I want to see... your face.
Ah!
I'm here to help!
STAY... BACK.

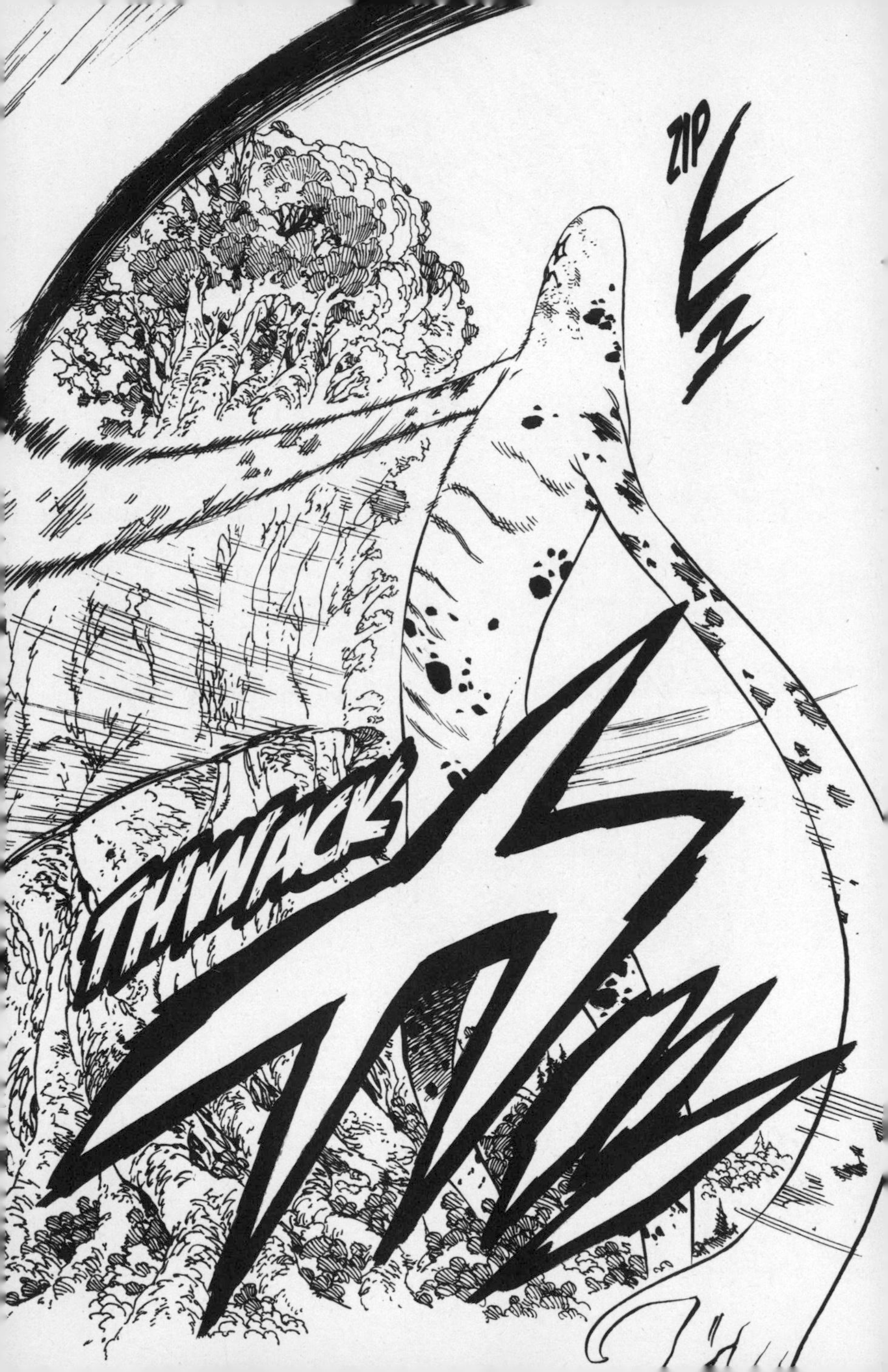
ZIP
THWACK

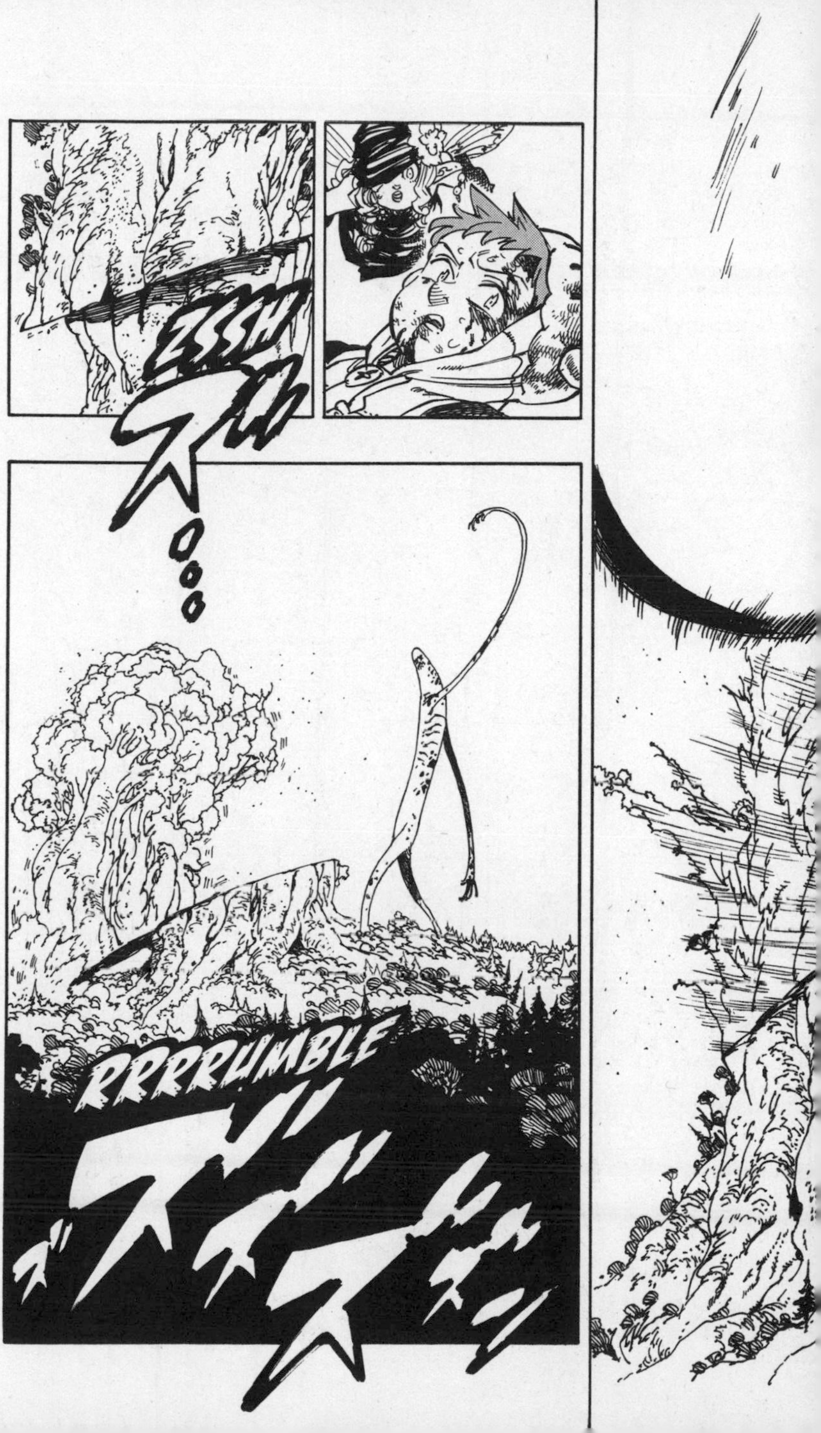
ZSSH
RRRRUMBLE

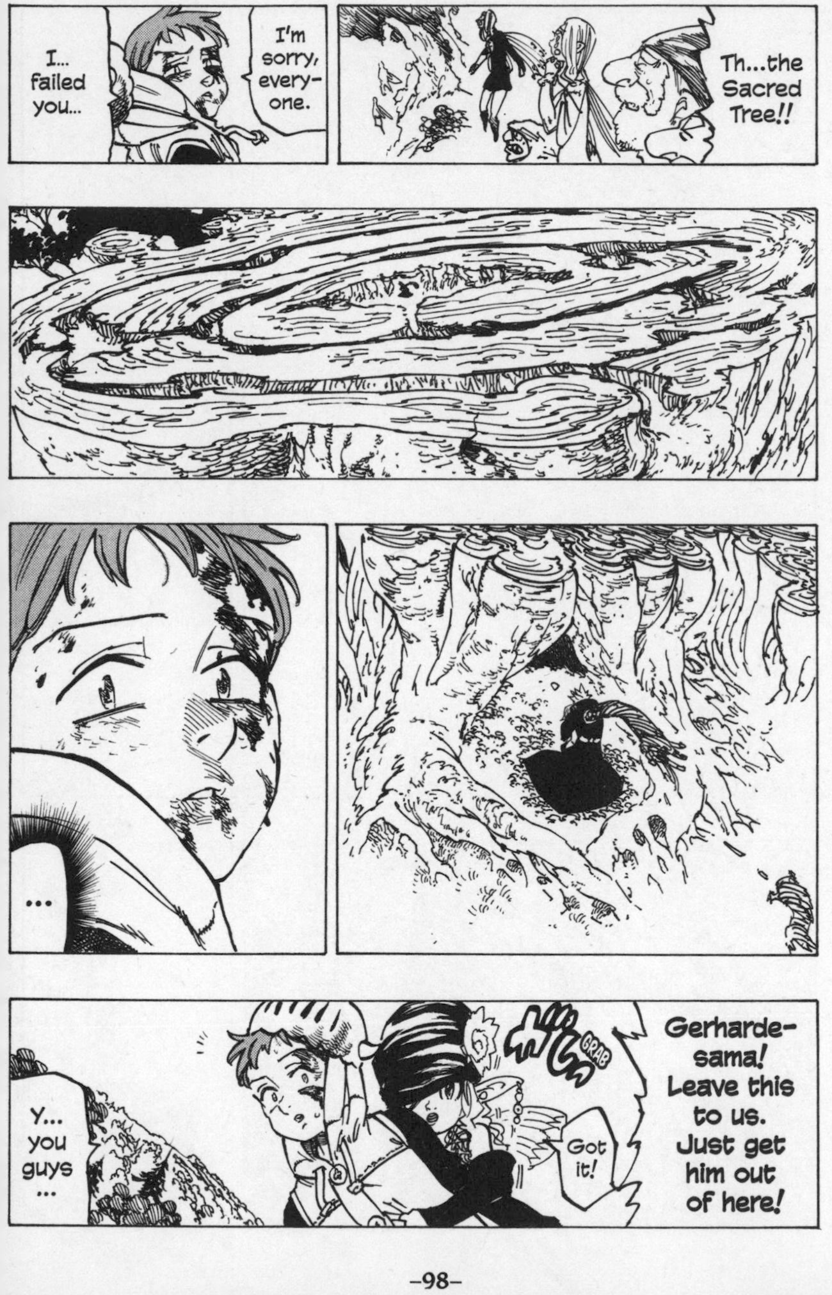
Th...the Sacred Tree!!
I'm sorry, every-one.
I... failed you...
...
Gerharde-sama! Leave this to us. Just get him out of here!
GRAB
Got it!
Y... you guys ...

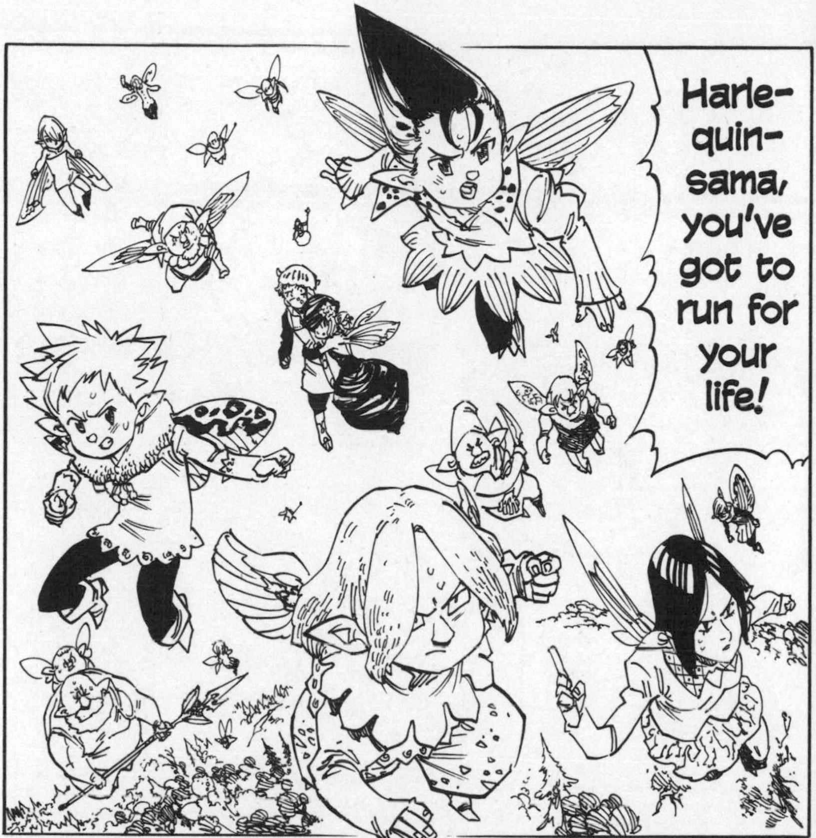
Harlequin-sama, you've got to run for your life!

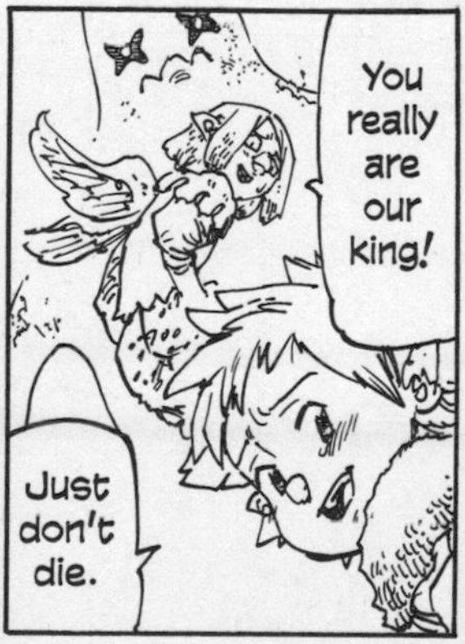
You really are our king!
Just don't die.

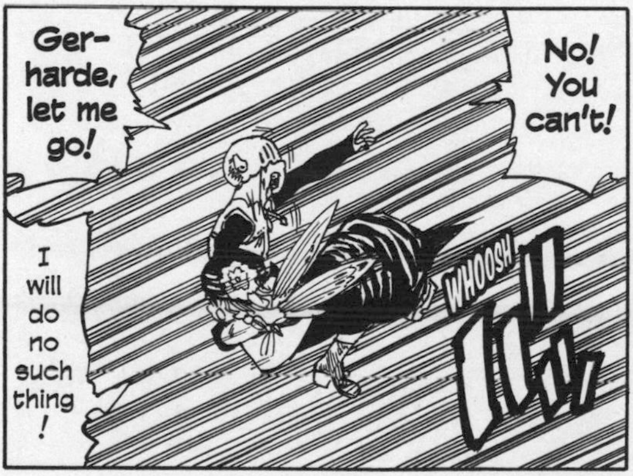
No! You can't!
Gerharde, let me go!
WHOOSH
I will do no such thing!

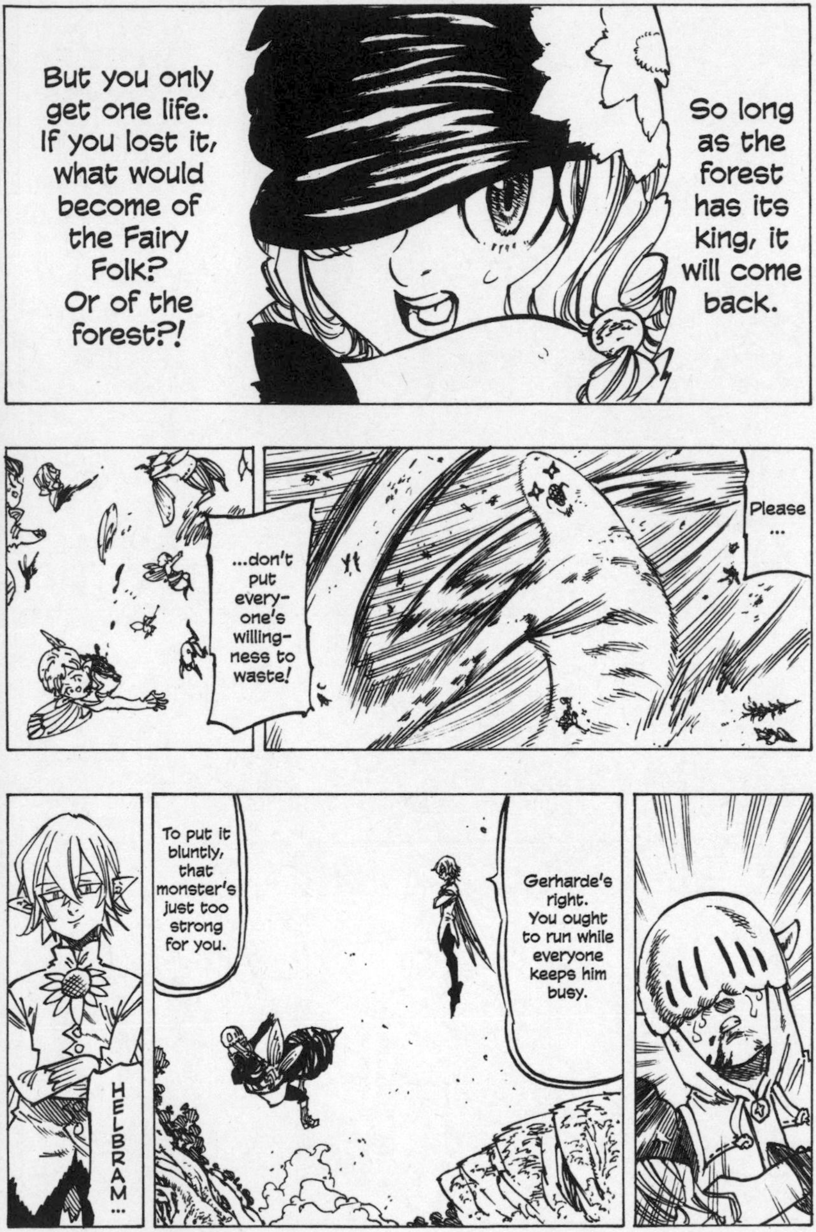
So long as the forest has its king, it will come back.
But you only get one life. If you lost it, what would become of the Fairy Folk? Or of the forest?!
Please...
...don't put everyone's willingness to waste!
Gerharde's right. You ought to run while everyone keeps him busy.
To put it bluntly, that monster's just too strong for you.
HELBRAM...

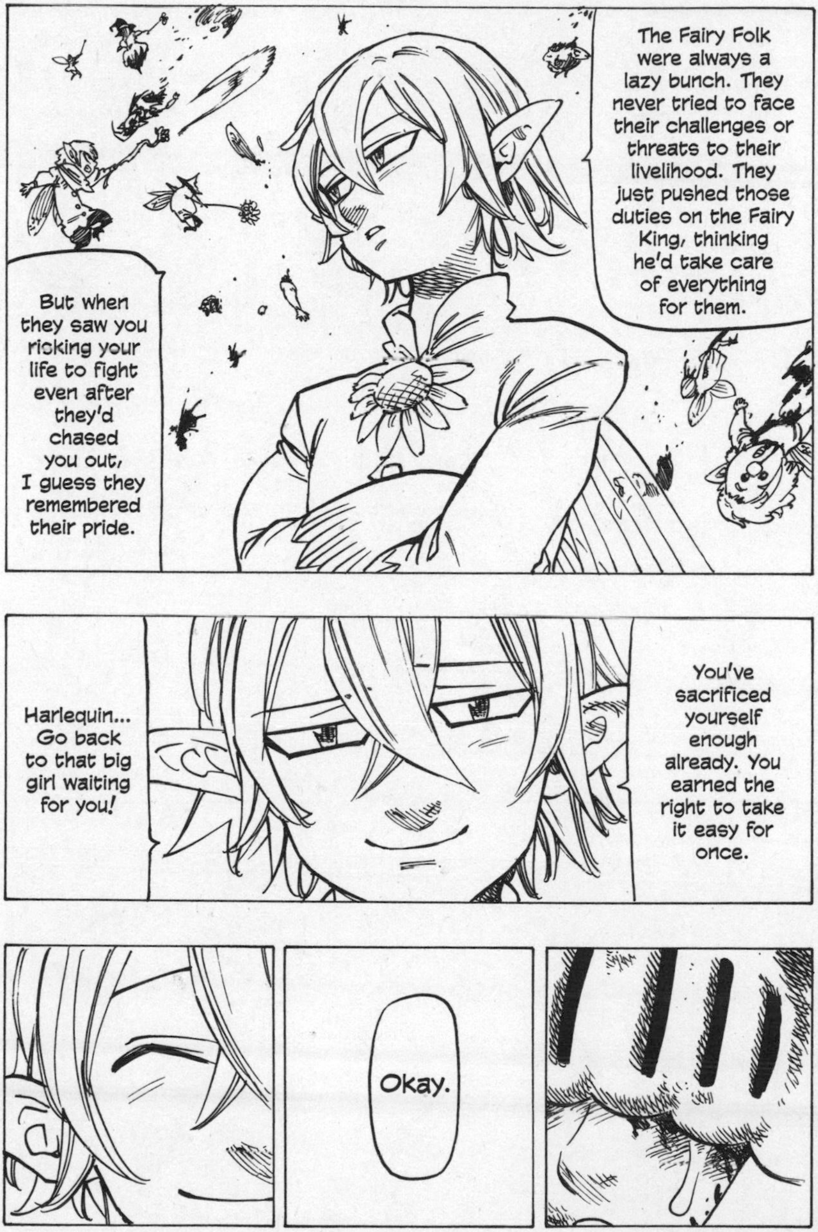
The Fairy Folk were always a lazy bunch. They never tried to face their challenges or threats to their livelihood. They just pushed those duties on the Fairy King, thinking he'd take care of everything for them.
But when they saw you risking your life to fight even after they'd chased you out, I guess they remembered their pride.
You've sacrificed yourself enough already. You earned the right to take it easy for once.
Harlequin... Go back to that big girl waiting for you!
Okay.

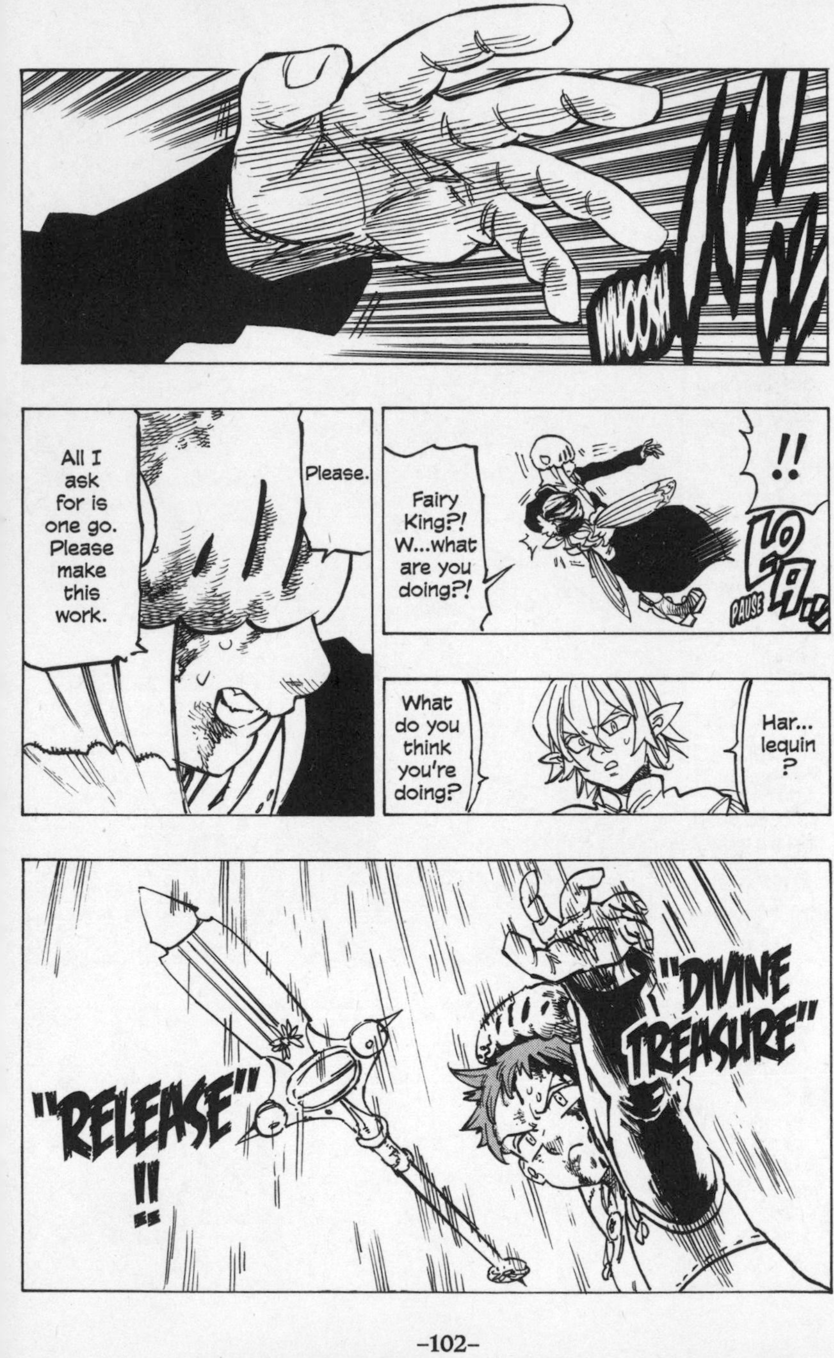
WHOOSH
!!
PAUSE
Fairy King?! W...what are you doing?!
Har... lequin?
What do you think you're doing?
Please.
All I ask for is one go. Please make this work.
"DIVINE TREASURE"
"RELEASE" !!

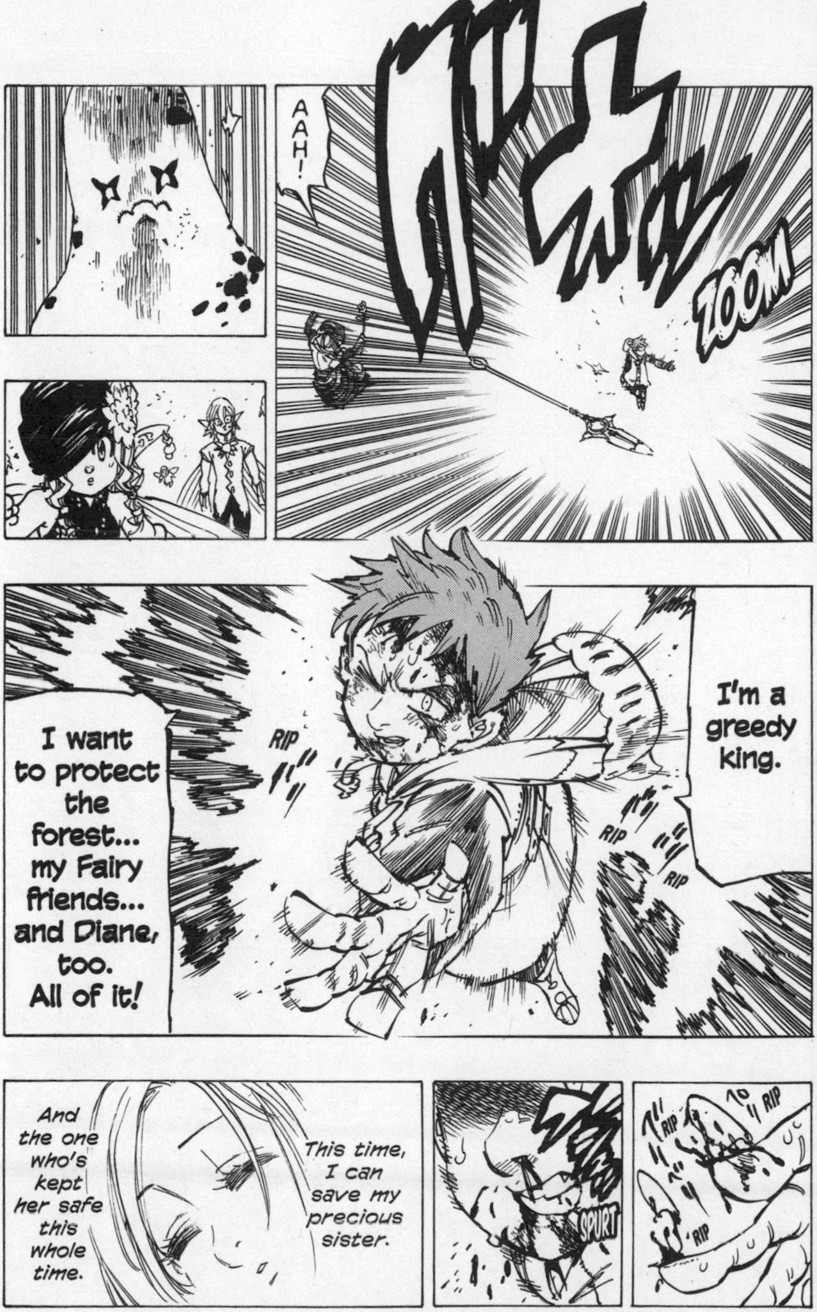
AAH!
ZOOM
I'm a greedy king.
RIP
RIP
RIP
I want to protect the forest... my Fairy friends... and Diane, too. All of it!
RIP
RIP
RIP
SPURT
This time, I can save my precious sister.
And the one who's kept her safe this whole time.

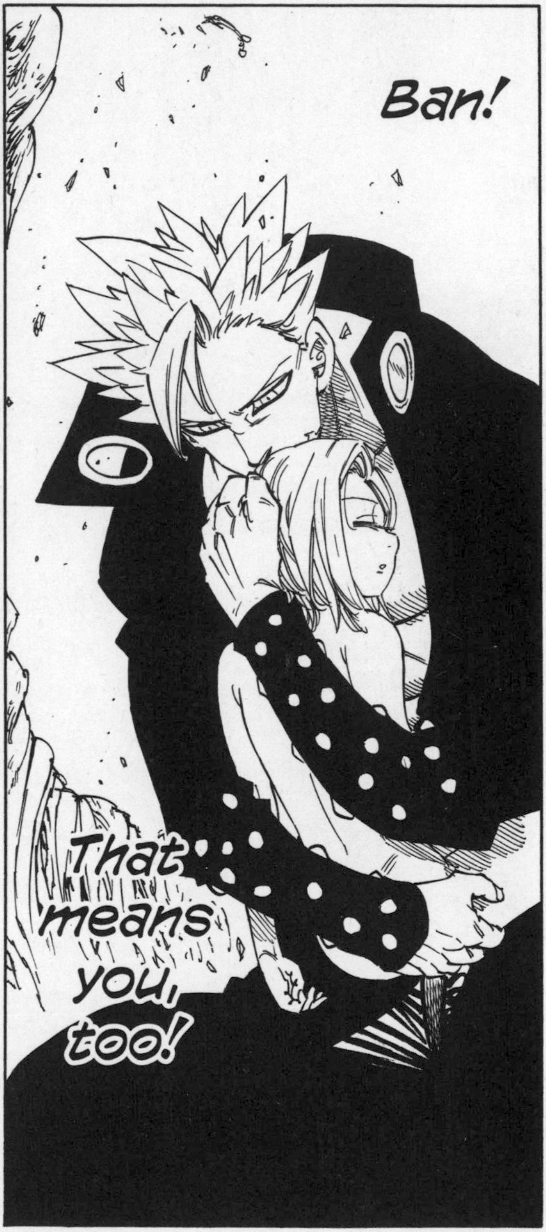
Ban!
That means you, too!

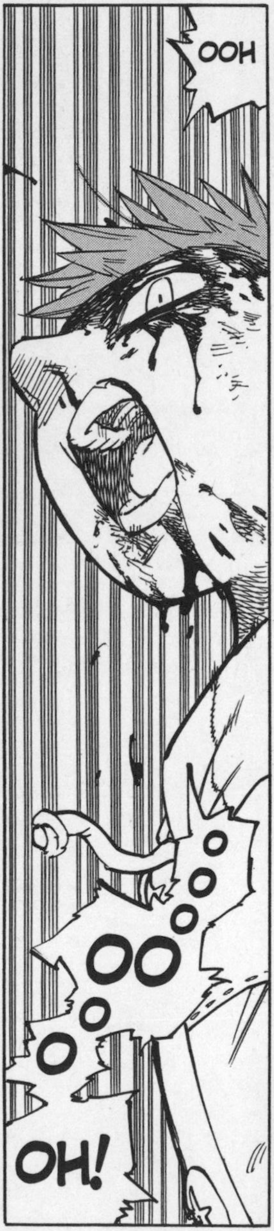
OOH
OOOOOOOO
OH!

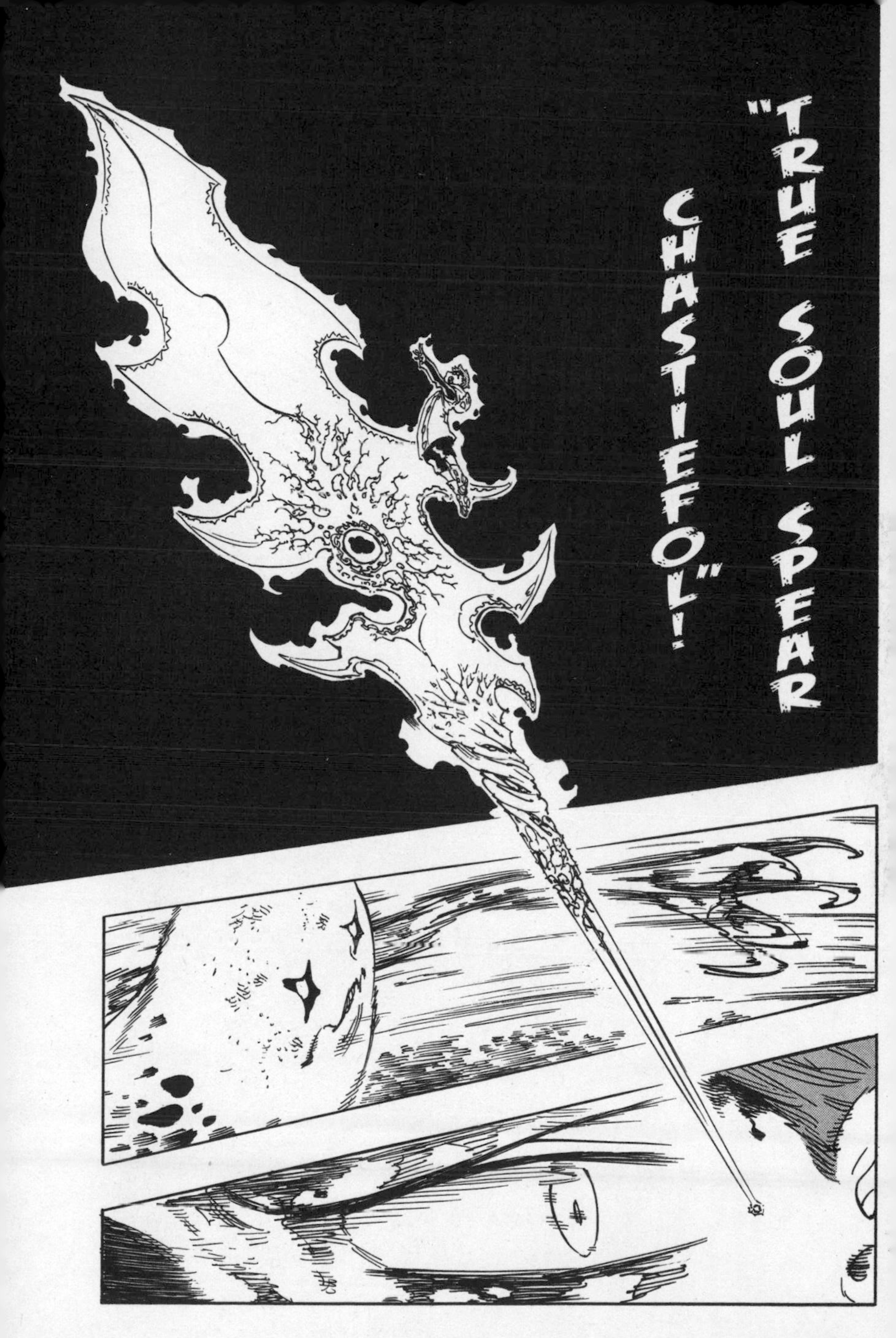
"TRUE SOUL SPEAR CHASTIEFOL!"

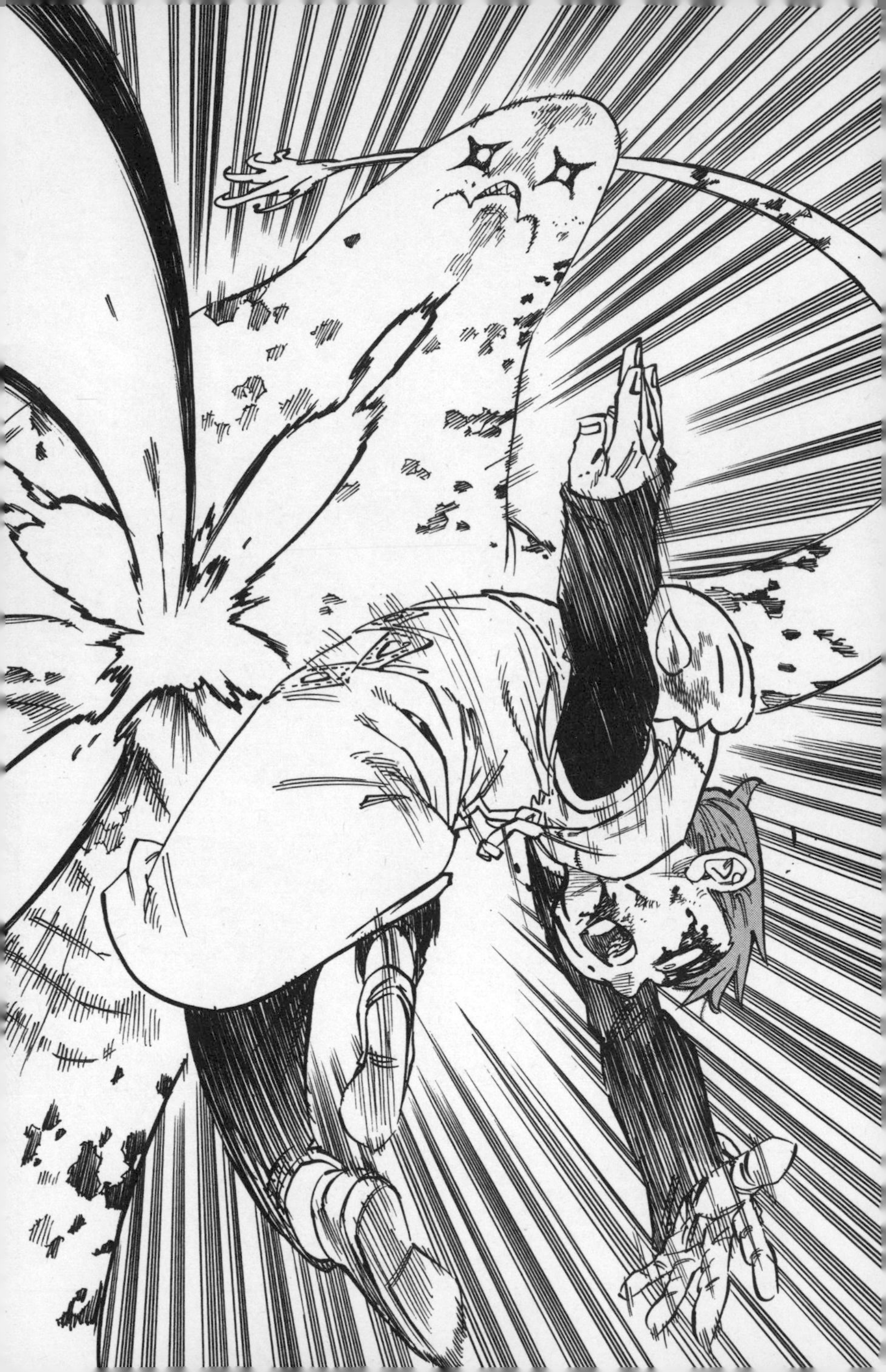

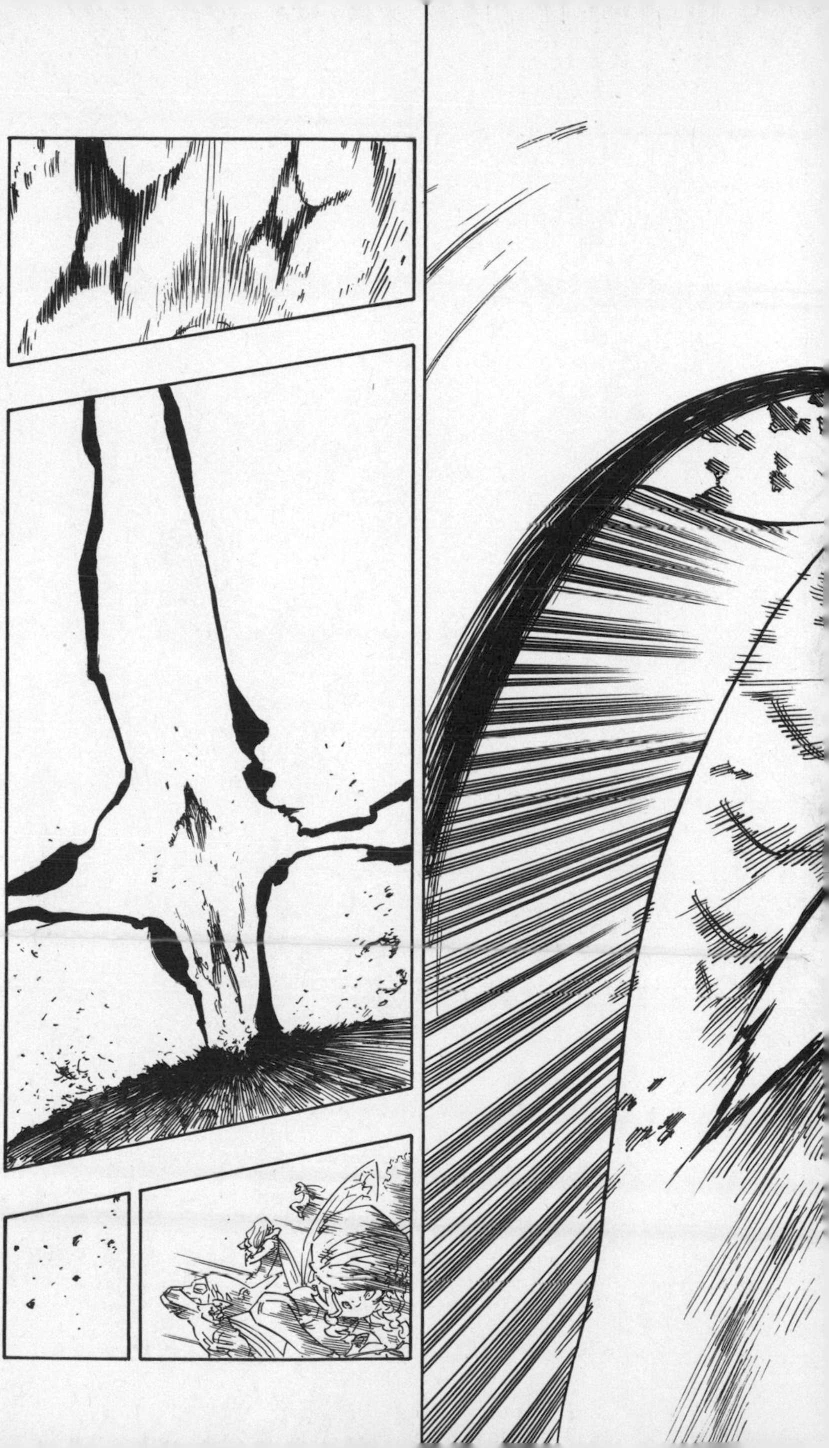

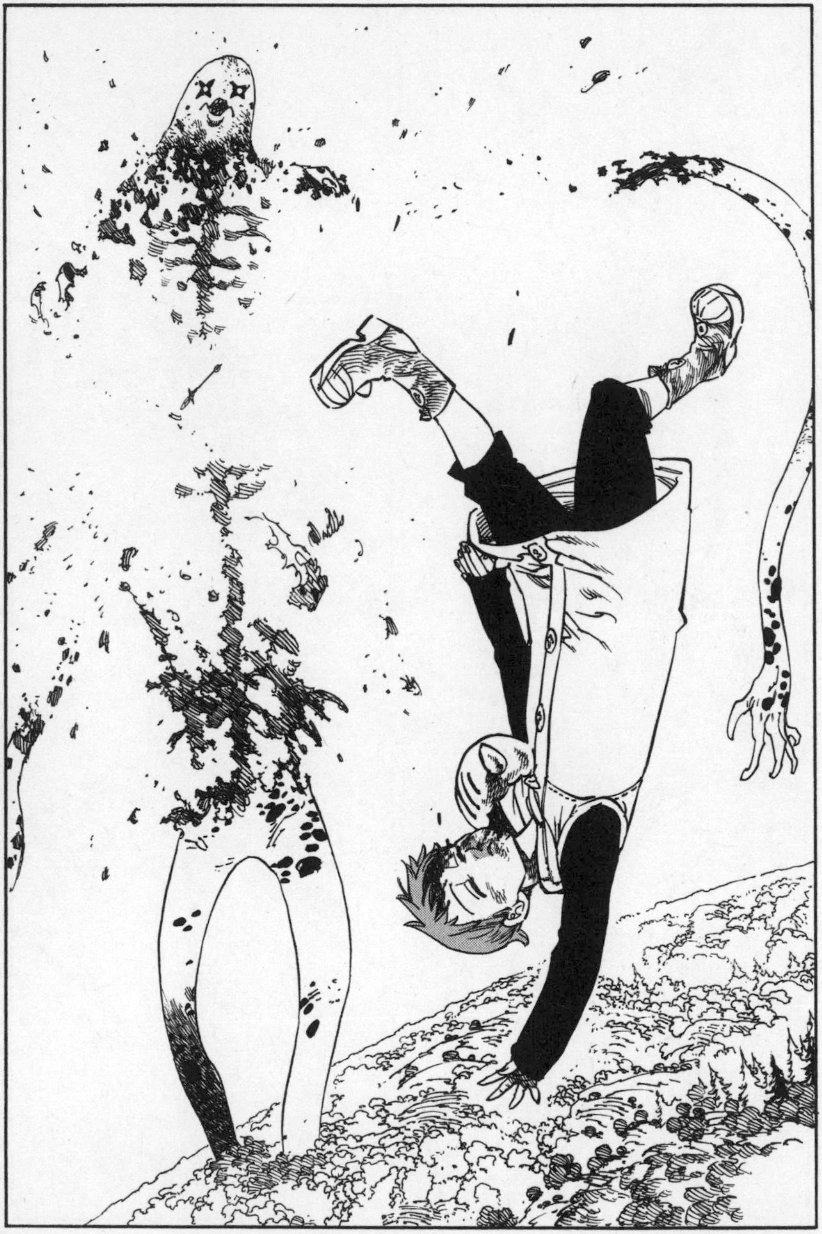

Chapter 119 - The Ten Commandments on the Move

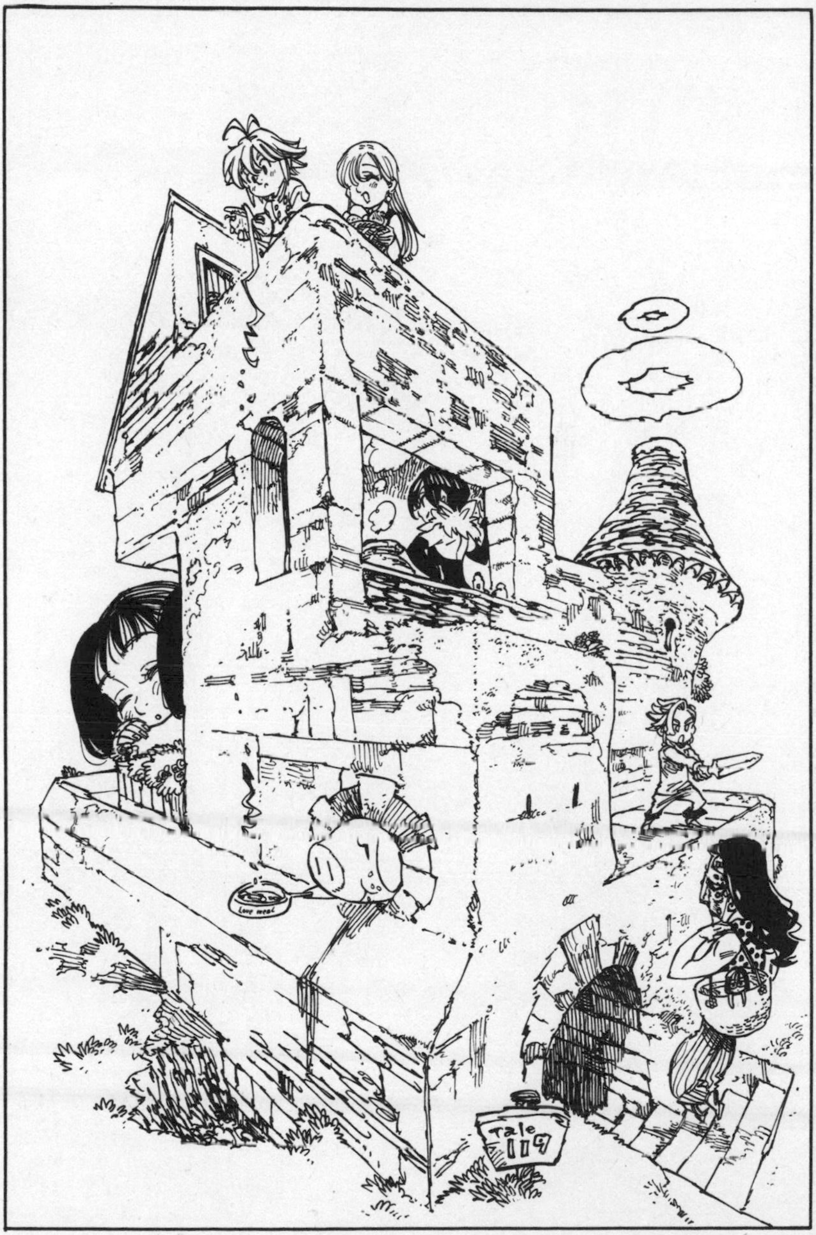
Love meal
Tale 119

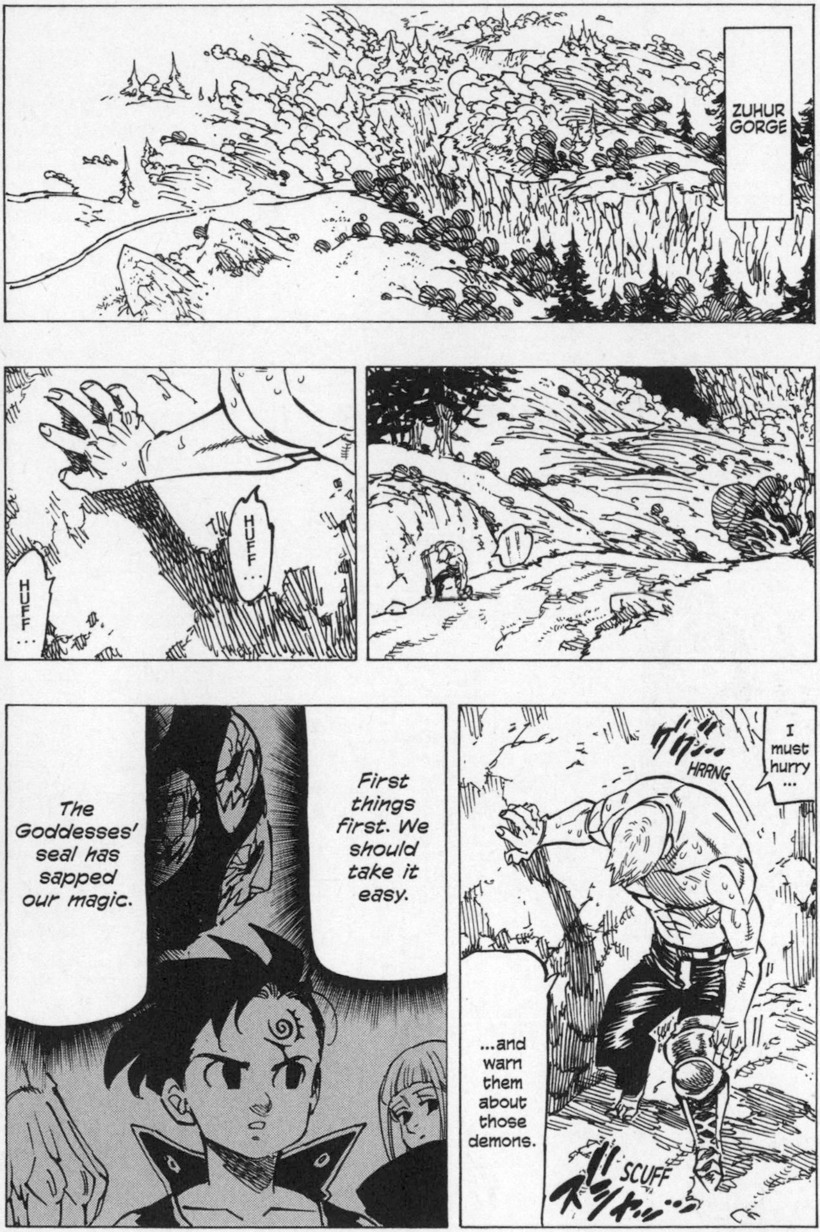
ZUHUR GORGE
HUFF...
HUFF...
I must hurry...
HRRNG
...and warn them about those demons.
SCUFF
First things first. We should take it easy.
The Goddesses' seal has sapped our magic.

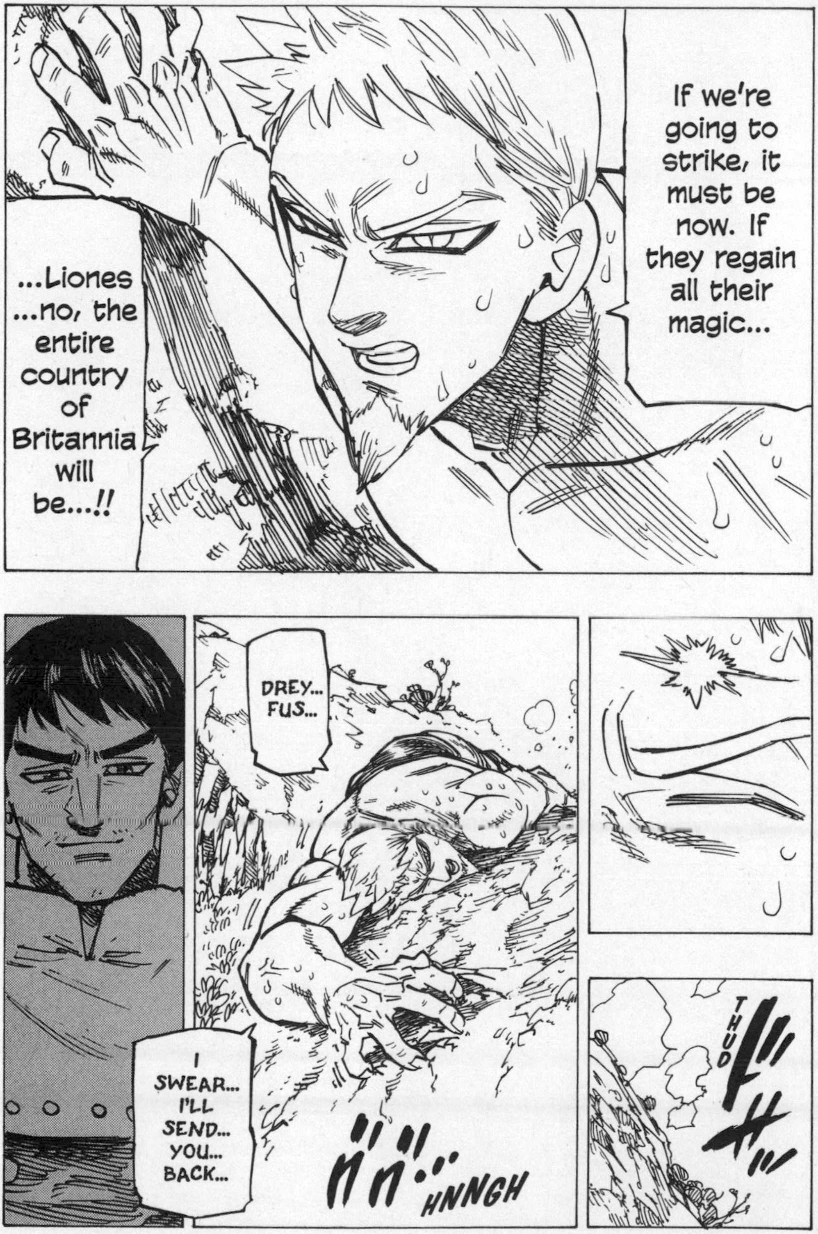
If we're going to strike, it must be now. If they regain all their magic...
...Liones ...no, the entire country of Britannia will be...!!
THUD
DREY... FUS...
I SWEAR... I'LL SEND... YOU... BACK...
HNNGH

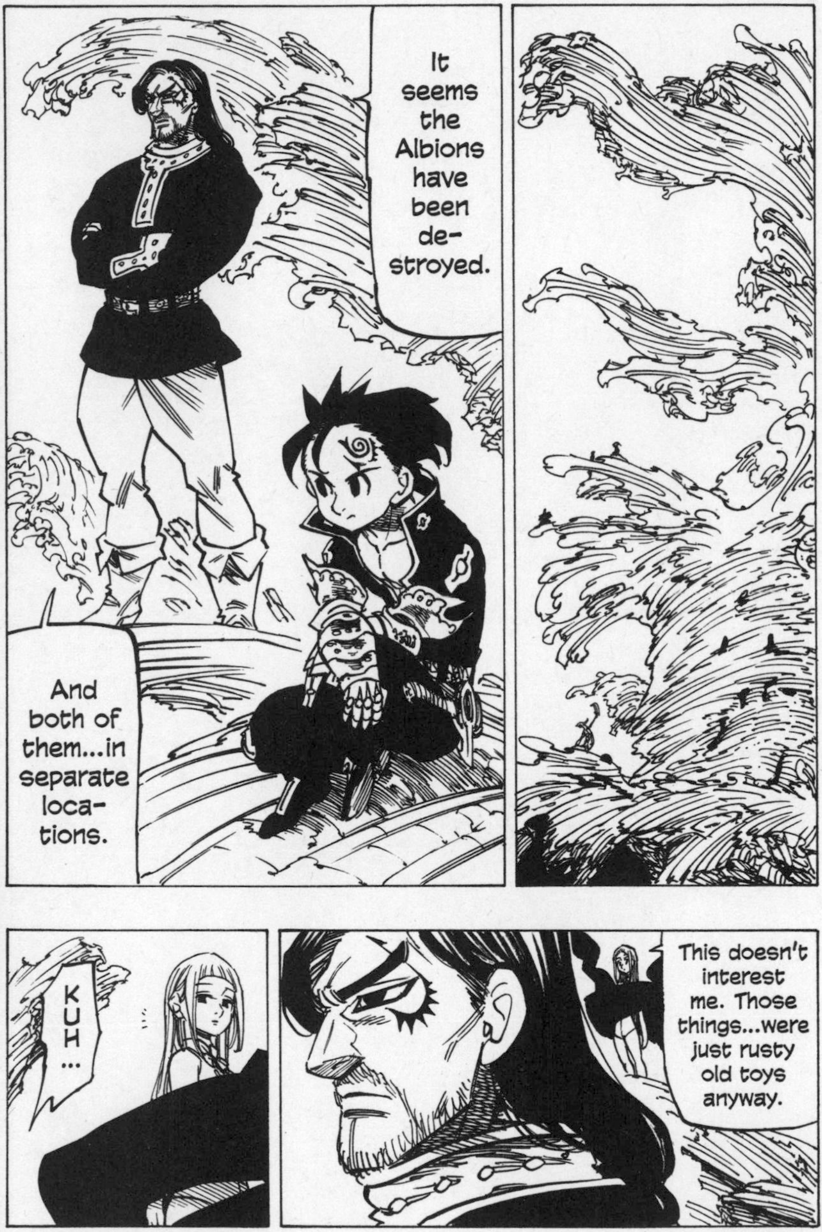
It seems the Albions have been de-stroyed.
And both of them...in separate loca-tions.
This doesn't interest me. Those things...were just rusty old toys anyway.
KUH...

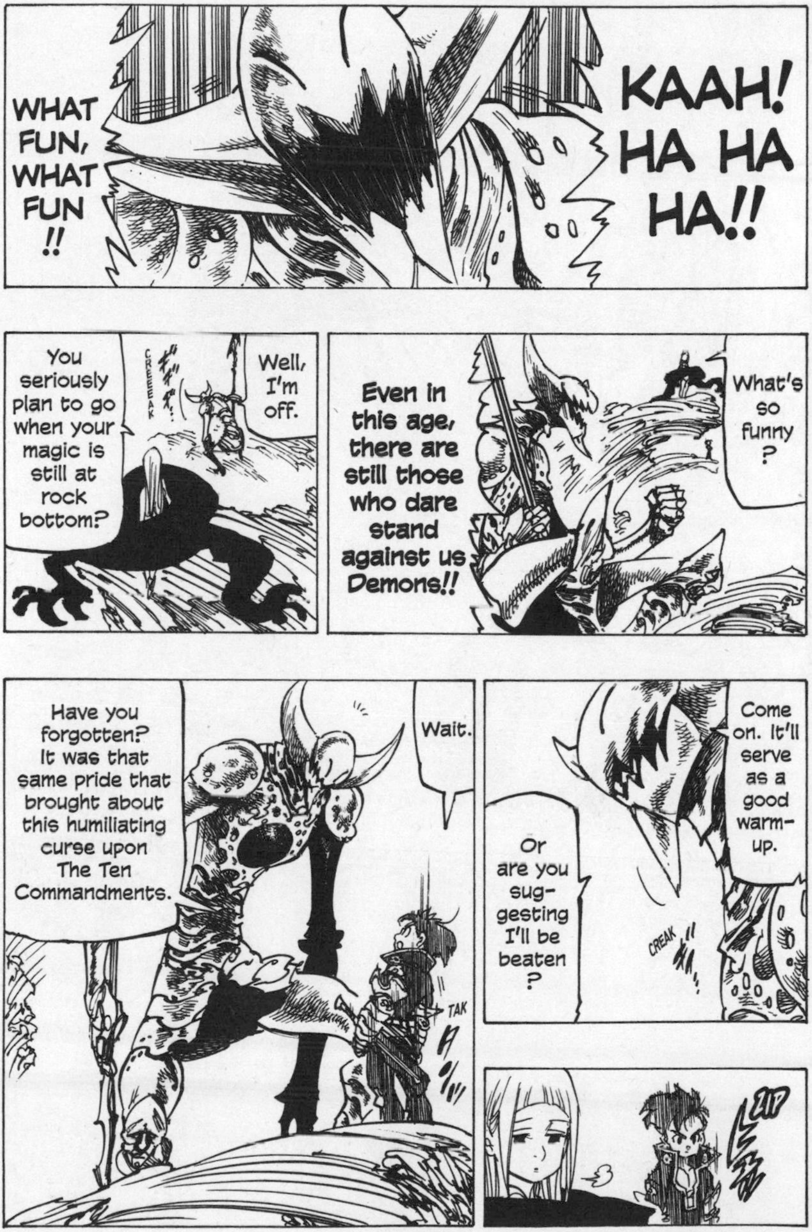
KAAH! HA HA HA!!
WHAT FUN, WHAT FUN!!
What's so funny?
Even in this age, there are still those who dare stand against us Demons!!
Well, I'm off.
CREEEAK
You seriously plan to go when your magic is still at rock bottom?
Come on. It'll serve as a good warm-up.
Or are you sug-gesting I'll be beaten?
CREAK
ZIP
Wait.
Have you forgotten? It was that same pride that brought about this humiliating curse upon The Ten Commandments.
TAK

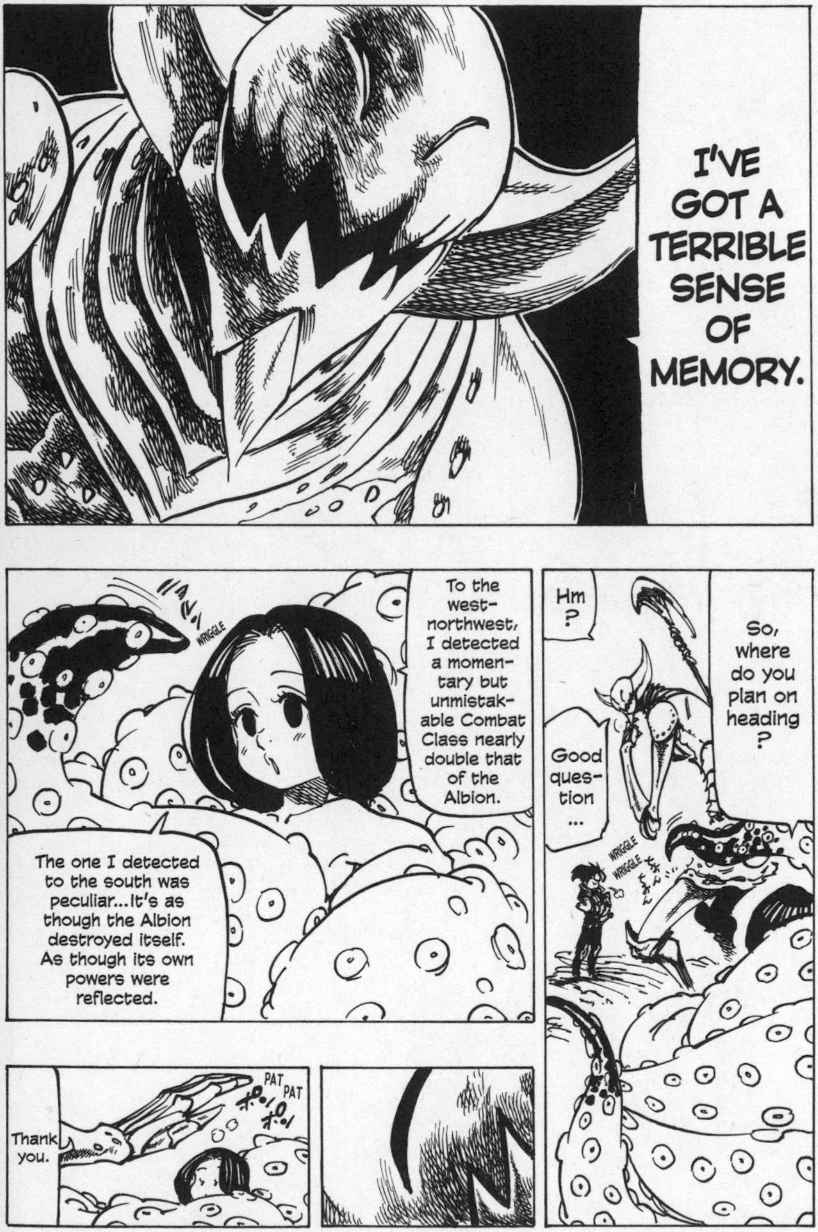

I'VE GOT A TERRIBLE SENSE OF MEMORY.
So, where do you plan on heading?
Hm?
Good question...
WRIGGLE
WRIGGLE
To the west-northwest, I detected a momentary but unmistakable Combat Class nearly double that of the Albion.
WRIGGLE
The one I detected to the south was peculiar...It's as though the Albion destroyed itself. As though its own powers were reflected.
PAT
PAT
Thank you.

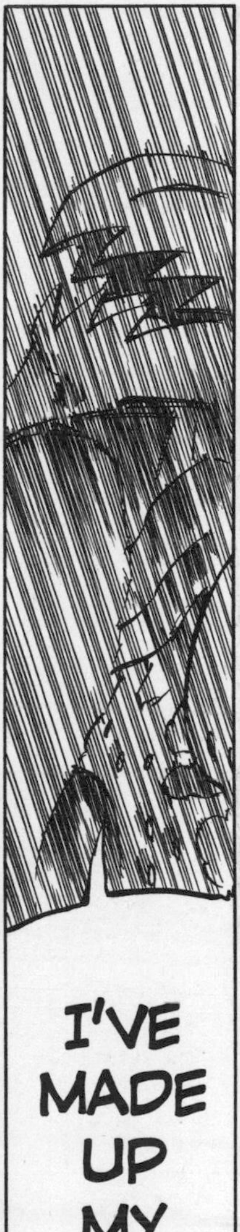
I'VE MADE UP MY MIND.
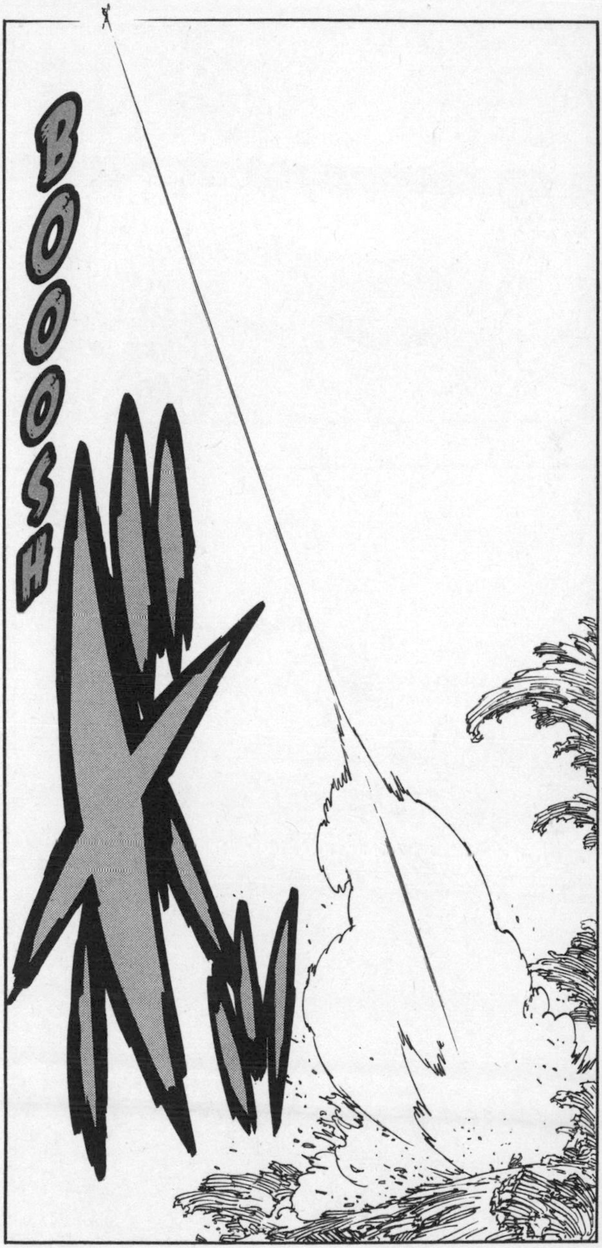
BOOOSH

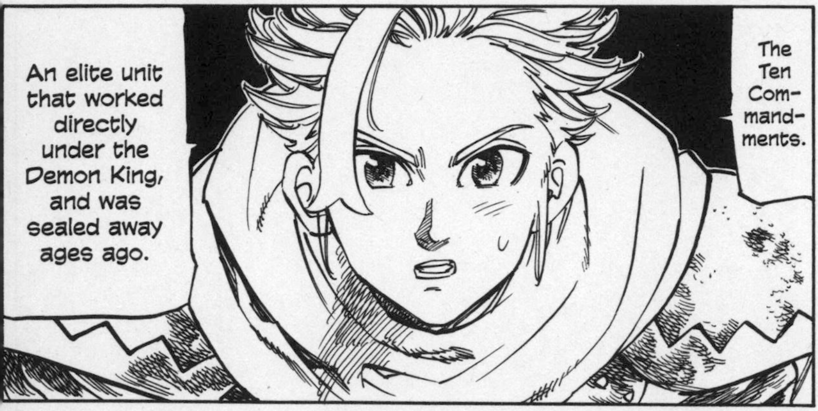
The Ten Commandments.
An elite unit that worked directly under the Demon King, and was sealed away ages ago.

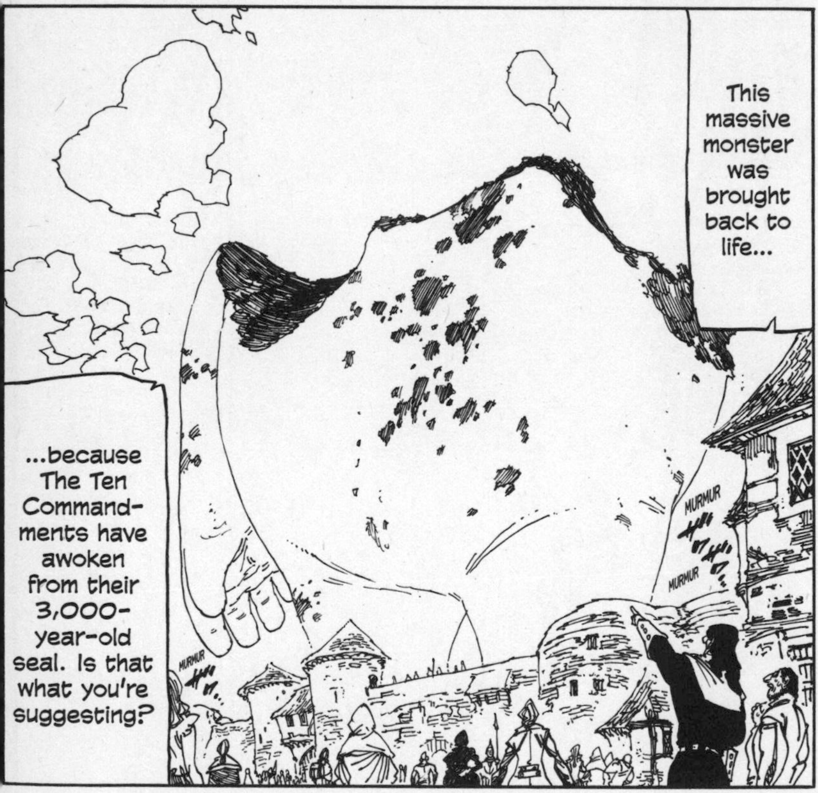
This massive monster was brought back to life...
MURMUR
MURMUR
MURMUR
...because The Ten Commandments have awoken from their 3,000-year-old seal. Is that what you're suggesting?

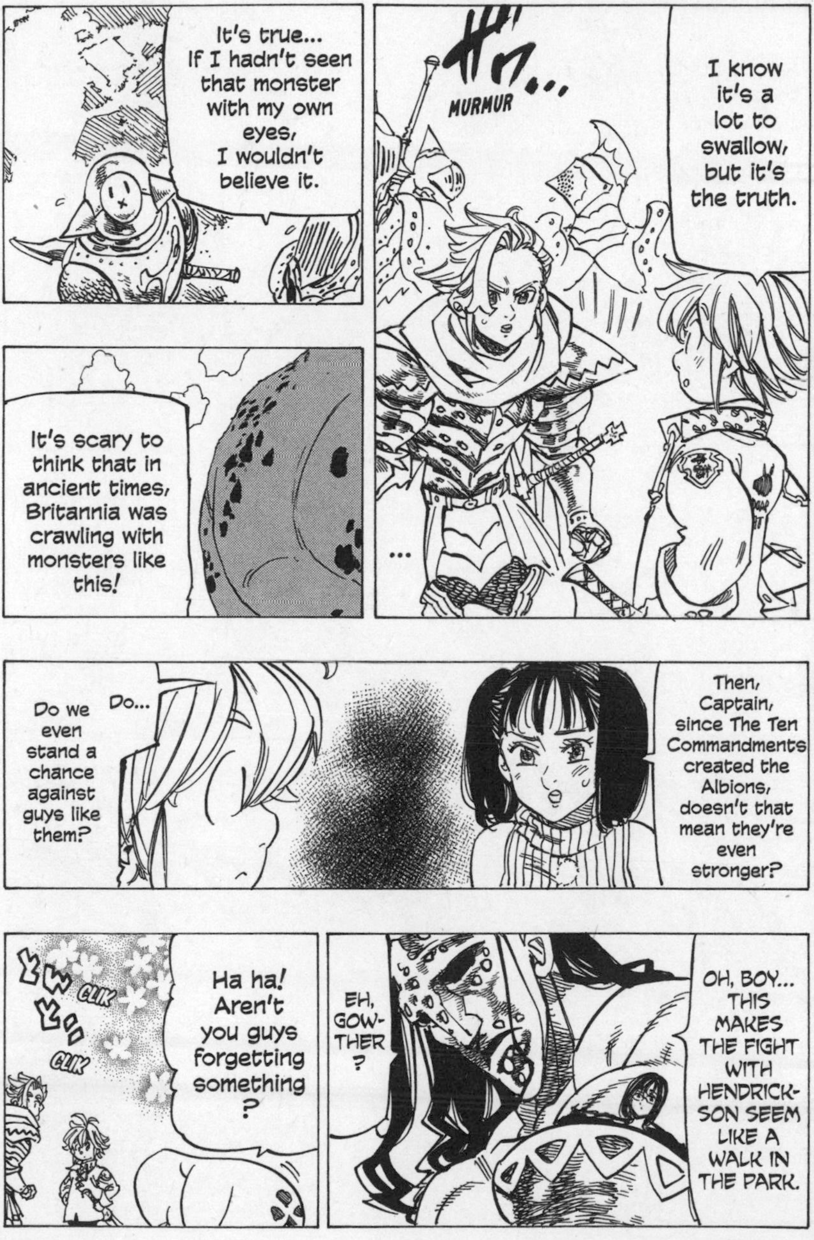
I know it's a lot to swallow, but it's the truth.
MURMUR
...
It's true... If I hadn't seen that monster with my own eyes, I wouldn't believe it.
It's scary to think that in ancient times, Britannia was crawling with monsters like this!
Then, Captain, since The Ten Commandments created the Albions, doesn't that mean they're even stronger?
Do...
Do we even stand a chance against guys like them?
OH, BOY... THIS MAKES THE FIGHT WITH HENDRICKSON SEEM LIKE A WALK IN THE PARK.
EH, GOWTHER?
Ha ha! Aren't you guys forgetting something?
CLIK
CLIK

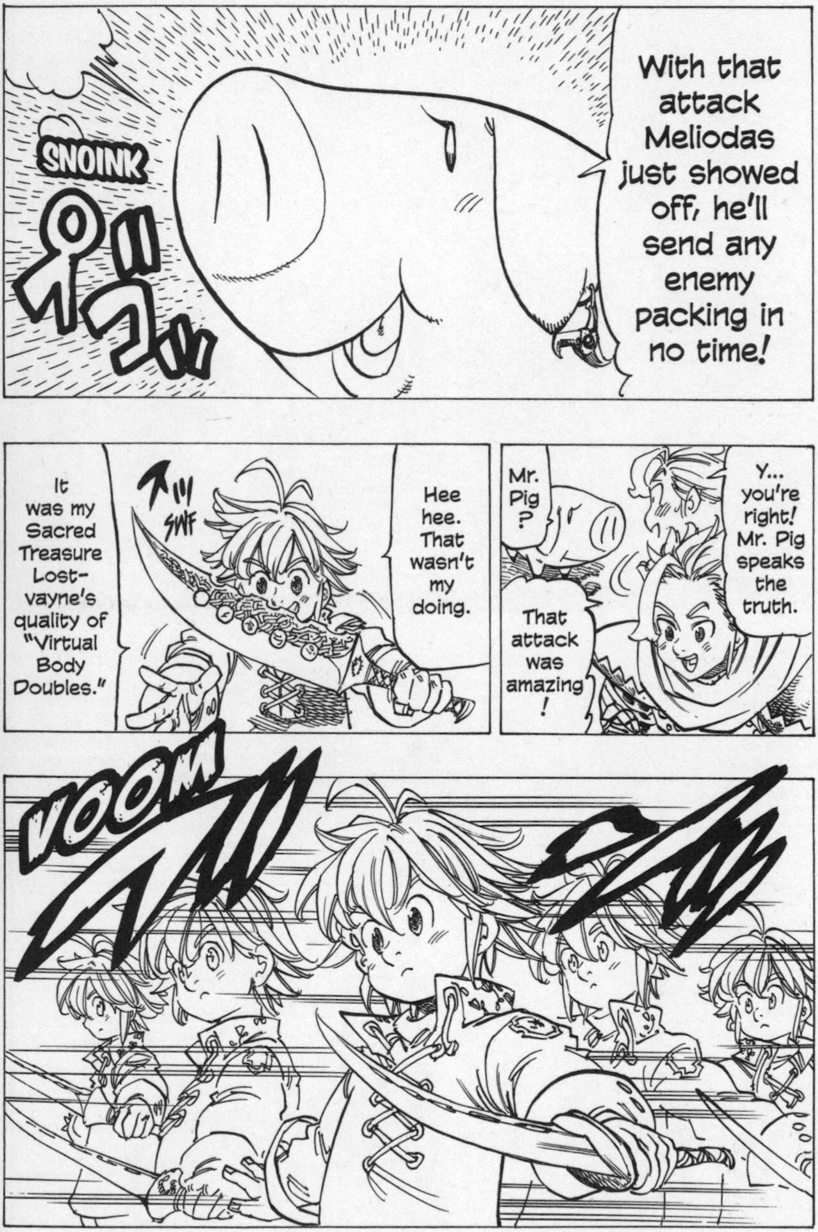
With that attack Meliodas just showed off, he'll send any enemy packing in no time!
SNOINK
Y... you're right! Mr. Pig speaks the truth.
Mr. Pig?
That attack was amazing!
Hee hee. That wasn't my doing.
SWF
It was my Sacred Treasure Lost-vayne's quality of "Virtual Body Doubles."
VOOM

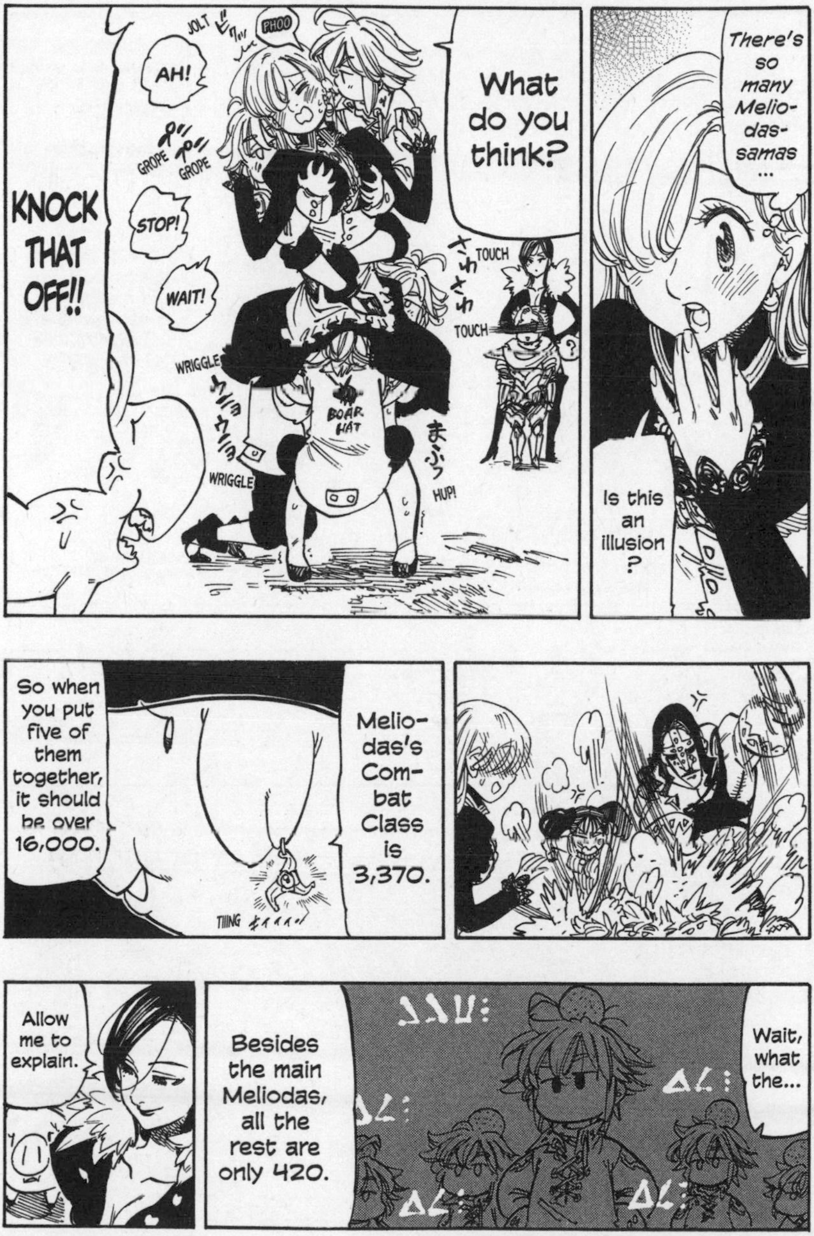
There's so many Melio-das-samas...
Is this an illusion?
What do you think?
JOLT
PHOO
AH!
GROPE
GROPE
STOP!
WAIT!
KNOCK THAT OFF!!
TOUCH
TOUCH
WRIGGLE
WRIGGLE
HUP!
Melio-das's Com-bat Class is 3,370.
So when you put five of them together, it should be over 16,000.
TIIING
Wait, what the...
Besides the main Meliodas, all the rest are only 420.
Allow me to explain.

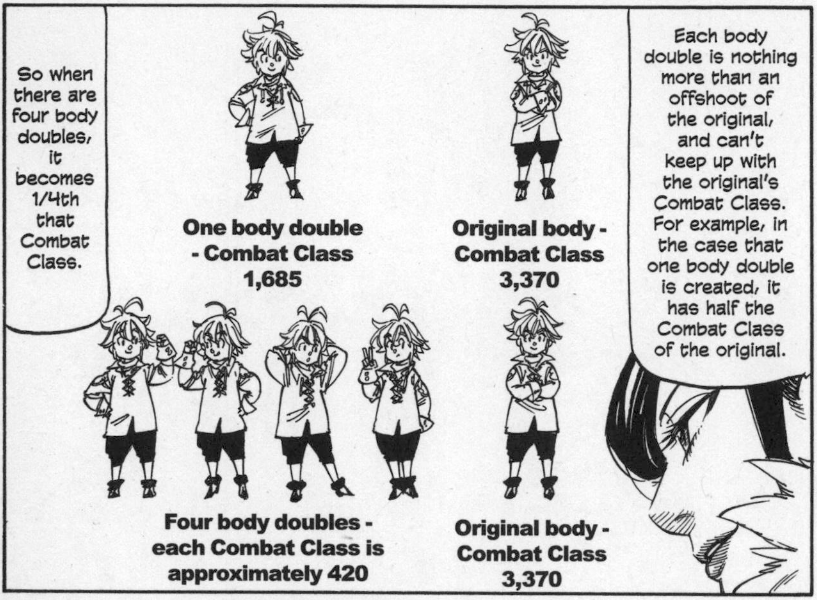
Each body double is nothing more than an offshoot of the original, and can't keep up with the original's Combat Class. For example, in the case that one body double is created, it has half the Combat Class of the original.
Original body - Combat Class 3,370
One body double - Combat Class 1,685
So when there are four body doubles, it becomes 1/4th that Combat Class.
Original body - Combat Class 3,370
Four body doubles - each Combat Class is approximately 420

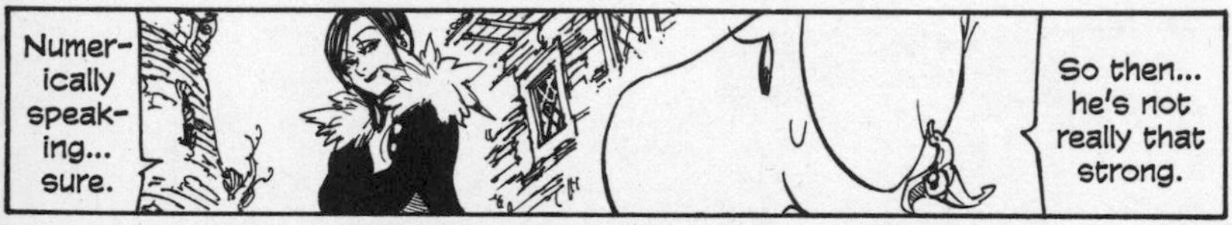
So then... he's not really that strong.
Numer-ically speak-ing... sure.

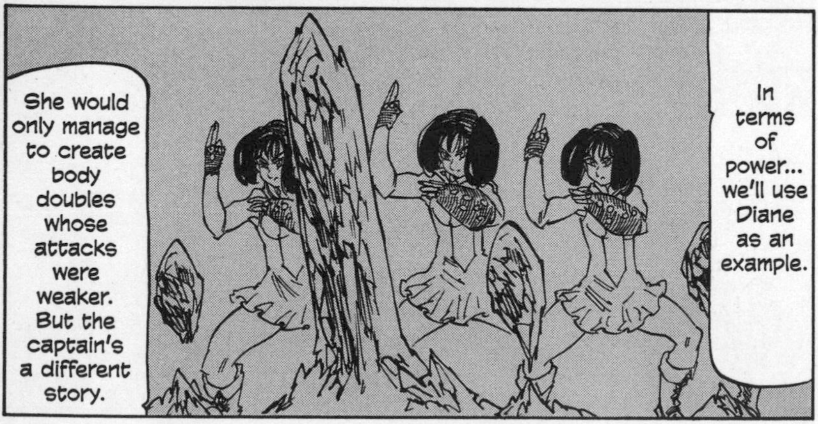
In terms of power... we'll use Diane as an example.
She would only manage to create body doubles whose attacks were weaker. But the captain's a different story.

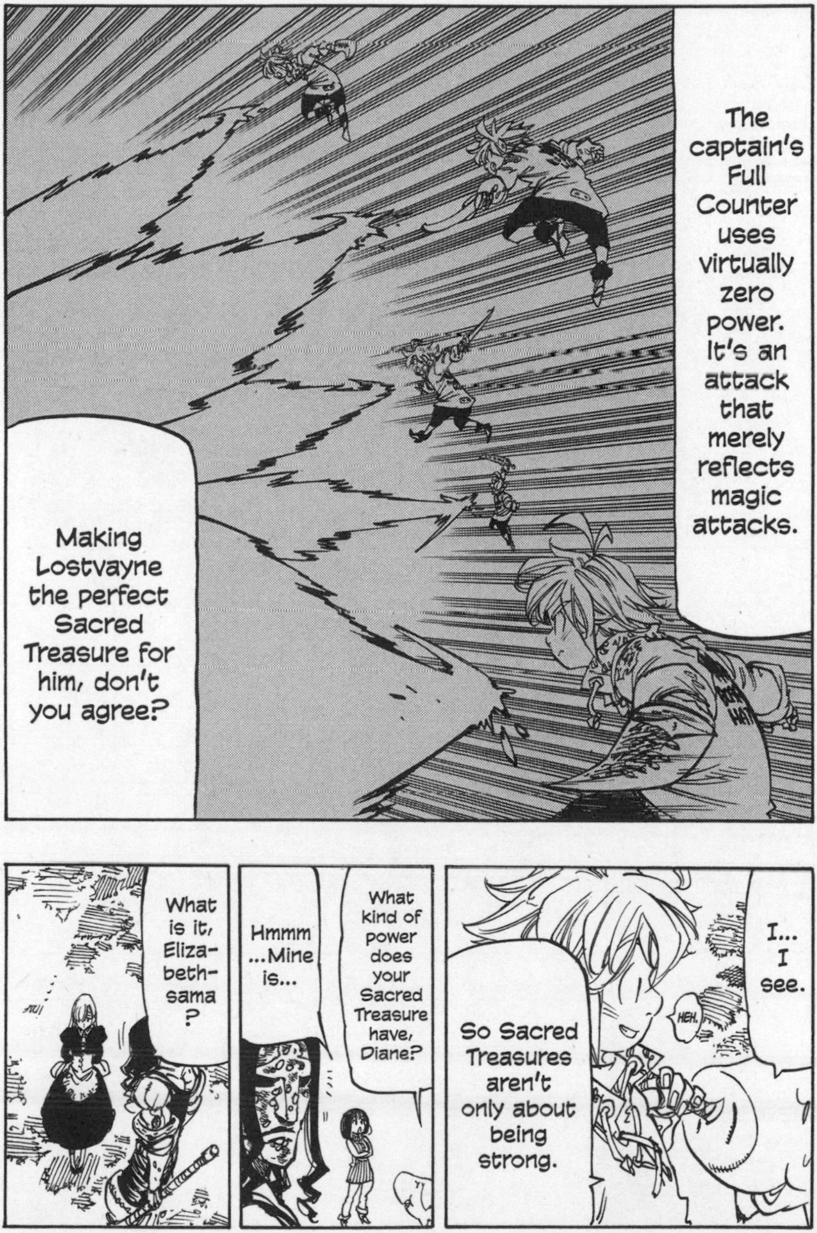
The captain's Full Counter uses virtually zero power. It's an attack that merely reflects magic attacks.
Making Lostvayne the perfect Sacred Treasure for him, don't you agree?
I... I see.
HEH.
So Sacred Treasures aren't only about being strong.
What kind of power does your Sacred Treasure have, Diane?
Hmmm ...Mine is...
What is it, Eliza-beth-sama?

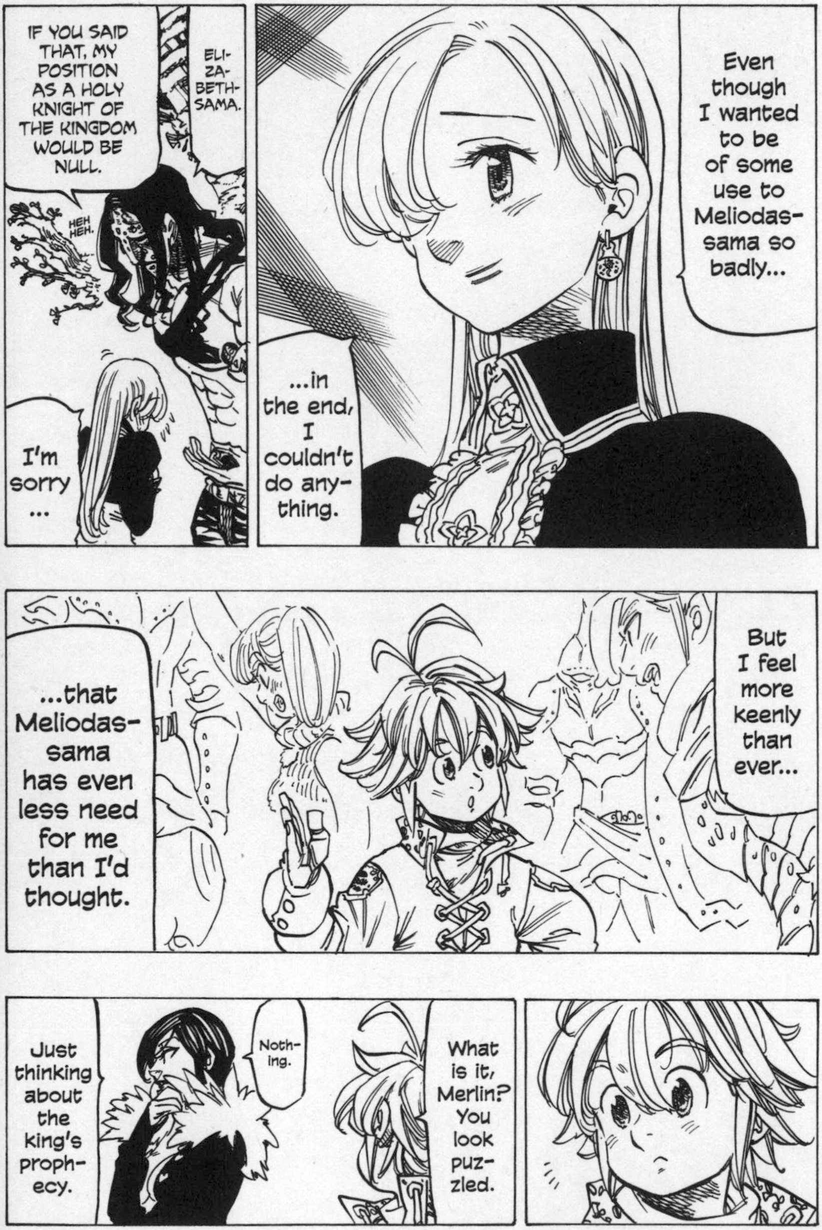

Even though I wanted to be of some use to Meliodas-sama so badly...
...in the end, I couldn't do anything.
ELI-ZA-BETH-SAMA.
IF YOU SAID THAT, MY POSITION AS A HOLY KNIGHT OF THE KINGDOM WOULD BE NULL.
HEH HEH.
I'm sorry...
But I feel more keenly than ever...
...that Meliodas-sama has even less need for me than I'd thought.
What is it, Merlin? You look puzzled.
Nothing.
Just thinking about the king's prophecy.

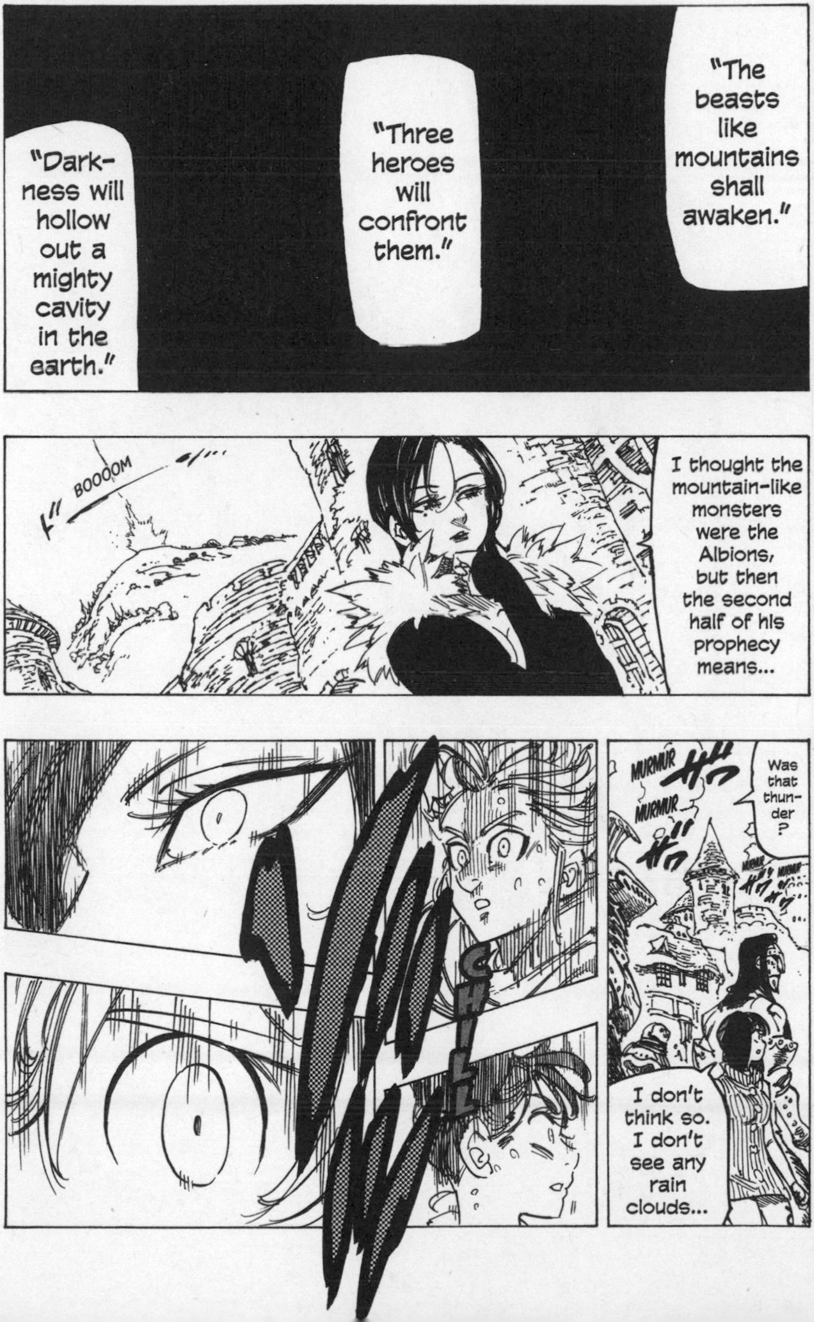
"The beasts like mountains shall awaken."
"Three heroes will confront them."
"Darkness will hollow out a mighty cavity in the earth."
I thought the mountain-like monsters were the Albions, but then the second half of his prophecy means...
BOOOOM
Was that thunder?
MURMUR
MURMUR
MURMUR MURMUR
I don't think so. I don't see any rain clouds...
CHILL

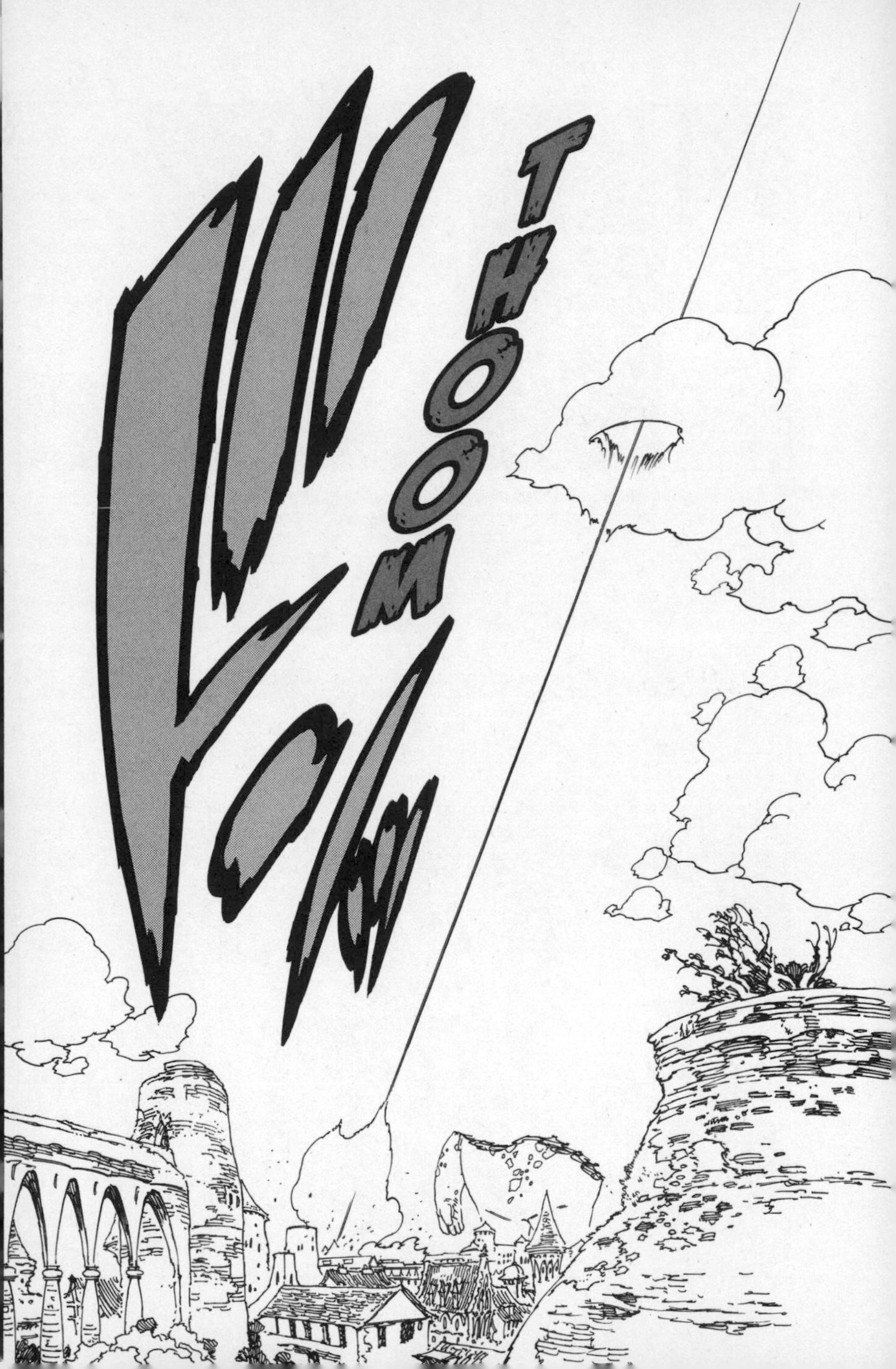
THOOM

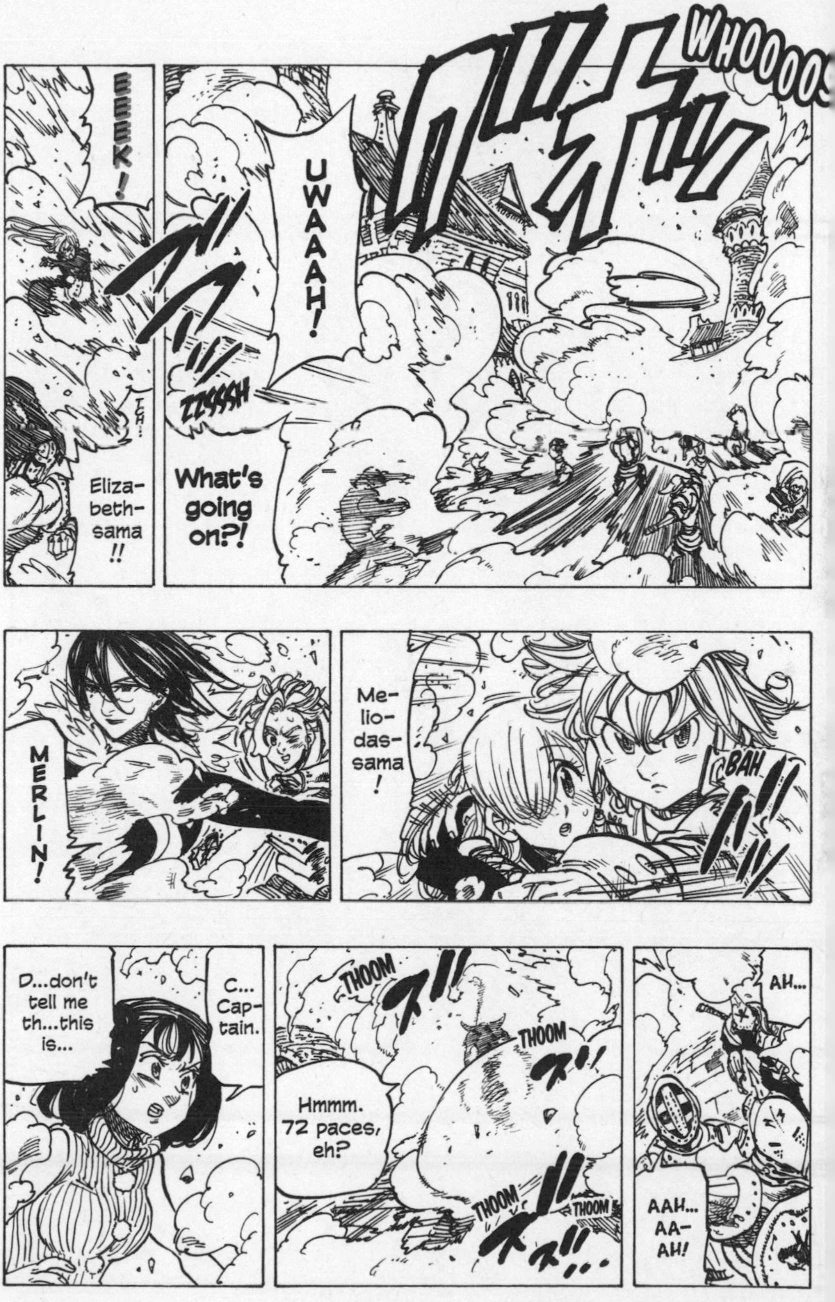
WHOOOOS
UWAAAAH!
What's going on?!
ZZSSSSH
EEEEK!
TCH!
Eliza-beth-sama!!
Me-lio-das-sama!
BAH
MERLIN!
AH...
AAH... AA-AH!
THOOM
THOOM
THOOM
THOOM
Hmmm. 72 paces, eh?
C... Cap-tain.
D...don't tell me th...this is...

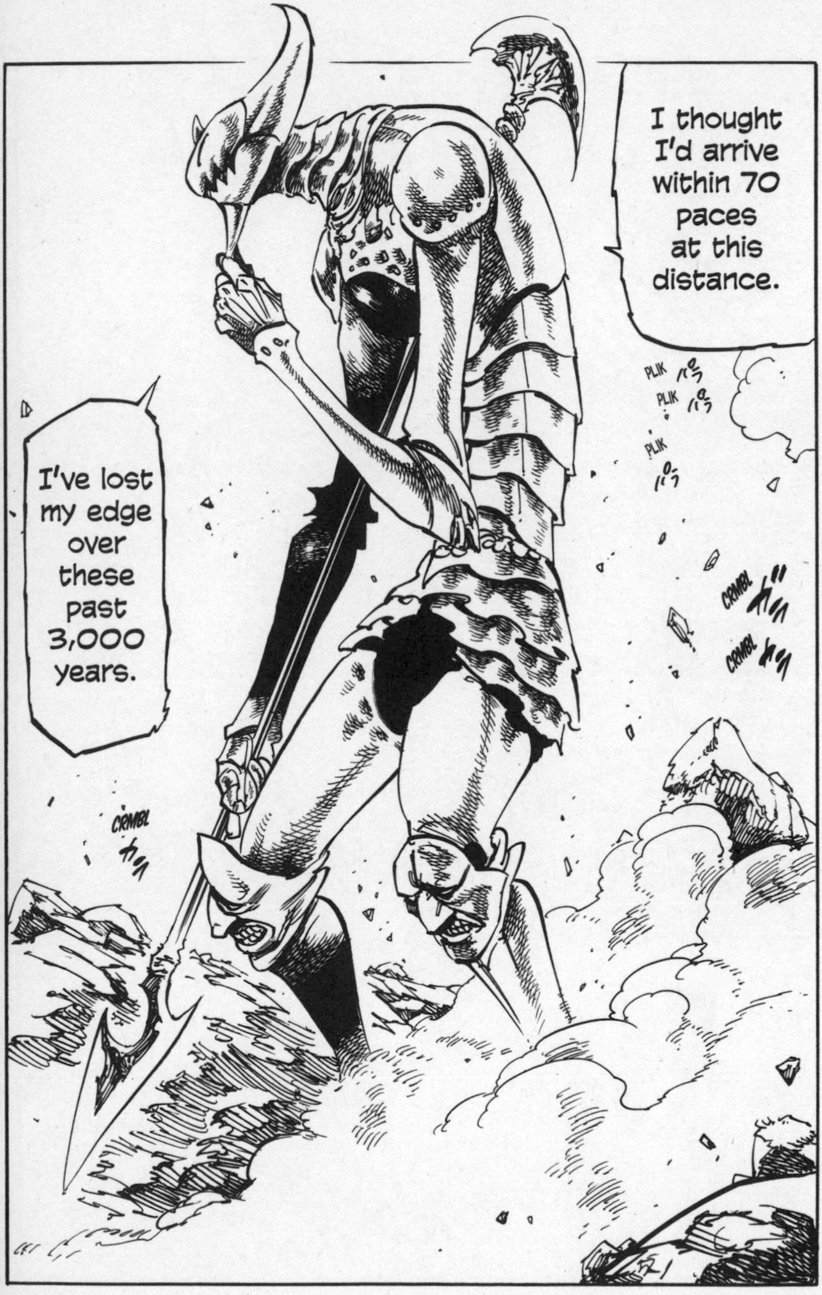
I thought I'd arrive within 70 paces at this distance.
PLIK
PLIK
PLIK
CRMBL
CRMBL
I've lost my edge over these past 3,000 years.
CRMBL

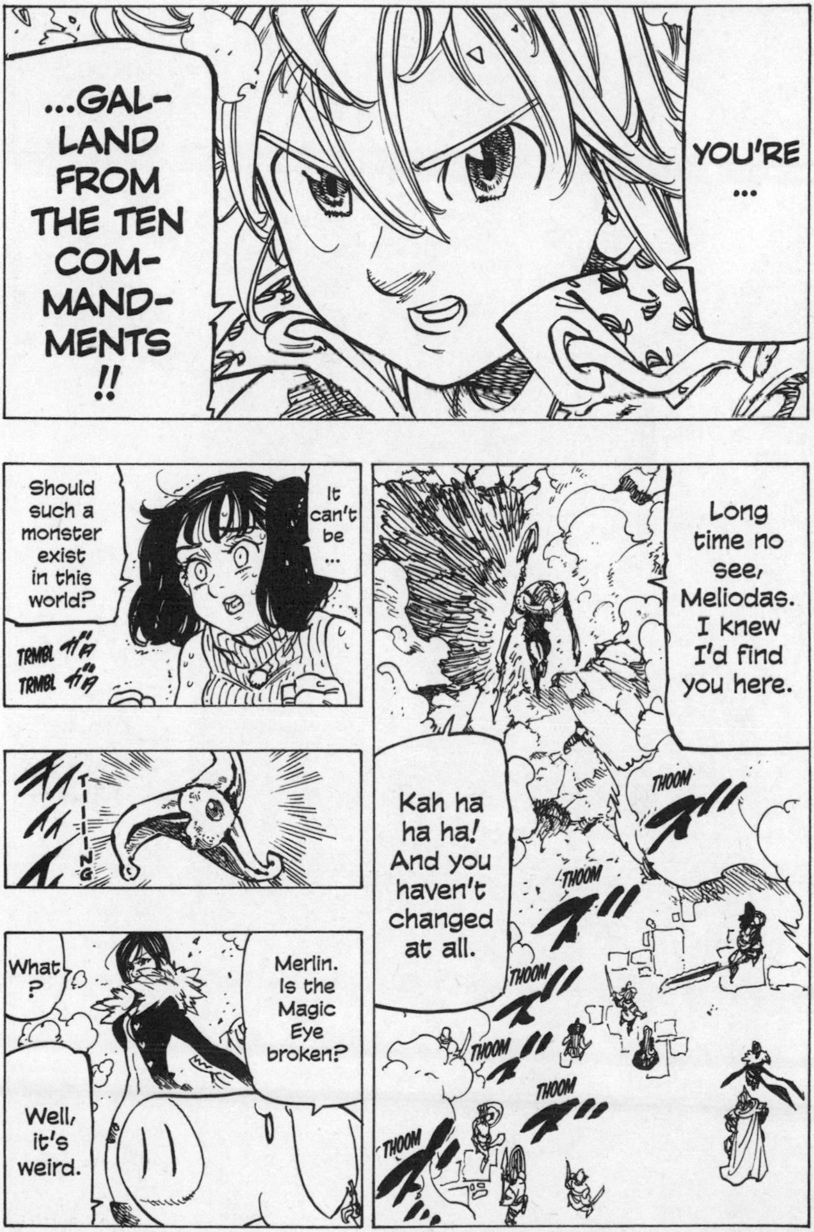
YOU'RE ...
...GALLAND FROM THE TEN COMMANDMENTS!!
Long time no see, Meliodas. I knew I'd find you here.
Kah ha ha ha! And you haven't changed at all.
THOOM
THOOM
THOOM
THOOM
THOOM
THOOM
It can't be ...
Should such a monster exist in this world?
TRMBL
TRMBL
TIIIIING
Merlin. Is the Magic Eye broken?
What?
Well, it's weird.

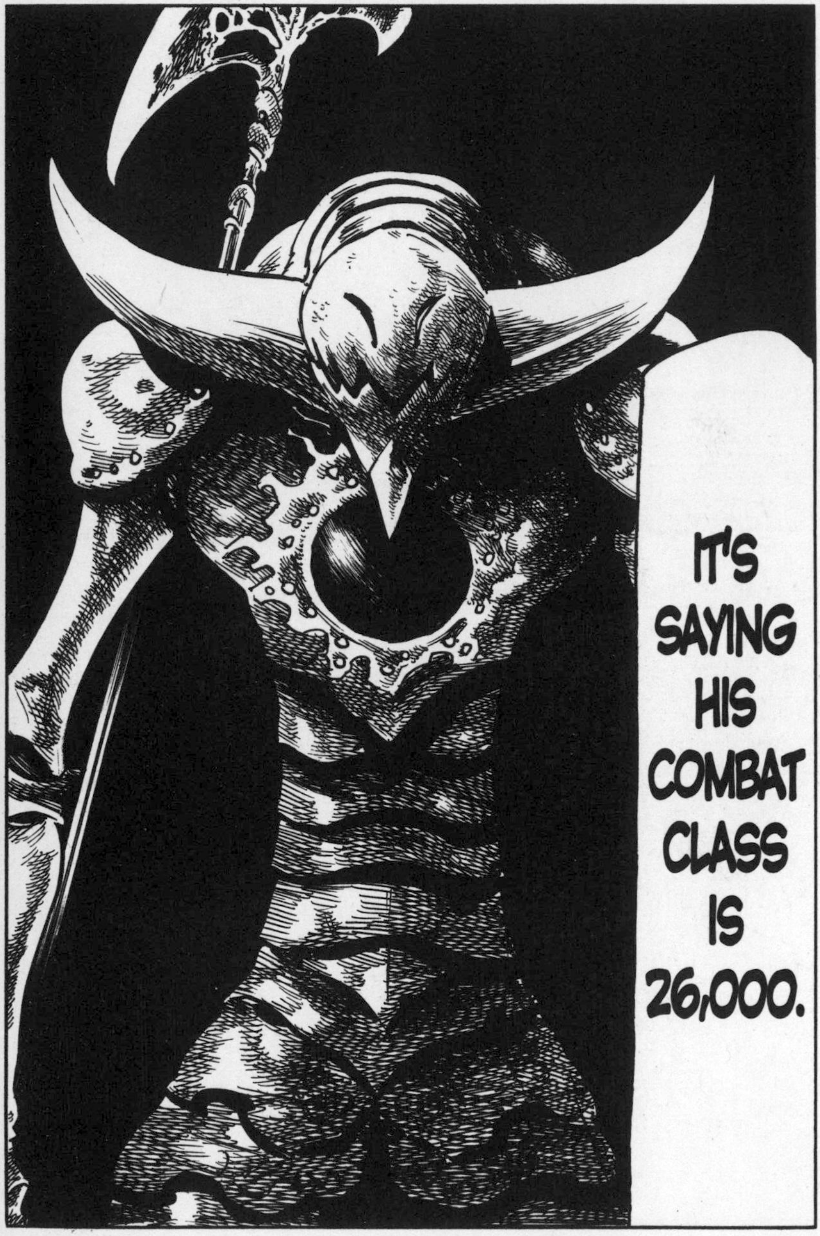
IT'S SAYING HIS COMBAT CLASS IS 26,000.

THE SEVEN DEADLY SINS

Chapter 120 - Overwhelming Violence

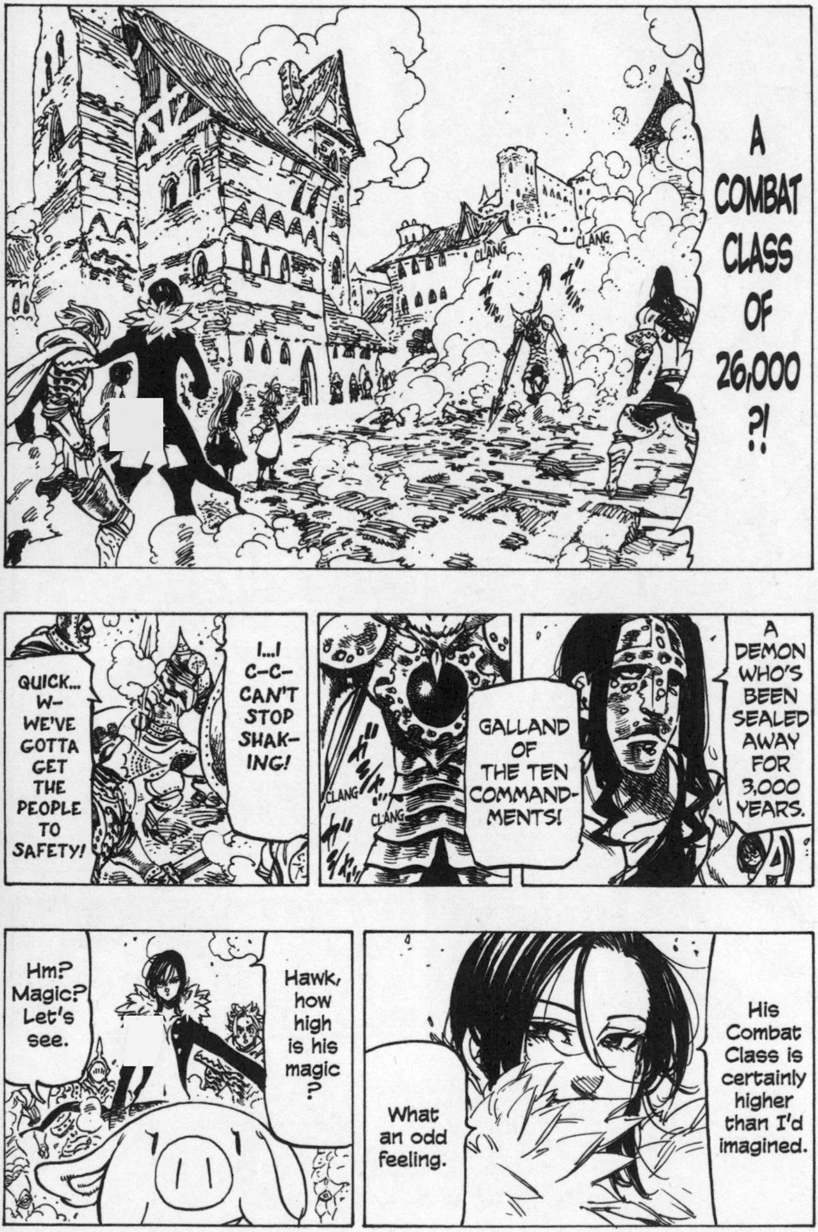
A COMBAT CLASS OF 26,000 ?!
CLANG.
CLANG
A DEMON WHO'S BEEN SEALED AWAY FOR 3,000 YEARS.
GALLAND OF THE TEN COMMAND-MENTS!
CLANG
CLANG
I...I C-C-CAN'T STOP SHAK-ING!
QUICK... W-WE'VE GOTTA GET THE PEOPLE TO SAFETY!
His Combat Class is certainly higher than I'd imagined.
What an odd feeling.
Hawk, how high is his magic?
Hm? Magic? Let's see.

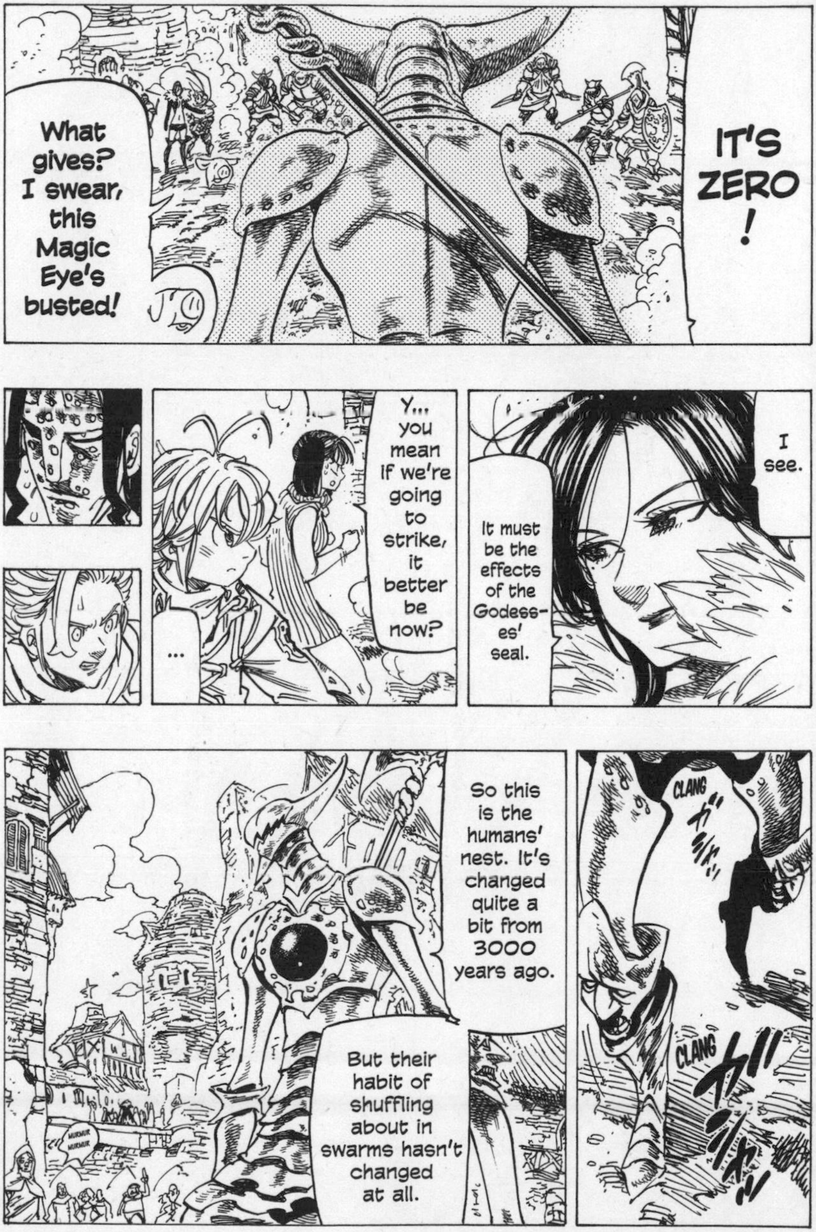
IT'S ZERO!
What gives? I swear, this Magic Eye's busted!
I see.
It must be the effects of the Godesses' seal.
Y... you mean if we're going to strike, it better be now?
...
CLANG
CLANG
So this is the humans' nest. It's changed quite a bit from 3000 years ago.
But their habit of shuffling about in swarms hasn't changed at all.
MURMUR MURMUR

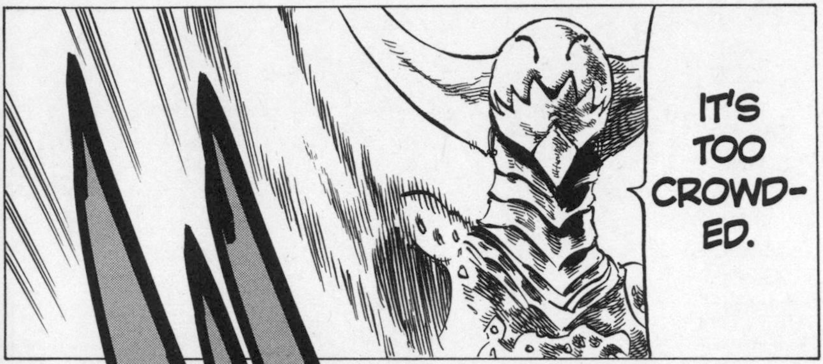
IT'S TOO CROWD-ED.
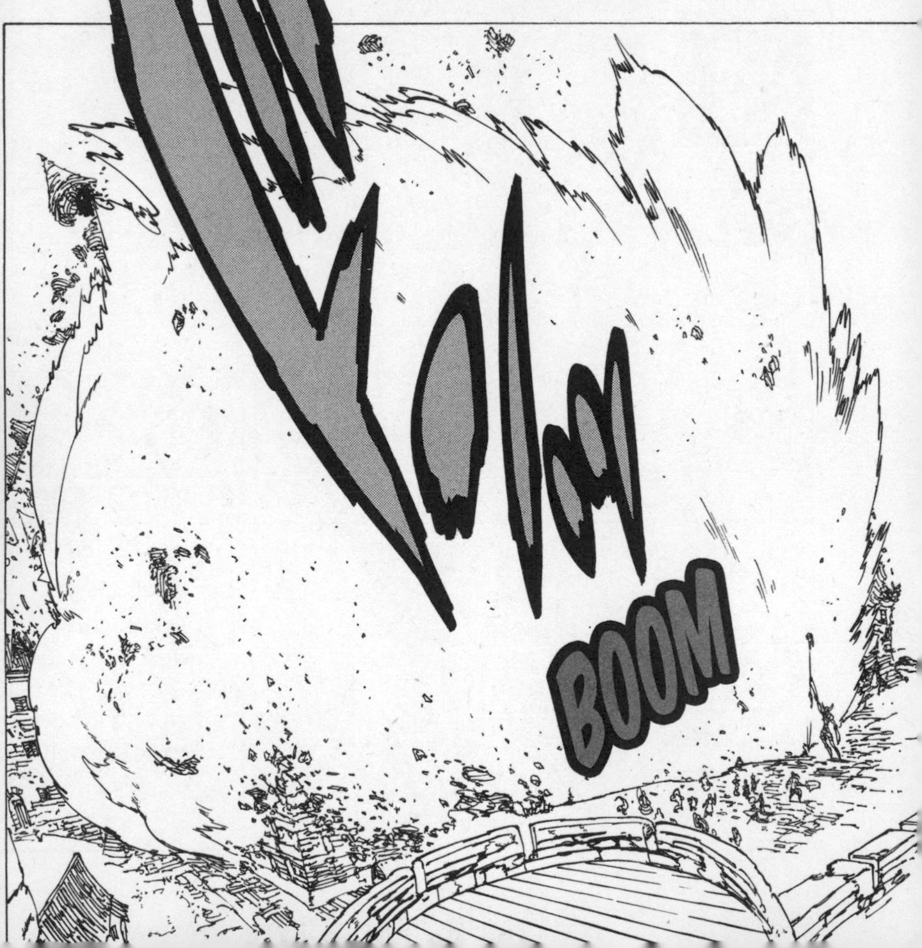
BOOM

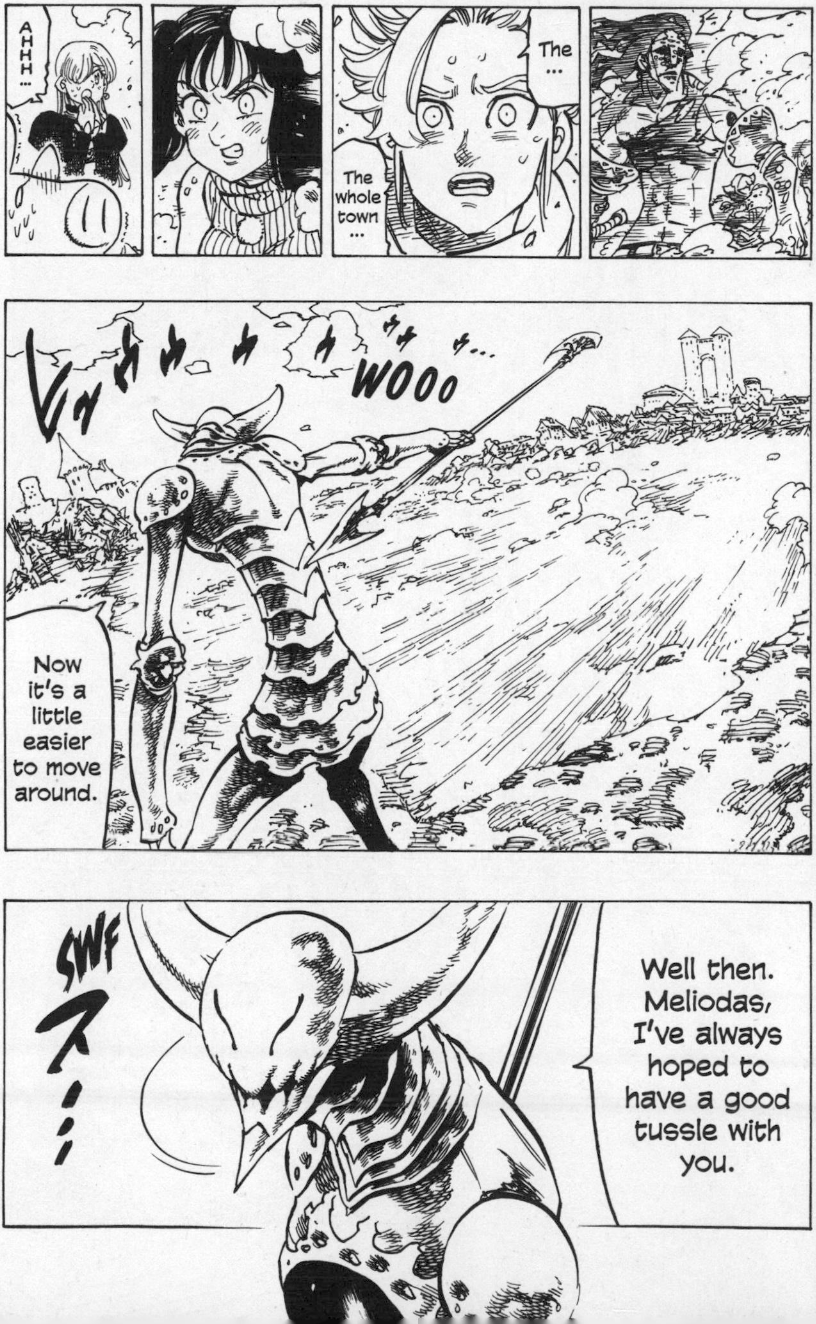
The ...
The whole town ...
AHHH ...
WOOO
Now it's a little easier to move around.
SWF
Well then. Meliodas, I've always hoped to have a good tussle with you.

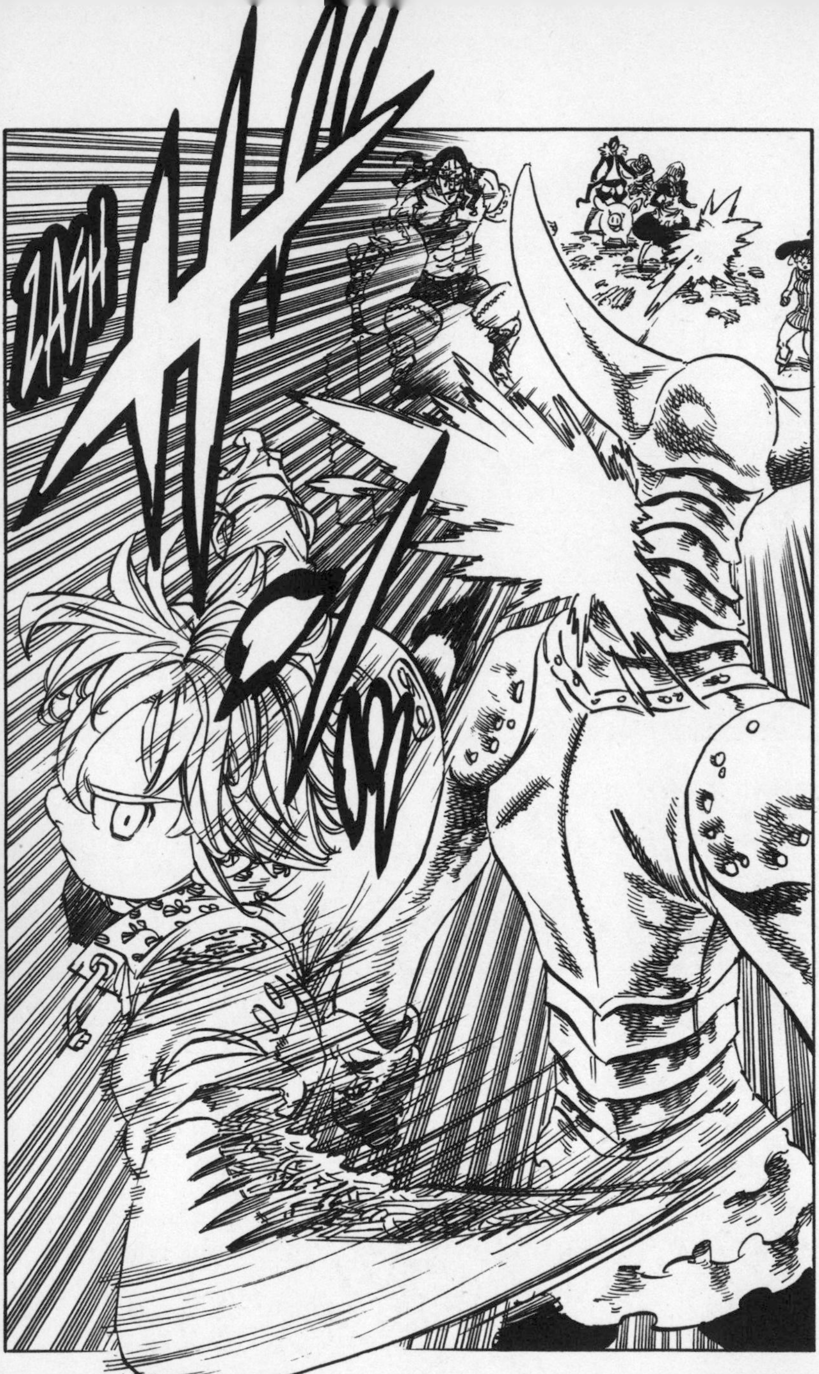
ZASH

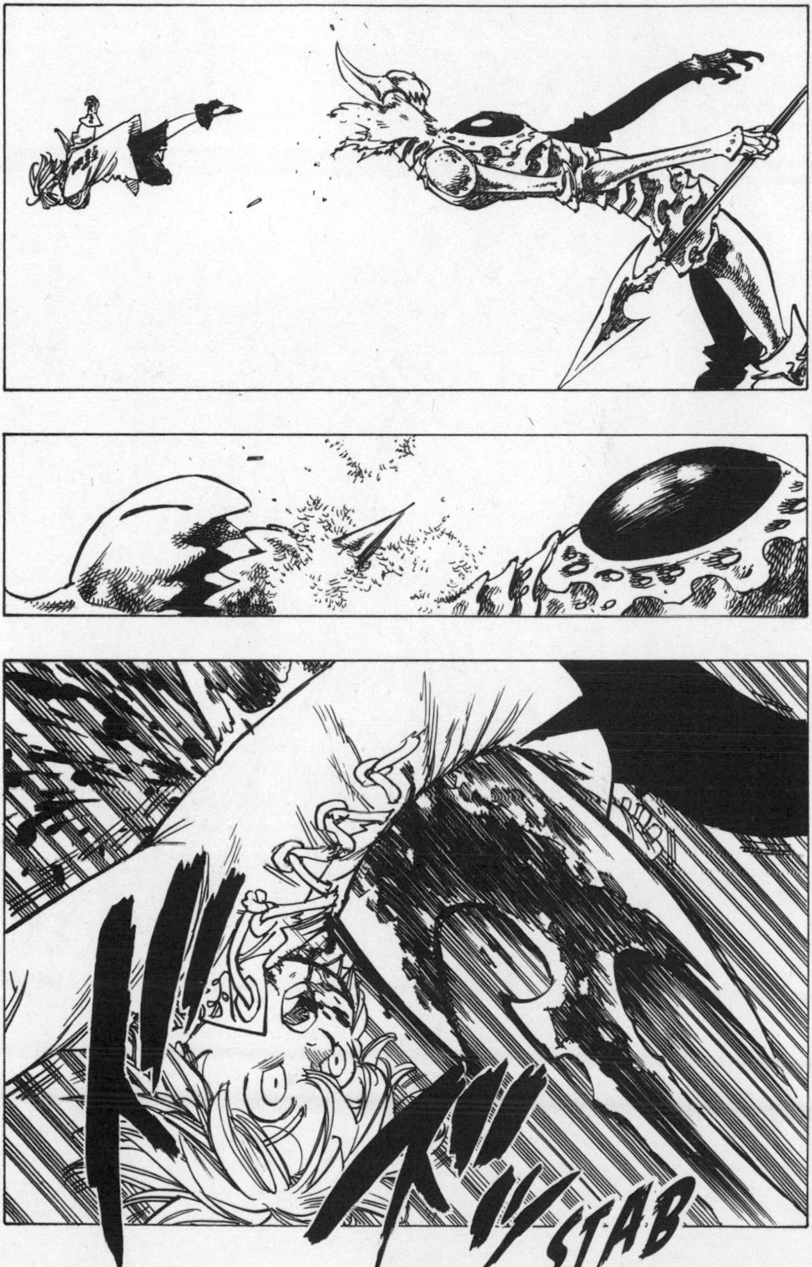
STAB

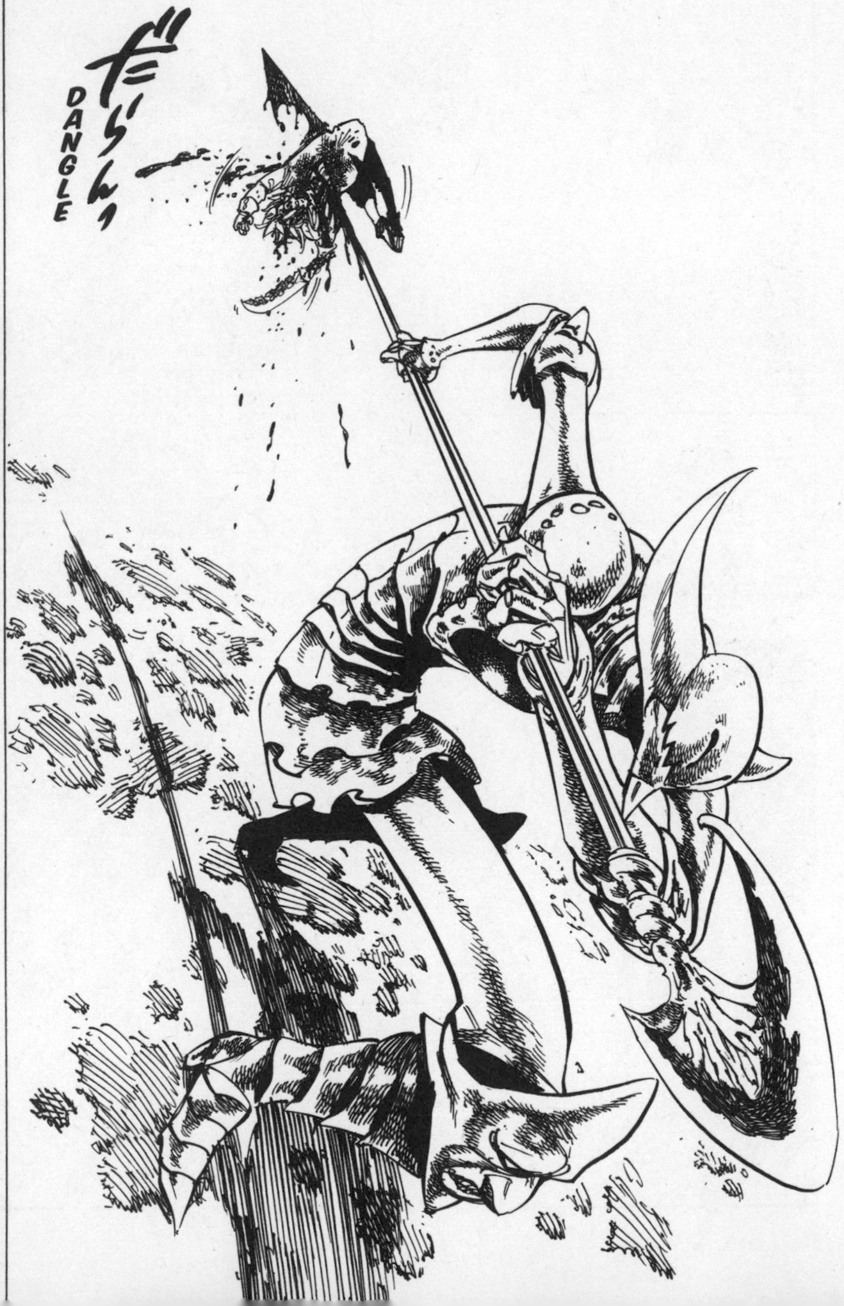
DANGLE

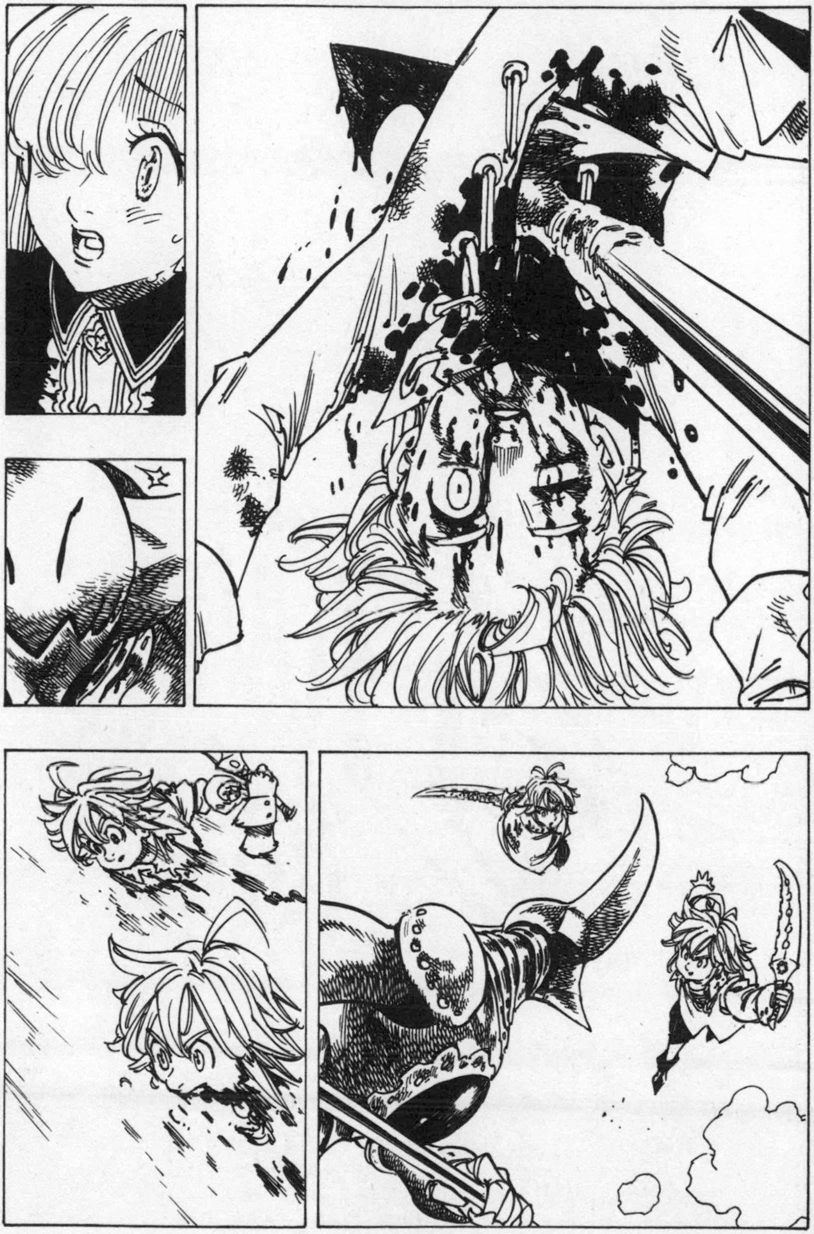

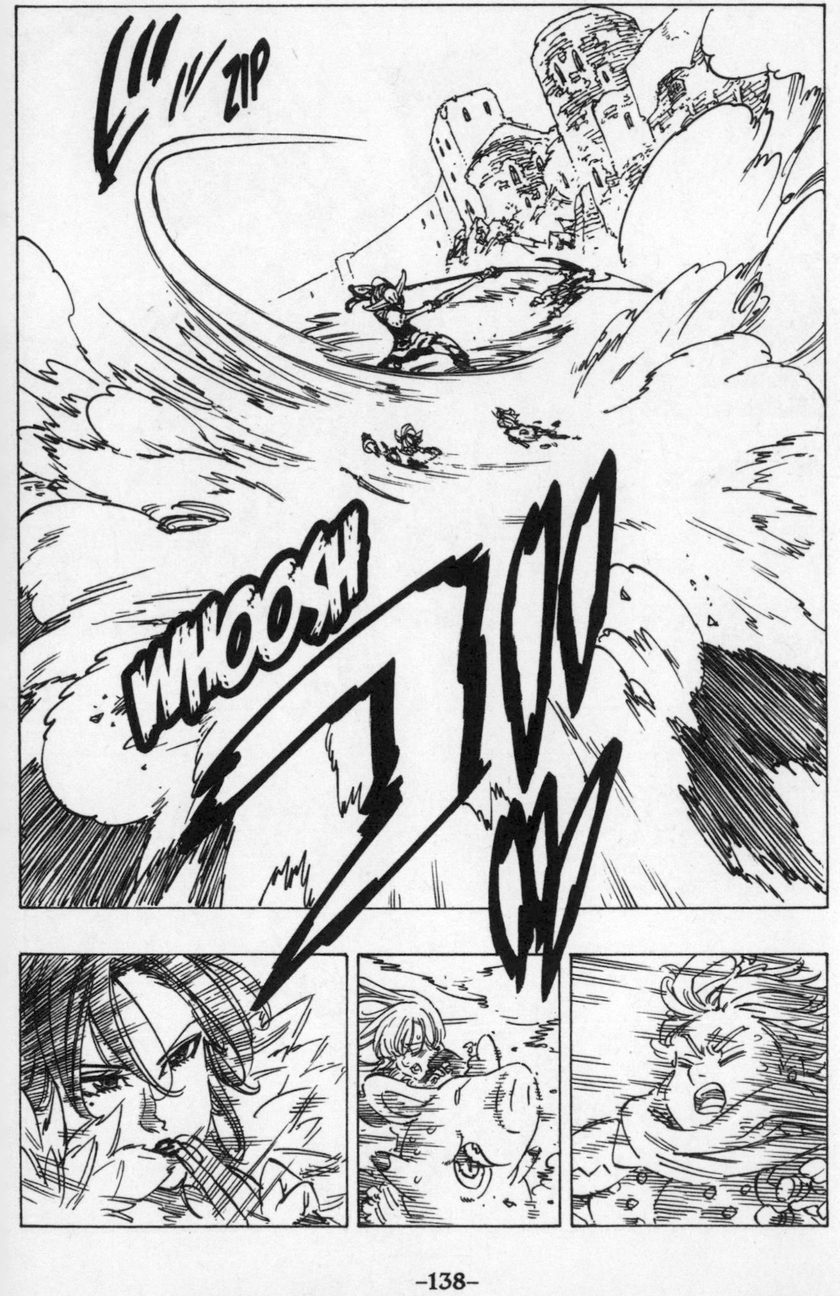
ZIP
WHOOSH

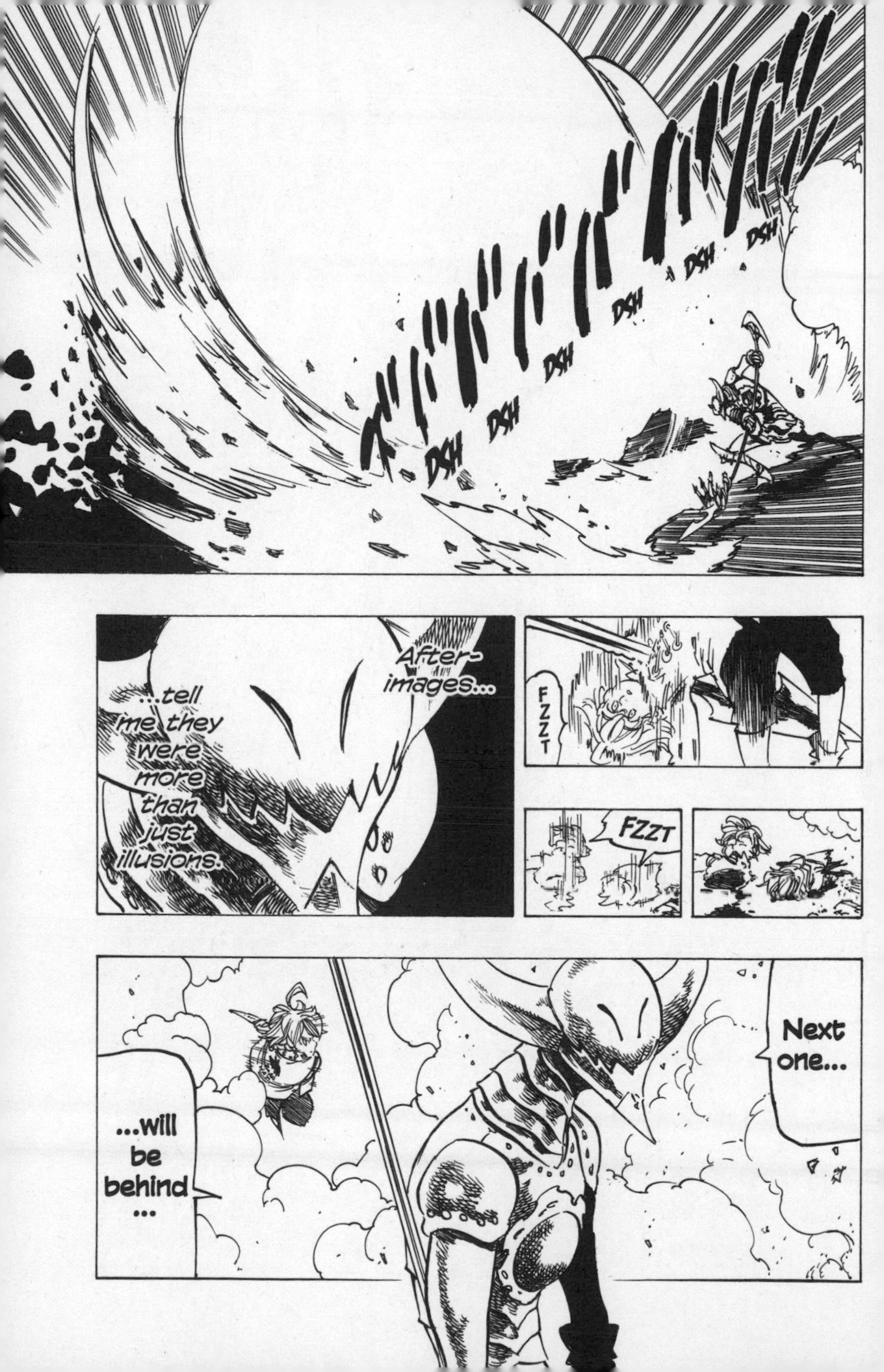
DSH
DSH
DSH
DSH
DSH
DSH
FZZT
FZZT
After-images...
...tell me they were more than just illusions.
Next one...
...will be behind...

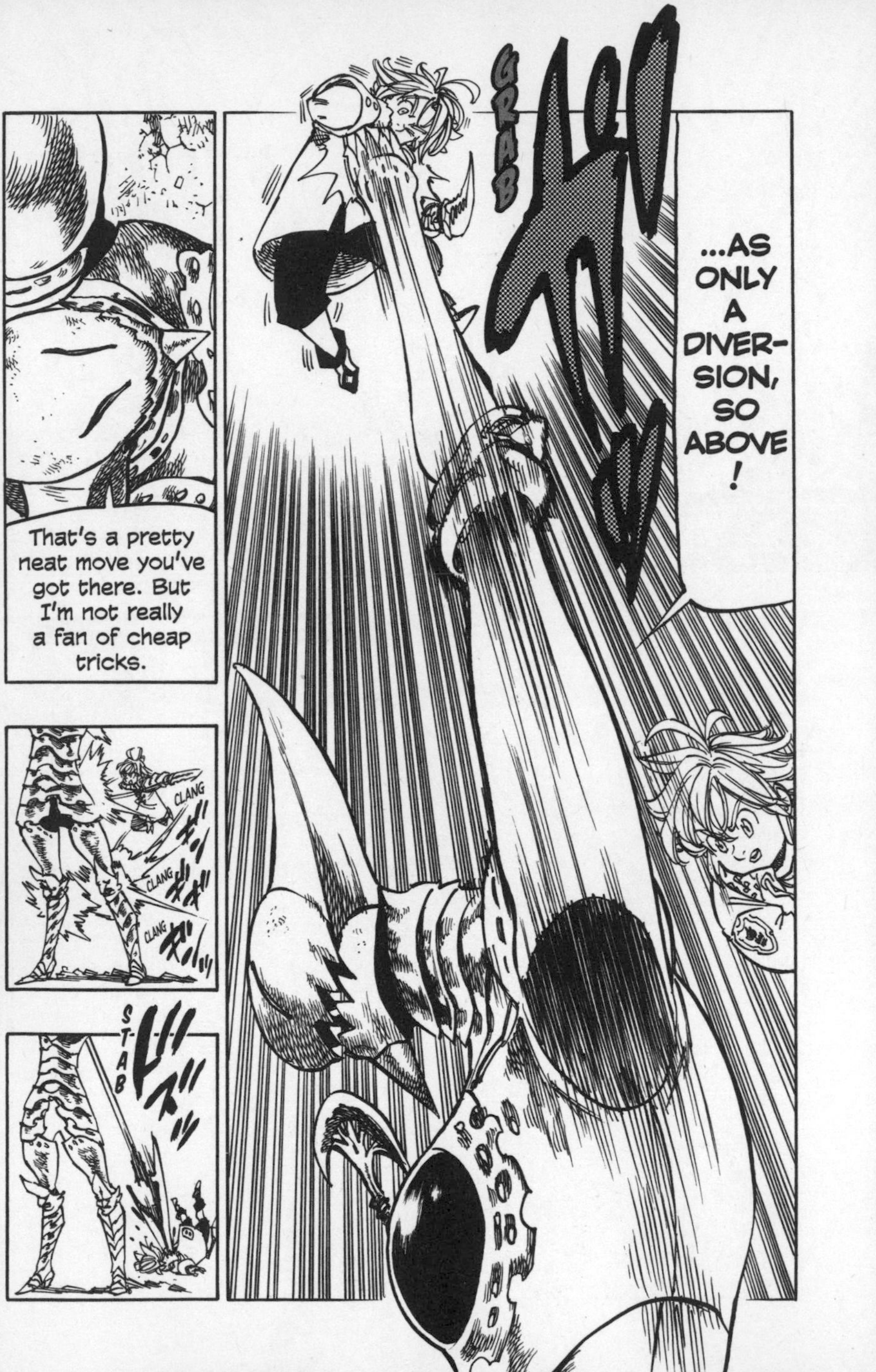
GRAB
...AS ONLY A DIVERSION, SO ABOVE!
That's a pretty neat move you've got there. But I'm not really a fan of cheap tricks.
CLANG
CLANG
CLANG
STAB

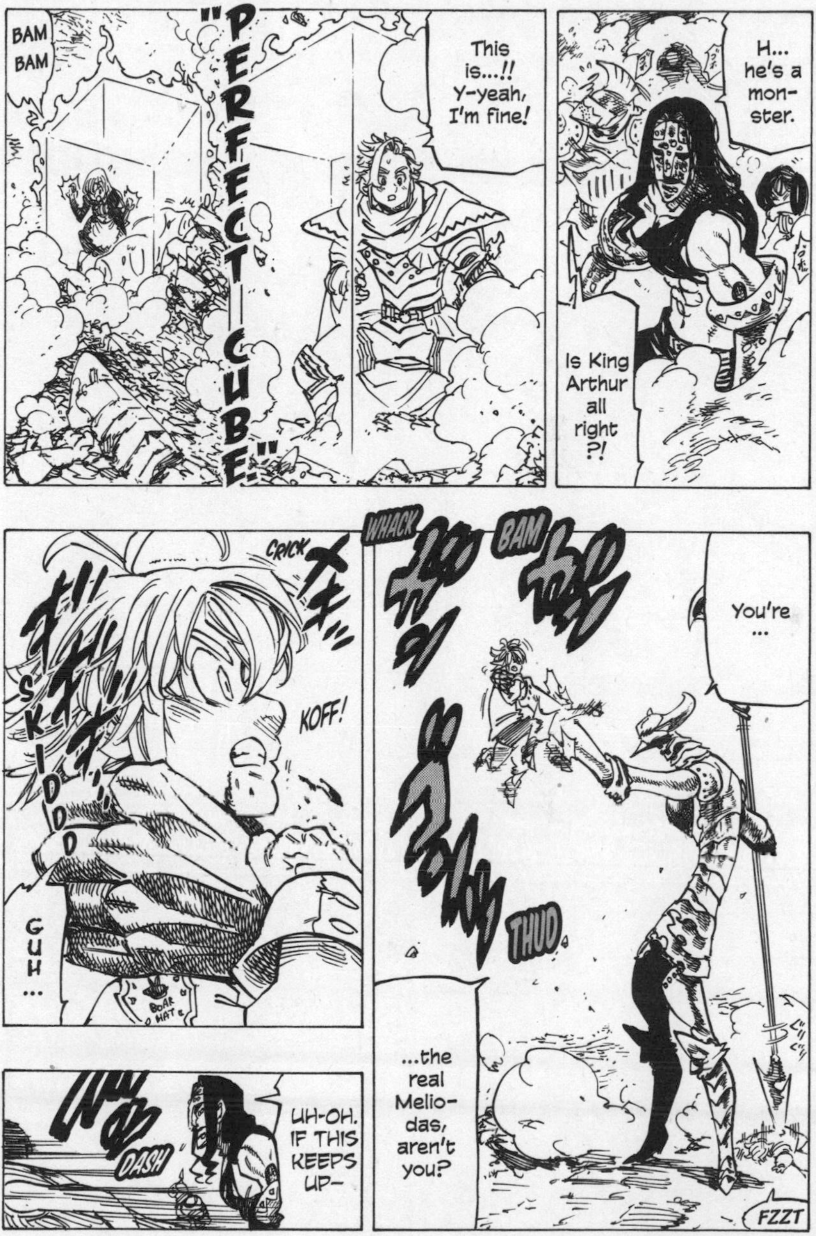
H... he's a monster.
Is King Arthur all right?!
This is...!!
Y-yeah, I'm fine!
"PERFECT CUBE."
BAM BAM
WHACK
BAM
You're...
THUD
...the real Meliodas, aren't you?
FZZT
CRICK
SKIDDD
KOFF!
GUH...
BOAR HAT
UH-OH. IF THIS KEEPS UP-
DASH

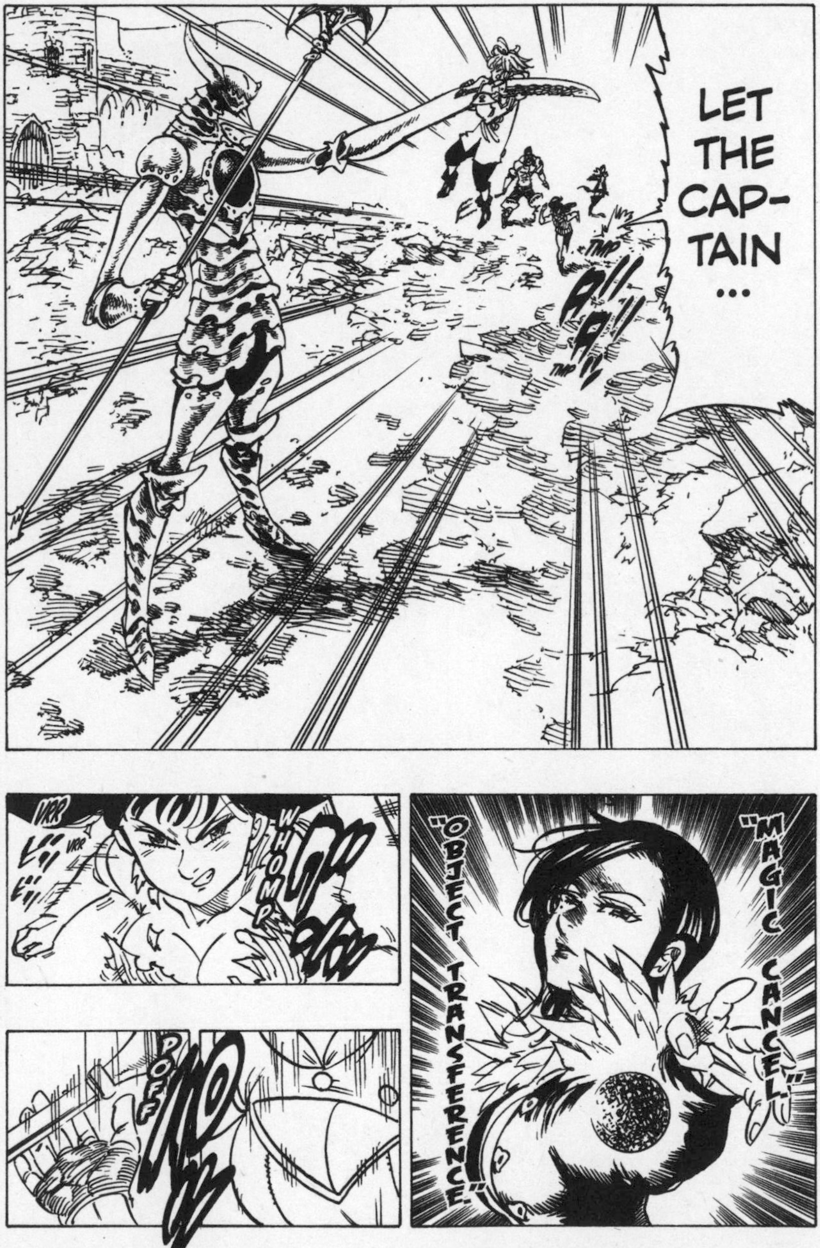
LET THE CAP-TAIN ...
TMP
TMP
"MAGIC CANCEL"
"OBJECT TRANSFERENCE"
VRR
VRR
WHOMP
POFF

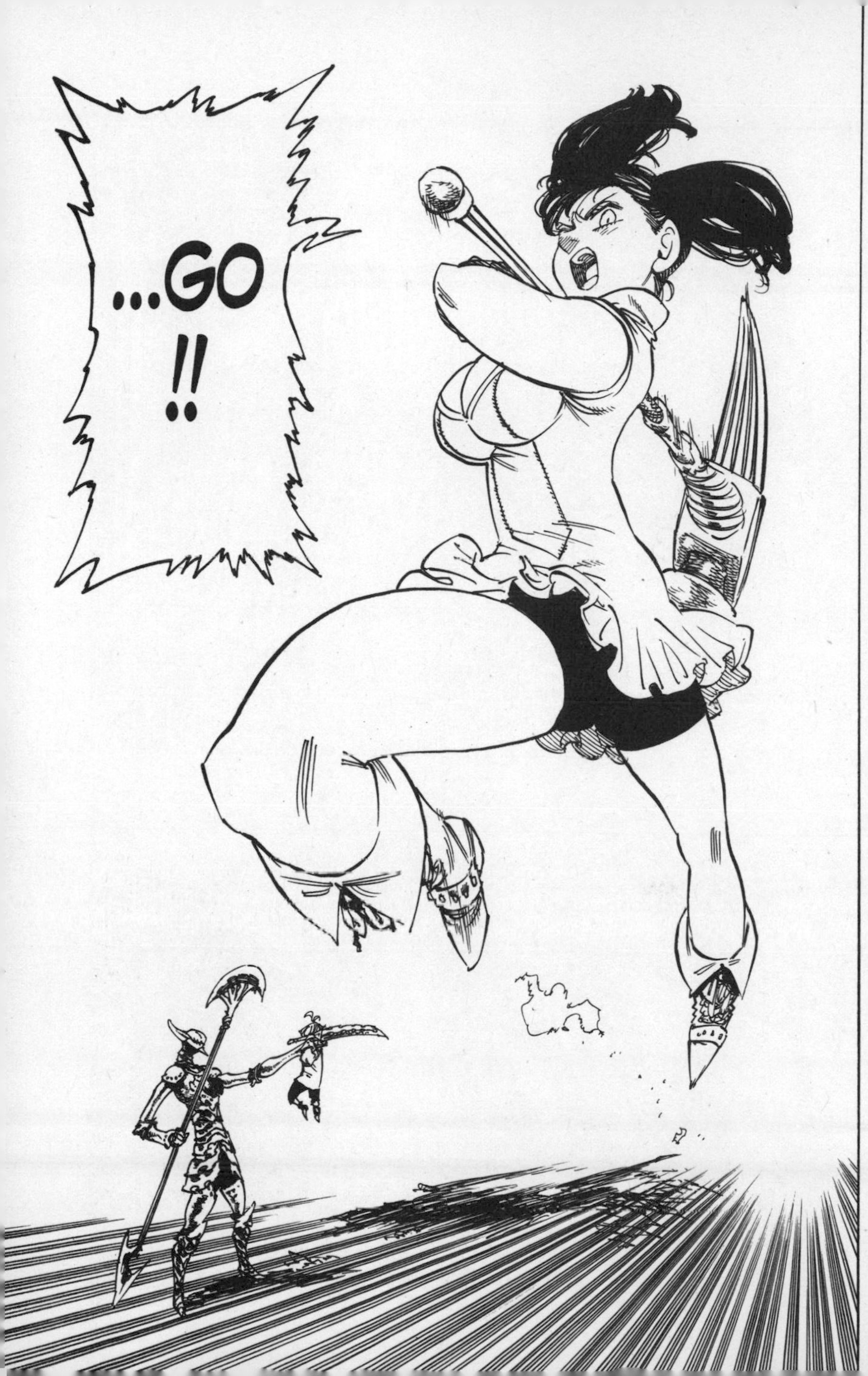

...GO !!

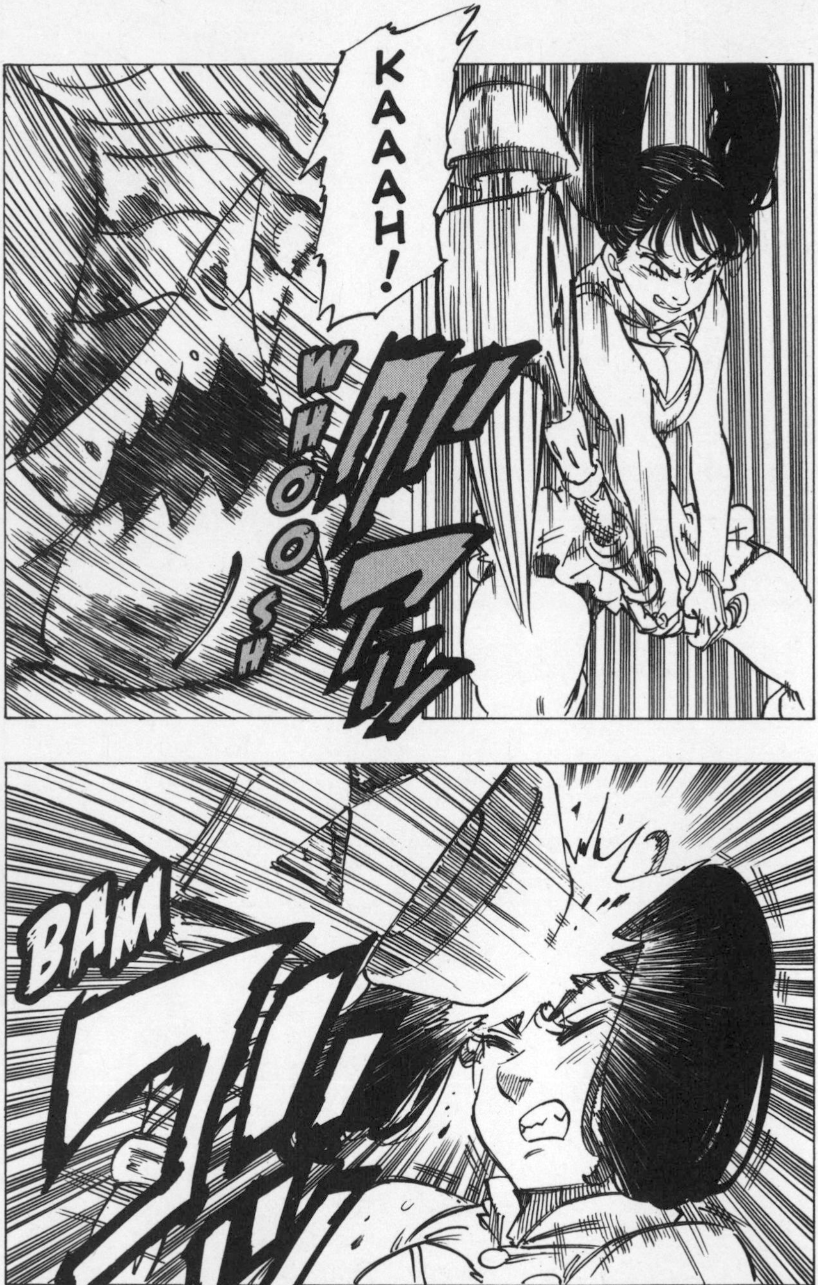
KAAAH!
WHOOOSH
BAM

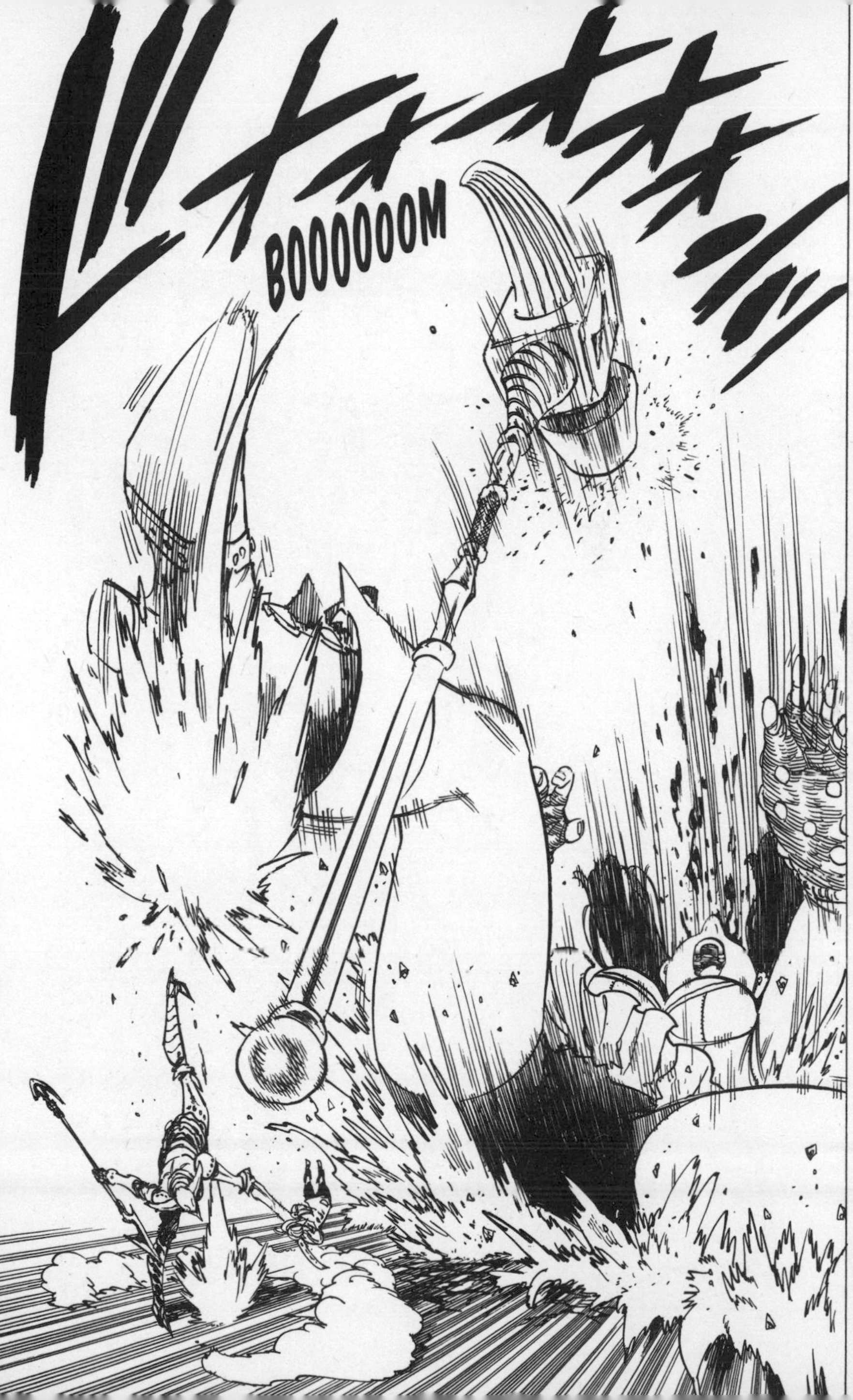
BOOOOOOM

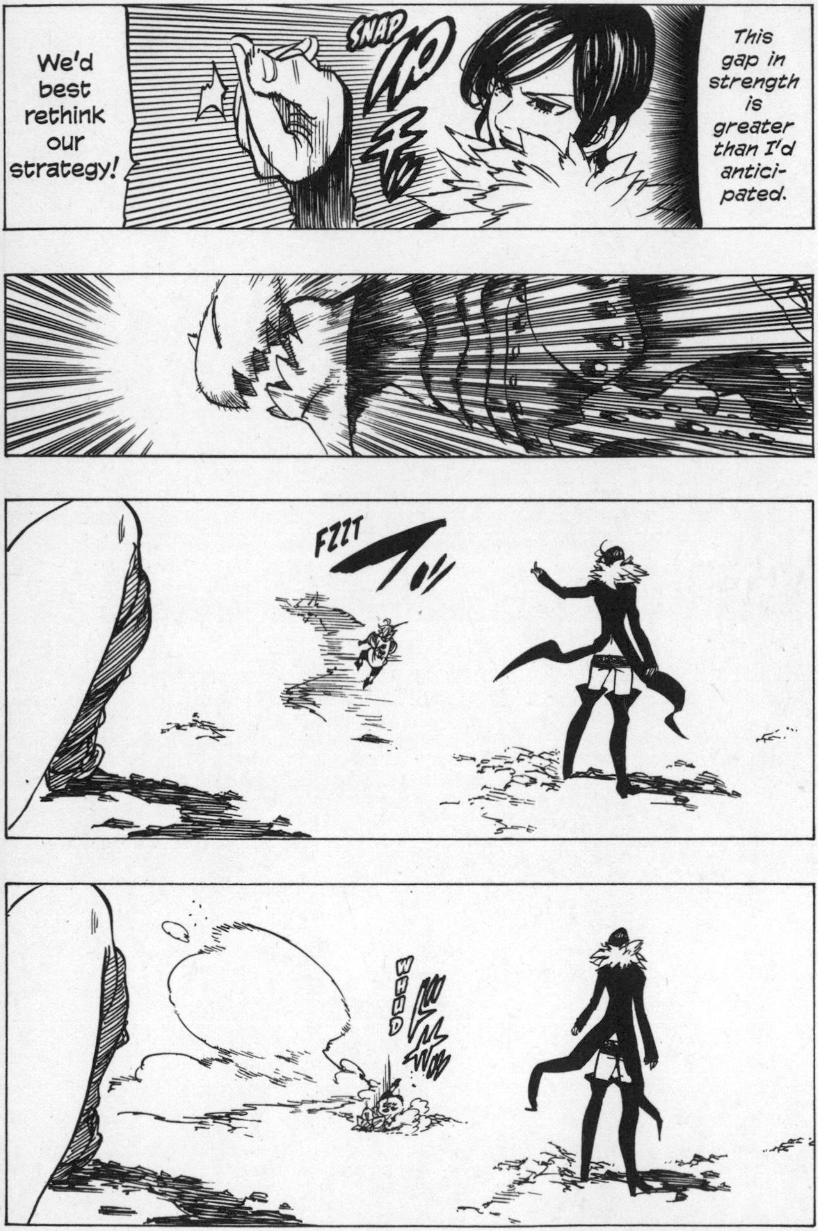
This gap in strength is greater than I'd anticipated.
SNAP
We'd best rethink our strategy!
FZZT
WHUD

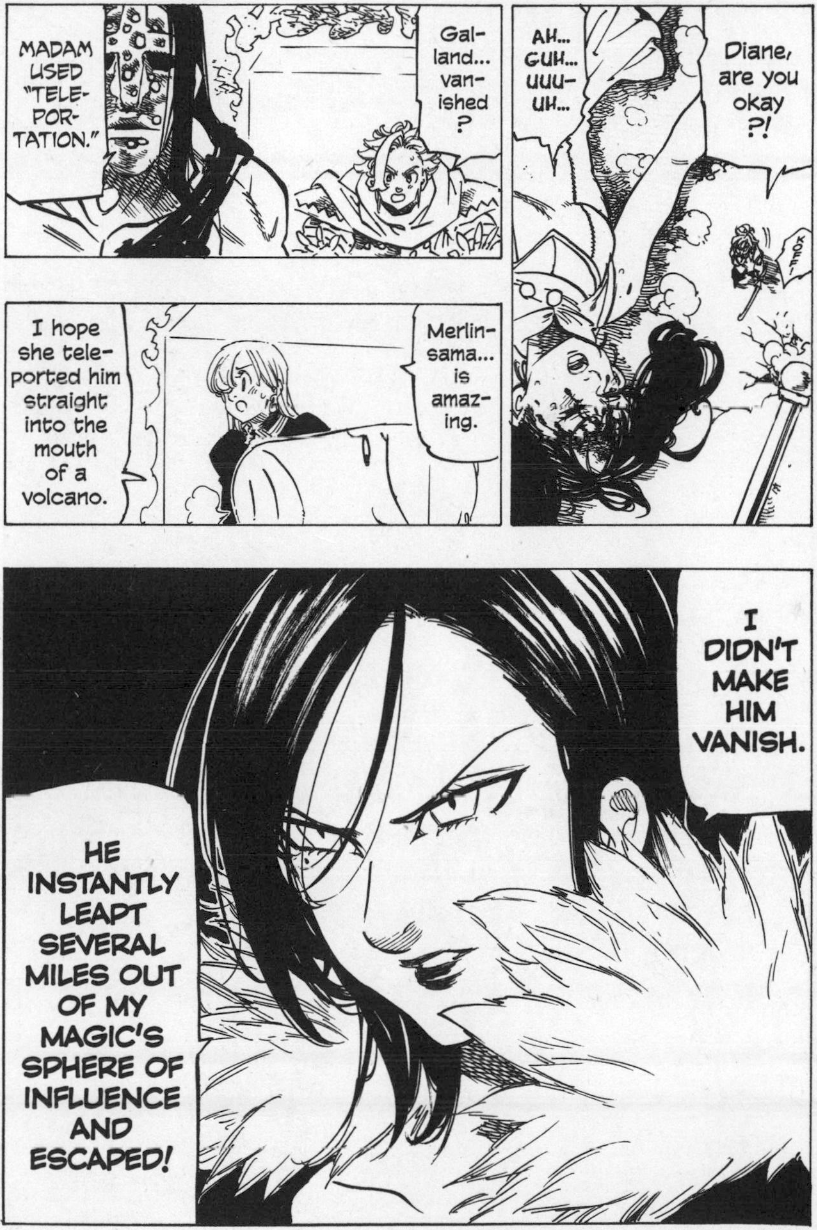
Diane, are you okay ?!
AH... GUH... UUU-UH...
KOFF!
Gal-land... van-ished ?
MADAM USED "TELE-PORTATION."
Merlin-sama... is amaz-ing.
I hope she tele-ported him straight into the mouth of a volcano.
I DIDN'T MAKE HIM VANISH.
HE INSTANTLY LEAPT SEVERAL MILES OUT OF MY MAGIC'S SPHERE OF INFLUENCE AND ESCAPED!

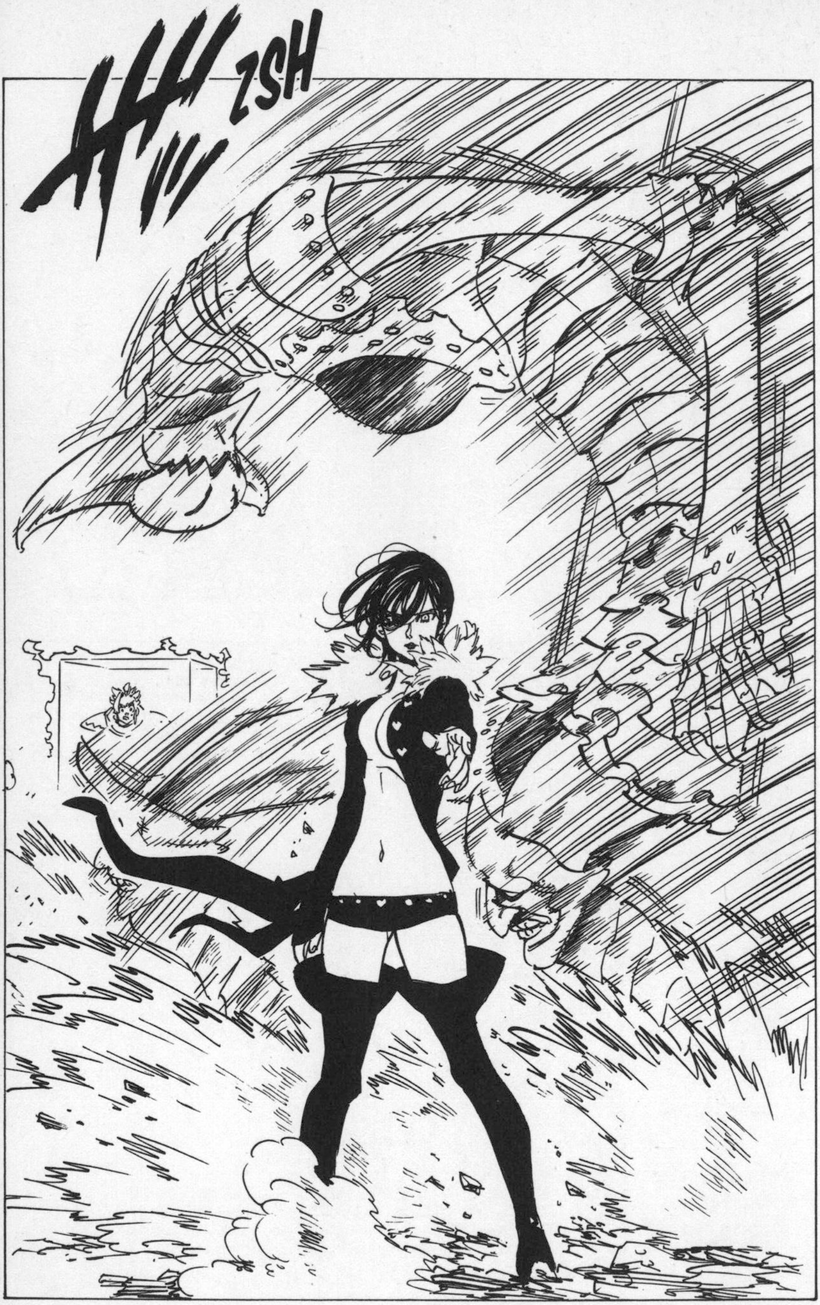
ZSH

GRAY DEMON

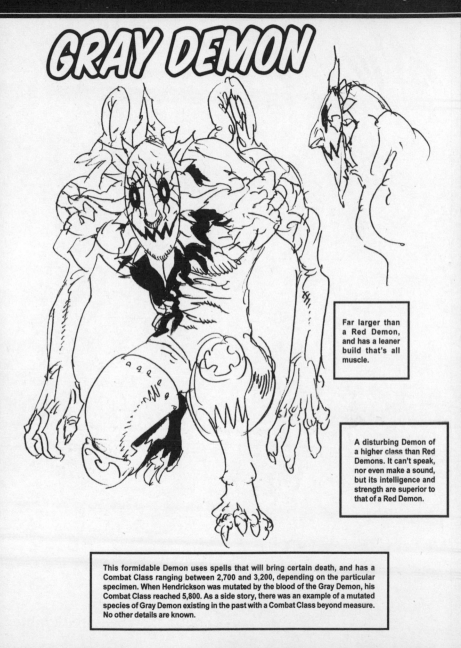

Far larger than a Red Demon, and has a leaner build that's all muscle.

A disturbing Demon of a higher class than Red Demons. It can't speak, nor even make a sound, but its intelligence and strength are superior to that of a Red Demon.

This formidable Demon uses spells that will bring certain death, and has a Combat Class ranging between 2,700 and 3,200, depending on the particular specimen. When Hendrickson was mutated by the blood of the Gray Demon, his Combat Class reached 5,800. As a side story, there was an example of a mutated species of Gray Demon existing in the past with a Combat Class beyond measure. No other details are known.

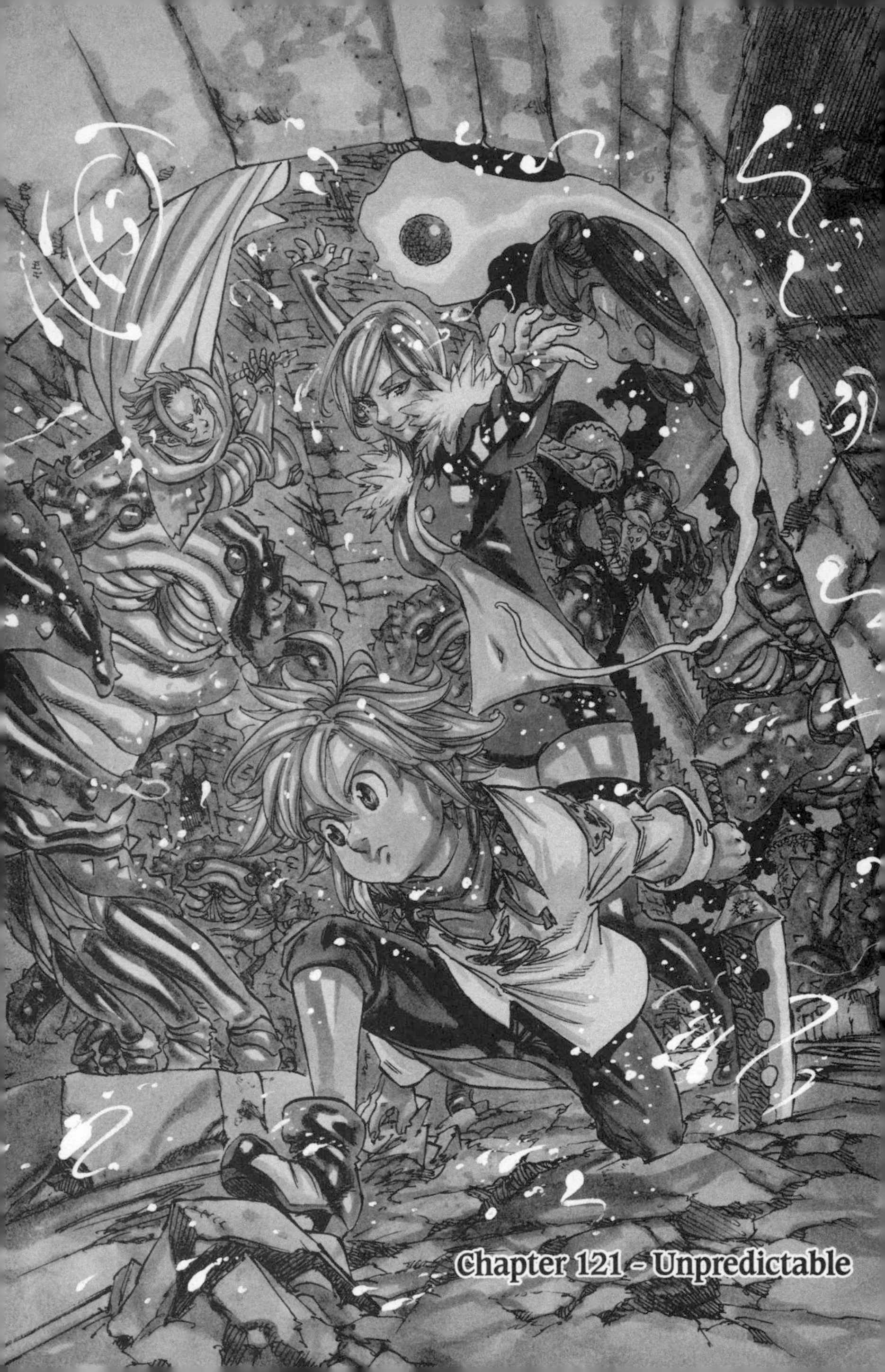
Chapter 121 - Unpredictable

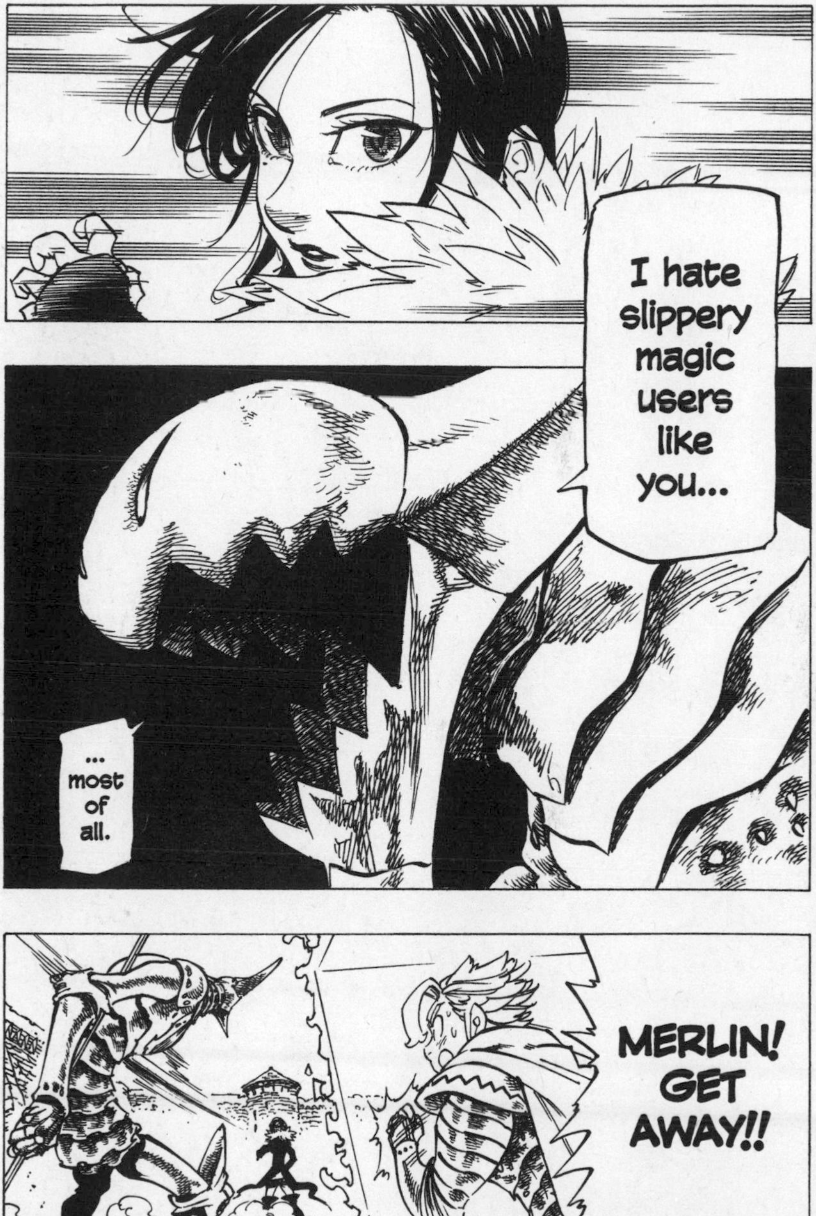
I hate slippery magic users like you...
... most of all.
MERLIN! GET AWAY!!

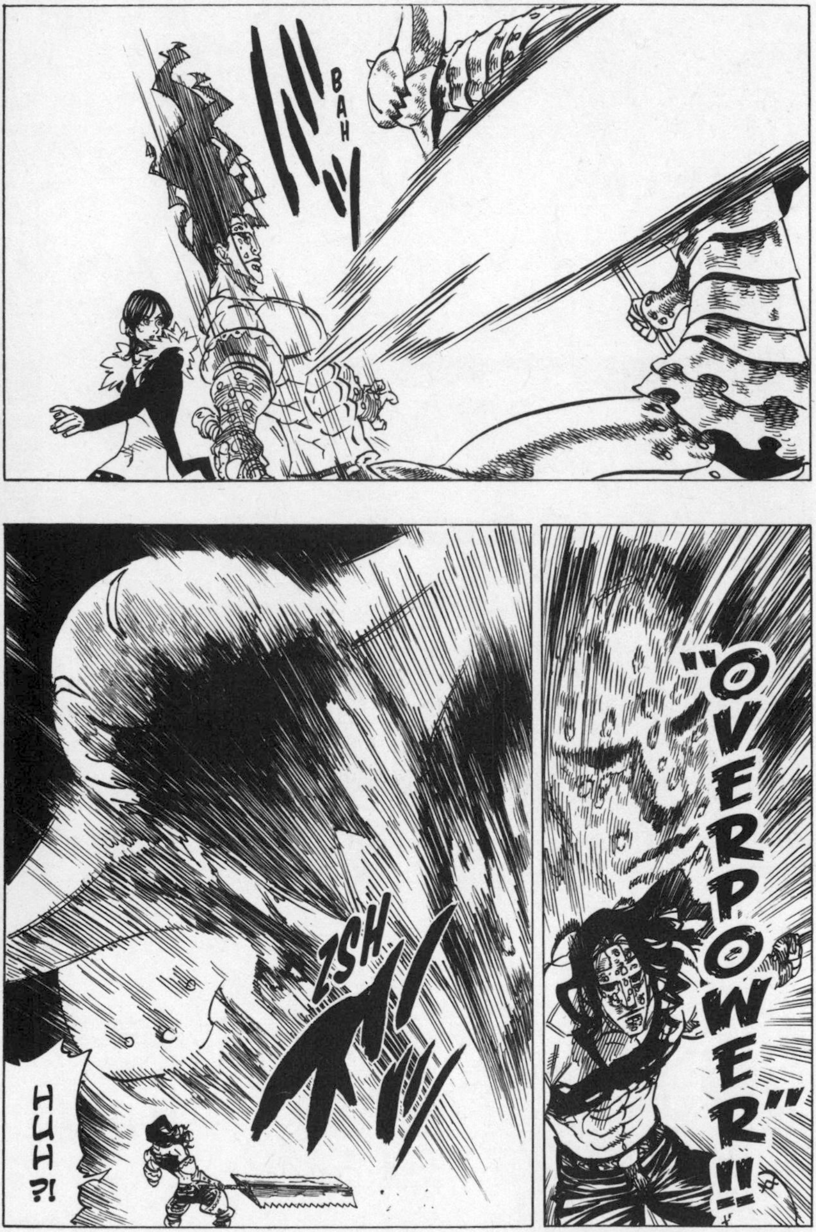
BAH
"OVERPOWER"!!
ZSH
HUH?!

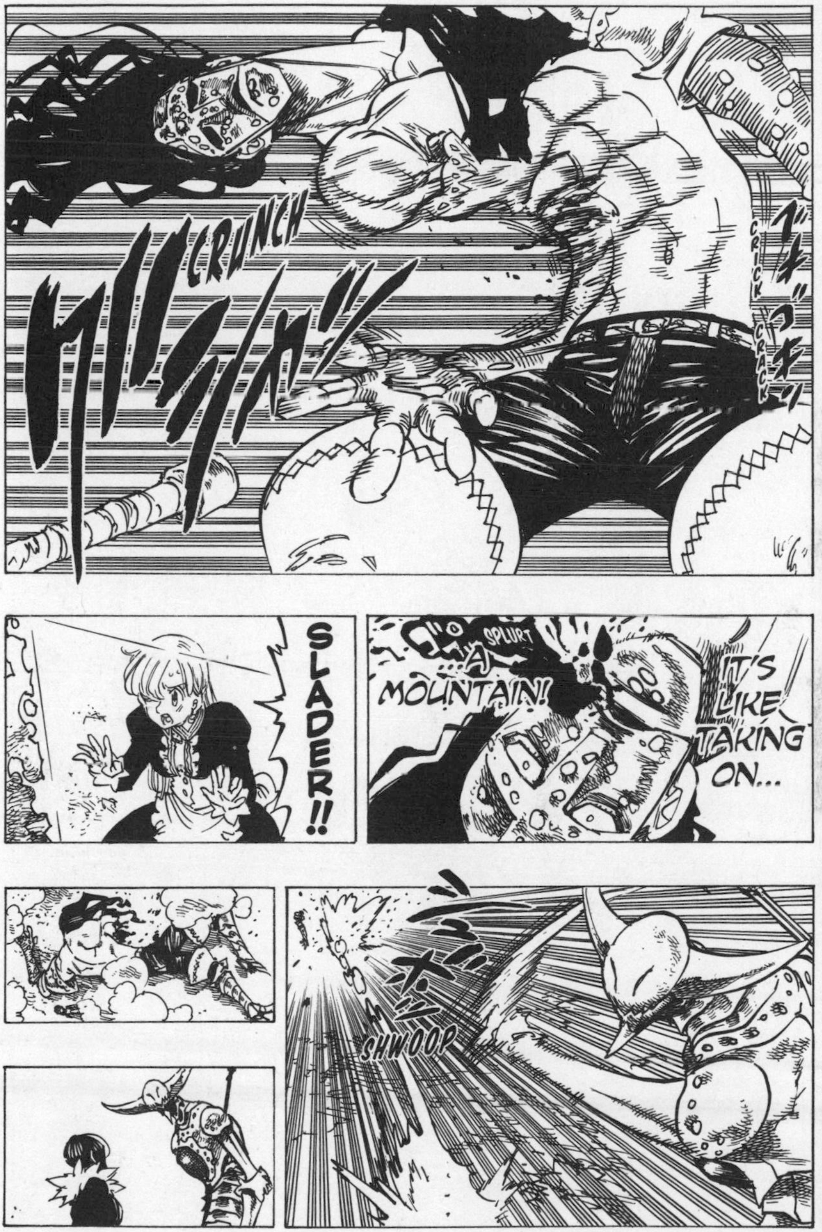
CRICK CRACK
CRUNCH
IT'S LIKE TAKING ON...
SPLURT
...A MOUNTAIN!
SLADER!!
SHWOOP

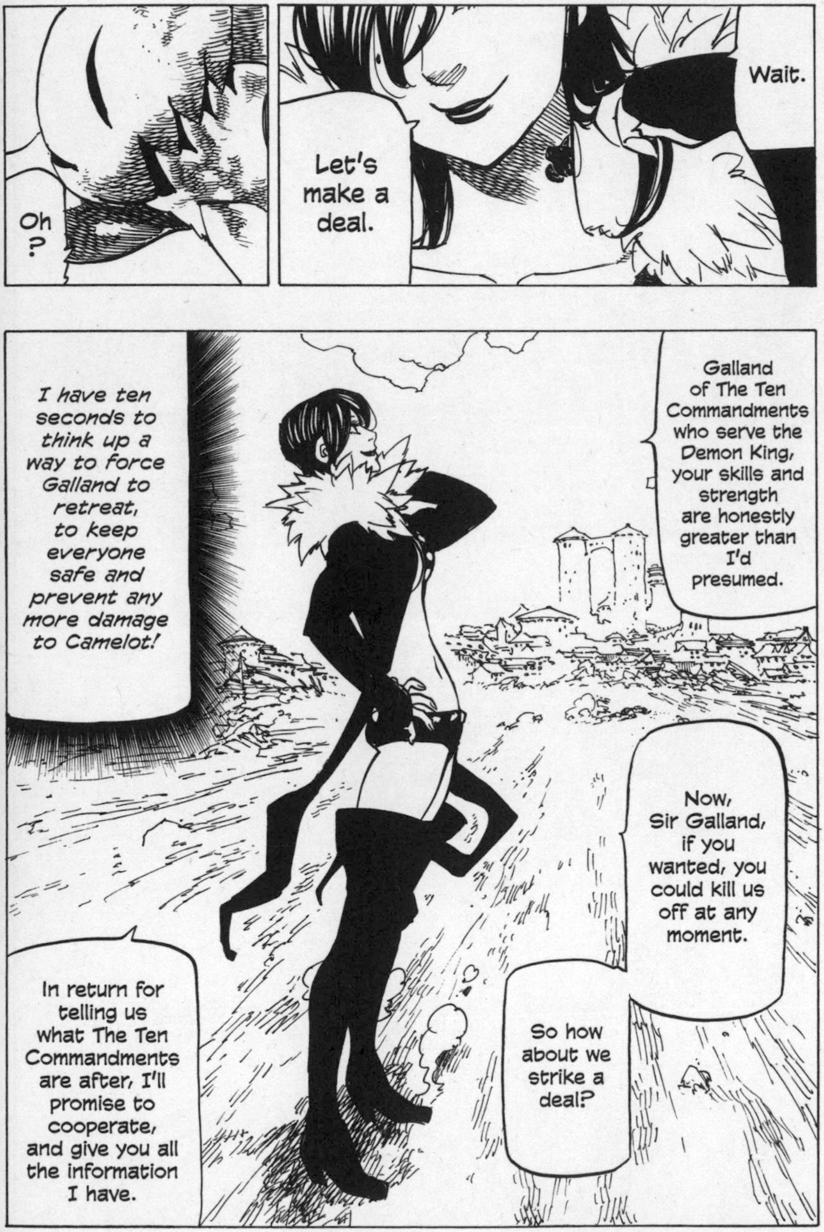
Wait.
Let's make a deal.
Oh?
Galland of The Ten Commandments who serve the Demon King, your skills and strength are honestly greater than I'd presumed.
I have ten seconds to think up a way to force Galland to retreat, to keep everyone safe and prevent any more damage to Camelot!
Now, Sir Galland, if you wanted, you could kill us off at any moment.
So how about we strike a deal?
In return for telling us what The Ten Commandments are after, I'll promise to cooperate, and give you all the information I have.

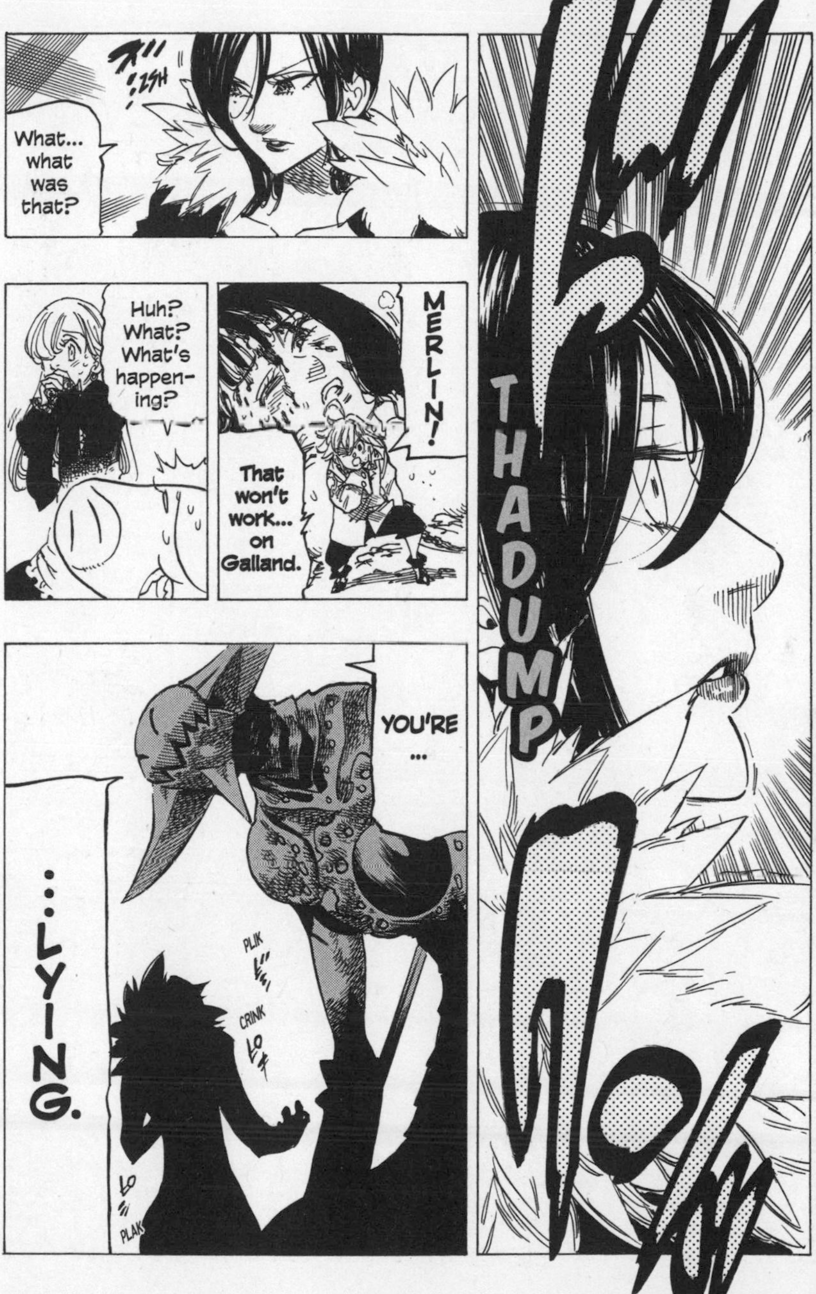
THADUMP
ZSH
What... what was that?
MERLIN!
That won't work... on Galland.
Huh? What? What's happening?
YOU'RE ...
...LYING.
PLIK
CRINK
PLAK

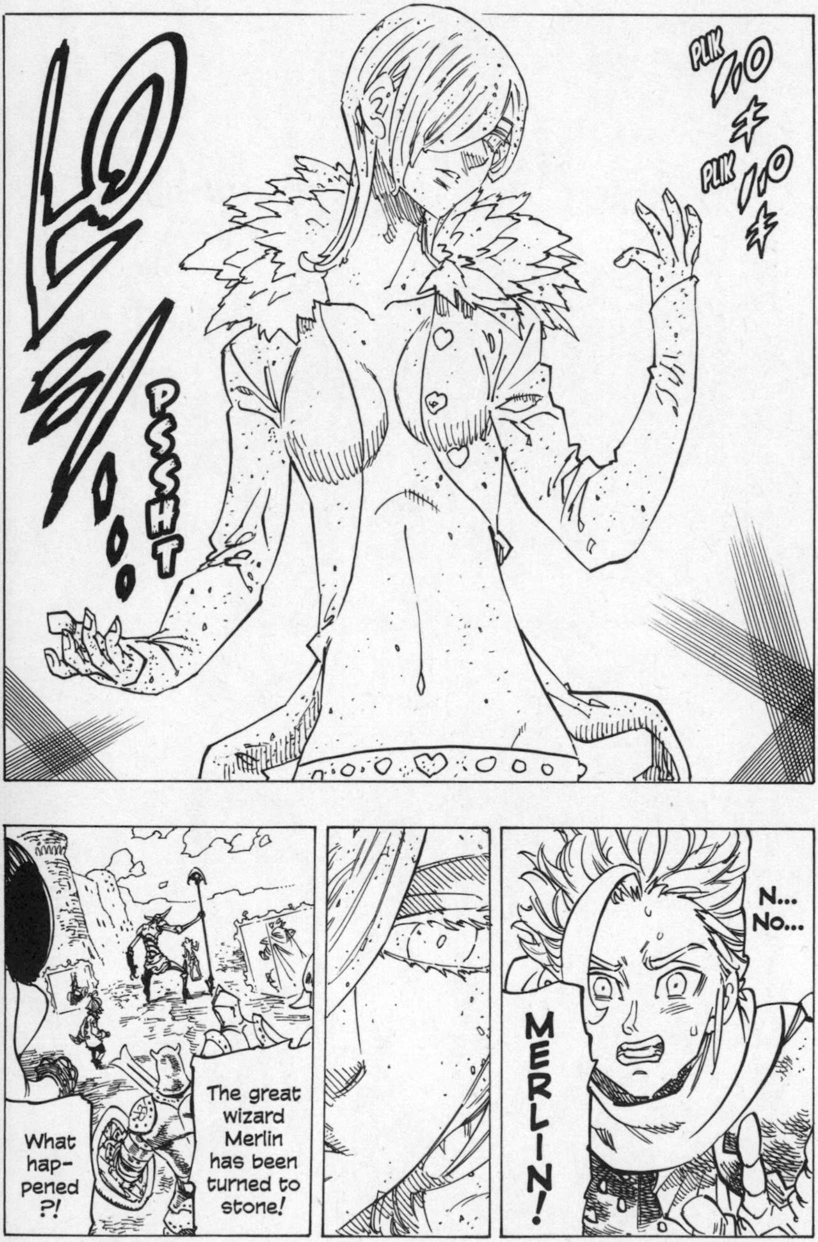
PLIK
PLIK
PSSHT
N... No...
MERLIN!
The great wizard Merlin has been turned to stone!
What hap-pened ?!

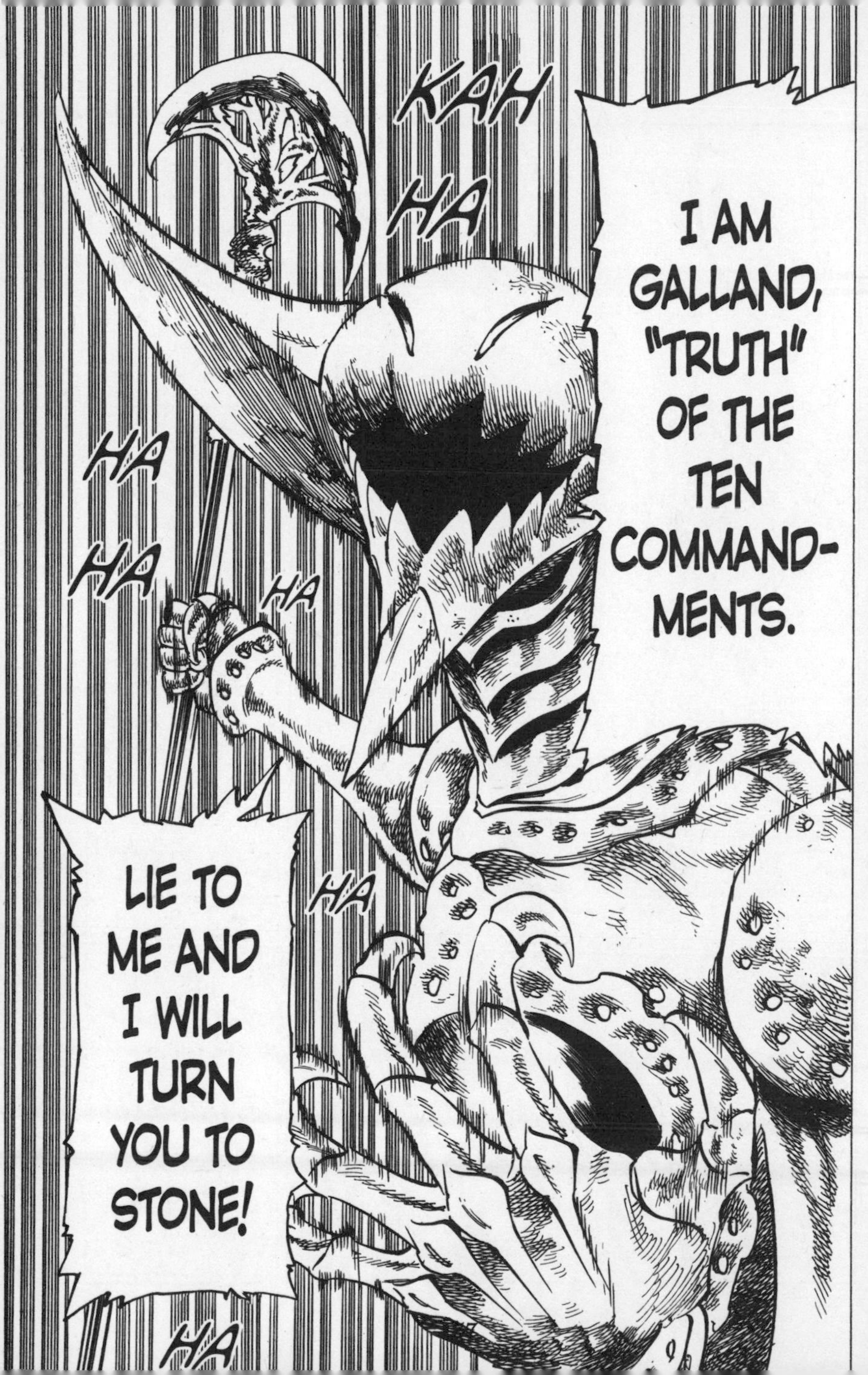
I AM GALLAND, "TRUTH" OF THE TEN COMMANDMENTS.
KAH HA
HA HA
HA
HA
LIE TO ME AND I WILL TURN YOU TO STONE!
HA

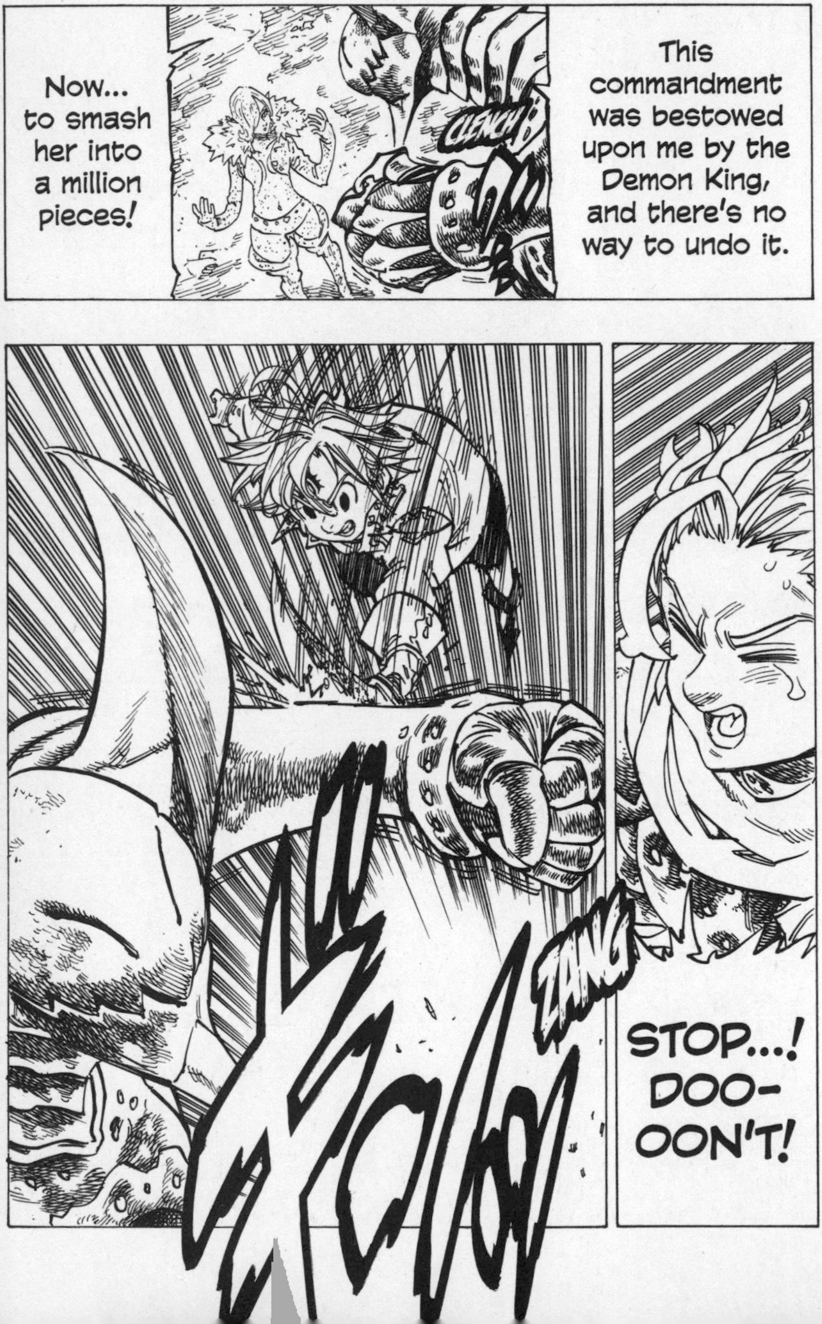
This commandment was bestowed upon me by the Demon King, and there's no way to undo it.
CLENCH
Now... to smash her into a million pieces!
STOP...! DOO-OON'T!
TANG

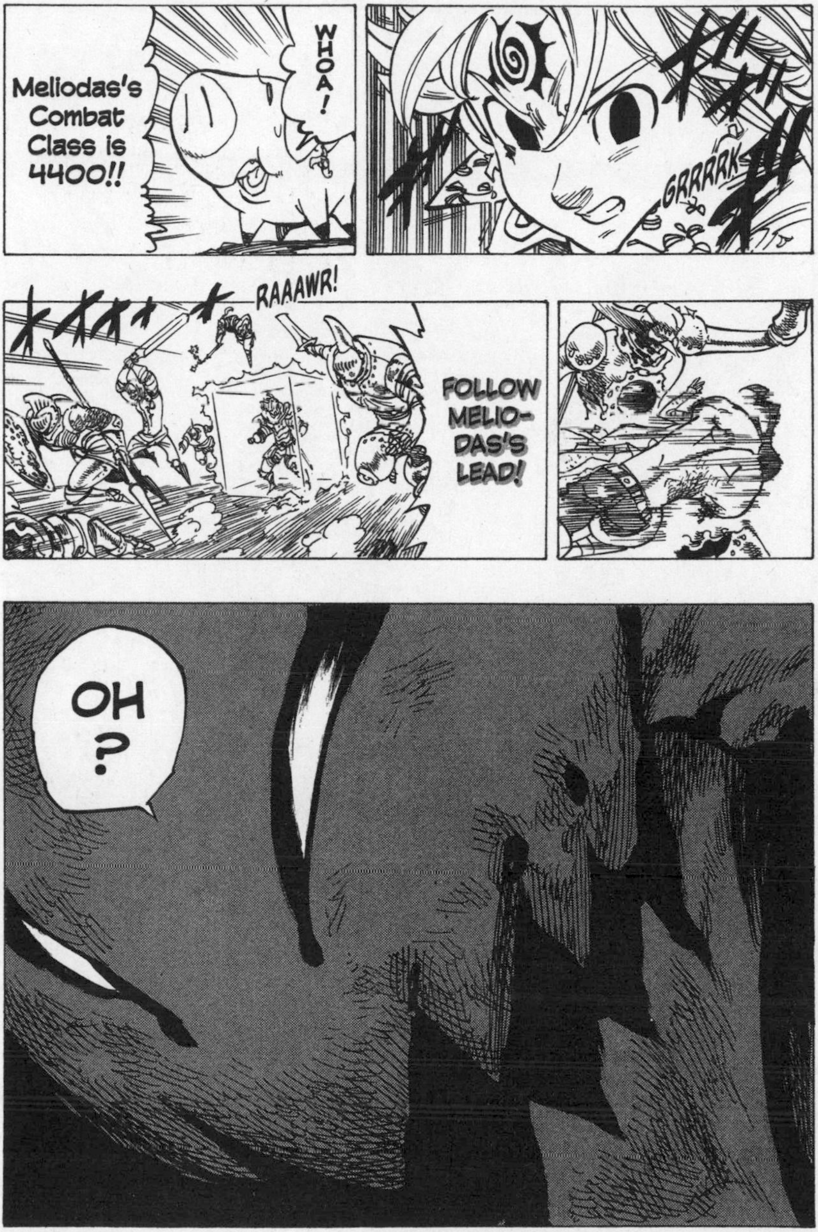
GRRRRK
WHOA!
Meliodas's Combat Class is 4400!!
RAAAWR!
FOLLOW MELIODAS'S LEAD!
OH?

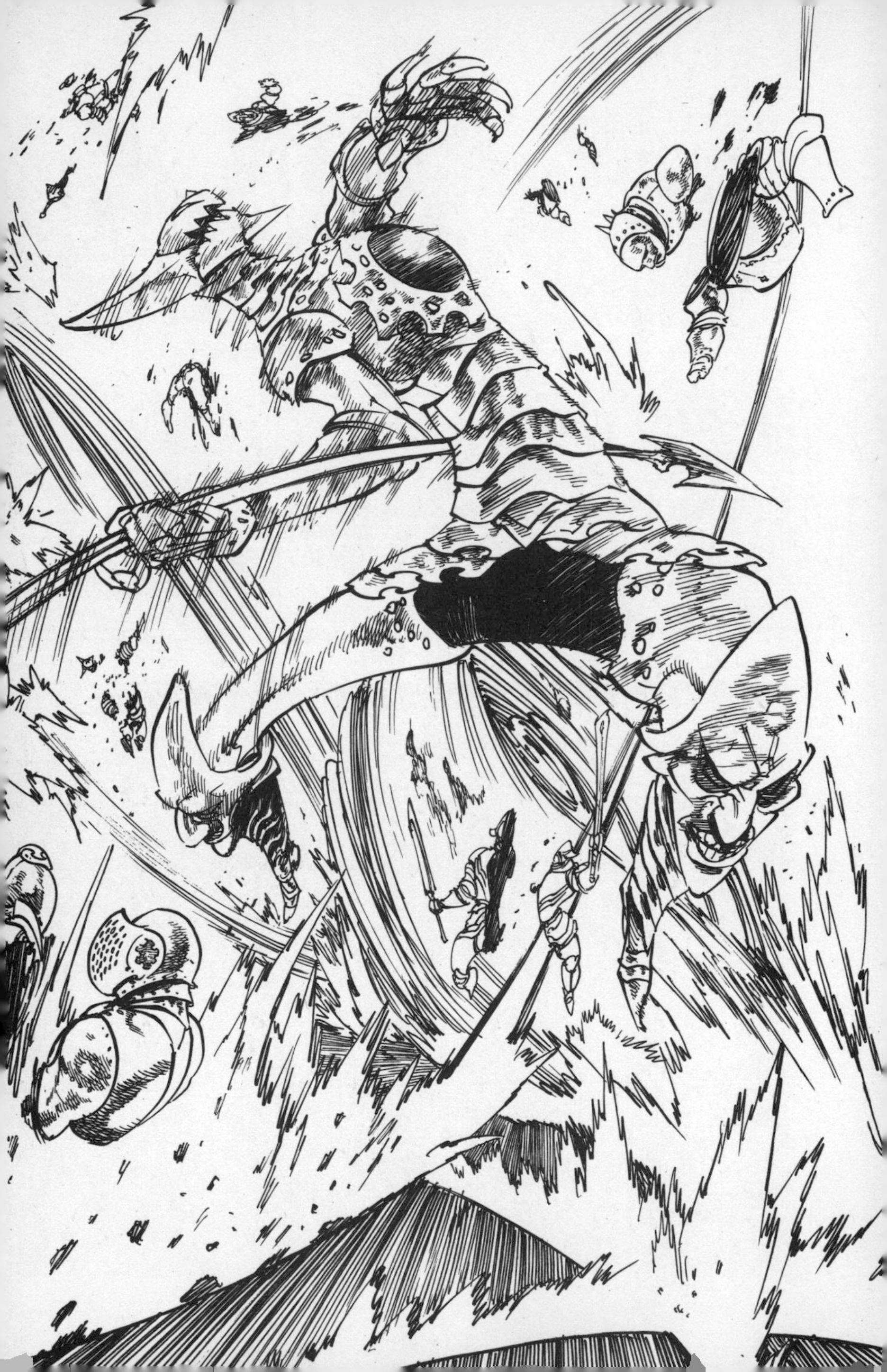

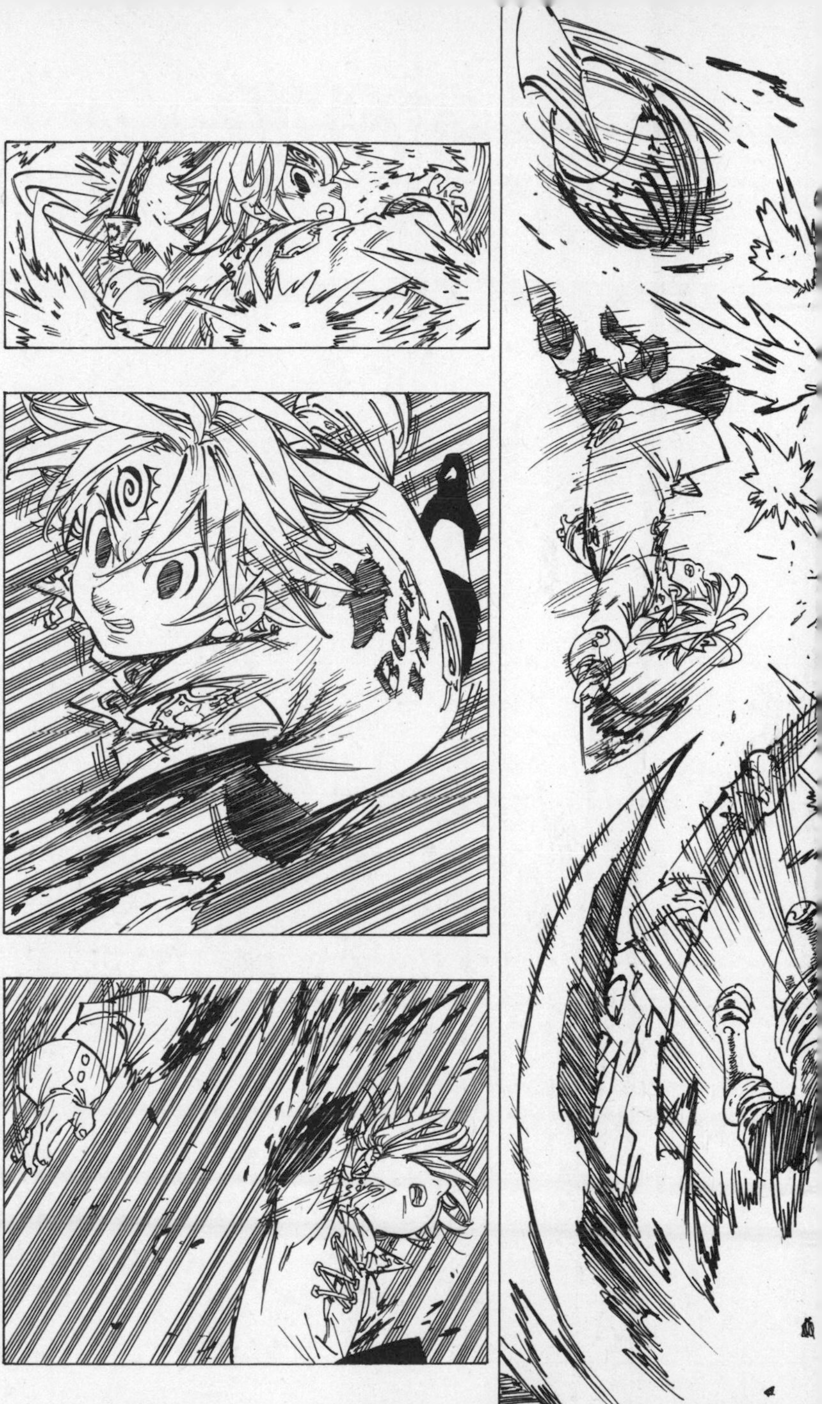

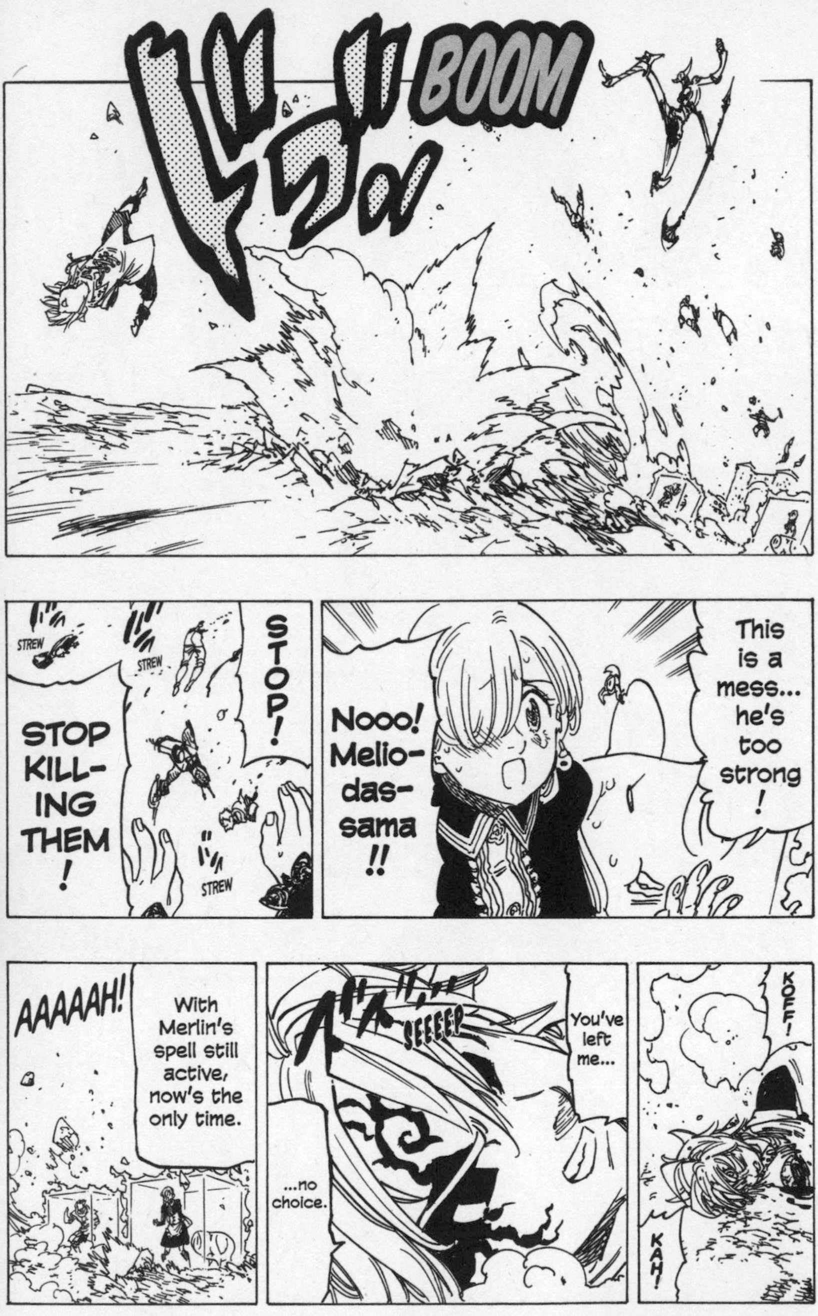
BOOM
This is a mess... he's too strong!
Nooo! Melio-das-sama!!
STOP!
STOP KILL-ING THEM!
STREW
STREW
STREW
KOFF!
KAH!
You've left me...
...no choice.
SEEEEP
AAAAAH!
With Merlin's spell still active, now's the only time.

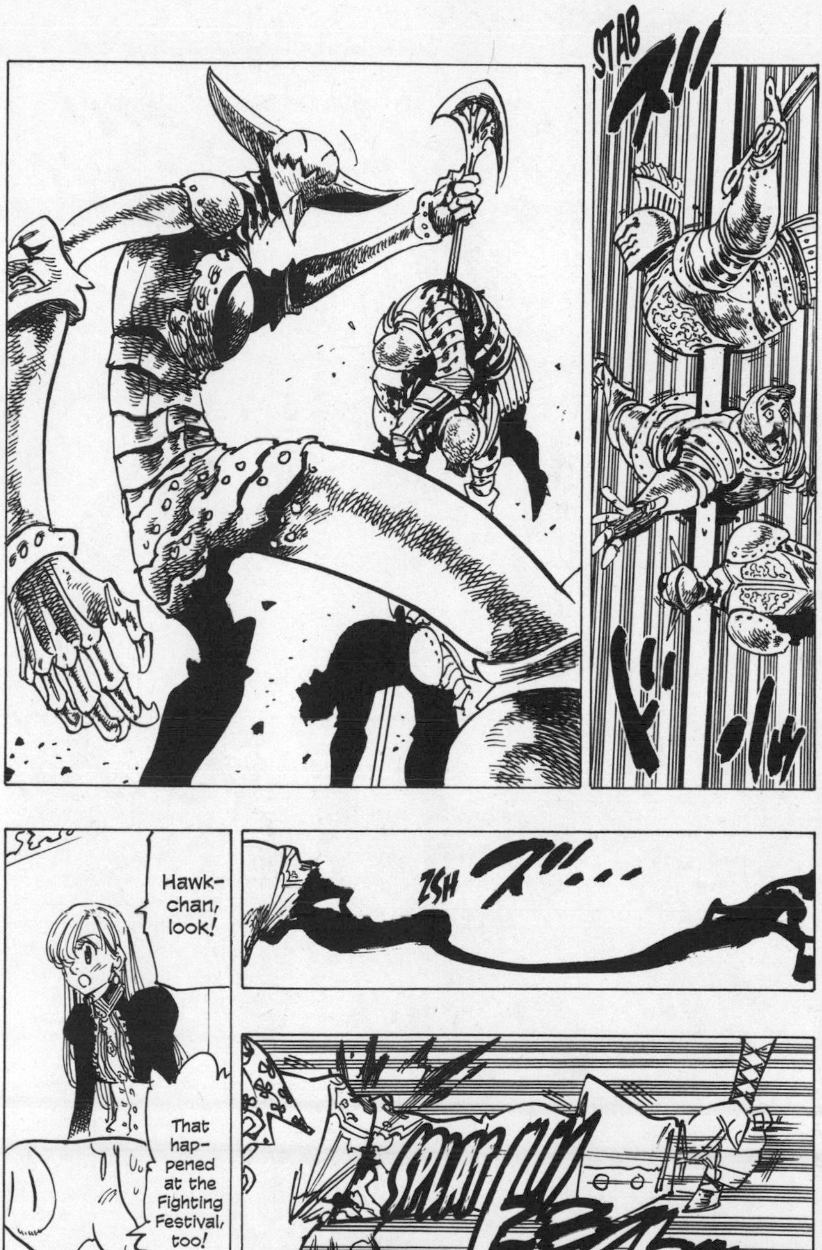
STAB
ZSH
SPLAT
Hawk-chan, look!
That happened at the Fighting Festival, too!

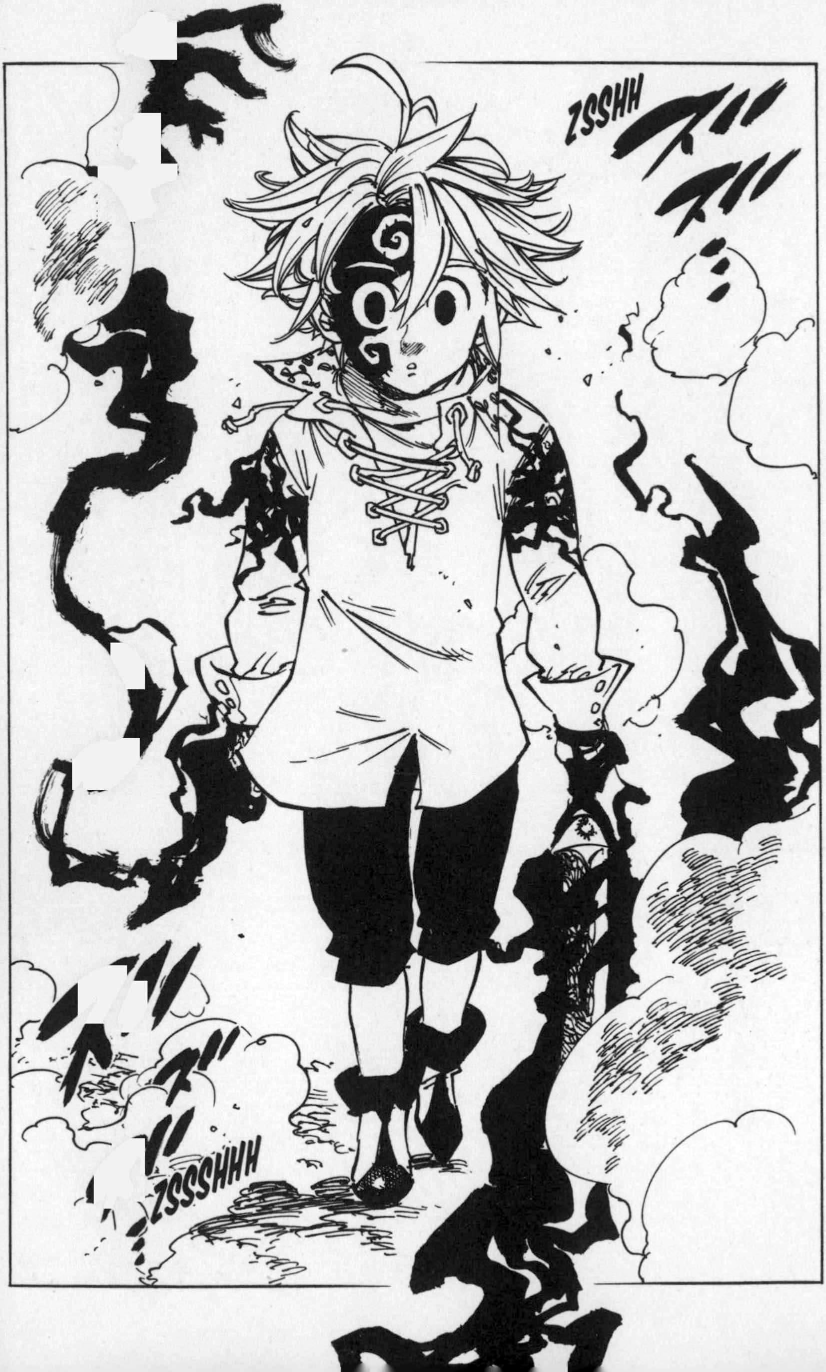
ZSSHH
ZSSSHHH

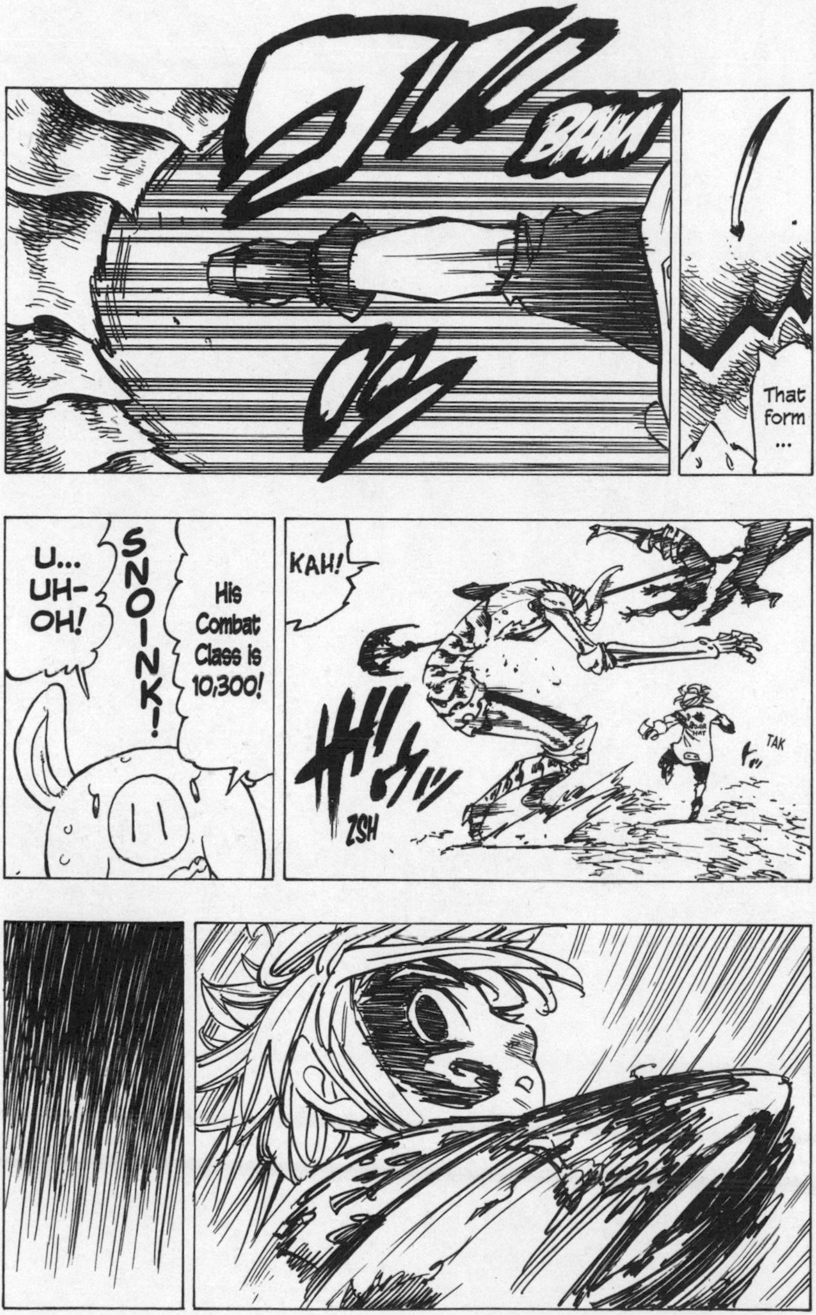
That form ...
BAM
KAH!
TAK
ZSH
His Combat Class is 10,300!
SNOINK!
U... UH-OH!

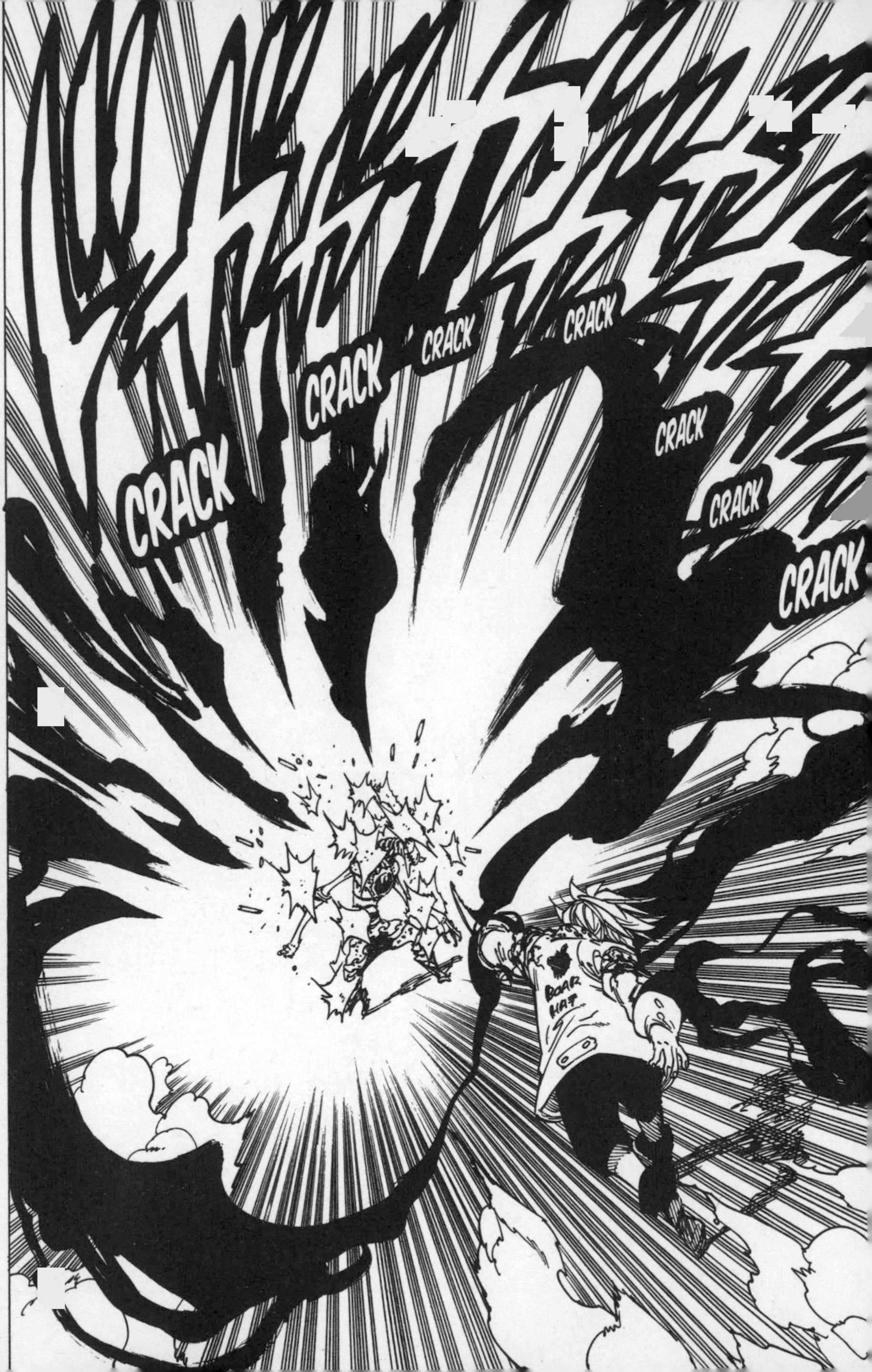
CRACK
CRACK
CRACK
CRACK
CRACK
CRACK
CRACK
CRACK
BOAR HAT

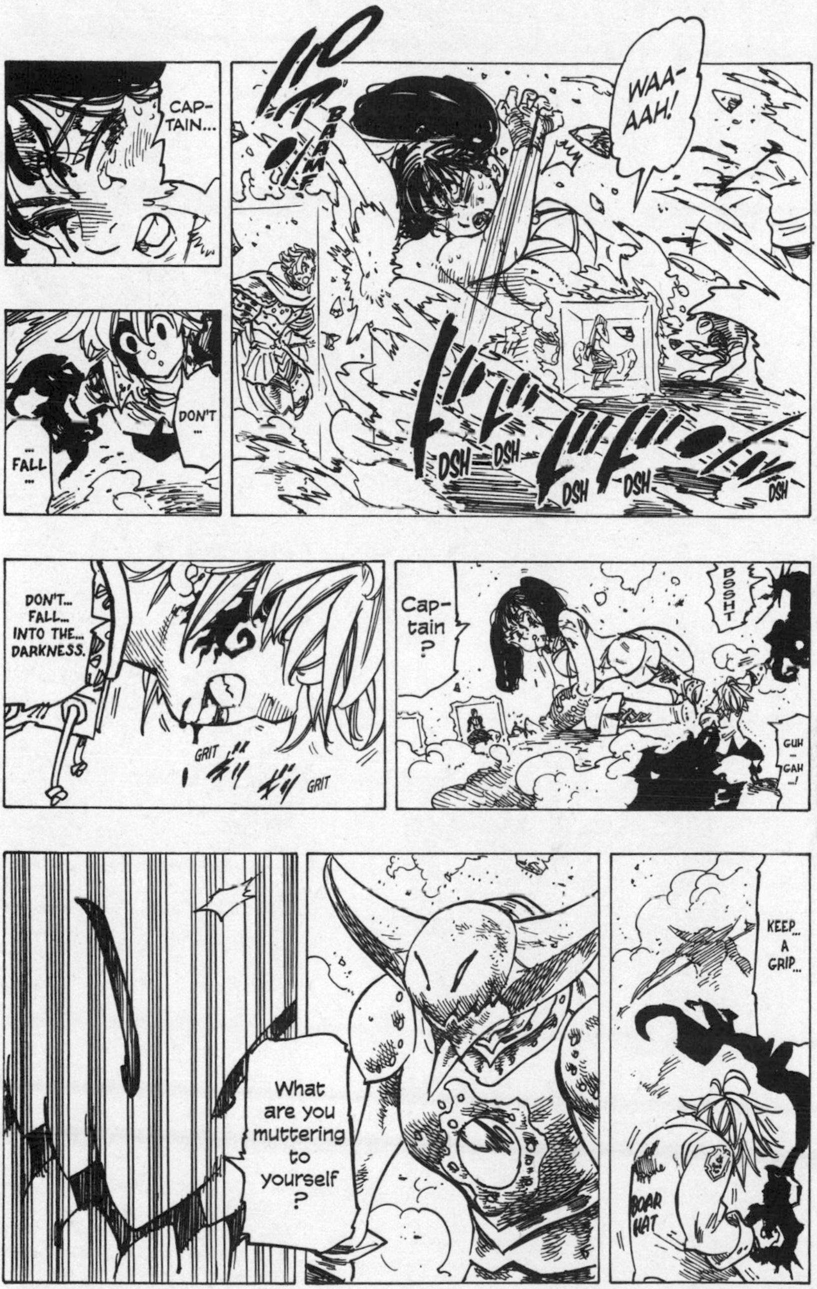
WAA-AAH!
BAAMF
DSH
DSH
DSH
DSH
DSH
CAP-TAIN...
DON'T ...
... FALL ...
Cap-tain?
BSSHT
GUH-GAH...!
DON'T... FALL... INTO THE... DARKNESS.
GRIT
GRIT
KEEP... A GRIP...
BOAR HAT
What are you muttering to yourself?

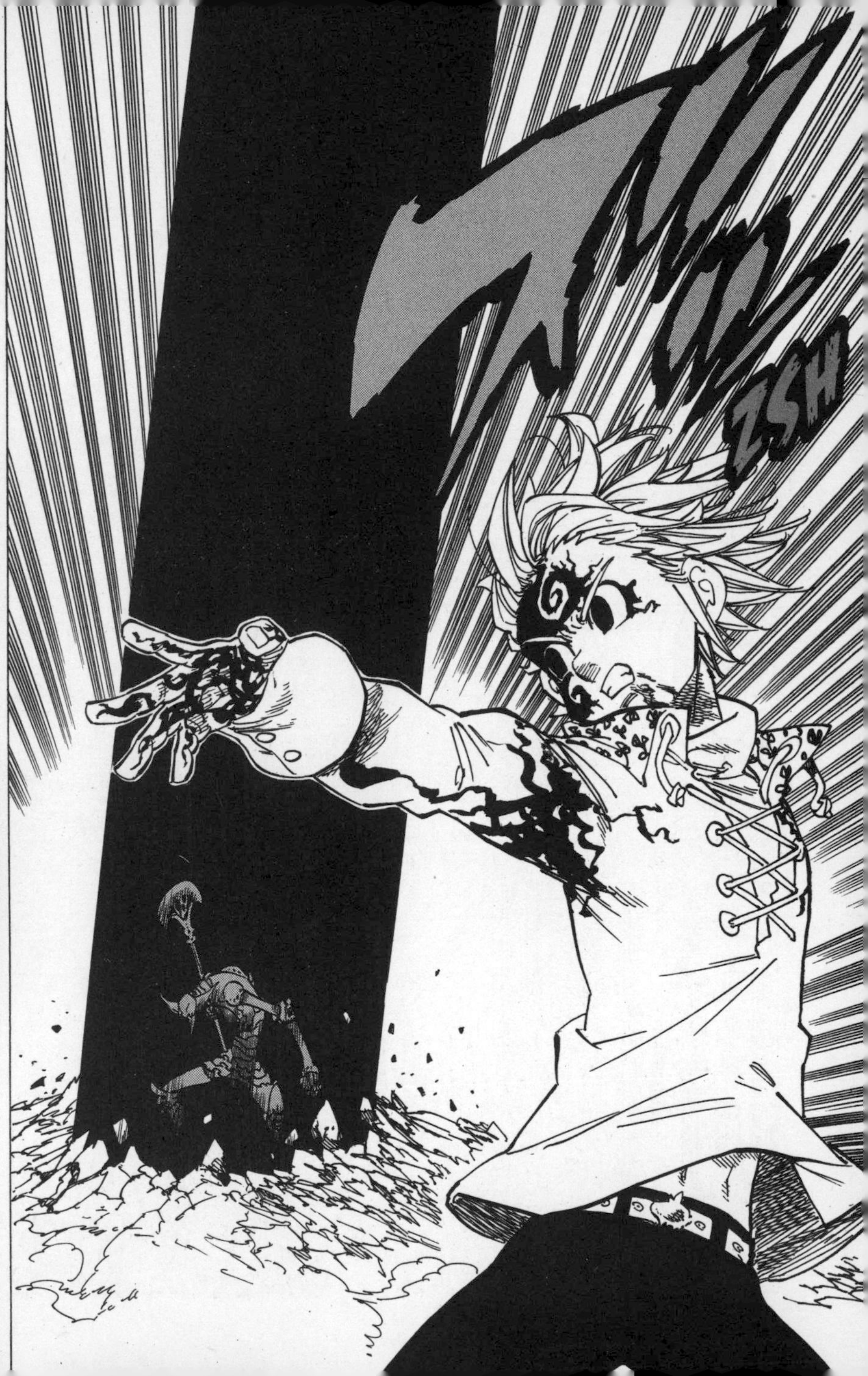
ZSH

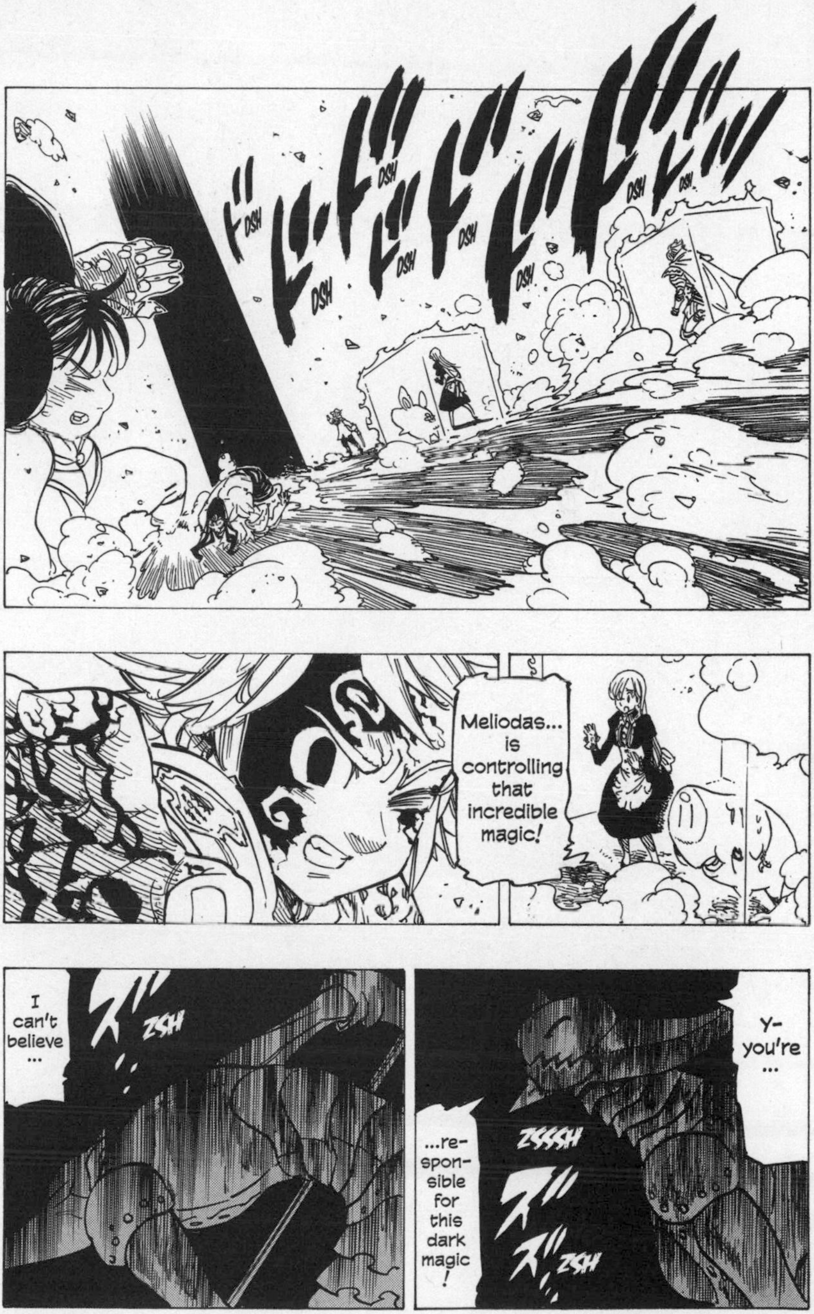
DSH DSH DSH DSH DSH DSH DSH DSH
Meliodas... is controlling that incredible magic!
Y-you're ...
ZSSSH
ZSH
...responsible for this dark magic!
I can't believe ...
ZSH

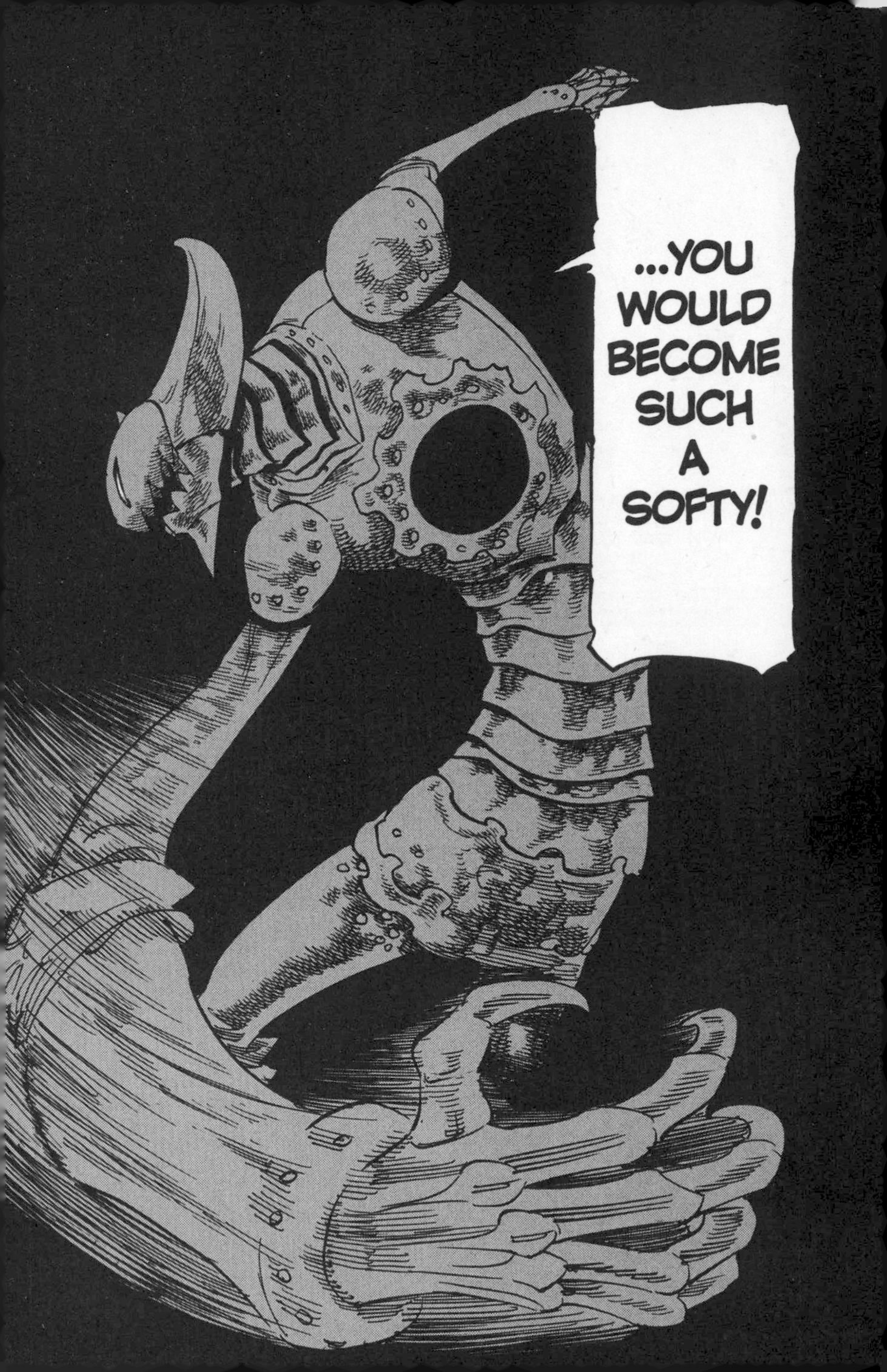
...YOU WOULD BECOME SUCH A SOFTY!

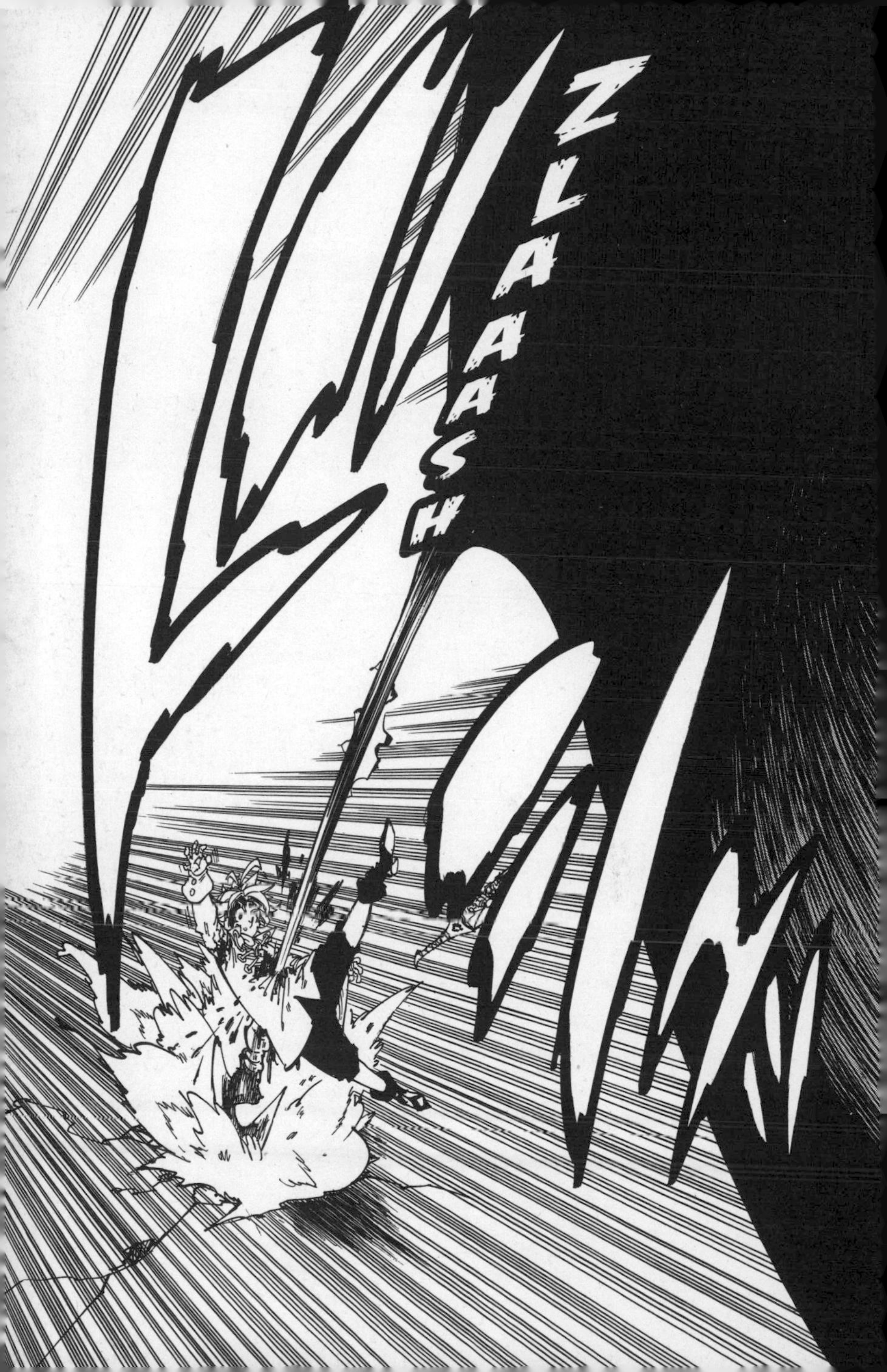
ZLAAAASH

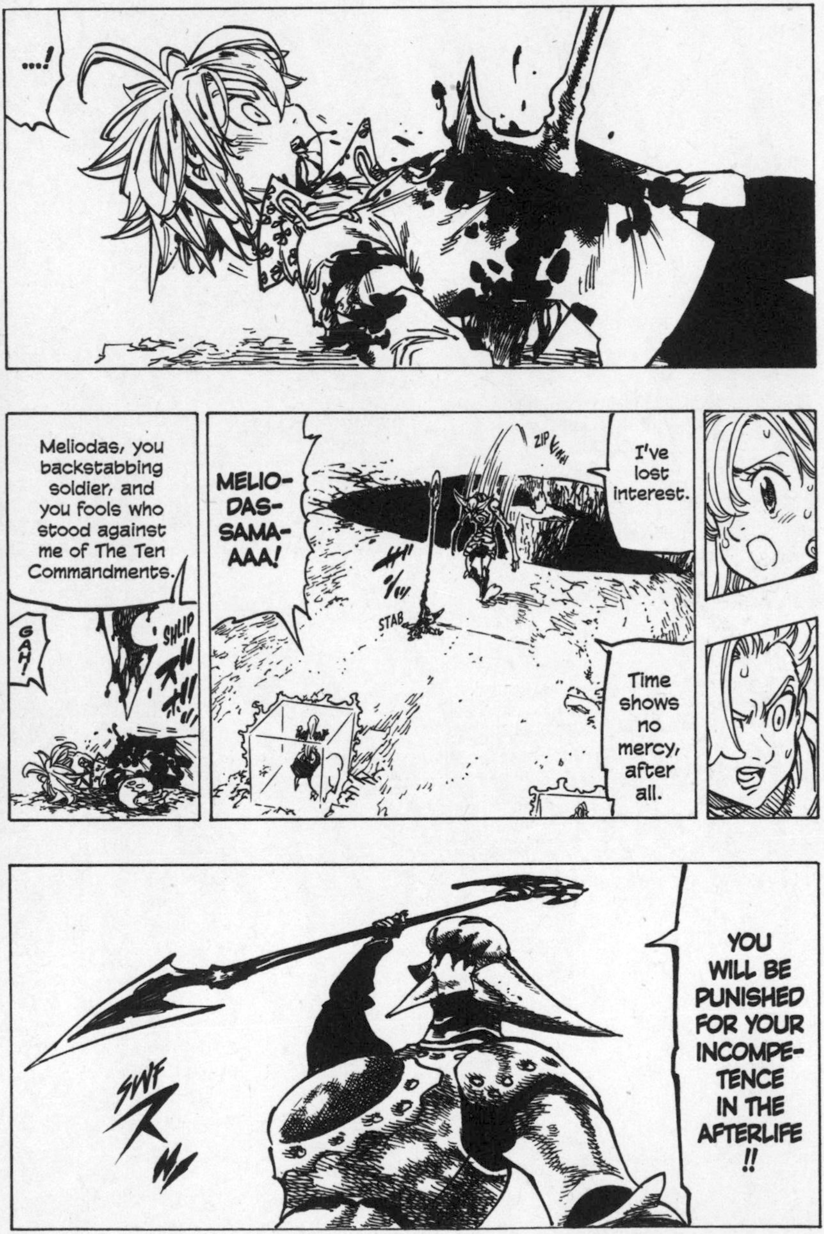
...!
I've lost interest.
Time shows no mercy, after all.
ZIP
MELIO-DAS-SAMA-AAA!
STAB
Meliodas, you backstabbing soldier, and you fools who stood against me of The Ten Commandments.
SHLIP
GAH!
YOU WILL BE PUNISHED FOR YOUR INCOMPETENCE IN THE AFTERLIFE!!
SWF

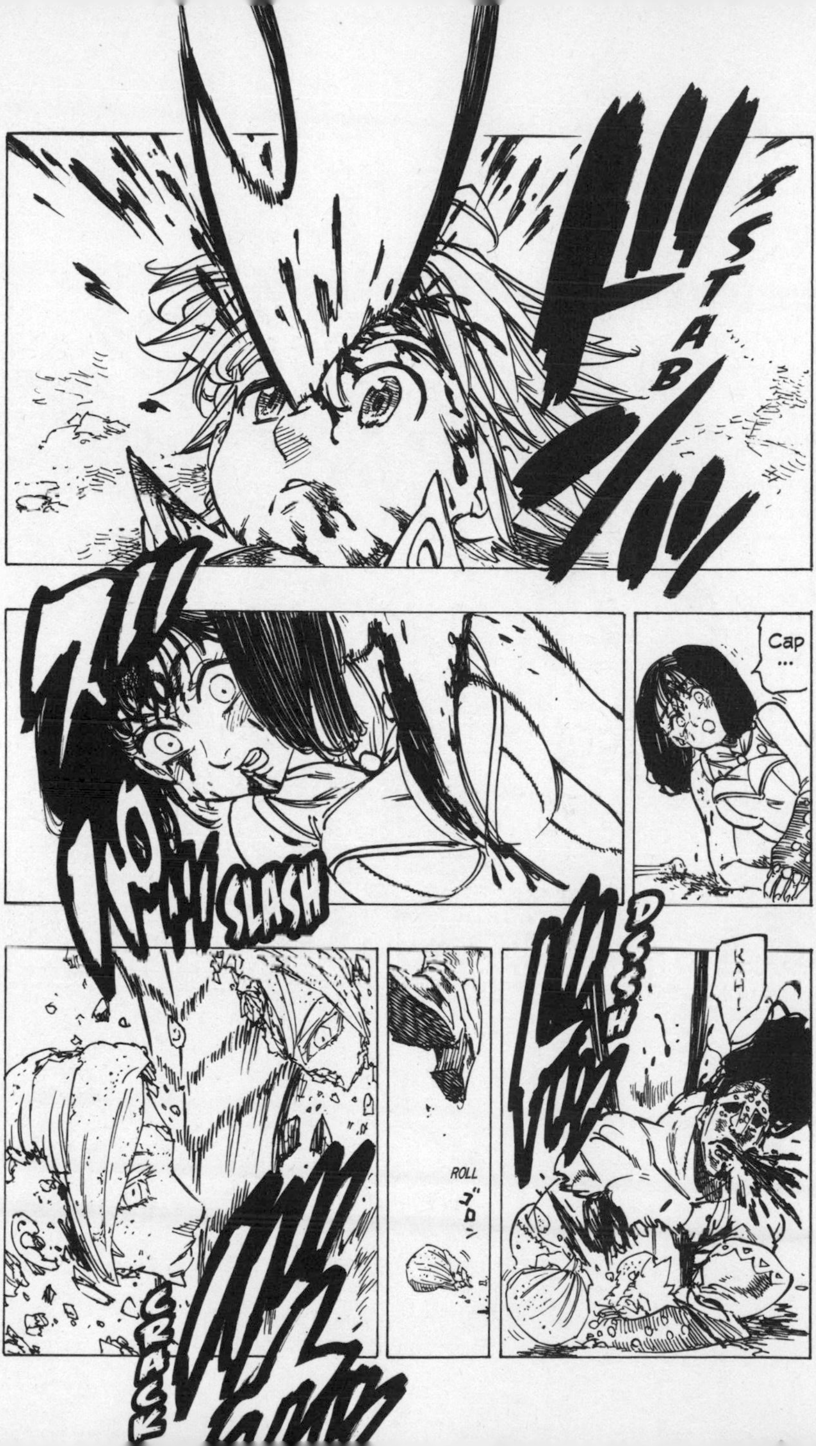
STAB
Cap ...
SLASH
DSSH
KAH!
ROLL
ゴロン
CRACK

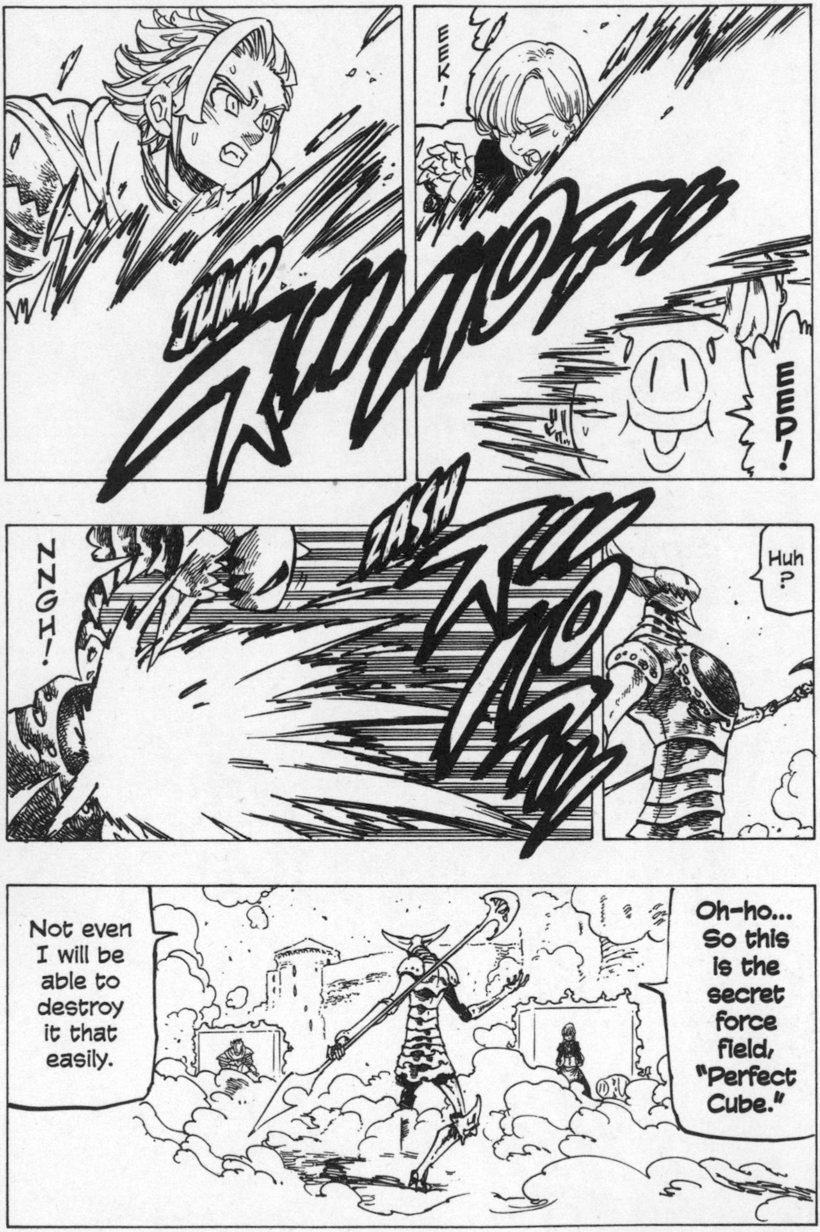
EEK!
EEP!
JUMP
Huh?
ZASH
NNGH!
Oh-ho... So this is the secret force field, "Perfect Cube."
Not even I will be able to destroy it that easily.

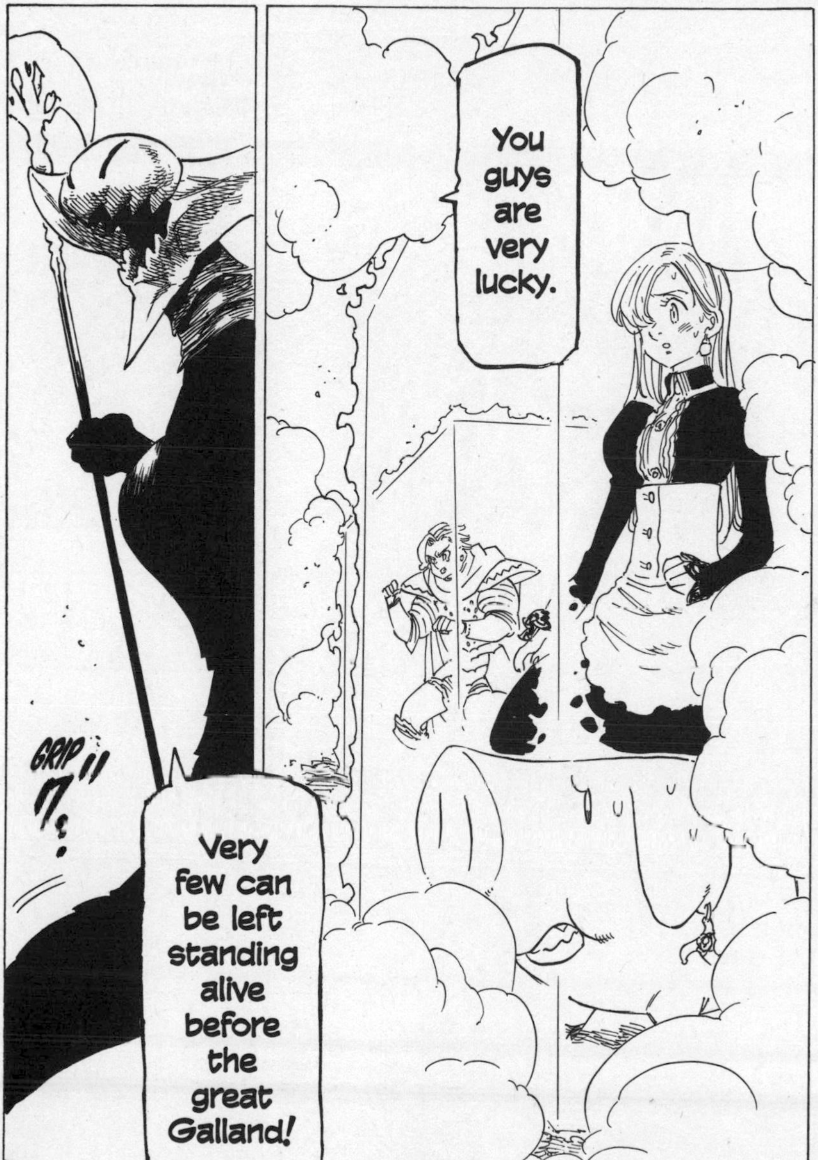
You guys are very lucky.
GRIP
Very few can be left standing alive before the great Galland!

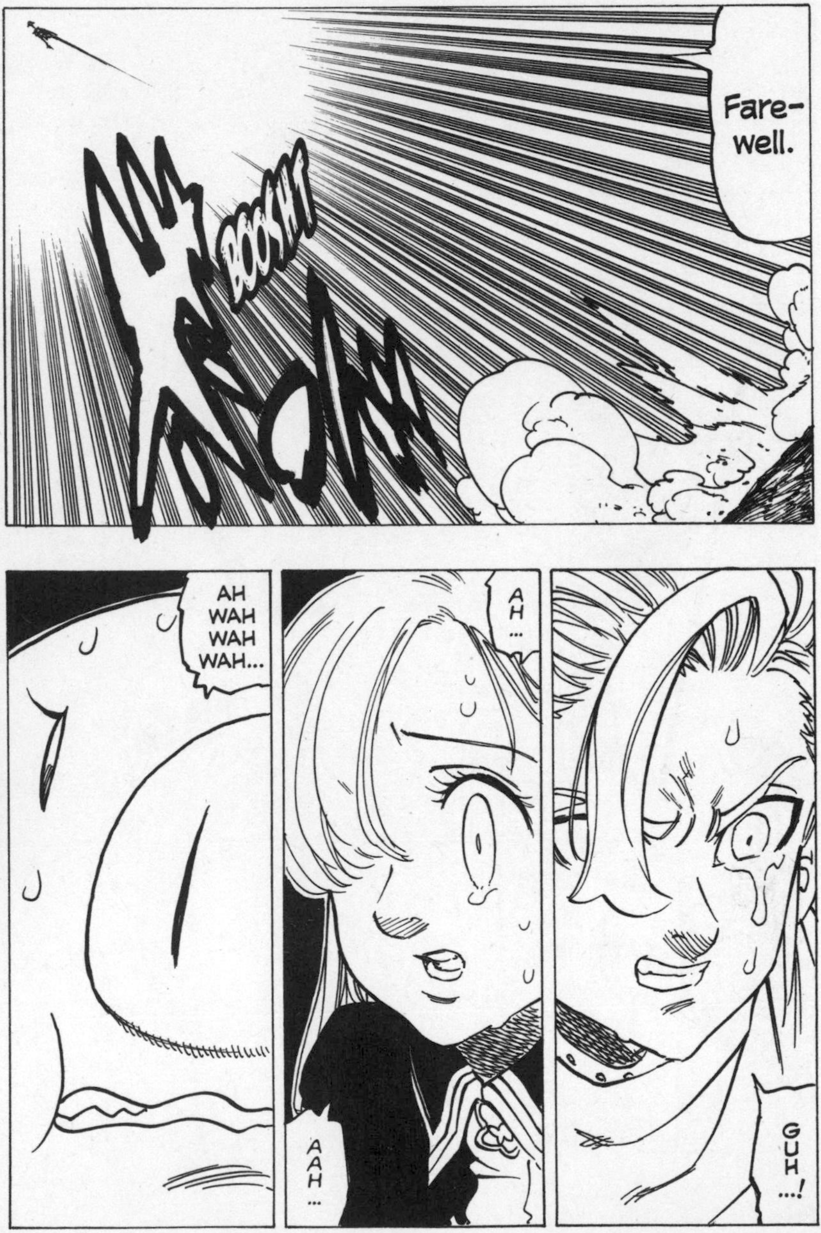
Fare-well.
BOOSH
GUH...!
AH...
AAH...
AH WAH WAH WAH...

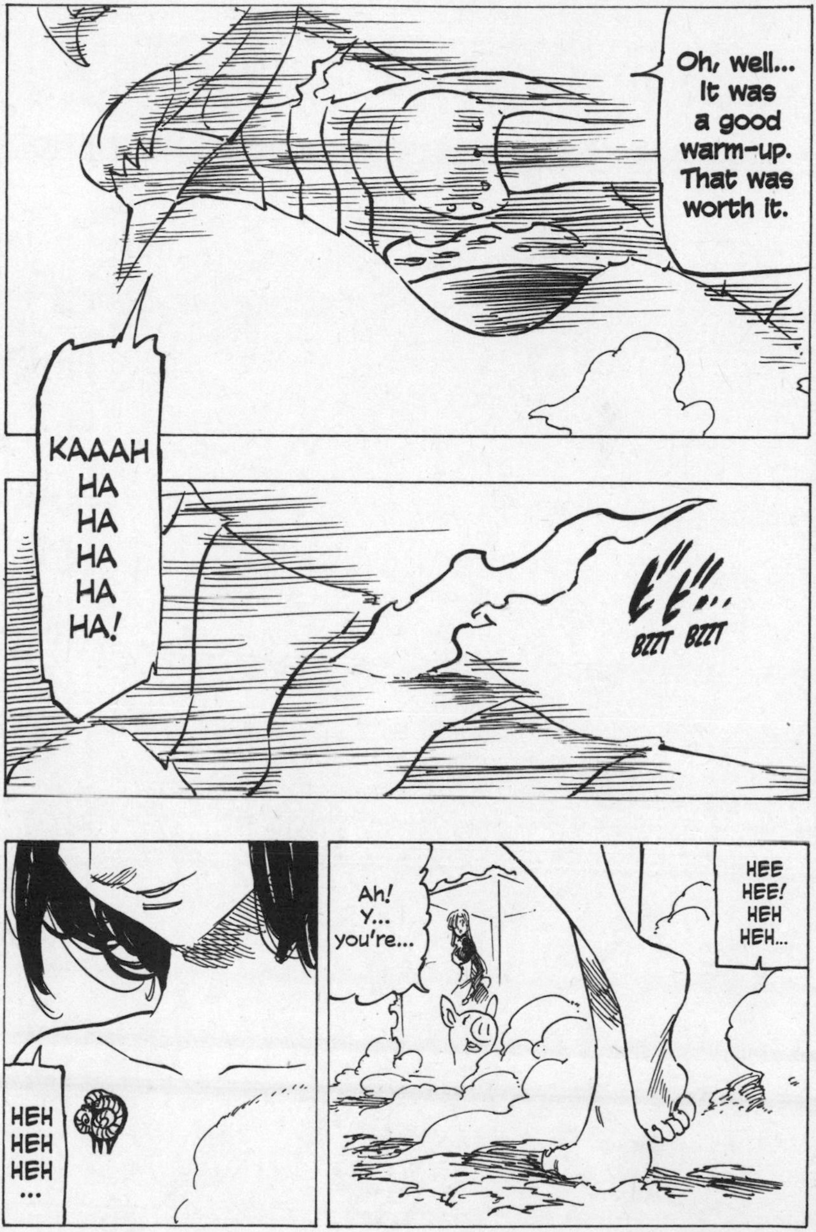
Oh, well... It was a good warm-up. That was worth it.
KAAAH HA HA HA HA HA!
BZZT BZZT
HEE HEE! HEH HEH...
Ah! Y... you're...
HEH HEH HEH ...

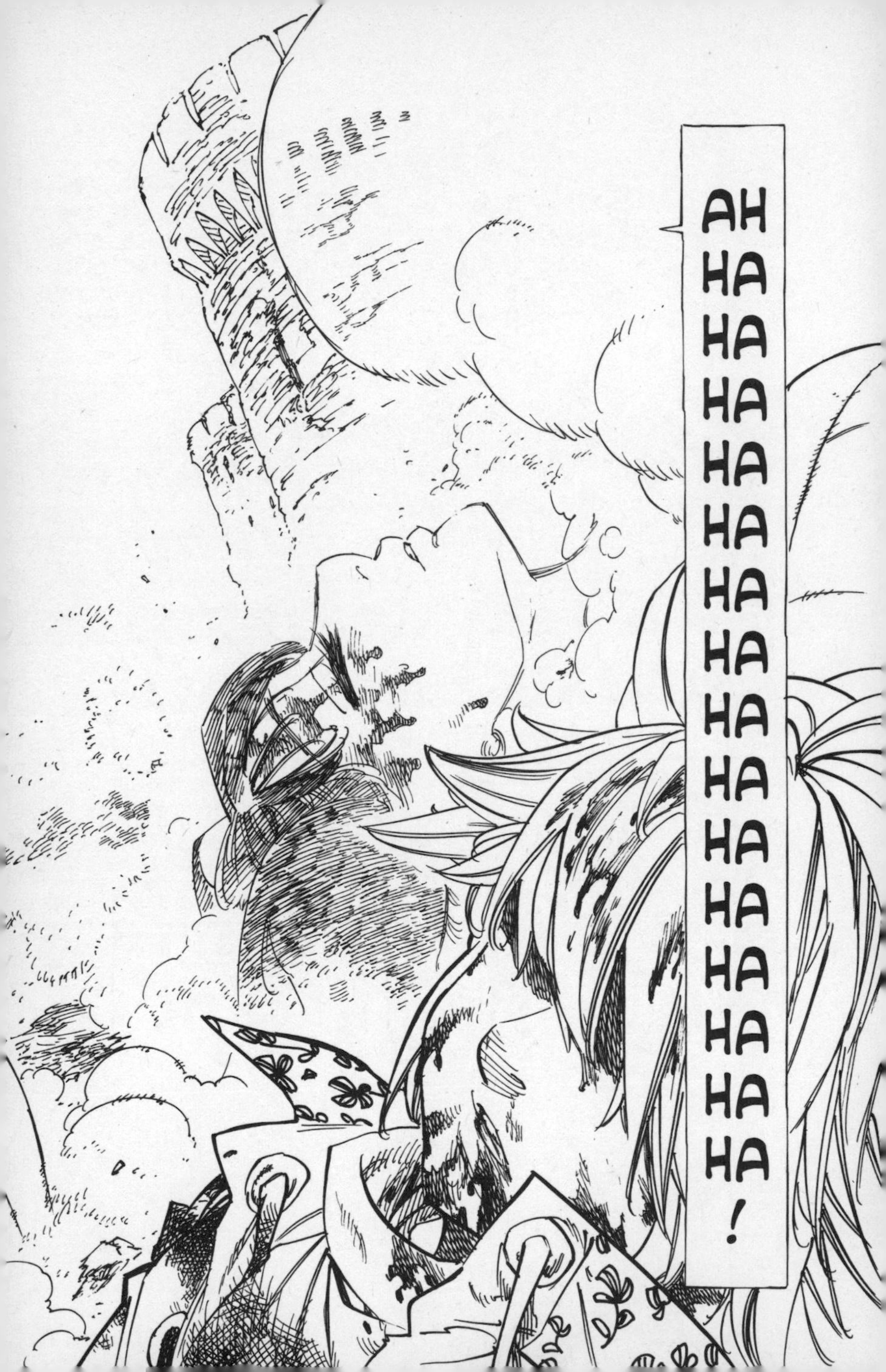
AH HA HA HA HA HA HA HA HA HA HA HA HA HA HA HA!

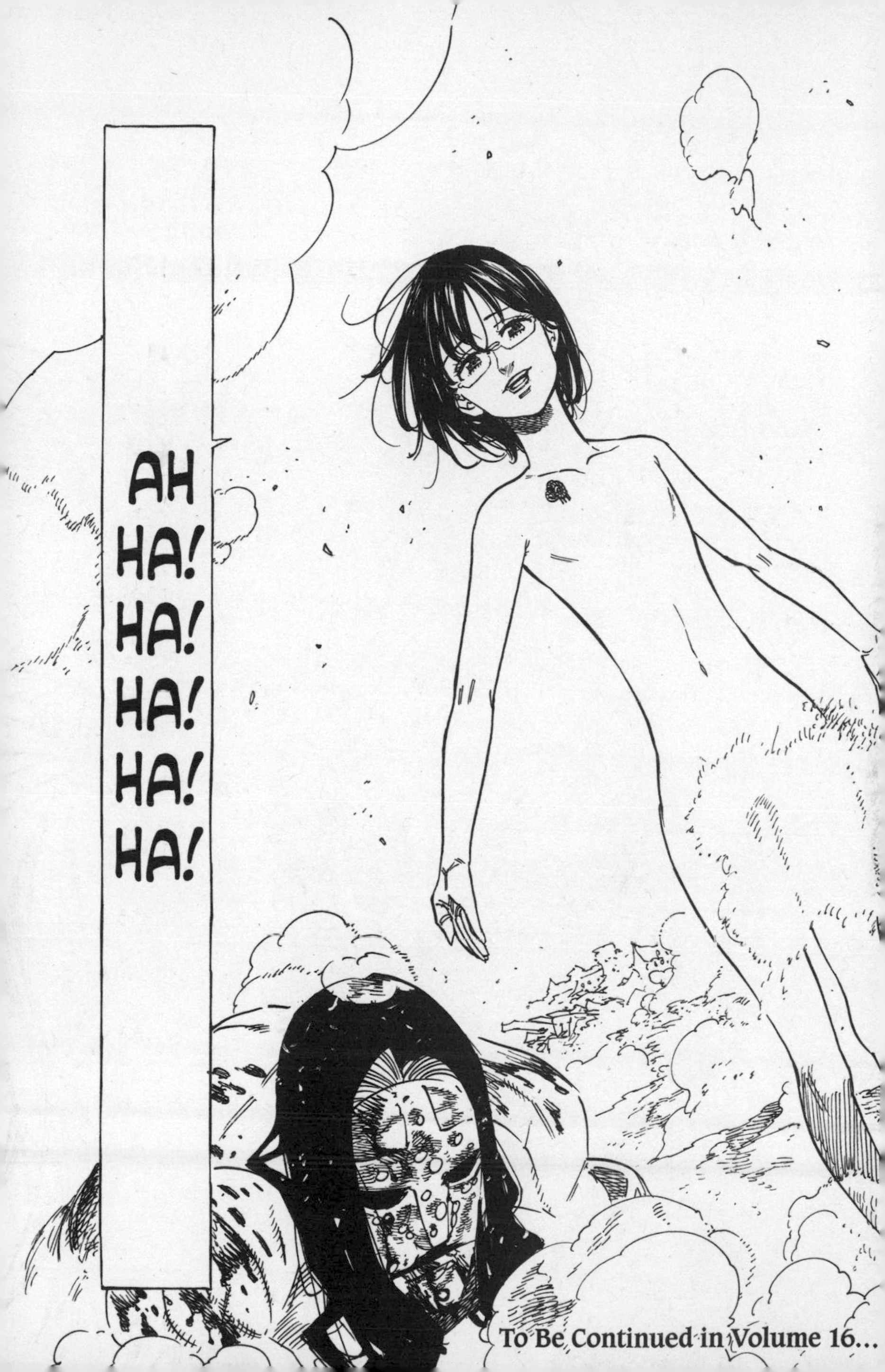
AH HA! HA! HA! HA! HA!
To Be Continued in Volume 16...

Bonus Story
Harlequin & Helbram

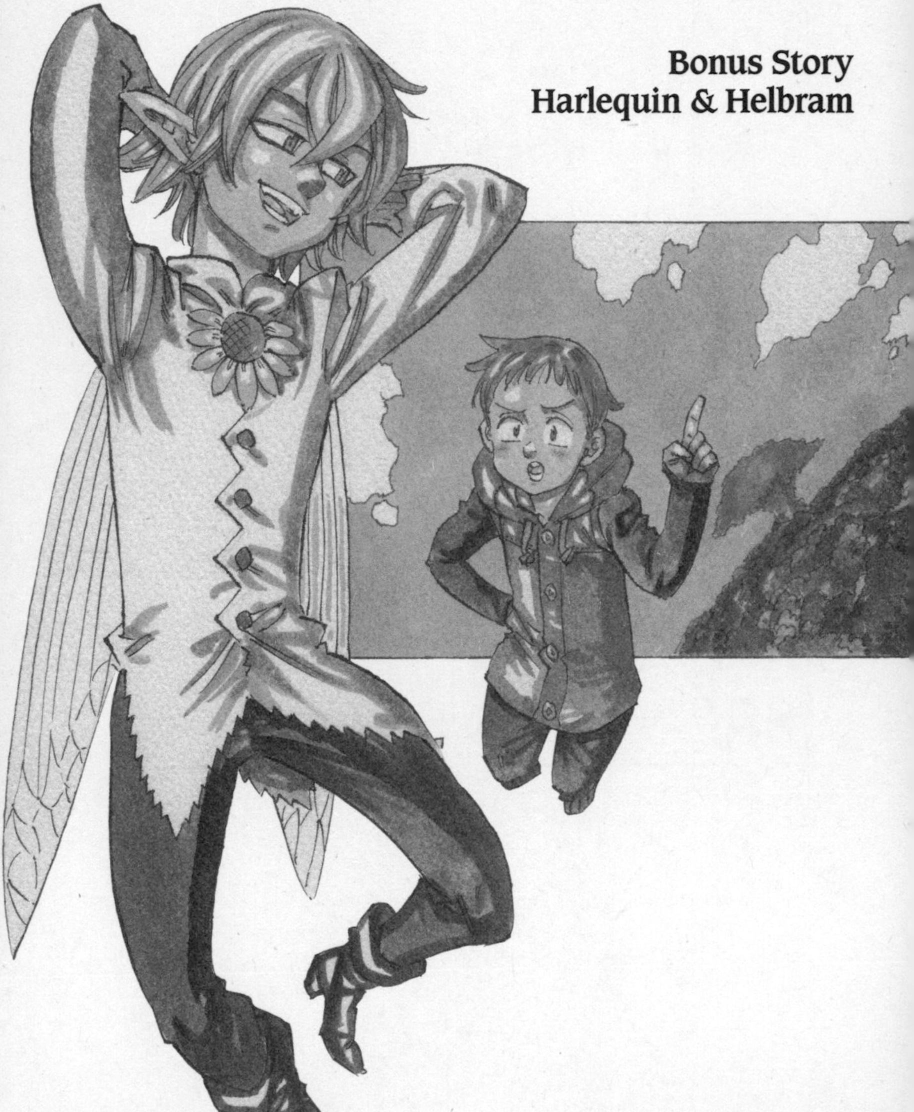

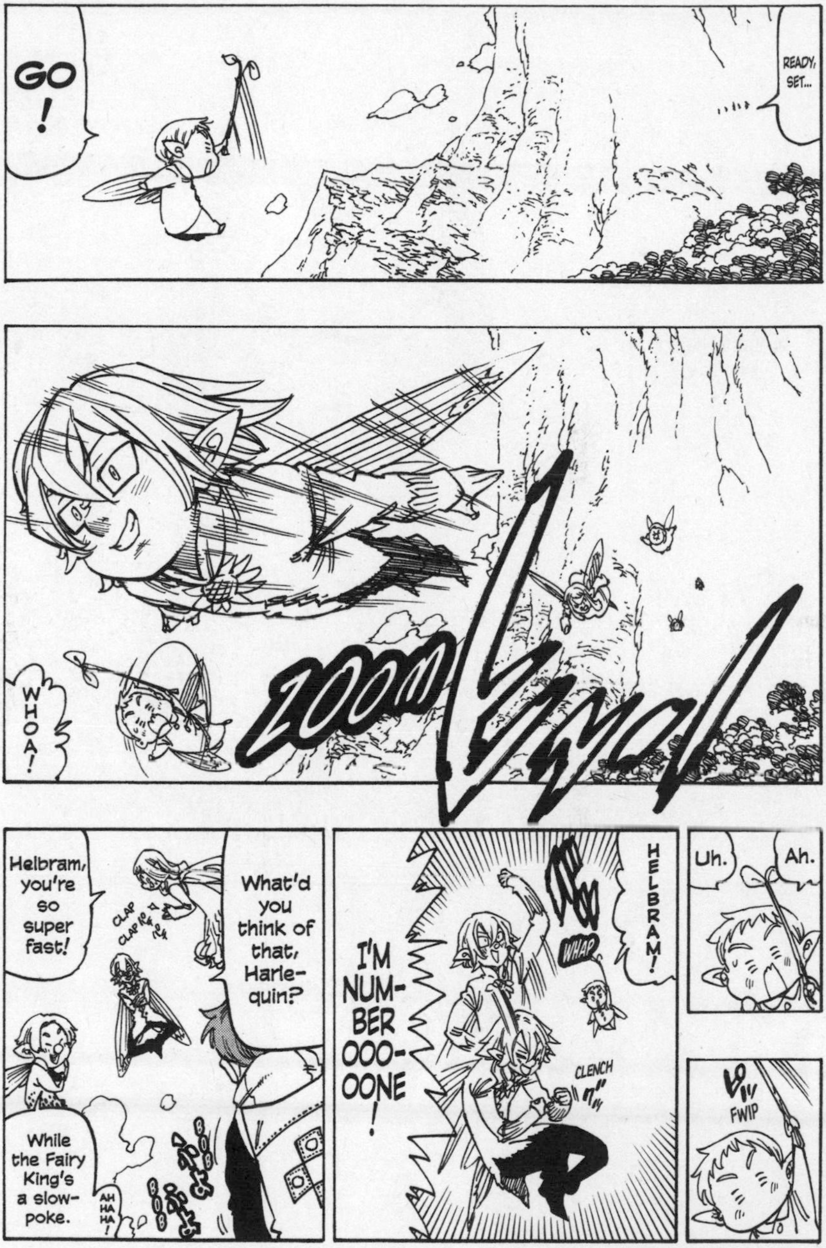
READY, SET...
GO!
ZOOOM
WHOA!
Ah.
Uh.
FWIP
HELBRAM!
WHAP
I'M NUMBER OOOOONE!
CLENCH
What'd you think of that, Harlequin?
Helbram, you're so super fast!
CLAP CLAP
While the Fairy King's a slowpoke.
AH HA HA!

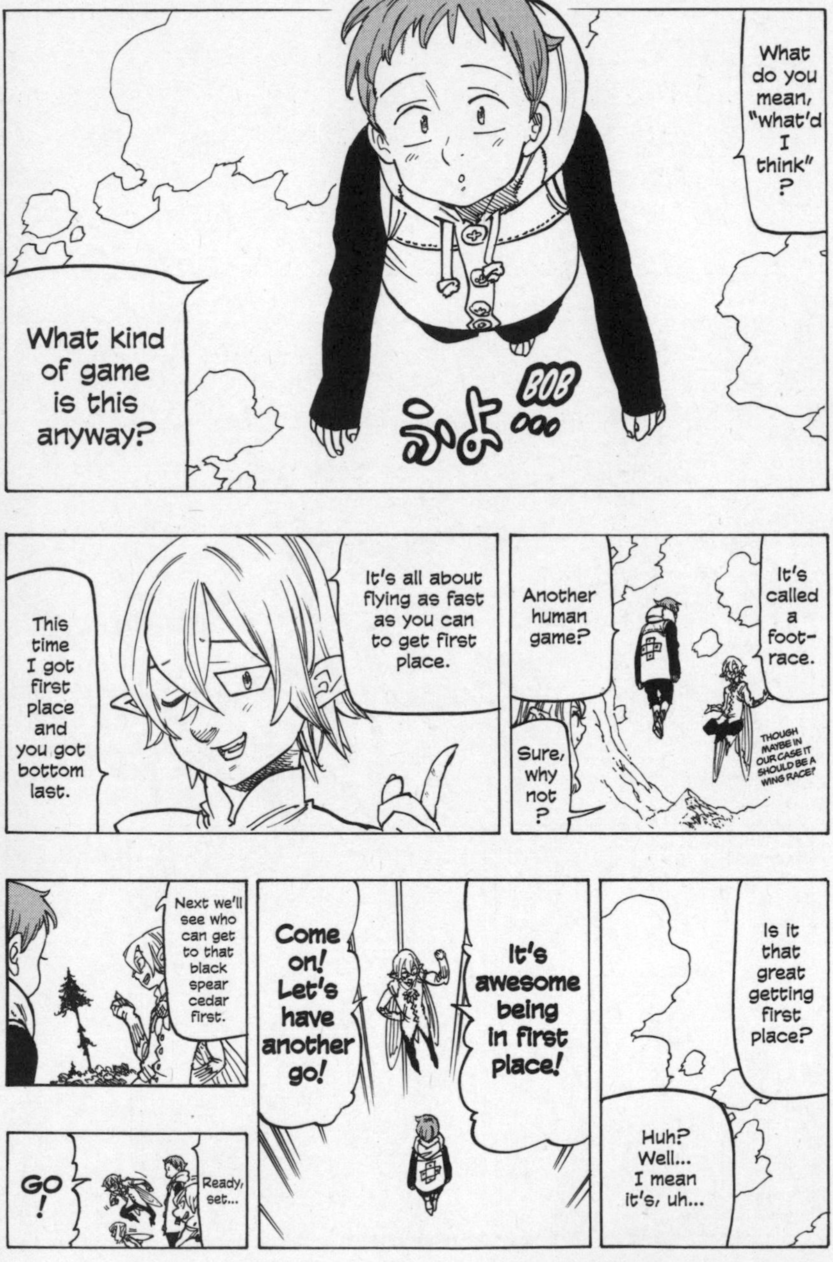
What do you mean, "what'd I think"?
BOB
ふよ…
What kind of game is this anyway?
It's called a foot-race.
THOUGH MAYBE IN OUR CASE IT SHOULD BE A WING RACE?
Another human game?
Sure, why not?
It's all about flying as fast as you can to get first place.
This time I got first place and you got bottom last.
Is it that great getting first place?
Huh? Well... I mean it's, uh...
It's awesome being in first place!
Come on! Let's have another go!
Next we'll see who can get to that black spear cedar first.
Ready, set...
GO!

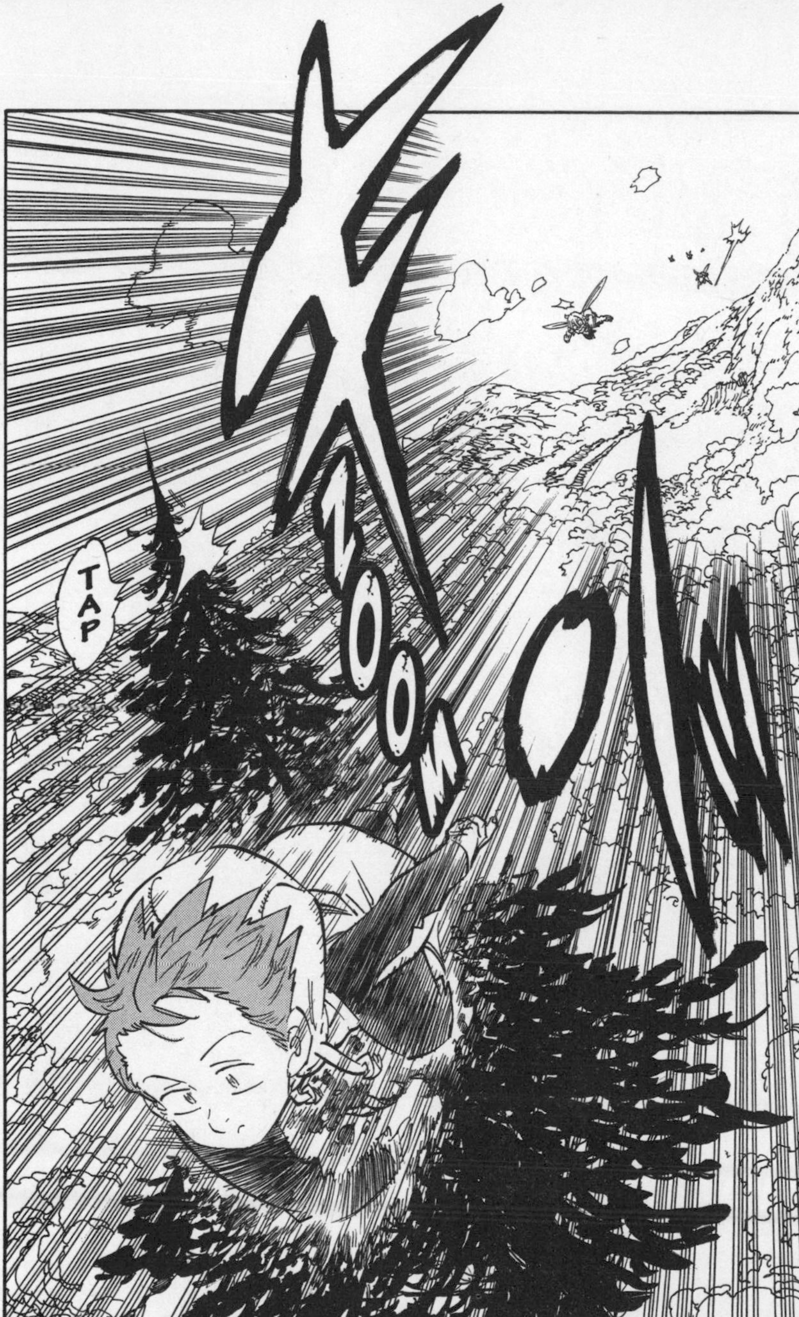
TAP

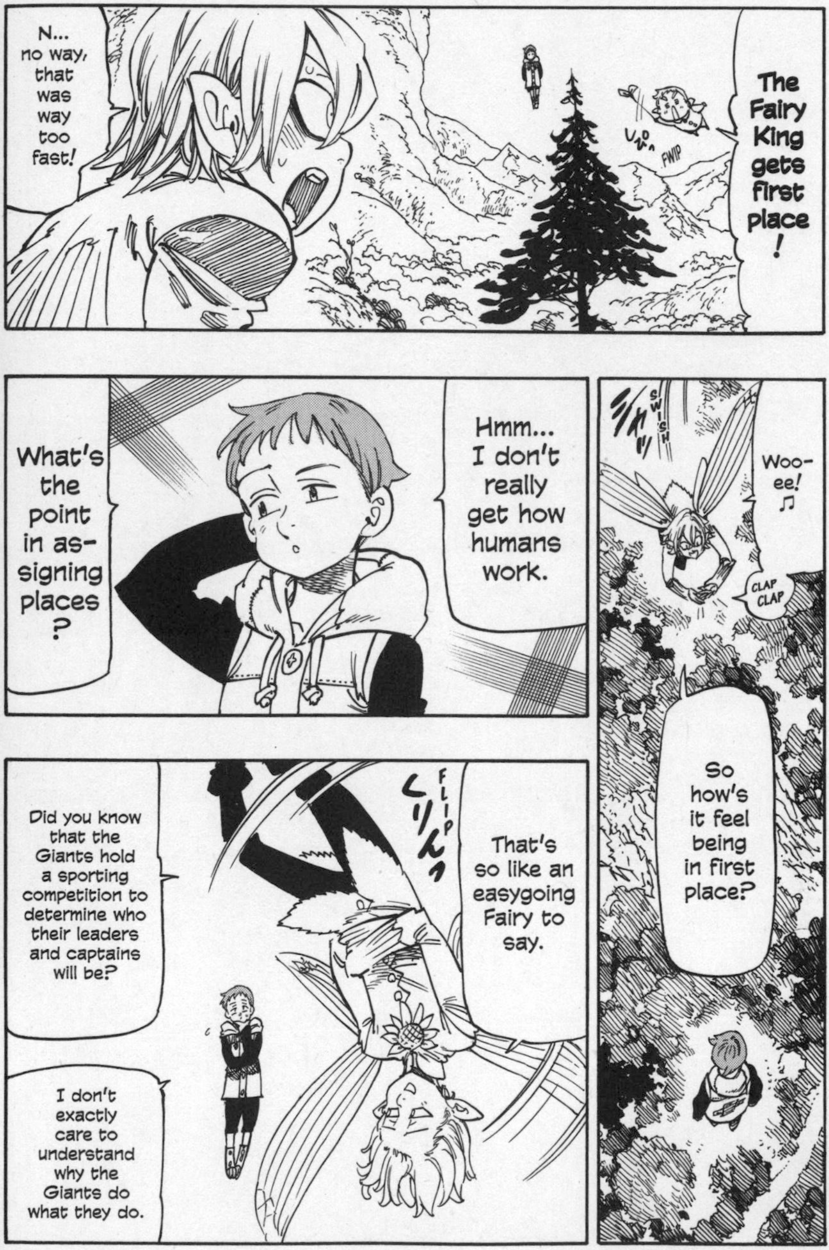
The Fairy King gets first place!
FWIP
N... no way, that was way too fast!
SWISH
Wooo-ee! ♫
CLAP CLAP
So how's it feel being in first place?
Hmm... I don't really get how humans work.
What's the point in as-signing places?
That's so like an easygoing Fairy to say.
FLIP
Did you know that the Giants hold a sporting competition to determine who their leaders and captains will be?
I don't exactly care to understand why the Giants do what they do.

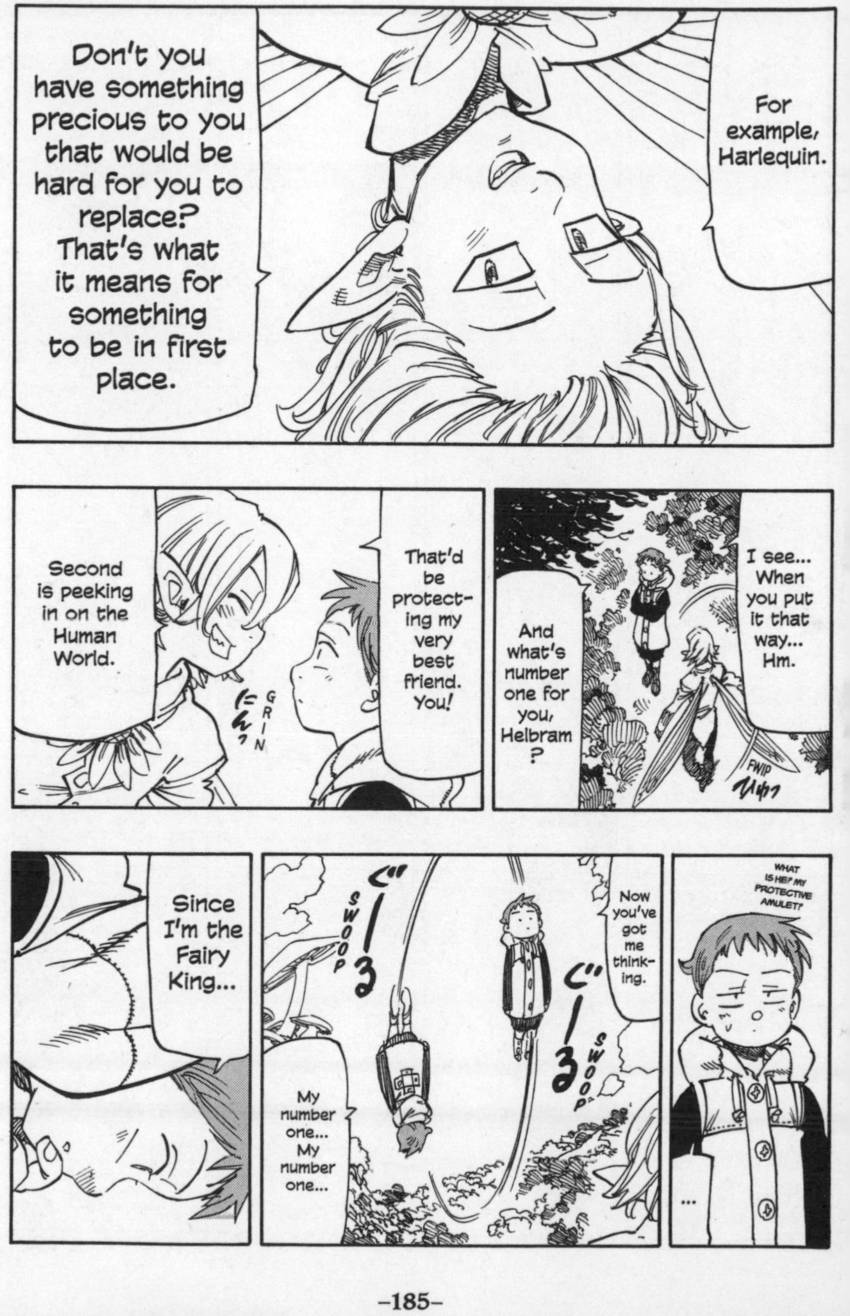
Don't you have something precious to you that would be hard for you to replace? That's what it means for something to be in first place.
For example, Harlequin.
I see... When you put it that way... Hm.
And what's number one for you, Helbram?
FWIP
That'd be protecting my very best friend. You!
Second is peeking in on the Human World.
GRIN
WHAT IS HE? MY PROTECTIVE AMULET?
...
Now you've got me thinking.
SWOOP
SWOOP
My number one... My number one...
Since I'm the Fairy King...

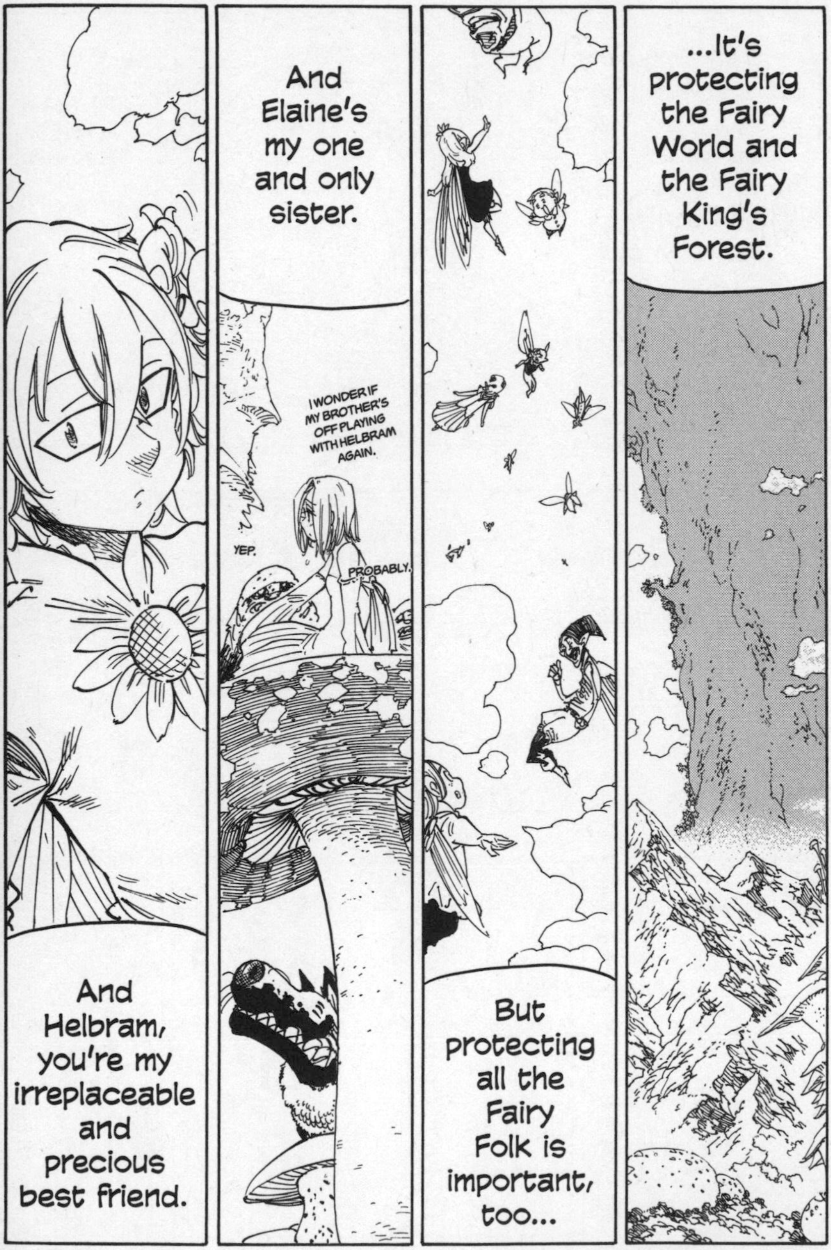
...It's protecting the Fairy World and the Fairy King's Forest.
But protecting all the Fairy Folk is important, too...
And Elaine's my one and only sister.
I WONDER IF MY BROTHER'S OFF PLAYING WITH HELBRAM AGAIN.
PROBABLY.
YEP.
And Helbram, you're my irreplaceable and precious best friend.

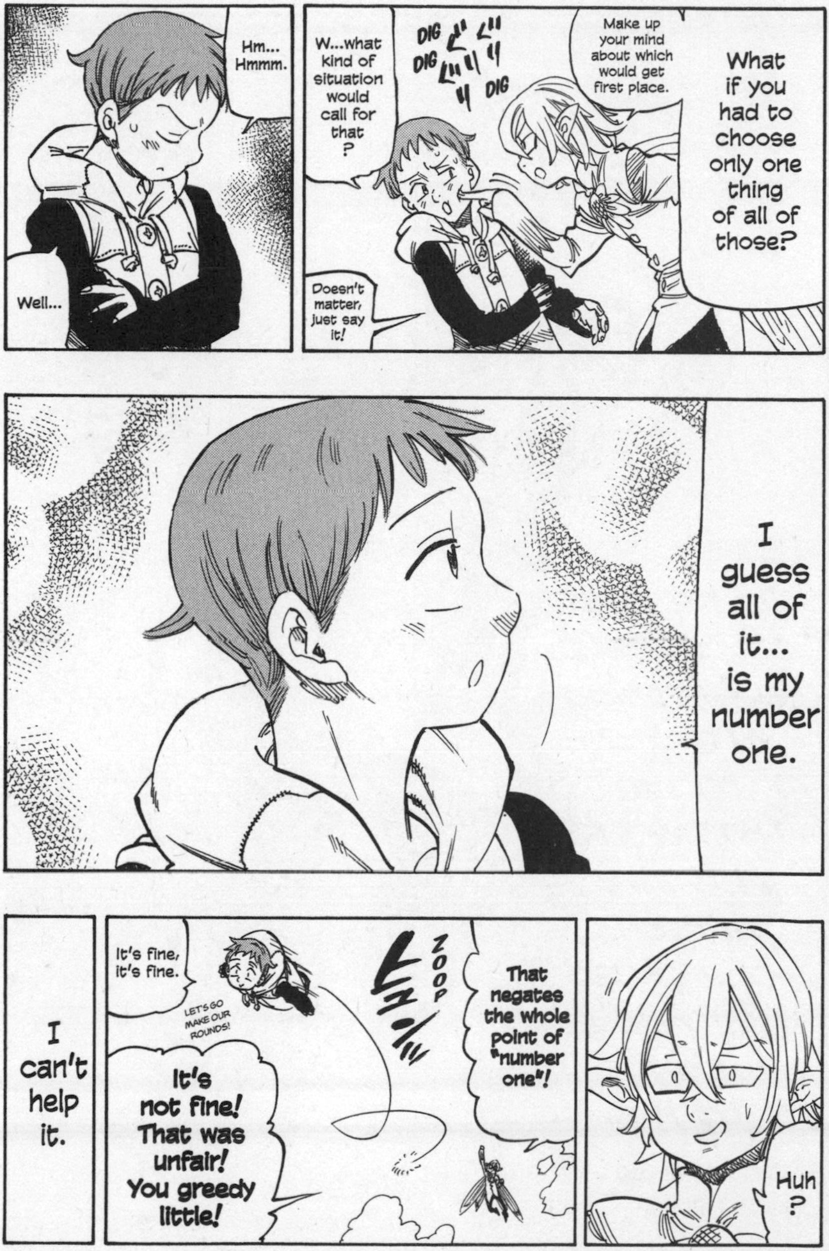
What if you had to choose only one thing of all of those?
Make up your mind about which would get first place.
DIG DIG DIG
W...what kind of situation would call for that?
Doesn't matter, just say it!
Hm... Hmmm.
Well...
I guess all of it... is my number one.
Huh?
That negates the whole point of "number one"!
ZOOP
It's fine, it's fine.
LET'S GO MAKE OUR ROUNDS!
It's not fine! That was unfair! You greedy little!
I can't help it.

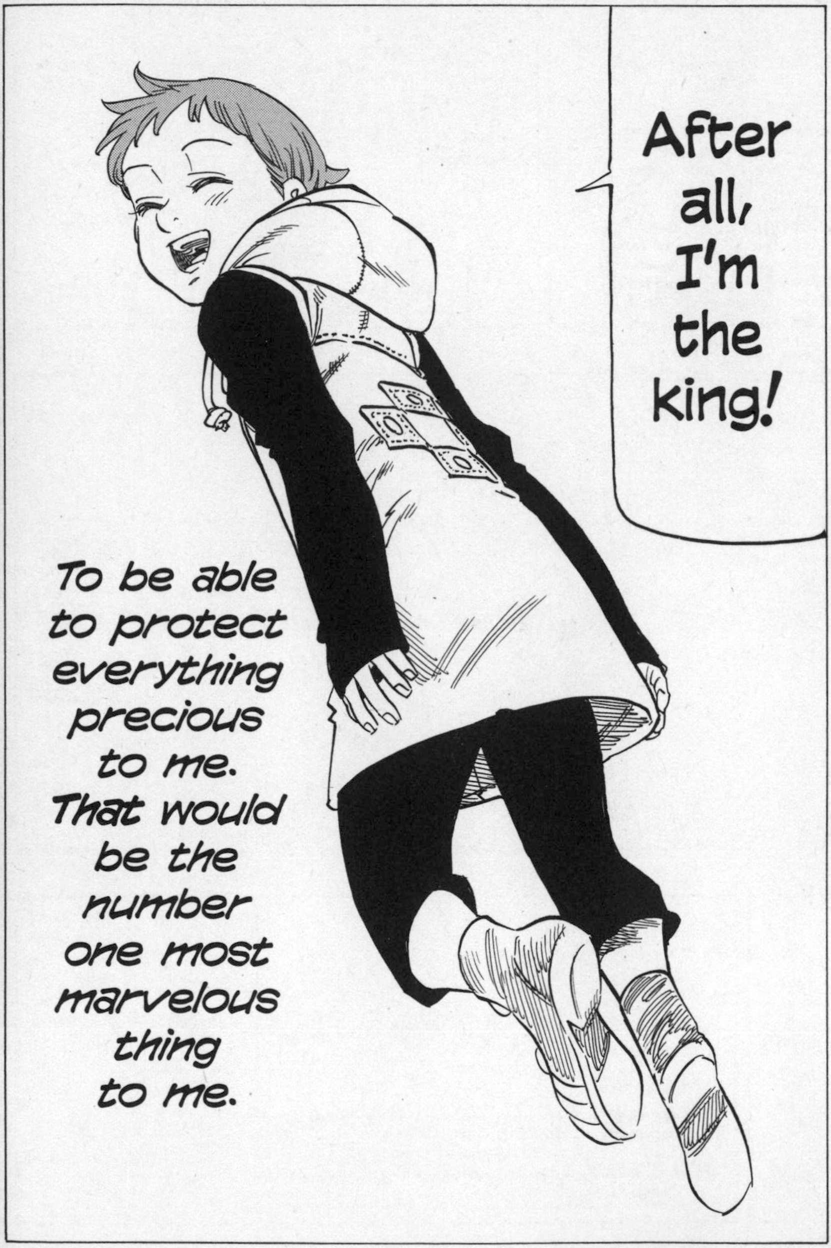
After all, I'm the king!
To be able to protect everything precious to me. That would be the number one most marvelous thing to me.

The End

These are Demon Golems that were created by the Demon Race during the Great War in the past. With their builds and caloric force, they would be better described as weapons. However, they say that The Ten Commandments would often play with them during their free time, thereby destroying them.

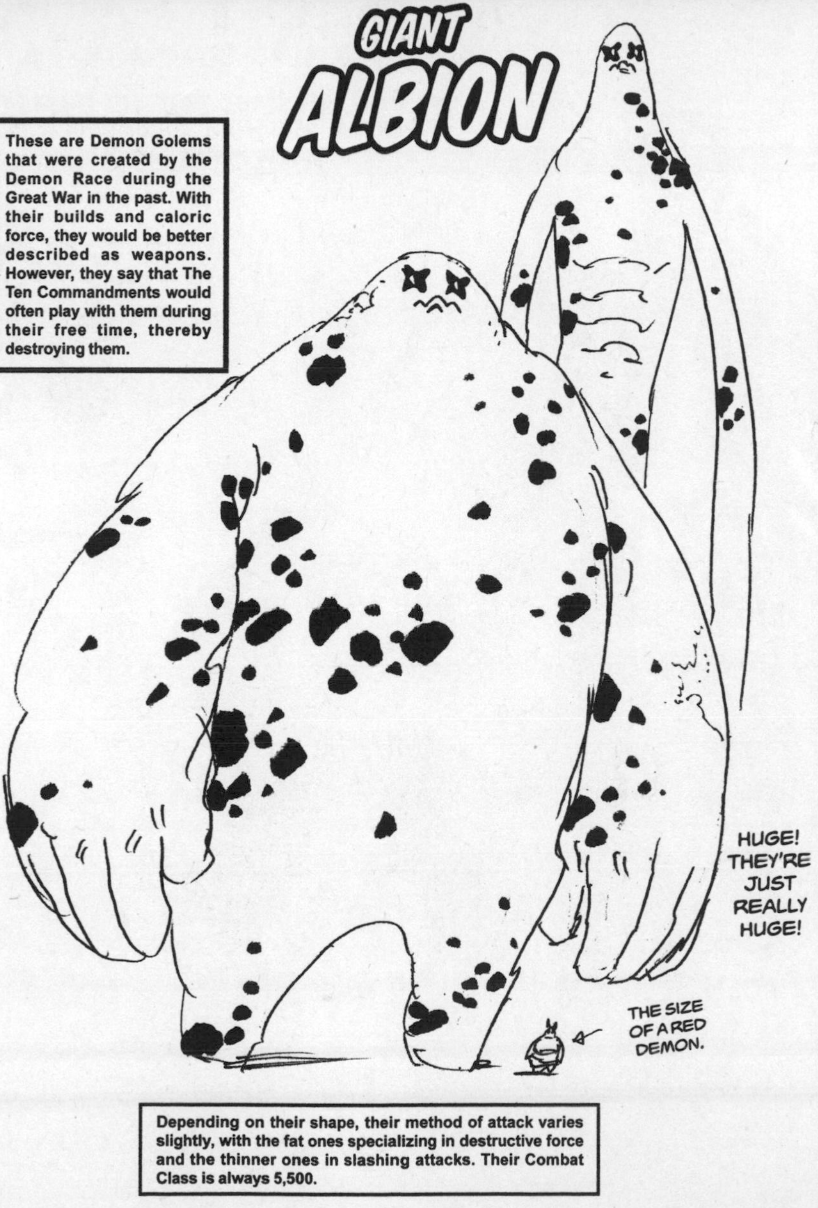
GIANT
ALBION
HUGE! THEY'RE JUST REALLY HUGE!
THE SIZE OF A RED DEMON.

Depending on their shape, their method of attack varies slightly, with the fat ones specializing in destructive force and the thinner ones in slashing attacks. Their Combat Class is always 5,500.

THE HEROIC LEGEND OF
ARSLAN

READ THE NEW SERIES FROM THE CREATOR OF FULLMETAL ALCHEMIST, HIROMU ARAKAWA! NOW A HIT TV SERIES!

3 9075 03920375 4

"Arakawa proves to be more than up to the task of adapting Tanaka's fantasy novels and fans of historical or epic fantasy will be quite pleased with the resulting book."
-Anime News Network

ECBATANA IS BURNING!

Arslan is the young and curious prince of Pars who, despite his best efforts doesn't seem to have what it takes to be a proper king like his father. At the age of 14, Arslan goes to his first battle and loses everything as the blood-soaked mist of war gives way to scorching flames, bringing him to face the demise of his once glorious kingdom. However, it is Arslan's destiny to be a ruler, and despite the trials that face him, he must now embark on a journey to reclaim his fallen kingdom.

Available now in print and digitally!

KC
KODANSHA
COMICS

DEVIL アビルサバイバー SURVIVOR

AFTER DEMONS BREAK THROUGH INTO THE HUMAN WORLD, TOKYO MUST BE QUARANTINED. WITHOUT POWER AND STUCK IN A SUPERNATURAL WARZONE, 17-YEAR-OLD KAZUYA HAS ONLY ONE HOPE: HE MUST USE THE *"COMP"*, A DEVICE CREATED BY HIS COUSIN NAOYA CAPABLE OF SUM-MONING AND SUBDUING DEMONS, TO DEFEAT THE INVADERS AND TAKE BACK THE CITY.

BASED ON THE POPULAR VIDEO GAME FRANCHISE BY ATLUS!

© Satoru Matsuba/Kodansha, Ltd. All rights reserved.

The Seven Deadly Sins volume 15 is a work of fiction. Names, characters, places, and incidents are the products of the author's imagination or are used fictitiously. Any resemblance to actual events, locales, or persons, living or dead, is entirely coincidental.

A Kodansha Comics Trade Paperback Original.

Published in the United States by Kodansha Comics, an imprint of Kodansha USA Publishing, LLC, New York.

Publication rights for this English edition arranged through Kodansha Ltd., Tokyo.

First published in Japan in 2015 by Kodansha Ltd., Tokyo.

ISBN 978-1-63236-270-4

Printed in the United States of America.

www.kodanshacomics.com

9 8 7 6 5 4 3 2 1

Translation: Christine Dashiell
Lettering: James Dashiell
Editing: Lauren Scanlan
Kodansha Comics edition cover design: Phil Balsman